Transition to Democracy in Poland

Other Works by Richard F. Staar

Arms Control: Myth versus Reality (editor)

Aspects of Modern Communism (editor)

Communist Regimes in Eastern Europe, 5th revised edition

East-Central Europe and the USSR (editor)

Effects of Soviet Political Fragmentation
on the Energy Infrastructure (coauthor)

Foreign Policies of the Soviet Union

Future Information Revolution in the USSR (editor)

Long-Range Environmental Study of the
Northern Tier of Eastern Europe in 1990-2000

The New Military in Russia: Ten Myths That Shape the Image

Poland, 1944–1962: Sovietization of a Captive People

Public Diplomacy: USA vs. USSR (editor)

Soviet Military Policy Since World War II (coauthor)

Transition to Democracy in Poland (editor)

United States-East European Relations in the 1990s (editor)

USSR Foreign Policies After Detente, 2nd revised edition

Yearbook on International Communist Affairs:
Parties and Revolutionary Movements (editor of 22 volumes)

Transition to Democracy in Poland

Second Edition

Edited by

Richard F. Staar

St. Martin's Press
New York

Transition to Democracy in Poland

ISBN 0-312-21247-X

Library of Congress Cataloging-in-Publication Data

Transition to democracy in Poland / Richard F. Staar. — 2nd ed.
    p.   cm.
    Includes bibliographical references and index.
    ISBN 0-312-21247-X
    1. Democracy—Poland.   2. Poland—Politics and government—1989–
I. Staar, Richard Felix, 1923–
JN6766.T73   1993
320.9438'09'049—dc21   98-9630
                                                                 CIP

Design by Letra Libre

First edition: March 1998
10   9   8   7   6   5   4   3   2   1

for Basieńka and Żywieńka

Contents

Tables and Figure

Acronyms

ABC	Association of Baltic Cities
AWS	Solidarity Electoral Action (*Akcja Wyborcza Solidarność*)
BBWR	Nonparty Bloc for Reform (*Bezpartyjny Blok Wspierania Reform*)
CBOS	Center for Study of Public Opinion (*Centrum Badania Opinii Społecznej*)
CBSS	Council of Baltic Sea States
CE mark	European Union Safety Certificate
CEEC	Central and East European Countries
CEFTA	Central European Free Trade Association
CEI	Central European Initiative
CFE	Conventional Forces in Europe, treaty on
CIS	Commonwealth of Independent States
CMEA	Council for Mutual Economic Assistance
CPI	Consumer Price Index
CSCE	Conference on Security and Cooperation in Europe (1975–1994); *see* OSCE
EBRD	European Bank for Reconstruction and Development
EC	European Community
EFTA	European Free Trade Association
EMS	European Monetary System
EMU	Economic and Monetary Union
EU	European Union
FDI	Foreign Direct Investment
G-7	The Group of Seven Economic Powers (Canada, France, Germany, Italy, Japan, United Kingdom, and United States)
GAO	U.S. General Accounting Office
GATT	General Agreement on Tariffs and Trade
GDP	Gross Domestic Product
GNP	Gross National Product
GSP	Generalized System of Preferences
GUS	Central Statistical Office (*Główny Urząd Statystyczny*)
IFOR	Implementation Force (renamed Stabilization Force)
IMF	International Monetary Fund

KLD   Liberal Democratic Congress (*Kongres Liberalno-Demokraty-czny*)
KO   Citizens' Committees (*Komitety Obywatelskie*)
KOR   Committee for Defense of Workers (*Komitet Obrony Robot-ników*)
KPEiR   Pensioners' Party (*Krajowa Partia Emerytów i Rencistów*)
KPN   Confederation for an Independent Poland (*Konfederacja Polski Niepodległej*)
KRS   National Judicial Council (*Krajowa Rada Sądownictwa*)
MFA   Multifiber Agreement
MFN   Most Favored Nation status
MP   Member of Parliament
NACC   North Atlantic Cooperation Council
NALG   National Assembly of Local Governments
NATO   North Atlantic Treaty Organization
NBP   National Bank of Poland (*Narodowy Bank Polski*)
NGO   Nongovernmental organizations
NIK   Supreme Control Board, the government's chief auditing agency (*Najwyższa Izba Kontroli*)
NJW   Special Vistula Units of the Internal Affairs Ministry (*Nadwiślańskie Jednostki Wojskowe*)
OBOP   Center for Public Opinion Surveys (*Ośrodek Badań Opinii Publicznej*)
OECD   Organization for European Cooperation and Development
OMRI   Open Media Research Institute (Prague, Czech Republic)
OSCE   Organization for Security and Cooperation in Europe (new name for CSCE since January 1995)
OPZZ   National Trade Union Accord (*Ogólnopolskie Porozumienie Związków Zawodowych*)
PC   Center Accord/Alliance (*Porozumienie Centrum*)
PdP   Alliance for Poland (*Przymierze dla Polski*)
PfP   Partnership for Peace
PGR   State-owned Farms (*Państwowe Gospodarstwa Rolne*)
PHARE   Poland-Hungary Aid for Restructuring the Economy
PK   Conservative Party (*Partia Konserwatywna*)
PPG   Polish Economic Program (*Polski Program Gospodarczy*)
PSL   Polish Peasant Party (*Polskie Stronnictwo Ludowe*)
PZPR   Polish United Workers' Party (*Polska Zjednoczona Partia Robotnicza*)
RdR   Movement for the Republic (*Ruch dla Rzeczypospolitej*)
ROAD   Citizens' Movement for Democratic Action (*Ruch Obywatelski Akcja Demokratyczna*)

ROP	Movement for Poland's Reconstruction (*Ruch Odrodzenia Polski*)
SD	Democratic Party (*Stronnictwo Demokratyczne*)
SdRP	Social Democracy of the Polish Republic (*Socjaldemokracja Rzeczypospolitej Polskiej*
SEED	Support for East European Democracy
SFOR	Stabilization Force
SK-L	Conservative-Peasant Party (*Stronnictwo Konserwatywno-Ludowe*)
SLCh	Peasant-Christian Party (*Stronnictwo Ludowo-Chrześcijańskie*)
SLD	Alliance of the Democratic Left (*Sojusz Lewicy Demokratycznej*)
SPR	Party of Political Realism (*Stronnictwo Politycznego Realizmu*)
ToT	Terms of Trade
TVP	National Television (*Telewizja Polska*)
UD	Democratic Union (*Unia Demokratyczna*)
UOP	Office of State Security (*Urząd Ochrony Państwa*)
UP	Union of Labor (*Unia Pracy*)
UPR	Union of Real Politics (*Unia Polityki Realnej*)
USAID	U.S. Agency for International Development
UW	Freedom Union (*Unia Wolności*)
WAK	Catholic Electoral Action (*Wyborcza Akcja Katolicka*)
WEU	West European Union
WTO	Warsaw Treaty Organization or World Trade Organization
ZChN	Christian National Union (*Zjednoczenie Chrześcijańsko-Narodowe*)
ZSL	United Peasant Party (*Zjednoczone Stronnictwo Ludowe*)
ZOMO	Motorized Units of Citizens' Militia (*Zmotoryzowane Oddziały Milicji Obywatelskiej*)

Preface

It had seemed natural to select Poland for a case study of transition to democracy in East-Central Europe. The country was the largest throughout the region in both area and population, had experienced a long tradition of modern political and social development that dated back to the eighteenth century, and was first to throw off the communist yoke that had been forcibly imposed by the Red Army of the Soviet Union toward the end of World War II.

The other consideration involved the availability of so many scholars in the United States who knew the Polish language and had done on-site research or teaching in Poland. All save one and a half of the chapters were written by such American experts. An attempt was made to pair each of the authors with a respondent from Warsaw, who would critique the draft papers on the basis of first-hand experience at the university, in government agencies, and international organizations. This approach proved successful.

All the participants in the conference held at the Hoover Institution during 23–24 November 1992 owed a debt of gratitude to Dr. Tomasz Gruszecki (European Bank for Reconstruction and Development, London); Mme Hanna Gronkiewicz-Waltz (president, National Bank of Poland); Professor Krzysztof Jasiewicz (Institute of Political Studies, Polish Academy of Sciences); Senator Andrzej Machalski (president, Confederation of Polish Employers); Dr. Christine Sadowski (Free Trade Union Institute, AFL/CIO), the exceptional American; Dr. Jacek Szymanderski (director, Center for Public Opinion Research, Warsaw); Minister Counselor Jacek Tomorowicz (embassy of Poland, Washington, D.C.); Mme Halina Wasilewska-Trenker (secretary of state, Central Planning Office, Warsaw); Jan B. de Weydenthal (then regional analyst for RFE/RL, Munich); and Justice Janina Zakrzewska (Constitutional Tribunal), who faxed her comments from Warsaw.

The editor expresses his personal thanks to Dr. John Raisian, director of the Hoover Institution, for opening the conference; and the Honorable George P. Shultz, former U.S. secretary of state and now distinguished fellow at the Hoover Institution, for his lengthy introductory remarks, which provided a stimulus that lasted throughout the proceedings. The foregoing resulted in a book, copublished in September 1993 by St. Martin's Press, the Hoover Institution, and Macmillan in England.

Since that time the Hoover Institution has continued research and support of events dealing with Poland. The editor visited Warsaw to participate in the 5th Congress of Central and East European Studies during 6–11 August 1995, specifically in a discussion of national security issues. He was interviewed on Polish television and, subsequently, has had several articles published in *Rzeczpospolita*.

Former president and Solidarity leader as well as Nobel Peace Prize recipient Lech Wałęsa addressed a standing room only audience in Dinkelspiel Auditorium, at Stanford University, on 31 May 1996. Introduced by the Honorable George P. Shultz, President Wałęsa also spoke briefly after a luncheon in his honor at Stauffer Auditorium, Hoover Institution. Later that same year, during 1–2 November 1996, a two-day seminar, "Transition to Constitutional Democracy and a Market Economy in Poland," was cosponsored by the Hoover Institution and the Center for Russian and East European Studies at Stanford University. Principal speakers included Bronisław Geremek, then chairman of the *Sejm* foreign policy committee; Lech Garlicki, justice of the Constitutional Tribunal; Jerzy Osiatyński, former minister of planning and later of finance; and John R. Davis, Jr., former U.S. ambassador to Poland. Unfortunately, a former prime minister and now justice minister, Mme Hanna Suchocka, was unable to attend.

These activities, in addition to changes that have taken place in Poland, suggested the need for a sequel to the original conference volume. Half of the fourteen contributors are new. As their identifications suggest, each has outstanding credentials for the subject matter under discussion. Given that a transition to democracy has indeed taken place in Poland, it seems only appropriate to recognize that a new phase of consolidating democracy is taking place.

The generous support of the Hoover Institution and its director, John Raisian; the Kościuszko Foundation and President Joseph E. Gore; the American Institute of Polish Culture and President Blanka A. Rosenstiel, as well as the United States Information Agency, for allowing us to co-opt one of its distinguished visitors from Poland during the original conference, are acknowledged with thanks.

The editor wishes to express appreciation to Jadwiga M. Staar for proofreading the text as well as checking the diacritical marks; his research associate Margit N. Grigory, managing editor of *Yearbook on International Communist Affairs* (1983–1991), who finalized this volume for submission to the press as well as prepared the detailed index; Maciej Siekierski, Hoover Institution curator of the European Collection, as well as East European specialist Zbigniew Stańczyk (who took the new cover photograph on the 4th of July in Warsaw), both of whom were most helpful in many ways. Jason Cohen and Dita Vyslouzil, the editor's research assistants at Boston University during 1997–1998, managed to produce a single IBM-compatible disk and helped gather materials for the editor's next book.

Richard F. Staar
Stanford, CA and Boston

Notes on Contributors

MARK F. BRZEZINSKI (J.D., Virginia; D Phil, Oxford) is an associate at the law firm of Hogan & Hartson, L.L.P. Between 1991 and 1994, he was a Fulbright Scholar attached to the Constitutional Tribunal in Poland, an Oxford-Soros lecturer at the University of Warsaw, and a research associate at the Helsinki Foundation for Human Rights, also in Warsaw. He has published a number of articles on Polish constitutional reform and is the author of *The Struggle for Constitutionalism in Poland* (New York and London, 1997).

GRZEGORZ EKIERT (Ph.D., Harvard) is associate professor of government and research associate with the Center for European Studies at Harvard University. He recently published *The State against Society: Political Crises and Their Aftermath in East Central Europe* (Princeton, N.J., 1996).

A. E. DICK HOWARD (LL.B., Virginia) is professor of law and public affairs at the University of Virginia. He was a Rhodes scholar at Oxford and served as law clerk for U.S. Supreme Court justice Hugo L. Black. Recent books include *Constitution-Making in Eastern Europe* (Washington, D.C., 1993). In 1996 the Union of Czech Lawyers, citing his "promotion of the idea of a civil society in Central Europe," awarded him their Randa Medal—the first time this honor had been conferred upon anyone other than a Czech citizen.

BARTŁOMIEJ KAMIŃSKI (Ph.D., Warsaw), an associate professor of government and a senior fellow at the Center for Study of Post-Communist Societies at the University of Maryland, is also a consultant in the international trade division of the World Bank. He most recently edited *Economic Transition in Russia and the New States of Eurasia* (Armonk, N.Y., 1996) and coauthored *Foreign Trade in Transition* (Washington, D.C., 1996).

NISSAN LIVIATAN (Ph.D., Hebrew University in Jerusalem) is a professor at Hebrew University and a former adviser to the Bank of Israel; he has been a visiting professor at MIT, the University of Chicago, the Wharton School, and the University of California at Berkeley. Author of several books, he also has published extensively in professional journals. His current fields of interests include monetary, exchange rate, and disinflation policies in developing countries.

ANDREW A. MICHTA (Ph.D., Johns Hopkins) is an associate professor and occupies the Mertie W. Buckman Chair of International Studies at Rhodes College. He is author of *Red Eagle: The Army in Polish Politics* (Stanford, Ca., 1990), *Government and Politcs of Post- communist Europe* (Westport, Conn., 1994), and *The Soldier-Citizen: The Politics of the Polish Army after Communism* (New York, N.Y., 1997).

DANIEL F. OKS (D.Phil., Oxford) is senior economist for Poland at the World Bank. He formerly taught at Buenos Aires University and has published several articles in professional journals. A research paper coauthored with Przemyslaw T. Gajdeczka won the special merit award of the American Express international competition.

ARTHUR R. RACHWALD (Ph.D., University of California at Santa Barbara) is a professor of political science at the U.S. Naval Academy and professorial lecturer at the Johns Hopkins University, School of Advanced International Studies, in Washington, D.C., as well as at the SAIS Bologna Center (1996–1997). He is the author of *Poland between the Superpowers* (Boulder, Colo., 1983) and *In Search of Poland: The Superpowers' Response to Solidarity* (Stanford, Ca., 1990), in addition to numerous chapters in books, articles, research papers, and commentaries.

JOANNA REGULSKA (Ph.D., Colorado) is an associate professor of geography and director of the Center for Russian, Central and East European Studies at Rutgers, the State University of New Jersey. She is completing a book entitled *Warsaw: Space, People, and Politics* (John Wiley & Sons) and an edited volume, *Gender and Citizenship: Contentions and Controversies,* with Nancy Leys Stepan.

RICHARD F. STAAR (Ph.D., Michigan), a senior fellow of the Hoover Institution at Stanford, is on leave during 1997–1999 as visiting research professor of international relations at Boston University and associate of the Kathryn W. and Shelby Cullom Davis Center for Russian Studies at Harvard.

RAYMOND TARAS (Ph.D., University of Warsaw) is visiting scholar of the Kathryn W. and Shelby Cullom Davis Center for Russian Studies at

Harvard during 1997–1998 and professor of political science at Tulane University. His interest in Poland stems from a Canada Council doctoral fellowship and a published dissertation, *Ideology in a Socialist State* (Cambridge, Eng., 1991). Most recently, he is the author of *Consolidating Democracy in Poland* (Boulder, Colo., 1995), and he edited *Post-Communist Presidents* (Cambridge, Eng., 1997).

SARAH MEIKLEJOHN TERRY (Ph.D., Harvard) is an associate professor of political science at Tufts University and a member of the Executive Committee at the Davis Center for Russian Studies, Harvard University. She is the author of *Poland's Place in Europe* (Princeton, N.J., 1983), edited *Soviet Policy in Eastern Europe* (New Haven, Conn., 1984), and coedited *The Soviet Empire Reconsidered: Essays in Honor of Adam Ulam* (Boulder, Col., 1994).

EWA M. THOMPSON (Ph.D., Vanderbilt) is professor of Slavic Studies at Rice University. She is the author of four books on Polish and Russian culture and politics, as well as of numerous articles in scholarly journals. A Chinese translation of *Understanding Russia* (Lanham, Md., 1987) was published in Hong Kong (1995).

JANINE R. WEDEL (Ph.D., University of California at Berkeley) is associate research professor of sociology and anthropology and a fellow of the Institute for European, Russian, and Eurasian Studies at George Washington University. She is also adjunct professor in the Graduate Public Policy Institute at Georgetown University. A three-time Fulbright scholar, her books include *The Private Poland* (New York, 1986), *The Unplanned Society: Poland during and after Communism* (New York, 1992), and *Collusion and Collision: The Story of Western Aid to Eastern Europe and the Former Soviet Union* (St. Martin's Press, 1998). She has contributed congressional testimony as well as studies for the Joint Economic Committee of Congress, the Atlantic Council, and the OECD.

ONE

Introduction: Future Prospects

Richard F. Staar

An old Chinese proverb states that predictions are difficult to make, especially about the future. Nonetheless, certain trends delineated by contributors to this book should become relevant as Poland enters the twenty-first century.

A survey of postwar history by Grzegorz Ekiert focuses on various forms of protest against communist rule and thus represents an excellent analysis of the foundations upon which to build a democracy that already has taken shape. His delineation of major crises, culminating in the "Polish October" of 1956 and through the period leading to the introduction of martial law on 13 December 1981, addresses the panorama of change brought about as a result of protest action always short of a national uprising.

The military junta did not solve any problems for the communist regime. Underground opposition surfaced in 1983 after martial law ended and intensified its activities, so that a noncommunist government could be formed in the fall of 1989. The Polish United Workers' (Communist) Party dissolved itself at the beginning of the following year. Collective protests continued even after these events, and the author concludes that such social activism manifested itself throughout Poland to a much larger extent than in any of the other postcommunist countries of East-Central Europe.

With this solid background, it becomes easier to comprehend what has occurred among voters and leaders of political parties. Raymond Taras analyzes parliamentary, presidential, and local elections from 1989 through 1997 as well as the referendum of 1996. He finds that the largest bloc within the electorate is comprised of nonvoters and explains the reasons for this phenomenon.

Former communists, who had renamed their movement Social Democracy of the Republic of Poland, took only 3 percent of the vote in 1990, which increased to 19 percent in 1993. This gave them (together with the former communist Polish Peasant Party) control over the national legislature. Two years later, Lech Wałęsa lost the presidency in a run-off by a small margin to Aleksander Kwaśniewski, who had been leader of the communist youth movement prior to 1990. Inability to unify the former Solidarity bloc led to Wałęsa's defeat. There are no parties in Poland today that have a mass membership. If anything, the political spectrum has become splintered for various reasons. Political leaders have been unable to counteract this development. The earlier elite from academia and the professions is being replaced by successful entrepreneurs from the business world.

Much of the foregoing had been sparked by the political activism of social movements in Poland. As pointed out by Ewa Thompson, the alliance that had united disparate groups (intelligentsia and workers, the church and secular intellectuals, farmers and city dwellers) disintegrated after 1990. Following the most recent presidential elections, five years later, realignment commenced along economic lines. This chapter analyzes political and economic attitudes among farmers and urban workers, which are far from monolithic. The author also discusses the impact of mass media and public opinion. Divisive issues include abortion, whereas political and social causes tend to unite the population. Polish society today is split along economic, ideological, and geographic lines rather than those of class. Such a development provides hope for the future.

The new political system that has been evolving represents a hybrid presidential-parliamentary one exhibiting considerable weakness, according to Andrew Michta. This weakness could be noted after the parliamentary elections in 1993, which placed former communists in control of the Sejm. It made differences between president and Parliament even greater. One of these involved control over the "presidential" ministries (defense, internal affairs, and foreign relations), which President Wałęsa used in his struggle against the Sejm.

After winning the 1995 presidential election by less than 3.5 percent of the popular vote, Aleksander Kwaśniewski may have wanted to retain these powers as well as a veto over the annual budget. However, the new constitution, adopted by Parliament on 2 April 1997, specifically denies such former prerogatives to the president. Kwaśniewski has had even less power since his ex-communists lost control over the government and Parliament after the 21 September 1997 election.

Joanna Regulska discusses local government reform, which goes back to the July 1989 parliamentary hearings on the subject of decentralization.

Both the political and economic rationale, with attendant benefits for the public, is analyzed. Major difficulties prevented rapid progress from taking place: the separation of powers between national and local levels remained unclear, the allocation of funds by central authorities had to be clarified, and the experience of local officials took time to acquire.

And yet by early 1998, several hundred training institutes and professional consulting organizations were actively engaged in building a professional cadre of local government officials. Citizens perceived local government as more efficient and responsive to their needs. Political institutions at the national level now support fiscal laws on behalf of and the transfer of primary education to local government. Stability is also suggested by the relatively small turnover of officials at lower levels. A study of 76 recall initiatives over a four-year period showed that these had resulted in 48 referenda. However, only three were adopted, in large part due to a low voter turnout, which invalidated the other outcomes.

The new constitution is analyzed by Dick Howard and Mark Brzezinski, both of whom are constitutional lawyers. They survey amendments to the 1952 document from the communist era through the work by constitutional committees, the so-called Small Constitution of 1992, and the new full-length constitution approved by a nationwide referendum on 25 May 1997. The coauthors of this chapter also discuss enforcement by the Constitutional Tribunal, which has become an activist institution, especially since 29 August 1997 when a law went into effect strengthening its powers and increasing the number of justices by three to fifteen. A table classifies 168 legal acts, including 75 parliamentary statutes and 93 substatutory regulations, which suggests that constitutional governance is on its way to firm establishment.

Nissan Liviatan and Daniel Oks discuss economic policy being pursued so as to qualify Poland for European Union (EU) membership in the year 2006. Growth has continued over the most recent six consecutive years, with inflation declining. Much of this is due to decisions made by the National Bank of Poland, the independence of which is being strengthened. The coauthors argue that social entitlements, the rate of unemployment (13 percent being forecast during 1997 and a drop to 9.5 percent for 1998), and unstable political alignments would recommend gradual disinflation. They are, in general, optimistic about Poland's economic future.

Although a dramatic reorientation of trade toward the West has been accomplished, Bartłomiej Kamiński warns that creeping government interventionism, if continued, will slow down integration with the world economy. Narrow sectoral interests have been skillfully exploited by the former communist Polish Peasant Party, whose economic philosophy is anti-free trade and strongly interventionist. This had brought agricultural protectionism to a new high and also contributed to the slowdown in privatization.

It would seem that commitments made under both the European Association Agreement with the EU as well as World Trade Organization membership would provide a powerful brake on bureaucratic temptation to micromanage economic processes. However, Polish authorities prior to the September 1997 elections had displayed considerable ingenuity in exploiting loopholes and circumventing corresponding provisions of respective international agreements. While these developments so far have not had a devastating effect on Poland's external performance, the accumulation of seemingly minor bureaucratic interventions (if continued) may have an adverse impact on exports under more competitive conditions in the future.

Sarah Meiklejohn Terry examines efforts to develop multilateral regional cooperation since the collapse of communism in 1989. Her primary focus is on the Visegrád group (Poland, Hungary, the Czech and Slovak republics) and the aspiration of its four members to join the European Union and NATO. A secondary focus is on broader regional concepts, such as the Central European Initiative (CEI) and the Council of Baltic Sea States. Despite early promises, these two groups have fallen into disarray. The potential of Visegrád was never achieved, due to fears that genuine success at the regional level would delay integration with Euro-Atlantic institutions. The breakup of Czechoslovakia, the disdain of Czechs for regional cooperation in the belief that they would qualify for early EU membership, and the increasingly aberrant behavior of Slovakia also contributed to failure. By contrast, the CEI fell victim to a combination of conflict in former Yugoslavia, inadequate funding, and politicization of its original pragmatic agenda around ethnic tensions.

Especially since 1993, multilateralism has been replaced increasingly with bilateral relations—some amicable, some less so—with neighbors to the west and east. Yet another disincentive to regional cooperation has been the emergence of an assertive Russia, intent on reclaiming its influence over both former "inner" and "outer" empires. This development has focused the attention of all Central European states on integration with the West. Unfortunately, even together, these states are incapable of ensuring their own security. As a result, Poles and Czechs (long estranged) have experienced an unexpected rapprochement. Poles and Ukrainians are well on their way to an historic reconciliation. Even the Partnership for Peace program, while in principle based on bilateral arrangements between each member state and the alliance, has fostered multilateral linkages. The NATO-Russia Charter of 27 May 1997 is also a positive signal that Moscow has begun to accept a mutual security regime rather than one based on territorial control and political or economic domination. As the Central Europeans approach membership in Western institutions, they are more likely to develop multifaceted cooperative relations with one another (and with their neighbors to the east), similar to those among present EU and NATO member states.

In her chapter on assistance to Poland from the Western democracies, Janine Wedel discusses the wide disparity between expectations by the recipient and actual performance. The idea of a Marshall Plan for all of East-Central Europe never materialized, perhaps because different actors (the G-7 countries, European Union members, and the United States) were unable to formulate a single master program. Idealism soon disappeared when it collided with reality.

The author contends that Western governments had been conditioned by their experiences in the Third World and that these represented a model applied to East-Central Europe, as well as by international financial institutions, nongovernmental organizations, and even "private" providers. A large part of this assistance came in the form of export loans and credits that had to be repaid. Many of the Western "consultants" attempted to apply Latin American models to a completely different situation in Poland. After seven years, however, Poles are consultants for the European Union in Romania and Ukraine. They even conduct a training program to reform the prison service in the former Soviet republic of Georgia.[1]

The final chapter in this volume is by Arthur Rachwald, who discusses national security and, specifically, Poland's entry into the North Atlantic Treaty Organization as well as other political and economic structures in Western Europe. The government in Warsaw had laid the foundations for this policy by concluding a special agreement with Germany in 1991. Relations vis-à-vis Russia have been less satisfactory, primarily because of Poland's frequently expressed desire to join NATO and the 9 July 1997 invitation from the latter to begin negotiations for membership by 1999.

The author explains this attitude in terms of past experience, which had emphasized bilateral agreements that failed and led to war. Polish culture is based on a Western orientation, and the success of "shock therapy" should facilitate integration with other private enterprise economies. Warsaw hopes to join the European Union after the year 2000—Poland is already a member of the Organization for Economic Cooperation and Development (OECD)—and to become a full-fledged participant in the Euro-Atlantic structure.

What, then, can one expect of the future? Despite apparent economic success, strikes and demonstrations probably will continue. Closure of the huge shipyard at Gdańsk, where Solidarity had been born in August 1980, resulted in layoffs for some 3,800 employees during 1997. A new joint venture with Pomorski Bank Kredytowy, the privately owned shipyard at Szczecin, and the Polish Steamship Company offered to build five vessels which would employ about half of the regular work force. Solidarity began issuing shares in a public offering to support the project. Other protests subsequently came from arms industry workers demanding higher subsidies from the government's budget. In the meantime, the European Bank for Reconstruction and Development offered $100 million as an investment for shipbuilding. Accession to NATO might solve these problems after the year 2000.

Another solution could be effected much sooner through the mass privatization of 512 former state-owned enterprises, shares in which have been traded on the stock exchange through 15 investment funds since June 1997. More than 25 million Polish citizens, or about 95 percent of those eligible, exchanged their privatization vouchers for shares. Results of a public opinion poll, published in mid-October, indicated that only 3 percent of the population kept savings at home and 40 percent had bank accounts. The government also announced that it would sell off its telecommunications company in 1998, valued at $15 billion, and open the market to competition in the following year. However, reprivatization of private property, confiscated by communist authorities at the end of World War II, still has many obstacles to clear.[2]

The U.S. business community already had invested about $3.2 billion in Poland when J. P. Morgan & Co. led a West European consortium in mid-1997 to acquire 24–30 percent of Bank Handlowy stock, the value of which amounts to $1 billion. Total foreign direct investment in Poland was expected to reach $18–19 billion by the end of 1997. The public sector still is responsible for about 40 percent of GDP, a drop from 70 percent in 1990.[3] Five years of sustained economic growth, averaging a 6 percent GDP increase, were accompanied by a decline of inflation rates from 18.5 percent to a projected 12 percent for 1997 and 9.5 percent in 1998.[4]

One cloud on the economic horizon is the foreign trade deficit, totaling $2.35 billion over a two-month period in 1997, compared with only $1.48 billion during the previous year. Most of this adverse balance of payments problem can be traced to relations with the European Community, from which $4.07 billion in goods was imported and to which only $2.69 could be exported. The new first deputy prime minister in charge of finances stated that Poland must reduce its budget deficit or face a crisis.[5]

Nevertheless, the European Commission had announced on 15 July 1997 its recommendation that Poland begin talks on accession to the

European Union. The following month, the government in Warsaw was invited to join the OECD as its twenty-eighth member. The then Polish finance minister announced a willingness to offer Russia technical assistance.[6]

Within all of East-Central Europe, Poland remains the largest trading partner of Russia. However, the Sejm adopted a resolution on 24 June 1997 that called upon the government to begin negotiations with Moscow on compensation for the 1.6 million Polish citizens deported to forced labor camps in Siberia, after the Red Army occupied eastern Poland during September 1939. Only about 100,000 former prisoners belong to an association of survivors, the vast majority of others having died in the Gulag archipelago.

Earlier that same month of June 1997, Poland's first deputy defense minister had met with his counterpart in Moscow. They agreed to "mutual and equal cooperation on a pragmatic basis." One of the results subsequently involved seven special operations officers from each side, spending two weeks in the Sahara desert of Tunisia for an anti-terrorist exercise. Others were being planned for Siberia and also the Amazon River jungle.[7]

In the meanwhile, Poland has not been ignoring relations with other neighbors to the east. At one time united in the Polish-Lithuanian Commonwealth, which extended from the Baltic to the Black Sea and incorporated much of Ukraine, this region may very well acquire an identity of its own. The presidents of Poland and Ukraine signed an agreement at Kiev on 23 May 1997 to pursue a common regional policy. Four days later at Tallin, they joined their counterparts from the three Baltic states in a pledge to cooperate on matters of security.[8]

These five chiefs of state also met with the presidents of Germany, the Czech Republic, Slovakia, and Hungary early in the following month at Gniezno in Poland for a mass celebrated by Pope John Paul II to commemorate St. Adalbert on the one-thousandth anniversary of his martyrdom. The missionary, a German-educated Slav from Bohemia, symbolized the Christian unity of East-Central Europe. Finally, the presidents from ten countries, including the prime minister of Russia met at Vilnius during 5–6 September 1997.

These summits could lead to a regional focus that encompasses security within the forthcoming NATO enlargement. Talks between representatives of the Polish government and NATO commenced in September 1997. That invitation did not come as a surprise in Warsaw. Stanisław Dobrzański, then defense minister, had published a well-reasoned article in a specialized Russian weekly newspaper,[9] in which he labeled Moscow's demands that Poland refrain from modernizing its freeways, airfields, and

sea ports as "not being serious." He stated that the Polish people are entitled to pursue economic development and that it is also in Russia's interest to have a prosperous rather than an impoverished neighbor.
Dobrzański had just visited the defense minister in Moscow and probably
told him much the same. At another level, Poland's first deputy prime
minister, Andrzej Karkoszka, met with his opposite member (also a civilian), Andrei Kokoshin. They discussed "in a business-like manner" mutual and equal cooperation on a pragmatic basis.[10]

In the future, the Polish armed forces will be reduced from 220,000 to
180,000 men and their organizational structure simplified by the year
2004. Defense expenditures are to increase two and a half times from the
2.5 percent level of GDP during 1997, depending on economic growth.
Investment for weapons is projected to grow from 15.7 to 37 percent of
the defense budget over the next fifteen years, according to Marek Siwiec,
who directs the national security office in Warsaw.[11] These developments
should close the readiness gap of 30–50 percent below NATO standards.
Holding maneuvers for British troops in the Pomeranian province along
the Baltic coast has proven to be less expensive than transporting troops
to Canada and also has brought Poland foreign exchange.

What will membership in NATO cost? According to a study group,[12]
headed by the current defense minister at Warsaw, integrating both command systems, ensuring the compatibility of telecommunications and air
defense, and modernizing airfields will total approximately $1.5 billion.
Poland would contribute $35–40 million annually over a ten-year period
by increasing its defense budget to 6 percent of GDP. (The current NATO
average is only 2.3 percent.)

According to a Department of Defense study, the United States government would be required to contribute only $150–200 million per year
during the next decade for all three new members of NATO, or less than
0.1 percent of the annual U.S. defense budget. A NATO study estimates an
even lower cost of $1.3 billion over a ten year period.[13] It remains uncer-
tain whether all 16 members of the NATO will approve this expansion
through their parliaments.

Since the president signed the new constitution on 16 July 1997, after
the Supreme Court had upheld the referendum results of 25 May, Poland
has been committed to the maintenance of democracy and the rule of law,
as well as ownership of private property and personal freedoms—basic
requirements for admission to NATO. The document went into effect
during mid-October, after eight years of provisional legislation.

Prior to the fall 1997 elections, on 3 August, a "lustration" (vetting) initiative became law,[14] requiring that all leading government officials—the
president, ministers, governors of provinces, deputies to Parliament, sen-

ators, judges, prosecutors, executive directors of province offices, heads of public radio, television, and press agencies—declare whether they had collaborated with the communist security agencies at any time during 1944–1990. Statements are to be verified by a Lustration Court, which will have access to official archives. False depositions may result in a ten-year ban from holding public office.

In a public opinion survey, fewer than 9 percent of respondents supported the SLD-PSL (former communists') alliance. Some 19 percent backed the Solidarity-led coalition[15] in July 1997, before parliamentary elections. Extensive flooding in the Odra River valley, which had engulfed more than 1,000 villages and towns in western Poland, with most homes uninsured because of high premiums, may have affected public perceptions. For example, then Prime Minister Włodzimierz Cimoszewicz was quoted as having told the 152,000 displaced flood victims that they should have taken out insurance. He later apologized. Recovery from the destruction will cost an estimated $2.8 billion.[16]

On that same election Sunday, the *New York Times* ran a story from its correspondent in Warsaw who reported that the SLD was "unlikely to command more than one-quarter of the votes, according to recent polls."[17] These same polls indicated that the Solidarity Electoral Action (AWS) coalition would receive about the same percentage of votes. Nobody expected it to win a plurality of 33.8 percent and 201 of the 460 seats in the Sejm as well as 51 of the 100 in the Senate.[18] The new speakers in these chambers of parliament both represent AWS: Solidarity activists Maciej Płażyński in the lower house and Alicja Grześkowiak for the upper chamber.

How did this happen? The new Solidarity leader, Marian Krzaklewski, is a 47-year old engineer with a doctorate in computerization of industrial processes who was born in southeastern Poland. During the last four years, he traveled around the country and by sheer force of personality brought more than 30 smaller political parties and trade union organizations into the AWS. Thus, the coalition included a cross-section of the entire Polish population. Krzaklewski was a researcher and an assistant professor at the polytechnic university in Katowice, where he became cofounder of Solidarity in 1980 at the Polish Academy of Sciences branch in Silesia. During the martial law period and until official recognition of that movement, he worked underground. Arrested in 1984, Krzaklewski spent several months in prison for these activities and was banned from teaching. He was elected to the national Commission of Solidarity in 1990 and a year later became its president.[19]

Reelected in 1995, Krzaklewski cofounded the Electoral Action Committee "Solidarity" (AWS) and was elected chairman. Although invited to become prime minister after the September 1997 election, he decided to remain a deputy to the Sejm and head of its largest faction. He probably will decide to run for the presidency of Poland in the year 2000. Krzaklewski nominated his former professor at the Institute of Industrial Chemistry in Gliwice for the premiership. Jerzy Buzek is a Lutheran and a member of the Evangelical Augsburg Church, the largest Protestant group in Poland. He chaired the first Solidarity congress in 1981 at Gdańsk, as well as two others, and had convinced Krzaklewski to become involved with politics. It should be noted that Professor Buzek had developed a strong interest in market economics during a fellowship at Cambridge University in England during 1970–1971.

After negotiating with their junior partners in the Freedom Union, 16 members of the new government took the oath of office on 31 October 1997, with 10 representing Solidarity (AWS) and six the Freedom Union (UW). See Table 1.1.

Prior to the fall elections, AWS chairman Marian Krzaklewski visited Washington, D.C. and spoke at a noon discussion.[20] He explained the strategy adopted after the former communists had "won" the 1993 parliamentary elections with only 20 percent of the popular vote. AWS represented a grouping that focused itself on problems confronting the nation. This, in turn, led to consolidation around Solidarity in terms of four issues: the constitution, privatization, social security, and health care.

Krzaklewski explained that AWS represented a social movement, not a political party, the only purpose of which had been to win the 1997 election, which it did. Already on 18 September, or three days before voting took place, AWS announced that it would convert itself into a Christian-Democratic political party. In the meanwhile, it would remain unified within Parliament. Registration papers were filed on 13 November 1997. The new party will seek to promote a market economy and Christian values.

Outside of government, their Christian-Democratic movement may even continue the innovative decision-making process which has assigned a number of "voting shares" to coalition members (parties, societies, organizations, foundations) within AWS, depending upon the size of membership, organizational level, technical capabilities and public support based on opinion surveys. An algorithm has been devised to allocate a percentage of votes to each group. To be binding, a decision required a two-thirds majority as well as approval by 75 percent of those present.

When presenting his program before Parliament, Prime Minister Jerzy Buzek outlined four major objectives: improving living standards, reforming government structures, strengthening national security, and reinforcing moral values. He won a 260 to 173 majority vote of confidence

Table 1.1   Government of Poland (as of 31 October 1997)

Name	Born	Portfolio	Affiliation
1. Buzek, Jerzy: chemistry prof.; chaired three Solidarity congresses; coordinated economists' team	(1940)	prime minister (PM)	AWS
2. Balcerowicz, Leszek: economics prof.; held same post in Mazowiecki and Bielecki govts.	(1947)	deputy PM (finance)	UW
3. Tomaszewski, Janusz: auto mechanic; headed Łódź region of Solidarity; originated AWS concept	(1956)	deputy PM (interior)	AWS
4. Geremek, Bronisław: medieval historian, former chmn. foreign relations committee of Senate	(1932)	foreign affairs	UW
5. Onyszkiewicz, Janusz: mathematician; Solidarity since 1980; held same post in Suchocka govt.	(1937)	national defense	UW
6. Wąsacz, Emil: electronics engineer; former director, Katowice and Szczecin steel mills	(1945)	state treasury	AWS
7. Steinhoff, Janusz: mining engineer; in Solidarity since 1980; chmn., Higher Mining Office, 1990–1994	(1946)	economy	AWS
8. Suchocka, Hanna: law prof.; mbr. Solidarity since 1980; former PM during 1992–1993	(1946)	justice	UW
9. Komołowski, Longin: employed by ship building firm at Szczecin; chmn., Solidarity for West Pomorze	(1948)	labor & social policy	AWS
10. Handke, Mirosław: chemistry prof.; since 1993, chaired conference of technical institute deans	(1946)	national education	AWS
11. Wnuk-Nazarowa, Joanna: since 1991, director of State Philharmonic in Kraków; Solidarity mbr. since 1980	(1949)	culture & arts	UW
12. Janiszewski, Jacek: held same position, 1993–1995	(1960)	agriculture & food economy	AWS

(continues)

Table 1.1 (continued)

Name	Born	Portfolio	Affiliation
13. Maksymowicz, Wojciech: M.D.; editor, Wiadomości Lekarskie	(1955)	health & social security	AWS
14. Morawski, Eugeniusz: chemist and economist; director of private company selling steel and computer equipment; dpty. industry minister in Suchocka govt.	(1950)	transport & marine economy	UW
15. Szyszko, Jan: PC dpty. chmn.; headed AWS ecology program; dir., national parks under Suchocka	(1944)	environmental protection, natural resources, forestry	AWS
16. Zdrojewski, Marek: ZChN mbr.; since 1990, with market economy inst. at Gdańsk	(1961)	communications	AWS

Source: Rzeczpospolita, 28, 29 and 30 October 1997, carried biographic sketches; printout from the Embassy of Poland in Washington, D.C. (November 1997).

for his program on 10 November 1997. Professor Buzek promised to "make up for time lost" during the preceding four years and that 1997 would be remembered as the year "when we began to repair the country and made a final break with a bad past."[21]

Although recent developments would seem to portend an optimistic future for Poland, they could also move in other directions. Much will depend not only on what happens inside the country but also on changes in the international scene. Developments could very well proceed along the following lines: a stand-off between parliament and president in Poland until the year 2000, when Aleksander Kwaśniewski is reelected chief executive and the following year former communists win control over both chambers of parliament; retrogression to conditions similar to those before 1989, before Solidarity began to erode communist power. The controlling element however, would be a resurgent Russia attempting to unite all Slavic peoples under its guidance.

This worst-case scenario is predicated on the assumption that by the year 2010, Russia will have recovered sufficiently to add certain former republics and parts of others from the old USSR as subordinate members of a "Slavic Peoples' Confederation." Belarus will be completely absorbed first, followed by the Russian-populated northern regions of Kazakhstan and Ukraine in the so-called "near abroad." (One should note that 44 percent of Ukrainians polled by the Kiev-based Social Monitoring Center supported joining the Russia-Belarus union.)[22]

By then, it may be time to begin pressuring Slovakia, the Czech Republic and, finally, Poland to join the Slavic Peoples' Confederation. Since these countries might not have yet become NATO members, due to procrastination in ratifying such a status, the West might be in no position to block the forced merger.

Even if the aforementioned sounds unbelievable, it still could happen and such a possibility should be considered. For example, Evgenii M. Primakov, before being appointed Russia's foreign minister on 9 January 1996, had served as director of foreign intelligence. In that capacity, he issued a report on "Russia and the Commonwealth of Independent States" or CIS.[23] This analytical study recommended a unified defense and economic zone for all former USSR republics, with the exception of the three Baltic States. Possible scenarios discussed included a much tighter Russian-led confederation, the possibility of each republic going its own way and, finally, several CIS states forming an even tighter union and ultimately merging with Russia. It is this last possibility that Primakov has been advancing.

However, the chances are better than even that a resurgent East will not represent a threat for many decades to come. That should provide ample time for Poland to expand its democratic roots through the efforts of future political leaders, many of whom will have been educated in Western Europe or the United States. Membership in NATO and the European Union as well as other linkages among neighboring countries between the Baltic and Black Seas may also finally convince even the most chauvinistic leaders in Russia that Poland will indeed remain off-limits to their dreams of expansion and regional hegemony. In time, the Polish people may even become a model in their own consolidation of democracy for another generation of Russians to emulate.

Notes

1. Jennifer Monahan, "Human Rights for Prisoners: Learning from Poland," *ODIHR Bulletin*, vol. 5, no. 3 (Fall 1997), 16–19; published by the Organization for Security and Cooperation in Europe.

2. René Höltschi, "The Polish Economy: From Big Bang to Boom," *Swiss Review of World Affairs* 47, no. 11 (November 1997): 29–30; Romuald Gilewicz, "Twardy orzech do zgryzienia," *Rzeczpospolita*, 7 August 1997, 13. Source courtesy of Dr. Eugene Zaleski in Paris.

3. "Foreign Investment in Poland," *RFE/RL Newsline*, 28 August 1997. See also Daniel Oks (task mgr.), *Poland: Country Economic Memorandum* (Washington, D.C.: World Bank, 15 July 1997), 138.

4. Embassy of Poland, *News from Poland* (July–August 1997), 1.

5. "Austerity Budget for Poland?" *RFE/RL Newsline,* 24 September 1997.

6. Valery Masterov, "Poland Joins Rich Nations' Club," *Moscow News,* 7–13 August 1996, 9.

7. "Grom v Sakhare," *Krasnaia zvezda,* 11 July 1997, 3.

8. Paul Goble, "The Spirit of Vilnius," *RFE/RL Newsline,* 8 September 1997.

9. Stanislav Dobzhan'ski, "Voenno-politicheskie vzgliady Varshavy," *Nezavisimoe voennoe obozrenie,* 21–27 June 1997, 1, 3.

10. "Vstrecha v Ministerstve oborony RF," *Krasnaia zvezda,* 5 June 1997, 1.

11. "Armed Forces Modernization," *News From Poland* (October 1997).

12. Janusz Onyszkiewicz, *Estimated Cost of NATO Enlargement* (Warsaw: October 1997).

13. Steven Erlanger, "A War of Numbers Emerges . . ." *New York Times,* 13 October 1997, A-1 and 10; "NATO Puts Growth at $1.3 Billion," ibid., 28 November 1997, A-15.

14. On the vetting law, see letter to the editor by Stash Pruszyński, "More Than Bad Behavior," *International Herald Tribune* (Paris), 12 September 1997, 9.

15. *RFE/RL Newsline,* 29 July 1997.

16. Ibid., 23 July 1997, and 7 October 1997.

17. Jane Perlez, "For the Poles, Brimming Baskets and a Vote too," *New York Times,* 21 September 1997, A-3.

18. *Rzeczpospolita* (25–26 September 1997).

19. Biography from Embassy of Poland, Washington, D.C.

20. "Solidarity's Revival and Polish Politics," *East European Studies Newsletter* (September–October 1997), 5–6; Woodrow Wilson International Center for Scholars.

21. Quoted in *RFE/RL Newsline,* 11 November 1997.

22. Cited in *RFE/RL Newsline,* 16 July 1997.

23. "Rossiia-SNG: Nuzhdaetsia li korrektirovka pozitsiia Zapada?" *Rossiiskaia gazeta,* 22 September 1994, 1 and 6.

TWO

Legacies of Struggle and Defeat

Grzegorz Ekiert*

Poland's postwar history shows the distinctiveness of that country's political development under communist rule in comparison with other parts of the region. The country experienced five major political crises (in 1956, 1968, 1970, 1976, 1980–1981) involving the massive mobilization of various social and professional groups. These events were characterized by a wide variety of collective protest and provoked coercive responses by the state. Moreover, Poland was the first Soviet bloc country in which the communists peacefully surrendered their power in 1989. It seems that among East-Central European regimes, the one in Poland represented an extreme example of both the institutional weakness of the party-state and the capacity of various groups within society to launch collective protest. It can be argued that in Poland, mass protests became a relatively routine way of exerting political pressure as well as defending collective interests that shaped institutional structures and political practices of the party-state.

This chapter focuses on the cycles of protest and opposition to communist rule in Poland and the forms they took. Without an accurate understanding of past strategies of resistance and instances of political mobilization, one can easily overlook or misjudge crucial facets of the

*This chapter is a slightly abbreviated version of the article "Rebellious Poles: Political Crises and Popular Protest under State Socialism, 1945–1989," in *East European Politics and Societies,* II, no. 2 (1997), published for the American Council of Learned Societies by the University of California Press at Berkeley. The author is grateful to Martha and Jan Kubik, Anna Grzymala-Busse, and Richard Staar for their comments on this chapter.

current social, political, and economic changes that are taking place. The historic patterns of collective protest have important consequences and manifestations in the current transition process and produce notable cross-regional differences in political developments among countries overcoming legacies from decades of communist rule.[1] It will be argued that the sources of Poland's uniqueness should be located, above all, in the pattern and outcomes of the de-Stalinization crisis during the 1950s. Paradoxically, Poland's successful and relatively peaceful dismantling of Stalinist rule became a serious liability for the country's post-Stalinist ruling elite. The de-Stalinization process, culminating in October 1956, engendered institutional, political, and cultural legacies that coalesced into a unique political opportunity structure. These specific institutional, political, and economic constraints set Poland apart from other East-Central European regimes. By comparison, the Polish regime became institutionally more diverse, culturally more tolerant, and economically more constrained. As a result, it appeared more vulnerable to collective action from below and, in the choice of its policies, more constrained by the real or anticipated opposition of various social groups. The Polish elite frequently resorted to corporatist practices, buying quiescence from strategic social and professional groups or regions and, in the process, imposing additional burdens on scarce resources and an inefficient economic system. In addition, Polish workers, students, and intellectuals became more defiant and willing to air their grievances and defend their interests through collective action than in other former Soviet bloc countries. Thus, since 1956, the trajectory of Poland's political and economic developments was unique. This fact raises a number of important questions that are still unanswered in comparative analyses of East European politics. To understand Poland's distinctive political experiences under communist rule, one should focus more on the contingent historical events that produce path-dependent political developments and less on either the systemic logic and institutional constraints common to all state-socialist regimes or singular factors specific to Polish culture and society.[2]

1. Collective Protest and Resistance in Poland: The De-Stalinization Crisis

Scholars have explained the extraordinary frequency of popular protest and political instability in post-1945 Poland in two ways. Some interpretations pointed to a number of peculiar factors characterizing society and the party-state that set the country apart from other state socialist regimes.[3] These factors reflected both Poland's past historical experiences as well as the peculiarities of the imposition and consolidation of the new regime. Scholars most often emphasized the following factors: the existence of an institutionally strong and politically independent Catholic Church, the survival of private land ownership and noncollectivized agriculture, a long history of strong anti-Soviet sentiments and uprisings against foreign domination, the strength and intransigence of the intelligentsia, the rebellious nature of the working class,[4] and the institutional weakness of the Polish party-state and its dismal economic performance. The second approach was based on systemic interpretations that emphasized the internal logic common to all state socialist regimes. According to these, state socialist institutional systems produced self-destructive tendencies and were highly crisis prone. By their nature, such regimes were not only highly repressive but also generated economic inefficiency, policy inflexibility, and underlying political instability. For a variety of unique historical factors, Poland was seen as the clearest example of such logic.[5]

It will be argued in the following section that neither social and historical factors peculiar to Poland nor a self-destructive logic of state socialism alone can explain Poland's political development under communist rule. Instead, in order to explain these distinctive developments one must focus on the country's particular political experiences, dynamics, and outcomes of political struggles and conflicts, as well as their cumulative political, institutional, and cultural consequences. In this section it will be shown that, above all, the specific resolution of the de-Stalinization crisis in 1956 created institutional and cultural foundations for Poland's subsequent turbulent political history. Peculiarities of Polish state socialism should be seen as resulting from a series of open confrontations between party-state elite and various forces within society that produced only temporary accommodations. From this perspective, Poland's postwar history may be seen as a long political learning process in which both sides in the confrontation developed new strategies of resistance and protest absorption; produced new institutional, political, and cultural resources; and traded concessions and defeats.

Resistance to Imposition of a Communist Regime

The imposition of a communist regime in Poland was accompanied by a period of open and intense resistance and political struggle. Organized forms of opposition and protest reached their peak in 1946 but quickly subsided in the face of relentless and brutal repressive actions conducted by Soviet forces and communist-controlled local security police and the army. Following rigged elections in January 1947, the victorious communists declared amnesty for members of the political and military underground. However, political repression only intensified, lasting well into the 1950s. This cycle of protest displayed the most varied repertoire of collective action in Poland's postwar history. According to Krystyna Kersten, forms of opposition against the communist takeover during this period included (1) everyday resistance and symbolic defiance; (2) public demonstrations and strikes; (3) political struggle by legal opposition forces; (4) the formation of underground political organizations; and (5) armed resistance.[6] Our knowledge about the strength and influence of antiregime movements and organizations as well as about the extent, forms, and intensity of protests is still relatively limited. Official communist data show that the number of illegal political and military organizations dropped from 1,057 in 1945 and 1,064 in 1946, to 721 in 1947, and 566 in 1948. The membership of these organizations was estimated at 80,296 in 1945, then 61,264 in 1946, then 46,084 in 1947, and 13,166 in 1948.[7] Between 1944 and 1948, the security police recorded 45,800 so-called terrorist acts against state authorities. During the same period, as a result of repressive actions against the opposition, 8,668 people were killed, about 150,000 arrested, and 22,797 sentenced by military tribunals.[8]

The cornerstone of legal opposition against the communists was the Polish Peasant Party (PSL), led by Stanisław Mikołajczyk. Other political forces such as the Labor Party and independent socialists or nationalists also attempted to organize legal political activities. Their efforts were quickly subverted by security forces. Leaders and activists of these parties were harassed and arrested. Communist agents infiltrated the leadership of such parties, in order to destroy them from within. As a result, all legally existing noncommunist forces were destroyed or forcibly merged with the Communist Party and its satellites. Mikołajczyk escaped from Poland after the communists declared victory in the falsified elections of 1947 and the wave of repression against independent politicians that followed. Remnants of the PSL were merged into the communist-controlled United Peasant Party, and the Polish Socialist Party was merged with the Polish Workers' Party in December 1948 to create the Polish United Workers' Party (PZPR). The period of legal political opposition was over.[9]

Armed resistance and legal opposition activities were also paralleled by other forms of collective protest. In May 1946, mass antiregime demonstrations in several cities were brutally dispersed by the security police and were followed by student strikes. During these events some protesters were killed, others wounded and arrested.[10] The country also experienced waves of workers' strikes, mostly caused by economic problems (low wages, excessive production quotas, lack of food, repression against workers' representatives). According to incomplete data collected by the Ministry of Labor and Social Welfare, during the last quarter of 1945, there were 42 strikes in 56 enterprises. In 1946, there occurred 136 strikes in several hundred factories.[11] Existing analyses of protest and resistance in Poland have focused on post-1956 events and have not paid sufficient attention to this early period of struggle. With the information now available, one can argue plausibly that specific features of Polish Stalinism, such as its notable self-limitation in comparison to other East European regimes, should be linked to the widespread and intense resistance and protest activities that occurred during the formative stages of the communist regime. Even though by 1948 organized resistance and open protests had been eradicated by political repression and consolidation of the party-state's institutional structures, important legacies from this period shaped the nature of Polish Stalinism as well as the de-Stalinization crisis in 1956. But the reemergence of collective protest in Poland after 1953 was a direct consequence of the political crisis that affected all Stalinist regimes in the mid-1950s.

The Transition in October 1956

The period between 1953 and 1956 was crucial for subsequent events that shook Poland in October 1956. This was a time of great uncertainties stemming from the gradual dissolution of the political order constructed by Stalin and his imitators in East-Central Europe. Stalin's death in March 1953 roused vague expectations and hopes for change. The dismal economic situation caused frequent outbursts of social unrest. The structure of political opportunities was gradually altered, with some groups, such as intellectuals and young party activists, benefiting more from the new situation than others. Reformist and more pragmatic factions inside the Communist Party were able to effectively challenge the Stalinist establishment for the first time. Internal debates and struggles that split the elite of state socialist regimes during that time focused on three general issues:

1. The problem of political and economic relations between the Soviet Union and its satellite regimes that arose after dissolution of a main tool of Stalinist policies in the region—the Information Bureau of the Communist and Workers' Parties (Cominform)—in April 1956, as well as formal normalization of relations between the USSR and Yugoslavia in June 1956;
2. Reassessment of domestic Stalinist policies, resulting in a complete reshuffling of the political elite, reorganization of the political police, rehabilitation and readmission to the Party of former leaders

accused of rightist deviations, the posthumous rehabilitation of some victims of Stalinist terror,[12] and the removal and indictment of several security force functionaries responsible for the most glaring abuses of power during the Stalinist years;

3. Reevaluation of Stalinist forced industrialization policies, which led to a debate over the ways to correct and rationalize the distorted economic system. At the center of these debates were collectivization policies, principles of investments and resource allocation, and the idea of a limited market. In general, this period of transition produced a highly chaotic political situation characterized by deep intra-elite cleavages and conflicts, a disastrous economic situation, continued Stalinist rhetoric in the media, abrupt shifts between old Stalinist and "new course" policies, and increasing social discontent and pressures for change. Poland was in the forefront of these developments.

On 28 June 1956, a peaceful workers' demonstration in Poznań—was transformed into a bloody revolt after security police fired into the crowd.[13] The situation in Poznań-Poland's fourth major industrial city—was tense for quite some time before the demonstrations and strikes erupted. Already in 1954 and 1955, workers were complaining bitterly about acute housing and food shortages, excessive production quotas and taxes, as well as inadequate supplies of components and raw materials, which prevented them from fulfilling production norms. The revolt began with a huge demonstration of workers from all the city's factories in front of town hall in response to rumors concerning the arrest of a workers' delegation from Poznań sent to Warsaw to present their complaints and demands. Within hours, after the security police had fired on the crowd approaching police headquarters, thousands of demonstrators were battling the regime's security forces, destroying police stations, seizing arms, and releasing prisoners. The omnipresent slogans—"We want bread," "We want freedom," and "Down with false communism"—aptly reflected workers' grievances and feelings. The Polish regime immediately mobilized massive armed forces of more than 10,000 troops and 360 tanks to quell the revolt and began repressive actions against workers who participated in demonstrations. During the revolt approximately 100 people were killed, 900 wounded, and 750 arrested. Among those arrested, 58 were later indicted and 27 were sentenced to prison.

Despite the brutality of this action, the general political situation deteriorated even further. During this time, almost the entire country was in a state of ferment. Public cultural life was blooming; certain journalists and newspapers were becoming less subservient to the Party's instructions; debating clubs of the intelligentsia were formed throughout the country; and student cabarets, theaters, and jazz clubs were established. Peasants began dismantling collective farms, and workers demanded higher wages and benefits as well as industrial self-government. Growing tensions and pressures for reform were coming from many quarters of society but, first of all, from inside the Communist Party and its proxy organizations. The party and mass organizations were split by internal conflicts; pressures for internal democratization and a change of leadership mounted. The transition process culminated in two plenary meetings of the Central Committee during July and October, which set the stage for a gradual and controlled turnover within the ruling elite. The October meeting, occurring within the context of Soviet pressure and great political activism in the country, made a symbolic break with the past and constituted the beginning of Poland's post-Stalinist regime.[14]

The political and institutional changes in Poland produced by the 1956 crisis were not only a reflection of intraparty struggles. The changes also reflected the fears of the communist elite, which were prompted by growing popular discontent and the links that were being established among intellectuals, students, radical party activists, and workers. The election of Władysław Gomułka as the new Party leader was greeted by enthusiastic mass rallies and demonstrations across the country. At the same time, thousands of meetings in factories, universities, and state institutions produced an avalanche of resolutions and demands that were sent to the Party's Central Committee. Mass mobilization had its climax on 24 October, when several hundred thousand Poles gathered in front of the Palace of Culture in Warsaw to listen to the speech of the newly elected party leader. The concluding passage of Gomułka's speech was an appeal for a return to work and a show of support for political change by increased productive effort. The period of social activism was far from over, however. In November and December, there were street demonstrations in several cities. In 1957 and 1958, industrial strikes were frequent. In October 1957, street demonstrations against the liquidation of the liberal weekly *Po prostu* were dispersed by the police.

The 1956 crisis brought great changes to Polish society and the composition and policies of the party-state's elite. To defuse political tension, significant economic concessions were offered. Military expenditures were reduced, investment increased in sectors producing consumer goods, and the discrimination and harassment of the private sector eased. Real wages in Poland increased by an average of 20 percent as a result of the crisis. Improvement of living standards was followed by political concessions. The security apparatus was reorganized, and amnesty was granted to political prisoners. Entire groups repressed under the Stalinist regime—including fighters of the noncommunist underground (Home Army), officers of the prewar Polish army, soldiers of the Polish armed forces in the West, and activists of the Polish Socialist and Polish Peasant parties—were rehabilitated. As a result of the October transition, the political leadership of the country was thoroughly changed, and a relatively open political discussion was carried out inside the party. Polish economists designed far-reaching reforms to improve the effectiveness of the economic system. New organizations emerged, while existing institutions and organizations elected new leaders. More autonomy was granted to many traditional "transmission belts," such as trade unions or student and youth organizations, as well as to the two communist-controlled political movements (the United Peasant Party and the Democratic Party). Spontaneously organized workers' councils in factories were legalized and traditional forms of cooperatives reestablished. Collectivization policies were halted and the majority of collective farms were dismantled. (Out of 9,975 collective farms in June 1956, only 1,934 remained.)

The institutional structure of the Polish party-state became more pluralistic than in any other state socialist country. New parliamentary elections were prepared for 1957 with a new electoral law allowing for a secret ballot and more candidates than the number of available seats. Also, a symbolic representation of independent Catholics in the Parliament was permitted. Censorship was drastically limited and Polish culture and intellectual life experienced a period of remarkable revival. The media discarded militant Stalinist language and experienced unprecedented programmatic changes.[15] In the education system, curricula were changed in all types of schools, and a new legal framework for universities, giving them a large measure of internal autonomy, was enacted. The Polish primate, Stefan Cardinal Wyszyński, was released from prison and promised significant concessions. Shortly after, other imprisoned priests were released, expelled bishops and priests assumed their former duties, lay Catholic organizations were formed, Catholic papers and publications were allowed to be published, and religious instruction returned to public schools.

Responding to strong anti-Soviet sentiments, relations with the USSR were altered. Soviet military advisers left Poland. Soviet Marshal Konstantin Rokossowski was relieved of his duties as Poland's minister of defense. The Polish debt to the USSR was cancelled on the basis of unfair pricing practices, and new credits were granted by the Soviet state. An official agreement was signed concerning the legal status of Soviet troops stationed temporarily on Polish territory, which stipulated that such a presence cannot infringe in any way on the sovereignty of the Polish state or allow any interference in Polish People's Republic internal affairs.

Finally, an agreement was signed concerning the repatriation of Polish citizens who remained in Soviet territories after the war. By March 1959, about 224,000 Poles were allowed to return to Poland. Promises of the new regime included economic reforms, decentralization and workers' self-government, freedom of expression in the arts and science, an end to foreign broadcast jamming, and guarantees of a secure existence to individual peasants and small private enterprises. The new party's leadership and its policies were accepted with great enthusiasm by large segments of the population. This was the only moment in the postwar history of Poland when the regime could claim a substantial measure of genuine popular support.

The dismantling of these achievements and a retreat from promises had already begun in the fall of 1957 and lasted for several years. Revisionist forces within the Party were quickly marginalized. Economic reforms were never implemented, and workers' self-government had been rendered meaningless by the end of 1958. The media's newly acquired freedoms were promptly rescinded. Religious instruction was banned from public schools, and the relationship between state and church deteriorated. Polish society was not able to defend the concessions granted to it by the regime in an hour of weakness. As Jakub Karpiński points out, "After October 1956, the program of the intelligentsia was quite often limited to simple trust and hope. Gradually these feelings turned to disappointments."[16] It can be argued that besides the weakness and fragmentation of reformist forces in Polish society, the tragedy of the Hungarian Revolution grossly contributed to such a reversal of policies by the new regime in Warsaw. These two 1956 events were closely interwoven and for years represented an example of the hopes, perils, and limits of liberalization attempts in the region. Over the long run, only the Polish church seems to have been an undeniable beneficiary of the Polish October. However, the intellectual elite also secured some limited autonomy, and the peasantry was saved from forced collectivization. During the 1956 crisis, as in all other cases of de-Stalinization, the principal political actors constituted an anti-Stalinist force within the party and among the intellectual elite and students. A very limited role was played by the church and Catholic circles, open anti-communist forces were absent, and neither workers nor peasants were able to organize and have visible impact on the political scene.[17] Thus, intellectuals and intelligentsia more generally were winners of the transition to a post-Stalinist environment. They extracted the most tangible concessions from the party-state. Their living standards, freedoms, and opportunities were greater than those of other groups in Polish society.

Despite the reversal of the October policies and promises made in 1957, since the beginning of the 1960s, Poland has remained the most liberal and open country in the Soviet bloc. The institutional, political, and cultural consequences of the Polish October can hardly be overestimated, especially if we compare them with the outcomes of two other major de-Stalinization crises—Hungary in 1956 and Czechoslovakia in 1968—as well as to the other state-socialist countries that survived de-Stalinization without an open political crisis. Krystyna Kersten argues that "in 1956, the change in power relations between the state and society took place. After 'October', the communists relinquished their ideological domination step by step. They focused on controlling only these actions which were significant from a political point of view. They accepted some elements of pluralism in culture, expanded freedom to pursue research in sciences, accepted the existence of private agriculture, and approved (despite some harassment and repression) the existence of the Catholic Church as an independent and powerful organization. Gradually, these forced concessions diminished the dependency of society making it possible for different social groups to articulate their aspirations."[18] Similarly, Jerzy Holzer points out that "Polish experiences in 1956 produced, on the one hand, the belief in power of society (the regime can be forced to make concessions). On the other hand, they produced self-assurance among the power elite (masses can be relatively easily pacified if one can wait long enough for political energy to burn down)."[19]

In sum, as a result of the post-October transition, Poland became a country with semiautonomous public spaces, an independent Catholic Church, a modicum of intellectual freedom, limited freedom to travel, an openness to the West in culture and the sciences, and a degree of institutional independence within the universities, and in media and professional organizations. These "unpatrolled spaces" became laboratories of experience that nurtured political dissent and opposition. In 1956, a new repertoire of collective protest emerged, and the culture of resistance among the educated classes was symbolically validated. Certain elements of the non-communist national tradition were resurrected and tolerated by the party-state. This situation differed radically from the outcomes of the 1956 de-Stalinization crisis in Hungary and 1968 in Czechoslovakia. In short, the political opportunity structure in Poland became significantly more open in comparison to other state-socialist regimes, even though the organizational and institutional structures of their party-states were similar.

2. Perils of Frozen De-Stalinization:
From March 1968 to Solidarity

In March 1968, a student revolt dramatically brought Poland's internal problems to the fore—worsening economic stagnation, growing intra-elite conflict, a steady retreat from the hopes and promises of October 1956, and an intensifying campaign against the intellectual elite.[20] The revolt was the desperate effort by groups of intellectuals and students to defend the remnants of the concessions achieved in 1956 and an attempt to force the regime to keep alive the legacies of 1956. It was also the political culmination of several years of growing disappointment and discontent, evidenced by the escalating conflict between the increasingly conservative Polish regime and the increasingly "revisionist" Polish intellectuals.

In February 1962, a debating society founded by Poland's leading intellectuals during 1956, the Club of a Crooked Circle, was banned. The following year, two influential cultural weeklies were liquidated; censorship was tightened; and certain liberal writers, artists, and scholars were sharply criticized by Party authorities. In response, in March 1964, a group of 34 writers and scholars sent a letter to Premier Józef Cyrankiewicz criticizing restrictions on artistic freedom and cultural production and protesting censorship, as well as demanding changes in the state's cultural and educational policies. The letter caused a considerable political stir. Exactly a year later, two young revisionist intellectuals— Jacek Kuroń and Karol Modzelewski—wrote an open letter to Party members that contained a critical analysis of party-state policies. In both cases, the regime responded with repressive actions against the signatories of the letters. Their books and articles were banned, contracts cancelled, passports confiscated, and official police investigations begun. Kuroń and Modzelewski were arrested and sentenced to prison terms; as was Melchior Wańkowicz, one of the signatories to the "Letter of 34." In 1965, state-church relations, which had become increasingly strained since 1958, deteriorated significantly following a letter sent by the Polish Episcopate to West German bishops. The letter was an official invitation for the latter to participate in the celebration of 1,000 years of Polish Catholicism and contained the phrase, "We forgive you and ask for your forgiveness." The government responded with an antichurch campaign built on the appeal to anti-German sentiments in Polish society. It also refused to allow Pope Paul VI to visit Poland, causing an international sensation. In 1966, during the tenth anniversary of the October 1956 transition, intellectuals criticizing regime policies during meetings organized to commemorate the events were expelled from the Party. Many others gave up their Party membership in a gesture of solidarity. A mass petition was signed by 1,200 students and academics protesting disciplinary proceedings instituted against students who participated in university-organized discussions and the suspension of Adam Michnik. At the same time, an anti-Semitic campaign was orchestrated by the conservative and nationalistic faction within the Party elite following the Arab-Israeli War in 1967 and Soviet-bloc support for the Arab countries. The country's political situation was fraught with tension, conflict, and confrontation. Intellectuals' discontent, the primitive anti-Semitic campaign, and the regime's increasingly repressive policies had the greatest impact on the political atmosphere in the major academic centers around the country.

During the 1967–1968 academic year, political tensions at Warsaw University were high. The catalyst for open confrontation was the decision to close production of a patriotic nineteenth-century Polish play by Adam Mickiewicz, *Forefathers' Eve*, at the National Theater in Warsaw. The play's final performance on 30 January, turned into a patriotic demonstration, after which a small student protest group was dispersed by the police. Two of the demonstration leaders, Adam Michnik and Henryk Szlajfer, were expelled from the university. Some 3,145 people in Warsaw and 1,098 in Wrocław signed a petition addressed to the authorities protesting the play's banning. The Warsaw branch of the Union of Polish Writers criticized the regime's cultural policies at one of its meetings and demanded that performances of *Forefathers' Eve* be allowed to continue unhampered. When a peaceful assembly of students at Warsaw University protesting the expulsion of Michnik and Szlajfer was attacked by the plainclothes security police forces on 8 March, a full-scale confrontation erupted. During the next two days, students organized rallies and street demonstrations, which turned into battles with the motorized police (ZOMO). In the space of a few days, the wave of student demonstrations spread to all major Polish academic centers. In several cities, students launched street demonstrations and fought with ZOMO. In other university towns, there were rallies and meetings. During street confrontations, students were brutally attacked with water cannons, tear gas, and truncheons. Faculty members were often beaten together with their students whenever the police invaded university buildings while pursuing demonstrators. Students launched occupation strikes at Warsaw University and the Warsaw Polytechnic. Students everywhere condemned police brutality and demanded the formation of an independent student organization, abolition of censorship, introduction of economic reforms, and observance of the constitution and political rights.

The regime responded with fury to the rebellion of students and intellectuals. Hundreds of students were expelled from universities, sentenced and jailed, or drafted into military service. Intellectuals who sympathized with students were attacked viciously in the press; universities were purged and their autonomy abolished. Authorities closed down the departments of economics, philosophy, sociology, and psychology at Warsaw University. A propaganda campaign in the mass media portrayed students and intellectuals as agents of Zionism, revisionism, German revanchism, and American imperialism. The anti-intelligentsia campaign was paralleled by an escalating anti-Semitic campaign. Hundreds of people lost their party membership and jobs because of their Jewish origins. As a result, following the March events, about 20,000 people (mostly Jews) were forced to emigrate from Poland. The Party attempted to create mistrust and division between workers and the intelligentsia. Party organizations mobilized groups of workers to stage protest meetings against "troublemakers" and "ungrateful" students and intellectuals who lived at the expense of the working class while shamelessly slandering the workers' state. This ugly and crudely manipulated repressive campaign found its unfortunate consequences in December 1970, when workers of the Polish coastal region went on strike to protest drastic price increases and a new austerity program, although students and intellectuals did not join their struggle.

The events of 1968 signified the final defeat of those groups and forces that had secured the most tangible concessions in 1956; that is, the intellectuals and reformist factions within the party. Jack Bielasiak argues that a major consequence of the 1968 upheaval was that "the liberal and revisionist elements within the PZPR [Polish United Workers' Party] were virtually eliminated from significant positions. More important, the revisionists, disillusioned by the wholesale attack on the intellectual community, ceased to believe that one could reform the system from within. They saw the 1968 attacks as evidence that the party cared exclusively about power, and that no meaningful political change was possible. Initially, and for some time, they therefore retreated into political passivity."[21] The merciless destruction of the Czechoslovak reform movement by the Soviets in the summer of 1968 supplied additional proof for what many saw as the impossibility of reforms from within. Whereas the March events with their ugly anti-Semitic and anti-intellectual campaigns represented a setback for the Polish intelligentsia and Polish culture in general, they also left important legacies that became evident only at the end of the 1970s.

First, defeat of the revisionist opposition changed the ideological orientation of intellectuals. According to Leszek Kołakowski, "March 1968, despite all prosecutions and repressions, finally liberated Polish culture from ties with the Communist system and its ideology. There was nothing left to 'revise' anymore, and nobody was ready to expect any improvement from one or another party faction."[22] Moreover, following a dramatic protest by independent Catholic deputies in Parliament against police actions in March, left-wing and revisionist opposition groups began to recognize independent Catholic circles as their natural allies. Adam Michnik emphasized this legacy of the 1968 events: "Bridging the artificial boundaries which separated a Pole-radical from a Pole-Catholic is, in my view, one of the most precious values of the March legacy."[23]

Finally, the March events became a formative political experience for the young Polish intellectuals who, for the first time, faced head on the repressive reality of state socialism. Tens of thousands of students participated in street demonstrations or strikes and were beaten up by the police. Thousands were expelled from universities and hundreds arrested. All experienced first hand the "organized lie frame-up" used by the authorities and the media to discredit protest participants. As Jerzy Holzer argues, "The entire generation of young intelligentsia—students and young intellectuals—inherited from the March events the awareness of their own weakness and the feeling of bitterness against the rest of society which refused to support them. But they also inherited the hatred against the regime which responded to a timid protest with violence and tear-gas, with lies in the media, with expulsion from universities and jobs, with arrest and trials."[24] It was this generation that returned to politics during the days of the Solidarity movement and rose to power after 1989. Jerzy Eisler is absolutely right in stating that "formation of the '68 generation was the most important and enduring value of the March events."[25] However, before defeated intellectuals and students mounted a new challenge to the regime, another collective actor unexpectedly entered the Polish political scene.

Workers' Revolts of 1970 and 1976

After the government announcement of substantial price increases in basic foodstuffs on 12 December 1970, workers in the coastal cities of Gdańsk, Gdynia, Elbląg, and Szczecin held mass meetings, elected strike committees, drew up lists of demands, organized marches to the local Party headquarters, and clashed inevitably with the police and military forces.[26] These events constituted the largest and most violent working class uprising in the history of state socialist regimes. The first protests and confrontations with police broke out in Gdańsk and Gdynia on 14 December. During the street riots, Party, trade union, and government buildings were burned down. Protesting workers were killed and wounded when the police opened fire. Strikes and violent street clashes continued the next day, and by 16 December, violent protests had spread to other coastal cities. The following day, workers in Szczecin (the second major industrial center of the coast) joined the rebellion with strikes and violent street demonstrations. In the course of the next few days, there were strikes in hundreds of factories throughout the region, repeated demonstrations and street battles between thousands of workers armed with bottles of gasoline and the police and military forces equipped with armored vehicles, tanks, and helicopters. In many instances, the police and the military fired at unarmed crowds, killing and wounding protestors. According to official data, between 14 and 20 December, about 45 people were killed, 1,165 wounded, and 3,161 arrested.[27]

As a result of the street riots, 19 public buildings were burned down, including the regional Party headquarters in Gdańsk and Szczecin, and 10 tanks, 18 armored personnel carriers, and some 60 police cars were destroyed. At the same time, massive forces of police and soldiers were concentrated in coastal cities, curfews were imposed, and the region's communications with the rest of the country were cut off in an effort to prevent further escalation of the strikes and demonstrations.[28] On 19 December, however, when the coastal region was already effectively pacified, strikes spread to other parts of the country. That day, there were about 100 strikes throughout Poland, but they all remained localized and ended by 22 December. There were also small street demonstrations in several cities that were dispersed promptly by the police. The brutality of the police action, the military occupation of factories, and the arrests of strike committee members, as well as a dramatic change in the country's leadership, contributed to the rapid decline of protests and the regime's recovery of political control in the region. Moreover, during this crisis the Polish intelligentsia, students, and the church, which had been pacified in 1968, did not join with the workers and remained remarkably silent. Thus, the workers lacked any influential allies. Their protests were easily suppressed and political tensions were promptly and skillfully defused. Although sporadic strikes occurred during the first months of 1971, workers were effectively silenced by the end of March.

The December 1970 revolt was a turning point in the tradition of workers' protest. The events created a historical memory of heroic struggle against the regime and became a symbolic reference point in working class resistance in much the same way that the 1956 and 1968 events had become a reference point for dissenting intelligentsia. For an entire generation of workers, especially those living in coastal cities who participated in strikes and demonstrations, the brutal and repressive nature of the regime was revealed. The revolt also signified the political awakening of the Polish working class. Workers' demands were not exclusively economic but covered an entire range of other issues pertaining to Poland's political situation. Such demands were heavily influenced by concepts of social justice and equality and focused on the functioning of public institutions, including trade unions and the media, economic reforms, the management and organization of production in enterprises, and broader social issues, such as health care, housing conditions, and public transportation.[29] The events produced a new repertoire of protest, a new collective action frame, and an experience of collective action that shaped patterns of worker protests in the years following 1970. Roman Laba strongly emphasizes this point, arguing that the "main characteristics of Solidarity, its master frames, were created autonomously by Polish workers six years before the creation of KOR and ten years before the rise of Solidarity. The sit-down strike and the interfactory strike committee are the organizational breakthroughs. The programmatic frame or breakthrough is the demand for free trade unions, independent of the party."[30]

The differences between the workers' demands and actions in 1970 and in 1980 should not, however, be disregarded. The 1980 demands were articulated in the clear language of political rights—this was absent in 1970. Ten years later, strikers demanded not only credible and truthful information in the media but above all the abolition of censorship and constitutionally guaranteed freedom of expression. Similarly, they demanded not only the democratization of existing trade unions but also the right to form new, independent unions.[31]

This difference was not a reflection of the "linguistic incompetence" of the 1970 strikers but instead indicated a fundamental change in the political imagination and the emergence of a new political discourse in 1980. Therefore, the argument that the Solidarity movement was the sole creation and expression of the long-lasting working class struggle in which the role of intellectuals, human rights organizations, and the church was not important is fundamentally flawed.[32]

The workers' rebellion sealed the fate of Gomułka's regime and closed a distinct period in Polish postwar history. The Party's divided leadership used the occasion to accomplish a long-overdue transition of power within the ruling elite. On 20 December, at the extraordinary seventh plenary Party meeting, Gomułka was demoted and his four closest associates removed from the Politburo. The new party leader, Edward Gierek, promised a two-year freeze on food prices and unspecified economic reforms. In spite of these pledges, there was a resurgence of strikes and protests that continued for another several weeks. Without further response in other parts of the country, they slowly subsided. Gierek's regime skillfully restored order by blaming all use of force on the departing leaders, by offering conciliatory gestures, and by making economic concessions. The original Five-Year Plan for 1971–1975 was redrafted and revised to satisfy more of the people's social and economic needs rather than to fulfill quantitative production targets. Also, a new agricultural policy was announced that abolished compulsory delivery quotas for private farmers. Real wages increased by 22 percent as an immediate result of the crisis.[33]

On 15 February, the government, responding to lingering strikes and workers' demands, cancelled all price increases and lowered food prices to the level prior to 13 December 1970. But the promises of the Gierek regime quickly turned into disappointments.

Gierek based his new economic policies and political promises on a massive influx of Western loans and an opening of the global market to Polish goods. He made no serious attempts, however, to reform Poland's economic institutions and practices. In the mid-1970s, this opening of the economy in the absence of systemic reforms backfired. The economic crisis that had already begun in 1974 became sharply visible in 1976. On 24 June 1976, the regime attempted to cope with the crisis by restructuring the prices of food and consumer goods and, in so doing, effectively cutting real wages. On 25 June, workers responded with mass revolts in two industrial cities in central Poland and short-lived strikes in many other locations. The strikes that took place in 130 factories across the country were generally peaceful. They lasted only for the day; that evening the price increases were revoked by the country's prime minister. In two cities, however, events turned violent and had lasting repercussions. During the street demonstrations in Radom, Party buildings were attacked and set on fire, and in Ursus, workers blocked the main railroad tracks in the country and fought with the police.[34]

As in 1970, the regime acted decisively. Street demonstrations were brutally dispersed by militarized police; hundreds of workers were arrested, beaten, and dismissed from their jobs. In Radom, two people were killed during the riots, 121 wounded, and more than 2,000 arrested. Also, 75 policemen were injured. Throughout the entire country several thousand people lost their jobs as a direct result of their participation in the protests, and 500 were indicted. The events ended with a series of trials in which 25 workers were sentenced to prison terms ranging from two to ten years. The repressions were followed by a propaganda campaign and orchestrated political rallies against "troublemakers" and "vandals." This time, however, the intellectual elite, already mobilized to prevent changes to the Polish constitution, recognized that real strength lay only in cooperating with and supporting the workers. In September 1976, a group of intellectuals founded the Committee for Defense of Workers (KOR) and demanded amnesty for all workers arrested and tried as well as an end to repression. They began publishing information on political persecution in Poland and collected funds to assist the victims of state repression. Also, the Catholic Church officially demanded an end to repression against the workers involved in protests.

In the aftermath of the June 1976 events, an alliance among workers, intellectuals, students, and the church began to emerge. The formation of

KOR stimulated the rapid development of independent groups, organizations, and initiatives across the country. Intellectuals, students, workers, and peasants formed their own organizations to monitor state repression and offer help and protection to the victims. Strictly political organizations were funded by some opposition activists. Underground publications flourished, and clandestine publishing houses and distribution networks were established. Independent self-education groups were formed, and unofficial "underground" universities were organized. The newly formed opposition groups secured their existence and consolidated the independent democratic space; they brought together committed groups of leaders and supporters who reevaluated past experiences and designed new strategies.[35] Meanwhile, the economic crisis engulfed all branches of the economy and eroded the official power structures. The growing moral and intellectual decay affected the entire institutional structure of the regime. The Marxist-Leninist project, which for years had supplied political imagination and self-justification to the Party elite, crumbled. Pope John Paul II's visit to Poland in 1979 amounted to an open symbolic confrontation with the regime, setting the stage for a new round of political struggle between the Polish party-state and society.[36]

Rise and Suppression of Solidarity

In the summer of 1980, when a huge wave of social unrest shook the country, the collective actors who entered the political stage this time were only nominally the same. For the first time in Poland's postwar history, social and political conflict transcended ideological categories developed in intraparty struggles and the symbolic cleavage between revisionists and dogmatists. It went beyond all traditional limitations, divisions, political visions, strategies, and concepts.[37] Moreover, the political and social gap between workers and intellectuals was bridged as a result of the post-1976 developments and opposition activities. In August 1980, a new national movement was ready to sign a genuine contract with the party-state. A new workers' organization, Solidarity, led by its grassroots leaders and supported by the church, intellectuals, and a majority of the nation, gained strength from day to day. With some 10 million members, Solidarity presented a powerful political force that was able to threaten not only the domestic order but also the entire political stability of the region. In contrast to earlier protests, demands of the union were distinctly political: freedom of association, freedom of conscience, freedom of the press, social autonomy and self-government, equality of rights and duties.

As Alex Pravda pointed out, "1980 brought an unprecedented expansion and politicization of workers' demands. Instead of pressing only for material security strikers asked for institutional change [and were] in the forefront of the struggle for civil liberties."[38] The crisis in Poland was primarily a political crisis. It indicated the collapse of a definite concept of social and political order, a concept that was manifested in the system of power established in Poland 40 years before. The August agreements that followed the nationwide strike action announced the formation of the first free trade unions in the communist world and established a completely new model of state organization. This model combined an authoritarian state that securely controlled national politics and vibrant, democratic politics where the state's control was no longer effective.

The successful conclusion and unexpected concessions forced on the Polish party-state by the strikers set this political conflict apart from events in the past. The summer of 1980 produced a rapid mass mobilization and unprecedented wave of strikes that involved all social strata and regions of the country. According to Piotr Marciniak, these strikes were characterized by (1) the absence of preexisting organizational resources within enterprises, such as independent employees' organizations; (2) a countrywide territorial scope and local universality; (3) long duration and a tendency for protests to expand and escalate; (4) strong bonds of solidarity among strikers that bridged factory, industry, and social divisions; (5) the dignified character of protest actions and the absence of violence; (6) a strong impact on significant segments of the establishment (local authorities, management, enterprise, Party, and union organizations); (7) the rapid development of strong organizational structures and a common identity, which quickly led to the formation of a nationwide movement.[39]

What was perhaps even more important was the movement's ability to win significant political concessions and the time necessary to secure and consolidate the achievements of the successful countrywide collective action. Thus, by the end of summer, Polish society had new organizational structures that had emerged during the strikes and a network of old embryonic opposition organizations that were formed at the end of the 1970s. For the first time, a state-socialist regime faced a highly organized, independent opposition movement with independent resources, experienced grassroots leaders, and the capacity to mobilize millions.

The institutionalization of Solidarity also provided the impetus for the independent organization of other social groups that were unable to join the union because they were not employees of state enterprises or public institutions. University students were the first group to start an independent organization and to press for reforms of the education system.[40] Establishing independent farmers' unions proved more difficult. Polish farmers did not represent a cohesive social group after four decades of exploitation, cultural and political mistreatment, and abuse by the state. Deep-seated grievances among farmers, however, very soon resulted in a campaign of protests in the countryside ranging from localized hunger strikes to spectacular demonstrations and the occupation of public buildings.[41] Artisans, craftsmen, and small businesspeople also organized independent unions.

Even the existing state-controlled organizations—professional and youth associations, the two existing political parties (the United Peasant Party and the Democratic Party), and the Communist Party itself—were transformed by the explosion of popular participation following August 1980. They underwent a rapid process of internal democratization and a change in their leaderships. As a result, organizations that used to act as liaisons between the party-state and society and that controlled the political sphere now acquired a significant degree of autonomy and often challenged the state's policies. Among the independent organizations that existed prior to the summer of 1980, those affiliated with the Catholic Church grew rapidly. The Catholic intelligentsia and many individual priests were deeply involved in the Solidarity movement, although the church hierarchy attempted to position itself as a mediator of conflicts between society and the state. Thus, the civic fever sparked by Solidarity spread to all groups, cities, and villages, and to all organizations and institutions of the Polish party-state. The self-governing spirit even affected the police and the military, as their members attempted to organize independent trade unions.

In a country of 35.5 million people, one-third of that number became members of independent professional, social, and political organizations. Moreover, the level of mass participation in various forms of collective action was phenomenal. By the end of the Solidarity period, one in five Poles had participated at least once in a collective protest. Predictably, only one in ten people living in the countryside participated in protest actions, whereas in cities the ratio was one in four. Twice as many men as women (more than 30 percent of whom were younger than 25) participated in protest actions. To sum up, Polish society experienced an unprecedented cultural and political revolution that altered all institutional structures, political attitudes, and modes of participation.[42] The emergence of a multidimensional, self-organized, strong, and independent democratic civil society that facilitated mass public participation became the most striking characteristic of the Solidarity period.

Solidarity evolved into more than an organized social force and a vehicle of political participation. It represented a distinct intellectual and symbolic formation that provided a multitude of groups and actors with a collective identity. During its existence, Solidarity was able to develop a coherent collective identity that reflected and reinforced the insurmountable division between the alien communist state "Them" and society "Us," as well as to establish a framework for a collective action based on the notion of inalienable human and political rights. Solidarity's distinctive alternative political discourse merged concepts and ideas developed by the democratic opposition in the 1970s with those promoted by the social and ethical doctrine of the Catholic Church. The movement also appropriated important segments of national and patriotic values and traditions. It found powerful symbolic expressions that appealed to the political imagination of diverse social groups within society. The collective identity of the movement was built around those symbols, values, and traditions, which set the movement apart from the official political language, values, and ideology.

Thus, Poland's political crisis did more than uproot a significant part of the state's theoretical and political foundations and undermine its routinely employed claims to legitimacy. The crisis generated two opposed and well-defined political forces representing the state and society and created two separate cultural and political idioms that appealed to different values and traditions and used different political calendars and symbols.[43] Solidarity emerged as a powerful defender of the Polish national tradition and values and as a representative of a powerful vision of reform and political change based on the self-organization of democratic society against a totalitarian state. It pushed the party-state elite into a position of guarantor for foreign political domination. However, they were considered indispensable only as long as the geopolitical balance of power in Europe remained unaltered.

The struggle that unfolded in Poland during the months following the August agreements and culminated in the imposition of martial law on 13 December 1981, also provided evidence of the regime's ability to survive and adjust to an unprecedented challenge from below. This was due in part to the pragmatism and flexibility of those in power, but it also resulted from Solidarity's own self-imposed limitations. Andrzej Walicki emphasized this paradox when he pointed out that "if Poland were not part and parcel of the Soviet empire, one would ask only why a powerful, all-national movement demanded so little, and how it would be possible to combine a full-fledged participatory democracy on the local level with communist-dominated government and, more important, with full communist control over the coercive powers." Furthermore, he asked how the Soviet Union could have accepted an arrangement where "communist power in Poland should be reduced to safeguarding the interest of the Warsaw Pact."[44]

On 13 December 1981, the imposition of martial law abruptly ended a precarious balance between political forces in Poland and reduced political uncertainties in the region. This was the most extensive internal military operation in the history of state socialist regimes. Poland's borders were sealed, communication systems cut off, a national curfew imposed, extraordinary repressive legal regulations introduced, all organizations suspended, and tens of thousands of Solidarity activists detained. Literally overnight, Poland changed from the most liberal to the most repressive regime in the Soviet bloc. In just a few years, however, it became clear that as with other historical parallels, similarities between Polish demobilization policies and their counterparts in Hungary after 1956 and Czechoslovakia after 1968 were rather superficial. Despite its startling short-term success, the imposition of martial law did not break the political stalemate between the state and society that emerged during the Solidarity period. Although Solidarity's legal organizational structures were destroyed and its resources dispersed, the movement soon emerged as a loose network of groups organized around territorial, institutional, professional, and personal bases, united on a set of common goals, values, and symbols.

These underground organizations formed the backbone of opposition and resistance against the post-martial law regime. During this period, public opinion polls consistently reflected that a significant segment of the population (approximately 25 percent) remained in strong opposition to the regime and that political divisions in the country persisted. As Krzysztof Jasiewicz concluded, "One of the most important results of the *Polacy '84* survey was the confirmation of the hypotheses that the political conflict which most sharply emerged in Poland in 1980–1981 was not resolved as a result of martial law and political events which followed its imposition. Quite to the contrary, it persisted although in less visible and spectacular forms."[45] The most visible forms of oppositional activities were street demonstrations and protests organized on the thirteenth of every month (marking the imposition of martial law) and other noncommunist national holidays. Street protests were most frequent and dramatic in 1982 and 1983, although they were usually confined to Solidarity strongholds in several large cities. The most important components of underground Solidarity activities, however, were the formation of independent educational as well as countrywide underground publishing and distribution networks.

Although the extent and intensity of oppositional activities and public support for underground Solidarity declined through the 1980s, groups of hard-core activists continued a broad range of clandestine activities in all regions of the country. Also, with the decline in political repression, legally existing groups and organizations gradually extended the limits of permissible activities. By the end of the decade, Poland again became the most politically liberal country of the Soviet bloc. Liberalization of the post-martial law regime, together with a declining capacity of the Solidarity movement to coordinate the struggle of oppositional groups, led to significant organizational and ideological fragmentation of the Polish opposition. Various political and social movements and parties filled the spectrum of available political options. Thus, at the end of the decade, the consensus and unity on the national level that had characterized the glory days of Solidarity gradually unraveled.

Although the imposition of martial law destroyed organized opposition and liberated the ruling elite from constant political pressure and threats, it did nothing to improve the party-state's capacity to deal with Poland's economic crisis. Also, with the passage of time, it became increasingly clear that the initial success in crushing independent organizations was not followed by consistent demobilization strategies through which the Polish party-state elite could again emerge as the unchallenged political force in the country and regain the political initiative. For a variety of reasons, the ruling elite refrained from massive political repression and searched for some sort of accommodation with representatives of the defeated opposition. This inconsistent demobilization process, during which both sides of the conflict frequently changed their strategies and failed to achieve convincing success, stretched over the entire decade and prolonged the political and economic difficulties that began in the 1970s.

In the spring of 1988, after several years of relative social peace, strikes and protests again erupted in factories and universities across the country. Students organized demonstrations on the anniversary of the March 1968 events and held occupation strikes at several universities in May. Independent street demonstrations took place in several cities on 1 May. In April and May, the former Solidarity strongholds—the Lenin Shipyard, Nowa Huta and Stalowa Wola steelworks—and a number of other factories went on strike. During these strikes, restoration of the Solidarity union and reinstatement of Solidarity activists fired during and after martial law became major demands. These political demands were, however, eclipsed by a large number of specific demands concerning wages and benefits as well as shop-floor issues applicable to a given enterprise. As a result of these actions, former leaders and activists of the Solidarity movement again became prominent in the country's political life. These strikes, however, failed to stimulate mass political mobilization and revive the spirit of 1980. According to Piotr Marciniak, they resembled "normal" strike waves that were taking place in many societies. These strikes were territorially limited and failed to achieve local universality. They were becoming shorter in duration and declining in number rather than expanding. Bridging the social boundaries became difficult. Strikes sharpened existing divisions and were not supported by any social elite of the country. Finally, they did not produce any new organizational structures and identities.[46]

Although the first wave of strikes did not bring any tangible political concessions, another wave during the summer of 1988 was more successful. This time, the strikes spread to Silesian coal mines and Solidarity strongholds in the regions of Szczecin and Gdańsk. Party-state authorities realized they were facing another potential political earthquake. Despite resistance from important segments of the ruling elite, Party leaders finally agreed to meet with representatives of the opposition, giving them quasi-legal status. In the fall of 1988, long preparations for the famous "Roundtable" negotiations began, which gave the initial stimulus to historical changes in East-Central Europe. Both the ruling elite and the Solidarity based opposition had to reach an internal consensus for entering the talks. Official negotiations began in Warsaw on 6 February 1989. They continued amid growing social tensions and multiplying protest actions. For example, in February 1989 there were 214 strikes in Poland, including 81 occupation strikes. During the first two weeks of March, work stoppages took place in 223 enterprises and strikes in 341, affecting all regions and all industries in the country.[47] During the same time, there were street demonstrations organized by students and ecological protests. Public opinion polls revealed that 4.4 percent of adult Poles participated at least once in strikes and demonstrations in 1988 and 8.4 percent in 1989. Among 314 protest events recorded by the Polish press in 1989, about 80 took place before the signing of the Roundtable agreements.[48]

There is a widely shared belief in the literature that the surrender of power by communist regimes during 1989 represented in essence a contractual transition accomplished through peaceful negotiations between reformists within the ruling elite and representatives of independent democratic groups; sustained mass mobilization supposedly did not occur and, therefore, had no significant impact on the transfer of power. Although this may have been the case in some countries, for example, Hungary, such a view should definitely be revised when it comes to Poland. The Roundtable negotiations and their final outcome were to a large extent the result of popular mobilization that began during spring 1988, peaked in the summer of 1988, and lasted well into 1989. In general, the 1989 transition was the direct result of a mass political movement that had emerged in 1980, remained a considerable political force after the imposition of martial law, and renewed its protest activities in 1988. Thus, Polish political developments reflected a powerful challenge from below that lasted over a decade, involved millions of people, and celebrated its final triumph in the events of 1989.

The Roundtable agreements, signed on 5 April, provided for re-legalization of Solidarity, Farmers' Solidarity, and the Independent Student Union. The opposition also gained limited access to the official political process through semidemocratic elections that were scheduled for June 1989. The results of the Roundtable negotiations set in motion a rapid process of liberalization, and the party-state elite very soon lost control over events. The parliamentary elections represented a clear moral and political victory for the restored Solidarity movement. By the fall of 1989, Poles had established the first noncommunist government in the region since the 1940s, and by January 1990, the Polish United Workers' Party ceased to exist. New political elite that emerged from the Solidarity movement led the country toward liberal democracy and a market economy.

3. Popular Protest and Resistance in Poland: Conclusions

This chapter examined Poland's experiences under communist rule from a specific theoretical angle. The focus is on the role of political crises and collective protest in shaping a distinct type of state socialist regime, one that was more tolerant, institutionally more pluralist, and more prone to public engagement and political crises. The high incidence of political conflict and collective protest cannot be attributed exclusively either to social, political, or historical factors specific to Poland or to general contradictions in the communist organization of the economy and politics. Instead, the source of Polish exceptionalism may be found in the country's unique political dynamics and its crisis-driven political development.

The postwar history of Poland may be conceptualized as a series of confrontations between ruling elite and various actors within society that altered the political opportunity structure, making it ever more conducive to organized challenge from below. In this sequence of confrontations, the pattern and outcomes of the de-Stalinization crisis of 1956 played the most important role in shaping Poland's political trajectory. The transition to the post-Stalinist regime produced distinctive institutional, political, and cultural legacies that resulted in notable institutional and cultural pluralism and set Poland apart from other state socialist regimes. It also made Poland's regime more vulnerable to various forms of popular mobilization and protest and provided political actors outside the party-state with important resources. As a result, different groups within Polish society periodically challenged the policies of the regime through mass political protest. These struggles were important generation-defining events and learning experiences. They also provided symbolic, intellectual, and social resources for future confrontations. Over time, various groups developed that cultivated and reworked their specific protest traditions, repertoires of contention, and frameworks for collective action, thus enhancing the opposition potential of society. This potential was sparked in subsequent political crises in which oppositional groups, despite their ultimate failure, were able to shape institutions and policies of the Polish regime and win tangible political and economic concessions. These different group-specific traditions of protest coalesced in the political crisis and mass mobilization of 1980, producing a sharp polarization between state and society and uniting various social groups in Polish society into a powerful revolutionary movement. The rise and legal existence of the 10 million-strong independent trade union movement, the self-organization of other social and political actors, and the appropriation of Polish national and democratic traditions by new political actors made the situation in Poland qualitatively different throughout the 1980s. As a result, Poland's political development and conditions departed even further from those in other Soviet bloc countries. Despite Solidarity's defeat in December 1981 and the imposition of a highly repressive regime, the party-state elite was never able to recover the political initiative and introduce effective economic and political reforms. By the end of the decade, the paralyzing political stalemate, the resurgence of opposition activities, and mass protest forced the regime to enter a controlled political transition. In 1989, the ten-year political struggle culminated in the downfall of the communist regime and the rapid democratization of the Polish political system. Thus, the process of deconstruction of the state socialist regime in Poland began in earnest during the 1980–1981 crisis, but its beginnings go back to the 1956 de-Stalinization crisis.

The post-1989 experiences of Poland's newly founded democracy reflect the legacies of popular struggles. Following the 1989 transfer of power, collective protest in Poland was intense. Waves of strikes swept entire sectors of the economy and huge demonstrations rocked Warsaw. Protest actions ranged from single isolated strikes and local actions organized by groups of activists to nationwide protest campaigns involving hundreds of public institutions and industrial enterprises as well as thousands of workers and public sector employees. They included hour-long warning strikes as well as protracted and desperate strike campaigns that lasted for months. The repertoire of protest was indeed diverse. It consisted of both violent and nonviolent street demonstrations, dramatic hunger strikes, huge rallies, boycotts, occupation of public buildings, blockades of roads and public spaces, rent strikes, and various forms of symbolic protest. Protest activities spread to all regions of the country and involved all social groups and categories, with workers, public sector employees, peasants, and the youth the most active participants. Comparative research indicates that Poland had the highest incidence of protest among all of the East-Central European postcommunist countries.[49] The high level of collective protest is not an exclusive result of costly economic and social policies introduced by the postcommunist governments. Other countries have been implementing similar measures to facilitate the transition to a market economy with much less opposition from groups and organizations within society. The situation in Poland reflects to a large extent past experiences of collective struggles. As was argued in this chapter, well before the fall of communism, various groups in Polish society developed considerable resources and expertise necessary for mounting successful collective action. The fragmentation of the political party system and volatility of the country's politics may be explained by the legacies of the past—the rise, suppression, and disintegration of the Solidarity movement. Thus, reexamination of political developments under state socialism is indispensable for understanding critical elements of the ongoing political transition in the region and the diverging experiences of the postcommunist countries.

Notes

1. See Grzegorz Ekiert, *The State against Society: Political Crises and Their Aftermath in East Central Europe* (Princeton: Princeton University Press, 1996), for a more detailed elaboration of this argument.
2. This argument is influenced by William Sewell's analysis in "Three Temporalities: Toward a Sociology of the Event," *CSST Working Papers*, no. 58 (Ann Arbor: University of Michigan, 1990), 17.
3. See, for example, George Schopflin, "Poland and Eastern Europe," in Abraham Brumberg, ed., *Poland: Genesis of a Revolution* (New York: Random House, 1983), 123–34.
4. Krzysztof Pomian describes Poland as the only Soviet-bloc country where "authorities were afraid of the working class, not the other way around," in *Wymiary polskiego konfliktu, 1956–1981* (London: Aneks, 1985), 10.
5. Abraham Brumberg, for example, argues that "nowhere had the endemic communist failures to erect an economic system at once rational, productive, and at least moderately equitable been so disastrous as in Poland." See his introduction to *Poland*, x.
6. Krystyna Kersten [J. Bujnowski], "O oporze 1944–1948 czyli o poszukiwaniu propozycji," *Krytyka* 17 (1984): 163–64. See also Barbara Otwinowska and Jan Zaryn, eds., *Polacy wobec przemocy, 1944–1956* (Warsaw: Editions Spotkania, 1996).

7. Zenon Jakubowski, *Milicja Obywatelska, 1944–1948* (Warsaw: PWN, 1988), 157.

8. See Maria Turlejska, "Komuniści wobec społeczeństwa polskiego. Ciągłość i zmiana techniki władzy," in Mirosława Marody and Antoni Sulek, eds., *Rzeczywistość polska i sposoby radzenia sobie z nią* (Warsaw: IS UW, 1987), 42–43.

9. See Andrzej Paczkowski, *Stanisław Mikołajczyk, czyli klęska realisty* (Warsaw: Omnipress, 1991).

10. See Wojciech Mazowiecki, *Wydarzenia 3 maja 1946* (Paris: Libella, 1989).

11. See Kazimierz Kloc, "Strajki w przemyśle w pierwszych latach Polski Ludowej," in Piotr Marciniak and Wojciech Modzelewski, eds., *Studia nad Ruchami Społecznymi* (Warsaw: IS UW, 1989), 5–41; Padraic Kenney, "Working-class Community and Resistance in Pre-Stalinist Poland: The Poznański Textile Strike, Łódź, September 1947," *Social History* 18, no. 1 (1993): 31–51.

12. These rehabilitations were restricted to former Party members and leaders purged by Stalinists during internal fighting for power. Most of them, like Gomułka, Spychalski, and Kliszko, played a crucial role in subsequent political events. In Poland, rehabilitation affected some 200 people, including the leaders of the prewar Polish Communist Party who had been killed by Stalin. Moreover, about 35,000 mostly political prisoners were released in the spring of 1956, and investigations of political offenses were terminated.

13. More detailed descriptions of the Poznań events and interpretations of the revolt can be found in Jarosław Maciejewski and Zofia Trojanowiczowa, *Poznański Czerwiec 1956,* 2nd ed. (Poznań: Wydawnictwo Poznańskie, 1990).

14. For detailed accounts of Party meetings and intraparty conflicts and struggles, see Wiesław Władyka, *Październik 56* (Warsaw: Wydawnictwa Szkolne i Pedagogiczne, 1994); Zbysław Rykowski and Wiesław Władyka, *Polska Próba. Październik '56* (Kraków: Wydawnictwo Literackie, 1989). See also George Sakwa, "The Polish 'October': A Re-Appraisal through Historiography," *Polish Review* 23: no. 3 (1978): 62–78.

15. See Jerzy Eisler, "Polskie radio wobec wydarzeń w kraju w 1956 r.," *Krytyka* 40 (1993): 146–63; Wiesław Władyka, *Na czołówce. Prasa w Październiku 1956 roku* (Warsaw: PWN, 1989).

16. Jakub Karpiński, *Count-Down* (New York: Karz-Cohl, 1982), 105.

17. See Krystyna Kersten, "Rok 1956—punkt zwrotny," *Krytyka* 40 (1993): 142–43.

18. Ibid., 145.

19. Jerzy Holzer, "Kryzysy i przezwyciężanie kryzysów w państwach komunistycznych," *Krytyka* 34–35 (1991): 40.

20. A detailed description and interpretation of the events can be found in Jack Bielasiak, "Social Confrontation to Contrived Crisis: March 1968 in Poland," *East European Quarterly* 22, no. 1 (1988): 81–105; and Jerzy Eisler, *Marzec 1968* (Warsaw: PWN, 1991).

21. Jack Bielasiak, "The Party: Permanent Crisis," in Brumberg, ed., *Poland*, 15.

22. Leszek Kołakowski, "The Intelligentsia," in Brumberg, ed., *Poland*, 62.

23. Adam Michnik, "Dziedzictwo Marca," in *Marzec '68. Sesja w Uniwersytecie Warszawskim 1981 r.* (Warsaw: Studencka Oficyna Wydawnicza SOWA, 1981), 2: 34.

24. Jerzy Holzer, *Solidarność 1980–1981. Geneza i historia* (Paris: Instytut Literacki, 1984), 19.

25. Eisler, *Marzec 1968*, 411.

26. For a more detailed analysis of December 1970 events in Poland, see Roman Laba, *The Roots of Solidarity* (Princeton: Princeton University Press, 1991), 15–82; Zygmunt Korybutowicz, *Grudzień 1970* (Paris: Instytut Literacki, 1983); Jerzy Eisler and Stanisław Trepczyński, *Grudzień '70. Wewnątrz 'Białego Domu'* (Warsaw: Colibri, 1991).

27. Jerzy Eisler, introduction to Edward J. Nalepa, *Wojsko Polskie w Grudniu 1970* (Warsaw: Bellona, 1990), 5–27.

28. During these events, regular military forces were employed in some 100 actions in all regions of the country, involving 61,000 soldiers, 1700 tanks, 1750 personnel carriers, and units of the air force and navy (Ryszard J. Kukliński, "Wojna z narodem widziana od środka," *Kultura* [April 1987]: 14). In the Baltic coast cities, 27,000 soldiers, 550 tanks, and 750 personnel carriers took part in pacifying the workers' rebellion.

29. See Beata Chmiel and Elżbieta Kaczyńska, eds., *Postulaty 1970–71 i 1980* (Warsaw: Uniwersytet Warszawski, 1988).

30. Laba, *The Roots of Solidarity*, 11.

31. See Piotr Marciniak, "Horyzont programowy strajków 1980 r.," *Studia nad ruchami społecznymi* 2 (1989): 153–54.

32. For the debate on the origin of the Solidarity movement, see Michael Bernhard, "Reinterpreting Solidarity," *Studies in Comparative Communism* 24, no. 3 (1991): 313–30; and Jan Kubik, "Who Done It: Workers or Intellectuals? Controversy over Solidarity's Origin and Social Composition," *Theory and Society* 23 (1994): 441–66.

33. See Jadwiga Staniszkis, *Poland's Self-Limiting Revolution* (Princeton: Princeton University Press, 1984), 257.

34. For a detailed analysis of June 1976 events, see Michael Bernhard, *The Origins of Democratization in Poland* (New York: Columbia University Press, 1993), 46–75.

35. For a detailed analysis of independent groups and initiatives, see Bernhard, "Reinterpreting Solidarity;" Jan J. Lipski, *KOR: A History of the Workers' Defense Committee in Poland, 1976–1981* (Berkeley: University of California Press, 1985); and Jerzy Holzer, *Solidarność 1980–1981* (Paris: Instytut Literacki, 1984).

36. For an insightful analysis of this period emphasizing the significance of papal visits to Poland for the emergence of the Solidarity movement, see Jan Kubik, *The Power of Symbols against the Symbols of Power: The Rise of*

Solidarity and the Fall of State Socialism in Poland (University Park, Pa.: Pennsylvania State University Press, 1994).

37. The period of Solidarity in Poland already has an extensive bibliography. Competent analyses of events can be found in Timothy Garton Ash, *The Polish Revolution: Solidarity* (New York: Vintage Books, 1985); David Ost, *Solidarity and the Politics of Anti-Politics* (Philadelphia: Temple University Press, 1990); Michael D. Kennedy, *Professionals, Power, and Solidarity in Poland* (Cambridge, Eng.: Cambridge University Press, 1991), in addition to books already cited above.

38. Alex Pravda, "The Workers," in Brumberg, ed., *Poland*, 68. See also Ireneusz Krzemiński, *Czego chcieli, o czym myśleli? Analiza postulatów robotników Wybrzeża z 1970 i 1980* (Warsaw: IS UW 1987).

39. Piotr Marciniak, "Strajki polskie lat osiemdziesiątych—ciągłość i zmiana," *Studia nad ruchami społecznymi* 5 (1990): 7.

40. See Andrzej Anusz, *Niezależne Zrzeszenie Studentów w latach 1980–1989* (Warsaw: Akces, 1991).

41. See Maria Halamska, "Peasant Movements in Poland, 1980–1981," *Research in Social Movements, Conflicts, and Change* 10 (1988): 147–60; and "Farmers' 'Solidarity,' 1981–1987," *Polish Agriculture* 8 (1988): 18–22.

42. The evolution of political attitudes is the best-documented aspect of Poland's development between 1980 and 1989, thanks to systematic empirical research conducted by a team of leading Polish sociologists. See Władysław Adamski et al., *Polacy '80: Wyniki badań ankietowych* (Warsaw: IFiS PAN, 1981); *Polacy '81: Postrzeganie kryzysu i konfliktu* (1982); *Polacy '84: Dynamika społecznego konfliktu i konsensusu* (1986); *Polacy '88: Dynamika konfliktu i szanse reform* (1989); *Polacy '90: konflikty i zmiana* (1991).

43. For an analysis of the cultural dimension of the political crisis in Poland, see Kubik, *The Power of Symbols*, and Irena Grudzinska-Gross, "Culture as Opposition in Today's Poland," *Journal of International Affairs* 50, no. 2 (1987): 367–90.

44. Andrzej Walicki, "The Main Components of the Situation in Poland," *Politics* 19: no. 1 (1984); 5.

45. Krzysztof Jasiewicz, Polacy '84 z półtorarocznej perspektywy. Raport wstępny z badania "Opinie Polaków—jesień '85" (Warsaw: UW, 1986), 9.

46. Marciniak, "Strajki polskie lat osiemdziesiątych," 8–9.

47. See Document no. 39, "Informacja o konfliktach społecznych i akcjach protestacyjnych w zakładach pracy i środowiskach zawodowych," in Stanisław Perzkowski, ed., *Tajne dokumenty Biura Politycznego i Sekretariatu KC. Ostatni rok władzy 1988–1989* (London: Aneks, 1994), 303–4; and Marek Pernal and Jan Skórzyński, *Solidarność 1980–1989* (Warsaw: Omnipress, 1990).

48. Data are from the project "Strategies of Collective Protest in Democratizing Societies: Hungary, Poland, Slovakia, and the Former East Germany, 1989–1994," directed by Grzegorz Ekiert and Jan Kubik.

49. For preliminary results of a four-country study on protest activities, see Grzegorz Ekiert and Jan Kubik, "Contentious Politics in New Democracies: Hungary, Poland, Slovakia, and the Former East Germany since 1989," Program on Central and Eastern Europe Working Paper Series, Center for European Studies, Harvard University, no. 41 (1997).

THREE

Voters, Parties, and Leaders

Raymond Taras

As remarkable as Poland's economic turnaround has been during the 1990s, it may be the country's political transformation that has confounded skeptics the most. In the decade following communism's collapse, Poland has seen four parliamentary elections (1989, 1991, 1993, and 1997), two presidential ones (1990 and 1995), two for local government offices (1990 and 1994), a five-part referendum in 1996, and a separate referendum in May 1997 to approve a new constitution. Governing parties have been voted out of office and replaced by opposition ones, while a legendary anticommunist incumbent president was defeated by the head of the former communist youth movement. In the 1990s, rumors of palace coups and charges that a prime minister had contacts with a Russian intelligence agent were never substantiated; the political system has been characterized by a commitment to outcomes determined by the democratic process. All other factors have been relegated to, at best, a secondary role. An interim "Small Constitution" was enacted in 1992, and five years later, a new, permanent one was approved by Parliament and the public. There appear to be no tests related to democratic consolidation left for Poland to meet.

In an authoritarian system such as communism, elite-focused research had its own rationale. By contrast, a study of an electoral democracy should naturally start with voters. This chapter begins, therefore, with an analysis of the attitudes and behavior of the electorate. Whom have they voted into power and why? Next is considered the role played by Poland's political parties—the aggregators of individual preferences. The consolidation of a party system has been one of the most notable political developments of the 1990s and worthy of particular attention. Finally, the nature of leadership is examined. Is the new group of political executives comprised of former communists or former opponents of the communist system? Or are the new leaders' career paths altogether different from the communist-era lineup? Voters, parties, and leaders are the principal components of a democracy.[1] Understanding their political preferences and behavior is to learn how far Polish democracy has come in the short space of a decade.

Voters

Two American political scientists have identified three basic types of political orientations on the part of voters: psychological involvement—the importance voters assign to politics; strength of partisan identification—the degree of attachment to a political party; and sense of contribution to the general welfare—the effort to expand collective goods.[2] It is ironic, then, that the largest single bloc of the electorate in Poland (but also in many other democracies) is comprised of nonvoters—those apparently not involved in, identifying with, or contributing to the public sphere at election time. At the same time, an indication that support for the democratic process has increased is the decline in the number of nonvoters with succeeding elections. For example, during the 1991 parliamentary elections, 59 percent of eligible voters did not cast their ballot—about the same level of abstention as in the May 1990 local elections. By the time of the runoff round of the 1995 presidential elections, only 32 percent of voters stayed away from the polls and did not register a preference between the incumbent, Lech Wałęsa, and his ex-communist challenger, Aleksander Kwaśniewski, a career *apparatchik* in the communist bureaucracy specializing in youth and physical education issues.

The traditional class explanation for nonvoting is that this group consists of the less educated, poorer, and more rural people in society. In Poland, political fatigue after the long struggle against the communist regime may have also accounted for greater citizen apathy. The opportunity to live one's life exclusively in the private sphere and ignore political involvement altogether was welcome after the constant mobilization and countermobilization of the previous decade. Some citizens derived enjoyment from having the chance to reject political participation, given how nonvoting under communism could lead to harassment by the authorities.

What, then, explains the variance in abstention levels between 1991 and more recently? One may suggest that the earlier absence of clear and consistent political orientations and programs advanced by parties may have produced equivocalness in voters, difficulty with partisan identification, and a sense of not being offered clear-cut choices. Both the 1995 presidential and 1997 parliamentary elections were, by contrast, precisely about a choice—between left-of-center and right-of-center candidates. A more transparent party system that more accurately reflected political differences within the electorate seems to be the main reason why Polish voters were more involved in the latter 1990s than the early 1990s, bucking conventional wisdom, which holds that popular enthusiasm with a new system fades in time as more cynical attitudes toward politicians develop.

This is not to suggest that the routinization of political life will not affect voter turnout. The 1996 referendum dealing with a battery of technical and noncontroversial questions (on four of the five questions, 90 percent of ballots cast were in favor of a particular proposal) was invalidated because only 32 percent of those eligible voted. A referendum on entry into the North Atlantic Treaty Organization (NATO) or into the European Union (EU) would spark greater interest. As elsewhere in electoral democracies, turnout at local elections in Poland is seldom above the 10 to 25 percent range. Parliamentary elections have not elicited the same level of voter enthusiasm as presidential ones. Stabilizing the voting population at about 60 percent, as appears to be happening in Poland, would reflect the same ethos as in most Western democracies.

When eligible voters do exercise their franchise, it is for reasons similar to those found in the West. First, they are concerned with pocketbook issues and support the party they consider will most expand benefits for people in their situation. Such voting behavior thus seeks to maximize expected utility. An electoral factor related to expectations is identity. As in Western democracies, voters use elections to affirm self- and group identity. In the case of a new market economy, voters seek to create *new* identities for themselves as young entrepreneurs, independent journalists, large-scale farmers, and so on. Voting can also originate in personalist politics—support for or opposition to individual politicians. Without a party of his own and not having fully succeeded in persuading voters that the 1995 presidential elections were a contest between the forces of the ancien régime and of the nouveau régime, Wałęsa became a leader supported or opposed primarily because of his personality.

Voting can be issue-oriented, too. Especially in the first years of a new political system, this might best explain electoral behavior. There is a plurality of alternative futures as voters and leaders select from a menu of choices: the role of government, the fate of the welfare state and the public sector, changes to social legislation, economic priorities, the status of minority and disadvantaged groups, foreign policy alliances. But there is a tendency on the part of the new rulers to treat these choices as too important for the electorate to make.

Despite a proliferation of parties, the party system paradoxically provided deceptively little choice in the first years of Polish democracy. Single-issue voting, whether on privatization, shock therapy, abortion, religious teaching in schools, or the welfare state was not possible. Parties across the spectrum, from the right-wing Confederation for an Independent Poland (*Konfederacja Polski Niepodległej*, or KPN) to the ex-communist Social Democracy of the Republic of Poland (*Socjaldemokracja Rzeczypospolitej Polskiej*, or SdRP), concurred on fundamental principles while disagreeing on methods and the pace of change. Once the civil society that mobilized against the communist system was transformed into an electorate under democracy, it could not decide the great issues of politics; issues of "high politics" were to be left for resolution by higher political circles. But issue salience in voting has increased as the major parties have established niches, each with specific policy programs and legislative records, each with recognizable voting patterns on legislation before Parliament. Thus, citizens' opportunities to influence issues have widened as the issues have become more narrowly defined.

As in the West, the consent Polish voters express for particular parties and leaders has different meanings. Prospective choice entails deciding which party can be trusted to govern the country most effectively for the next term. In the 1991 parliamentary elections, the electorate endorsed the choice that had already been made in June 1989, when the "contract" Sejm (with 65 percent of seats assigned to the communist bloc and 35 percent contested at the ballot box) was selected: the loose Solidarity coalition returned to office. Retrospective choice is passing judgement on incumbents: do we want another term of this? In 1993 voters said "no" to this question, and in part by default, the ex-communist party came to power.

Selecting a benevolent, enlightened, charismatic, or strong leader is another consideration of voters at the polls. Both the 1990 and 1995 presidential contests were essentially referenda on Wałęsa; a campaign poster for his reelection proclaimed: "There are many other candidates, there is only one Wałęsa"—the latter fact troubling a majority of voters. Finally, voting is a symbolic act that supports the democratic process, whereas nonvoting provides evidence of eligible voters' sense of political inefficacy, irrelevance, cynicism, or bewilderment. In the second half of the 1990s, retrospective voting appeared to be the main motivation of the electorate.

Elections

As noted earlier, between 1989 and 1997, Polish voters went to the polls four times to elect a parliament and two times to elect a president. What have been the results of these elections? Which factors were decisive in determining outcomes? Can we discern a pattern in Polish electoral behavior?

Elections to the Sejm (lower house of Parliament) in June 1989 were to be "competitive but not confrontational," as agreed at the Roundtable. The competitive aspect was to apply only to 35 percent of Sejm seats, and all 100 seats of the reconstituted Senate; the governing coalition was given patronage over 65 percent of Sejm seats, locking in a majority for itself. Considering the stakes, the campaign was brief, lasting only two months.[3] The Solidarity camp sought to depersonalize the elections and described itself as a more competent, democratic, and viable alternative to the incumbent communists. By contrast, the "governing coalition" of communists and their supporters campaigned on the basis of personalist politics, urging electors to "choose the best."

The turnout for the first round of these historic elections was just 62.7 percent of eligible voters. All but one of Solidarity's candidates won the seats they contested; only a handful of party candidates secured the necessary 50 percent majority in the first round to be elected. About 40 percent of all voters struck off the names of all communist coalition candidates. The Senate results proved an even more spectacular Solidarity victory: it captured 99 of 100 seats, even though its share of the vote was less than in the contested Sejm seats. About two-thirds of votes went to Solidarity candidates, up to one quarter for party candidates, and the remainder for independents.[4]

The unintended consequences of the 1989 elections—installation of a Solidarity government by September—overshadowed the planned result: political pluralism and power-sharing. The ramifications of these elections were felt throughout the Soviet bloc. No communist government in the region was safe from electoral defeat. Indeed, the outcome of Poland's pioneering elections was mild compared to what was to follow for communists elsewhere.

A discernible change in the electorate's attitude took place before the first presidential elections were held in November 1990. Approval of the government, Sejm, and Senate fell from 85 to 55 percent. The proportion of respondents asserting that living standards were bad increased from 65 to 80 percent. The Solidarity camp, organized as the Solidarity Citizens' Committees (KO), was Wałęsa's principal support base in his campaign for the presidential office. The Center Accord (PC), the first political group to demand the resignation of General Wojciech Jaruzelski—a communist holdover chosen by Parliament to be president—and the Christian National Union (*Zjednoczenie Chrześcijańsko Narodowe,*or ZChN), a Catholic movement with great influence in rural areas, also were key organizational pillars of Wałęsa's bid.

The main challenger to the former Solidarity trade union head was Prime Minister Tadeusz Mazowiecki, a highly respected journalist and Catholic intellectual who, however, lacked a strong organization and depended on his Citizens' Movement for Democratic Action (*Ruch Obywatelski Akcja Demokratyczna*, or ROAD) to create campaign committees spontaneously. The SdRP, the overhauled Communist Party that constituted the anchor for the broader left-of-center coalition called the Alliance of the Democratic Left (*Sojusz Lewicy Demokratycznej*, or SLD), did have organizations throughout the country and a relatively large membership (about 60,000) but suffered from association with the ancien régime. It selected Włodzimierz Cimoszewicz as candidate. The largest membership (about 400,000) of any party was that of the Polish Peasant Party (*Polskie Stronnictwo Ludowe*, or PSL), seeking to shake off its former status as a satellite of the Communist Party. Its candidate was Roman Bartoszcze. The most virulent anticommunist candidate was Leszek Moczulski of the KPN. In total, thirteen individuals announced they were running for president.[5]

In the first round, Wałęsa topped all vote-getters but was far short of the 50 percent needed to avoid a runoff (Table 3.1). The biggest shock of the elections was the second-place showing of outsider Stan Tymiński, eclectic head of the eclectic Party "X," who beat out Mazowiecki to get into the runoff. Held two weeks later, the second round brought fewer voters to the polls, perhaps because almost all losing candidates climbed on the bandwagon with Wałęsa against Tymiński, making the outcome a foregone conclusion. Moreover, 34 percent of first-round Tymiński supporters abstained in the second round, content that they had registered an antiestablishment protest once. Wałęsa thus received a mandate to serve as president, securing nearly three-quarters of votes cast.

The next step in legitimizing Poland's democratic system was election of a parliament in October 1991 that would be untainted by compromises reached with the communists. Rules governing elections for the Senate, or upper chamber, were simple compared to those for the Sejm. Similar to the United States, voters would choose two senators by plurality in each of the country's 47 provinces and three each from the densely populated metropolitan areas of Warsaw and Katowice, for a total of 100 seats. For the Sejm, 37 constituencies were created that would return anywhere from seven to 17 members each, depending on size, for a total of 391 seats.[6] Sixty-nine other deputies would be elected indirectly: parties would provide national lists of candidates and would be apportioned seats based on the number of votes they received in the constituencies.[7]

The electoral law was designed to give representation to even the smallest parties, since no minimum threshold was established for securing Sejm

Table 3.1   Presidential Election Results, 25 November and 9 December 1990

First Round (25 November; turnout of 61 percent)

	Votes	Votes Cast (percentage)	Electorate (percentage)
Lech Wałęsa (Solidarity KO)	6,569,889	40.0	23.9
Stanisław Tymiński ("X")	3,397,605	23.1	13.8
Tadeusz Mazowiecki (ROAD)	2,973,264	18.1	11.8
Włodzimierz Cimoszewicz (SdRP)	1,514,025	9.2	5.5
Roman Bartoszcze (PSL)	1,176,175	7.2	4.3
Leszek Moczulski (KPN)	411,516	2.5	1.5

Second Round (9 December; turnout of 53 percent)

	Votes	Votes Cast (percentage)	Electorate (percentage)
Lech Wałęsa	10,622,696	74.3	38.7
Stanisław Tymiński	3,683,098	25.7	13.3

Source: Główny Urząd Statystyczny, Mały Rocznik Statystyczny 1994 (Warsaw: GUS, 1994), 71–72.

seats. Although the party system had been fragmenting anyway as the Solidarity camp splintered, the law institutionalized this fragmentation. Yet it should come as no surprise that such a law was adopted. The architects of the new system wanted to be certain that no political force went unrepresented and found incentives to participate in the fledgling democracy. Put differently, small political groups had more to lose from opting out of democracy than from staying in, winning some representation, and trying for a better showing next time.

Three major issues shaped party programs at the time of the 1991 elections: (1) the drastic program of economic reform (sometimes called the "big bang" approach, sometimes shock therapy), which entailed rapid privatization and price liberalization; (2) the role of the Catholic Church in society, in particular its commitment to religious instruction in school and opposition to abortion; and (3) the scope and nature of decommunization—lustration, or the exposing of former communists, and political exclusion (whether to include the postcommunist SLD).

To summarize the key parties contesting the 1991 election, the left-of-center Democratic Union (Unia Demokratyczna, or UD) and right-of-center Liberal Democratic Congress (Kongres Liberalno-Demokratyczny, or KLD)—both offshoots from Solidarity—had different approaches to economic reform but represented the "new democrats." The peasant parties (PSL and others) rejected neoliberalism in attracting a constituency. The SLD offered a benign assessment of the previous communist regime but attracted voters because of its anticlerical policies. The KPN and PC had the greatest appeal among radical anticommunists, whose numbers in the country were diminishing. Finally, Christian democratic and nationalist orientations were incorporated into Catholic Electoral Action (*Wyborcza Akcja Katolicka,* or WAK), a coalition headed by the ZChN.

The 1991 election results (Table 3.2) demonstrated no overwhelming support for any one political field. Neither decommunization nor anticlericalism became the key campaign issue. Neither blanket rejection of nor full support for the economic reform program guaranteed a party electoral success. In returning a splintered parliament, the electorate compelled political leaders to build elaborate coalitions in order to govern.

The most important lesson of the 1991 elections was the need to revise the electoral law in order to create a stronger party system. For the next parliamentary elections held in September 1993, a total of 391 seats were to be contested in multimember constituencies, while 69 others

Table 3.2 Parliamentary Election Results, 27 October 1991[*]

	Percentage	Sejm (N = 460)	Senate (N = 100)
Democratic Union (UD)	12.3	62	21
Alliance of the Democratic Left (SLD)	12.0	60	4
Catholic Election Action (WAK)	8.7	49	9
Center Accord (PC)	8.7	44	9
Polish Peasant Party (PSL)	8.7	48	8
Confederation for an Independent Poland (KPN)	7.5	46	4
Liberal Democratic Congress (KDL)	7.5	37	6
Peasant Accord (PL)	5.5	28	7
Solidarity	5.1	27	12
Friends of Beer Party (PPP)	3.3	16	0
19 other parties	11.9	43	20

[*]Turnout was 41 percent.
Source: Frances Millard, "The Polish Parliamentary Elections of October 1991," *Soviet Studies* 44, no. 5 (1992): 846–47.

were to be distributed to parties receiving more than 7 percent of the national vote.[8] A threshold of 8 percent was established for electoral alliances (such as the SLD) to gain seats. For individual parties, the threshold was set at 5 percent.

The SLD's victory in 1993 (Table 3.3) came as no surprise, given the changed electoral law that disproportionately rewarded the top vote-getting parties and the changed mood of the electorate, which had grown disillusioned with what Wałęsa had called "the war at the top" within Solidarity ranks. For its part, the ex-communists had completed a remarkable comeback nationwide and in specific regions. In the mining center of Sosnowiec, for example, support for the SLD increased from 3 percent in the 1990 presidential elections to 19 percent in the 1991 parliamentary ones to 34 percent in 1993. In Warsaw, then-SLD leader Kwaśniewski placed far ahead of other party leaders in votes received, obtaining 149,000, as compared to 87,000 for Ryszard Bugaj of the Union of Labor (*Unia Pracy,* or UP); 57,000 for Bronisław Geremek of the UD; and 54,000 for Jan Krzysztof Bielecki of the KLD.[9] The fact that, among these party

Table 3.3 Parliamentary Election Results, 19 September 1993*

	Percentage	Sejm (N = 460)	Senate (N = 100)
Alliance of the Democratic Left (SLD)	20.6	171	37
Polish Peasant Party (PSL)	15.3	132	36
Democratic Union (UD)	10.7	74	4
Union of Labor (UP)	7.2	41	2
Confederation for an Independent Poland (KPN)	5.6	22	0
Nonparty Bloc for Reform (BBWR)	5.4	16	2
German minority	0.6	4	1
Fatherland Alliance (*Ojczyzna*)	6.4	0	1
Solidarność ("S")	4.6	0	9
Center Accord (PC)	4.5	0	1
Liberal-Democratic Congress (KD-L)	3.8	0	1
Others	14.8	2	7

*Turnout was 51 percent.

Source: Główny Urząd Statystyczny, *Mały Rocznik Statystyczny 1994* (Warsaw: GUS, 1994), 67–8.

leaders, the top three vote-getters in Warsaw were on the left further underscored the electorate's shift in this direction. Kwaśniewski's impressive showing augured well for a presidential challenge.

Within the SLD alliance, 61 deputies belonged to the former communist trade union, the National Trade Union Accord (*Ogólnopolskie Porozumienie Związków Zawodowych,* or OPZZ). Led by Ewa Spychalska, the union distrusted "liberals from the SLD" and meant to keep the SLD firmly on the left. If the PSL was treated as ex-communist because of its origins, then the proportion supporting the left in September 1993 represented just over one-third of voters. Even though it won the election, the left was outperformed, therefore, by the post-Solidarity bloc—UD, UP, a Catholic electoral alliance called Fatherland (*Ojczyzna*), the Nonparty Bloc for Reform (*Bezpartyjny Blok Wspierania Reform,* or BBWR), the Solidarity trade union ('S'), the PC, KLD, and the Movement for the Republic (*Ruch dla Rzeczypospolitej,* or RdR)—which received about 45 percent. To be sure, the social democratic Union of Labor, with 7 percent of the vote, could just as easily be regarded as a leftist party.

If electoral support for the outgoing coalition made up of the UD, Fatherland, and KLD parties were aggregated, it added up to 21 percent of all votes; adding BBWR votes would bring the total to 26 percent. These calculations suggest that, in sum, personal rivalries and internal disputes within the Solidarity camp allowed the SLD to come to power.

Zbigniew Brzezinski, former national security adviser to President Jimmy Carter and pioneering Kremlinologist, elaborated on the reasons for the ex-communists' victory.[10] While giving credit to the SLD's better organization, he contended that its leaders were never held accountable for their communist past. The victory of the left was highly contingent on the pain many citizens suffered during the transition to a market economy,[11] the refusal of the Solidarity government to concede wage increases to public sector employees, the unpopular anti-abortion law championed by what was perceived as a meddling church, and the continual conflicts within the liberal democratic camp.

The presidential election campaign began shortly after the parliamentary elections. Popular dissatisfaction with the volatile Wałęsa continued to grow, opening the field to new candidates. Any of the four Solidarity ex-prime ministers—Mazowiecki, Bielecki, Jan Olszewski, Hanna Suchocka—could legitimately aspire to the office. Among former prime ministers, only Olszewski and Pawlak of the PSL became presidential candidates. Clearly, the main challenge would be mounted from the resurgent left.

In the run-up to the 1995 elections, Wałęsa and Kwaśniewski made different tactical decisions about their main organizational bases. Wałęsa quarreled with the Solidarity trade union he had helped found and even failed to show up for an annual convention. An eleventh-hour patching up of relations did not regain lost support. By contrast, only after winning the presidency did Kwaśniewski resign from the party he had headed (the SdRP), since it had replaced the old Communist Party in January 1990. As with parliamentary elections, the SdRP served as the cornerstone of an elaborate postcommunist electoral bloc unifying a large number of organizations, including the old communist trade union.

The official three-month-long election campaign saw a dramatic resurgence in Wałęsa's popularity. Results of public opinion polls conducted in the spring and summer of 1995 indicated that his level of support seldom rose over 10 percent and that he would lose to any other party leader in a head-to-head contest. But from September onward, he overtook such center-right candidates as Olszewski and Hanna Gronkiewicz-Waltz, president of Poland's National Bank and candidate of the Christian National Union party. During the campaign it became clear that Wałęsa was the only "electable" candidate of the center-right. On television he no longer appeared rash and inarticulate but thoughtful and sensible.[12]

In the first round, Kwaśniewski (35 percent) and Wałęsa (33 percent) garnered about two thirds of all votes cast (Table 3.4). Left-of-center candidates trailed far behind: former dissident Jacek Kuroń (9 percent) represented the declining Freedom Union (*Unia Wolności*, or UW)—a shaky merger of the UD and KLD; ombudsman Tadeusz Zieliński (4 percent) was the nominee of the Union of Labor. Waldemar Pawlak, twice prime minister and head of a pivotal party in parliament, the PSL, received only 4 percent.

It is worth considering whether splintering within the noncommunist left allowed Kwaśniewski to squeeze into the runoff and become the representative of the social democratic orientation of the Polish electorate rather than, say, Kuroń. According to the political scientist Jerzy Wiatr (himself a cabinet minister in the SLD-dominated government), the left-of-center bloc was indeed weakened when delegates to the UP convention refused to throw party support behind Kuroń—despite the wishes of the UP leadership—and instead chose Zieliński as UP candidate. The effect was to deprive Kuroń of the ability to project himself as a candidate transcending party politics; instead, he was perceived as a representative of the UW alone.[13]

The collapse of support for Gronkiewicz-Waltz, at one time poised (according to polls measuring voting intentions) to eliminate Wałęsa as candidate of the right-of-center bloc, also needs elaboration. Arguably, the most convincing explanation of her "shooting star" candidacy was

Table 3.4   Presidential Election Results, 5 and 19 November 1995

First Round (5 November; turnout of 65 percent)

	Votes	Votes Cast (percentage)	Electorate (percentage)
Aleksander Kwaśniewski (SLD)	6,274,670	35.1	22.3
Lech Wałęsa (nonparty)	5,917,328	33.1	21.0
Jacek Kuroń (UW)	1,646,946	9.2	5.9
Jan Olszewski (RdR)	1,225,453	6.7	4.4
Waldemar Pawlak (PSL)	770,419	4.3	2.8
Tadeusz Zieliński	631,432	3.5	2.2

Second Round (19 November; turnout of 68 percent)

	Votes	Votes Cast (percentage)	Electorate (percentage)
Aleksander Kwaśniewski	9,704,439	51.7	34.6
Lech Wałęsa	9,058,176	48.3	32.3

Source: Krzysztof Jasiewicz, "Poland," in *Political Data Yearbook 1996*, special issue of *European Journal of Political Research* 30, nos. 3–4 (1996): 533.

that she became a "hostage" of the Catholic Church as the election campaign progressed. According to Zbigniew Nosowski, writing in the Catholic journal *Więź*, Gronkiewicz-Waltz initially had strong popular support due to her widely viewed professionalism as president of the Polish National Bank. But the church forced her to become "an ostentatious Catholic" during the campaign, highlighting her religiosity and family values.[14] This boomeranged on her candidacy. Wałęsa already had impeccable credentials as a devout Catholic and, coupled with growing societal distaste for the church's involvement in politics, running on a program emphasizing Catholicism rather than professional expertise proved to be Gronkiewicz-Waltz's undoing.

Going into the second round, then, Wałęsa had both the political momentum and the expectation of capturing most of the votes of eliminated candidates. During the two-week interval between rounds, Kwaśniewski sought to attract Zieliński voters while Wałęsa tried to make all votes cast for his former Solidarity associates—Kuroń's 9 percent, Olszewski's 7 percent, Gronkiewicz-Waltz's 3 percent, and 4 percent for minor candidates —his own. Unifying the Solidarity bloc in the second round would have mathematically put Wałęsa over the top. By contrast, previous elections indicated that ex-communists seemed unable to surmount a 40 percent threshold of support.

Perhaps the decisive event of the campaign was the first of two television debates between Kwaśniewski and Wałęsa. Their political style appeared in sharpest relief: Kwaśniewski's youth, eloquence, and calm versus Wałęsa's churlishness, demagoguery, and combativeness. Indeed, Wałęsa appeared so ill-tempered that he opened the second debate by apologizing for his behavior in the first.[15] He repeated that Poland had to do away with communism once and for all—a refrain that had lost its appeal. Kwaśniewski countered by charging that Wałęsa was a man of the past. As one Polish journalist noted, "Kwaśniewski didn't gain much from the debates, but Wałęsa lost considerably."[16]

In the end, however, Wałęsa had so antagonized his former associates in Solidarity that many of their supporters refused to vote for him in the runoff. Predictably, two-thirds of voters who supported Zieliński and Pawlak in the first round now switched to Kwaśniewski. But, surprisingly, more than 40 percent of Kuroń voters switched support to the ex-communist, and even 25 percent among backers of Olszewski—the uncompromising anticommunist—did likewise. To underscore his eroding support, Wałęsa even lost 3 percent of his first-round supporters to Kwaśniewski. As a final humiliation, in the town in which he was born, Popowie, Wałęsa lost by a margin of 13 percent.[17]

Wałęsa's support was strongest in a handful of provinces throughout the conservative, religious southern part of the country and the poor rural east, though he also did well in the cities.[18] During the runoff he won a majority of votes cast by those over 50; by private entrepreneurs, pensioners, and housewives; and by those with primary and also those with higher education—a reversal of the first-round pattern, where Kwaśniewski captured the intelligentsia.

Kwaśniewski swept the more populated mining and industrial regions in western and coastal Poland. (He is from Koszalin, a province along the Baltic Sea.) He registered a sizable margin of victory over Wałęsa among the twenty-somethings and the baby boomers. Farmers, office workers, manual laborers, and the unemployed backed the ex-communist. While rural women supported Wałęsa for his strongly expressed religious beliefs, including his presidential veto of legislation that would have liberalized abortion, more secular, urban, and educated women preferred Kwaśniewski.[19]

One final observation on the 1995 presidential campaign concerns the impact of the system of election on the outcome. There is no question that direct presidential elections are supported by an overwhelming number of citizens. An opinion poll conducted in April 1994 found that 89 percent of respondents approved of the direct election of the president; only 6 percent preferred that Parliament elect the president (the way Jaruzelski was selected in 1989). Just after the 1995 election (in January 1996), the respective numbers were 94 percent and 4 percent.[20] But for one political observer, Radisława Gortat, direct elections have proven dysfunctional in Poland: "If parliamentary elections contribute to the crystallization of the party system, general presidential elections cause fragmentation of existing parties and hinder the emergence of a structured party system." She argued that the system of direct elections was partial: "This method is not unbiased politically. It strengthens the successor to the former communist party and weakens parties emerging from the split of the former opposition movement."[21] Unquestionably, direct presidential elections favor the candidate best able to construct a wide coalition of voters and place the candidate at the head of a disunited camp at a disadvantage. It is this lesson that generated the birth in 1996 of Solidarity Electoral Action (*Akcja Wyborcza "Solidarność,"* or AWS).

In explaining why such a recently formed alliance (it was not a political party, though efforts were undertaken in 1997 to turn it into one) was able to win the September 1997 elections, it is enough to recall the 1993 results. Right-of-center parties had captured close to two-thirds of the popular vote then but obtained only one-third of parliamentary seats. All these parties had to do to defeat the ex-communists was to unite—an arduous task but one having major incentives, i.e., capturing power. Indeed, in 1997 the SLD actually increased its share of the vote by 6.5 percent (see Table 3.5 on p. 63), which reflected positively on the performances of President Kwaśniewski and Prime Minister Cimoszewicz. But the SLD's coalition partner, the PSL, was decimated, losing 105 seats. Its makeshift cooperation with the ex-communists, Pawlak's uninspiring leadership, and a too secular policy orientation made the PSL easy prey in the countryside for the more religious anticommunist peasant groups (like the ZChN).

The anchor of the AWS was the still-existent Solidarity trade union, now led by a technocrat Marian Krzaklewski. He successfully re-keyed the union from a mere political instrument of Wałęsa, at the same time exploiting worker discontent with the burgeoning patronage network of the governing SLD. Krzaklewski's most significant achievement was to bring together over 30 quarreling right-of-center parties and persuade them to get behind a labor movement—an unusual alliance to be sure. Even though he led the AWS to victory, the union head declined the post of prime minister and instead nominated Jerzy Buzek, a veteran Solidarity activist (he had organized the 1981 Solidarity congress), chemistry professor from Silesia, and Evangelical Lutheran (his wife and children, however, are Roman Catholic). In his desire to influence politics from behind the scenes, Krzaklewski was accused of wishing to form a new Politburo (the unelected executive committee that held power under the communist regime). More probable was the positioning of himself to run for the presidency in the year 2000.

The AWS did not hold absolute majority of seats in the Sejm and needed a partner to form a government. The obvious choice was the Freedom Union (UW), the third-largest vote-getter in 1997. Sometimes called the party of prime ministers, because it included many of Poland's best-known political leaders, under Leszek Balcerowicz the UW was committed to speedy market reform to a greater degree than the somewhat etatist-orientated AWS. Balcerowicz, historian Bronisław Geremek, and former prime minister Suchocka all had to be given important posts in an AWS-UW coalition government. The 1997 electoral victory by a conservative bloc was tempered, therefore, by its need to come to terms with neoliberal and secular elements.

Parties

The dismantling of the communist party in 1990 has left no political parties in existence in Poland that can claim to have a mass membership. Parties today are primarily electoral ones, and, once they secure representation in the Sejm, they become parliamentary ones. Conversely, political participation is now rarely channeled through activity in a party; citizen activity is limited to the ballot box in a way that did not occur during the communist period. This can be viewed as a positive sign that the political system is not overloaded with demands.

Politics has become professionalized since 1989. There are no lathe operators, surface miners, or state farm workers in parliament as during the communist period—only elected politicians. Parties do not have juggernaut bureaucracies, as the communist party did, but their leaders do work in politics on a full-time basis. The sham amateurism of the old system has given way to unambiguous professionalism.

In the early 1990s, political parties splintered frequently. Just as often, they entered into electoral pacts with other parties in order to capture votes. They adopted different names when contesting elections, and their elected members formed clubs with even different names once they entered parliament. We have the example of the ZChN, a conservative clerical party. It ran in the 1991 parliamentary elections under the label Catholic Election Action (*Wyborcza Akcja Katolicka,* or WAK). For the 1993 elections, a similar Catholic alliance was called "Fatherland." For the 1995 presidential elections, the ZChN formed part of the Alliance for Poland (*Przymierze dla Polski,* or PdP). And for the 1997 legislative elections the party joined with the Solidarity trade union in the AWS. In a similar way, numerous peasant parties have formed parliamentary blocs and electoral pacts. Even the SLD, as we have noted, is a coalition of various political groups tracing their origins to former communist organizations. The fluidity of individual parties and party alliances made keeping track of them very difficult up to 1993. Since that time the party system has crystallized into a smaller and more constant group of parties. Of crucial importance to democracy is that all of these have accepted the rules of the game and abide by outcomes generated by these rules. There is no threat, even by former communists, to use extraparliamentary means to obtain power.

In the first years after the democratic breakthrough, there was a return to narrow national and religious loyalties. As one author noted at the time, "The new parties in Polish politics are Catholic, nationalistic, and right wing. They claim for themselves a continuity of resistance against communism, and they reject dissident intellectuals as left wing and cosmopolitan, elitist and alienated."[22] These parties attacked the liberal-democratic center but succeeded only in weakening it as well as themselves.[23] By the second half of the 1990s, the parties that survived were not Catholic, nationalist, and right wing. However, centrist parties were not strong either. Generally, political parties became more secular, pragmatic, and European than before. Table 3.6 (on p. 68) gives a notional understanding of the policy orientations of Poland's major parties and their leaders in 1997.

Over the past five years, the largest party in terms of both membership and vote-getting has been the SLD, the social-democratic successor of the former communist party. Because its origins lay in the communist regime, it was frozen out of all government coalitions up to 1993. The SLD could only hope to gain power through electoral appeal, not by playing the coalition game in parliament. To be sure, it lent informal support to the governments headed by Olszewski and Suchocka. In return, it was defended from rightist attacks by the UD. The modus vivendi established between the SLD and UD (now UW) had its origins in the 1989 Roundtable talks, when communists and dissidents agreed on power-sharing. Right-wing politicians have been quick to see a conspiracy whenever such "collaboration" exists between communists and crypto-communists. There is more often a meeting of minds between SLD and UW leaders than between SLD leaders and those of any other party, including its troublesome one time coalition partner, the PSL.

From among many peasant parties formed after 1989, the PSL emerged for a time as the strongest in the Polish countryside. Also a descendant of a communist-era party, the PSL has effectively defended private farmers,

Table 3.5   Parliamentary Election Results, 21 September 1997[*]

	Percentage	Sejm (N = 460)	Senate (N = 100)
Solidarity Electoral Action (AWS)	33.8	201	51
Alliance of the Democratic Left (SLD)	27.1	164	28
Freedom Union (UW)	13.4	60	8
Polish Peasant Party (PSL)	7.3	27	3
Movement for Reconstruction (ROP)	5.6	6	5
Union of Labor (UP)	4.7	0	0
Pensioners' Party (KPEiR)	2.2	0	0
Union of Real Politics (UPR)	2.0	0	0
German minority	0.6	2	0
Independents and other parties	3.3	0	5
Totals	100.0	460	100

[*]Turnout was 48 percent.
Note: Data compiled by author.
Source: Rzeczpospolita (25–26 September 1997).

whose economic interests are threatened by market economics. Poland's rural population accounts for 37 percent of the electorate, so the PSL is likely to be a strategic actor for some time, but internal leadership struggles eroded much of its support in 1997. Regular attempts were made by parties from the Solidarity camp to lure it away from the SLD, but its refusal of such overtures marginalized the party after 1997.

The strongest electoral showing of any party in 1991 was that of the Democratic Union; indeed, the first postcommunist government headed by Prime Minister Mazowiecki was a precursor of the UD, which was officially founded in December 1990. Though consisting of a seven-party coalition, Suchocka's government (in power during 1992–1993) was also primarily a UD progeny. The party's leaders claimed not to have any particular ideology or program, and the UD held together for a long time by being liberal on social issues but monetarist on economic ones. Early on, the UD consisted of a recognizably left-wing ROAD group, centrist Mazowiecki supporters, and a right-wing faction under Aleksander Hall. The latter broke away in 1992 to form the Conservative Party (*Partia Konserwatywna,* or PK). But two years later, the UD merged with the Liberal Democratic Congress, as neoliberal a party as the PK, to form the Freedom Union and was again beset with internal disagreements. Its presidential candidate in 1995, the well-liked former dissident Kuroń, proved no match against political heavyweights of the class of Wałęsa or Kwaśniewski. The UW then chose a neoliberal, Leszek Balcerowicz, architect of Poland's market reform program, to lead the party into the 1997 parliamentary elections, in which its loss of 14 seats compared to 1993 but its inclusion in a coalition government produced bitter-sweetness. With a remarkable first few years as a party, storied political leaders, a handful of former prime ministers, and the political liberalism characteristic of Western political parties, the UW has proven to be Poland's most underachieving party.

The Freedom Union has not been the only one that has failed to become a strong party of the center. In 1993 Wałęsa gave his endorsement to the setting up of a moderate presidential party that would contest parliamentary elections and give him direct representation and leverage in the Sejm. The middle-of-the-road BBWR that he helped create did not capture the imagination of voters, even though it was modeled on interwar leader Józef Piłsudski's parliamentary appendage. During the 1993 elections, it just reached the minimum 5 percent threshold needed for representation. In 1996, BBWR signed the agreement that set up Solidarity Election Action. However, most of the 20 or so parties joining the AWS were right of center. In 1997 Wałęsa announced that he would form a new Christian Democratic Party of Poland, but its future was unclear.

A key constituent member of the AWS was the right-wing ZChN, which formed a pillar of the Olszewski government that lasted from late 1991 to spring 1992. Another was the Conservative-Peasant Party (*Stronnictwo Konserwatywno-Ludowe*, or SK-L), a recent amalgamation of Hall's Conservative Party (PK) and the Peasant-Christian Party (*Stronnictwo Ludowe-Chrześcijańskie*, or SLCh) of Artur Balasz. Both factions of the nationalist Confederation for an Independent Poland (led by Moczulski and Słomka) also signed the AWS agreement, clearly tilting the alliance toward the right. The Solidarity trade union anchoring the AWS was committed to defending workers, however. Its more liberal orientation was bolstered by an important defection from the Freedom Union, that of Jan Maria Rokita's group. The very number of parties that entered the AWS coalition and the area of the political continuum they covered, from center to far right, made it Poland's newest umbrella party. Not surprisingly, its original founding document spoke in generalities of the movement for which "truth, justice, and interpersonal solidarity are the essential components in the building of an independent, just, and democratic Poland."[24]

Former Prime Minister Olszewski also did not give up his search for a viable right-wing party. His respectable performance during the 1995 presidential elections inspired him to establish a conservative bloc, the ROP, which won six seats in the 1997 parliamentary elections. Olszewski remained a political presence, deriving grudging respect from both left and right as the prime minister who challenged both Wałęsa and the ex-communists and was unseated from office in the closest thing that Poland has known to a coup.

One last noteworthy party is the Union of Labor. The only left-of-center group that was descended from Solidarity, it defied expectations that it would quickly disappear from the political scene. The UP program seeks to halt privatization of state companies and to pass a government budget that would be decoupled from International Monetary Fund deficit-reduction targets. It also is committed to maintaining many social programs earmarked for cuts. Its leadership has included Bugaj, a respected economist, as well as the former ombudswoman Ewa Letowska, the onetime Solidarity fugitive Zbigniew Bujak, and ex-dissident Karol Modzelewski. In 1997, it barely failed to obtain the 5 percent electoral support needed for parliamentary representation.

Although the principal electoral coalitions and parties examined here are themselves made up of many former political parties and groups, it is now possible to speak of Poland as a fairly stable multiparty system.

Executives and Leaders

A strong executive is an unlikely outcome of the transition from communist rule. Indeed, the raison d'être for extrication from authoritarianism is to create institutional pluralism, where many parties and institutions share power and balance one another. Furthermore, keeping actors committed to democracy means dispersing power widely. But political leadership remains pivotal during a transition. Whereas adversarial politics within the elite may deepen fragmentation found in society, consensual elite behavior can counterbalance societal cleavages and produce consociational democracy, a system in which the spoils of politics are divided on the basis of segmental interests.[25]

A number of interrelated aspects of leadership merit attention: (1) the structure of the executive branch; (2) the personalities and political styles of leaders; and (3) leadership skills and qualifications. Each of these is considered in the following pages.

The constitutional role of the presidency is circumscribed. According to the 1992 Small Constitution, Poland is described as having "a presidential-parliamentary system of government." But the 1997 constitution dropped even this recognition of presidential authority and, in Article 10.1, declares that "the system of the Polish Republic is based on the separation and balance of legislative authority, executive authority, and judicial authority."[26] Chapter 5 of this constitution enumerates the specific powers of the president, such as the right to designate the prime minister (though not cabinet ministers), initiate legislation, veto bills (which the Sejm can override by a three-fifths majority), under certain conditions dissolve Parliament and call early elections, and oversee defense and national security matters. When the president issues decrees (*akty urzędowe*), they need the prime minister's countersignature.

The 1992 Small Constitution, granting the president modest authority, was not the legal framework that Wałęsa had in mind for himself. Nor did he approve of the 1997 act, though by then he was out of office and not affected by its further limitations on the powers of the president. During his five-year term as president, Wałęsa tried to prevent a parliamentary system from being institutionalized. But the Sejm rebuffed his attempts to expand presidential power, and also defeated him on the key issue of the electoral law, which legislators insisted should be more proportional than Wałęsa wanted.[27] The SLD victory in the 1993 parliamentary elections brought into question whether Wałęsa still possessed a popular mandate. When, in 1995, the Sejm began to consider various drafts of a new constitutional act to replace the Small Constitution, Wałęsa's was the only version of seven that proposed a presidential system. In contrast, his 1995 presidential opponent, Kwaśniewski, placed himself in the mainstream, stressing that he was a parliamentarian. By voting against Wałęsa in the 1995 elections, voters were also indirectly expressing their opposition to presidentialism.[28]

Wałęsa's political style—populist forays into factories and dairy cooperatives—was also criticized: it brought the dignity of the presidency into question. His response was that he had no interest in becoming a champagne-drinking president: instead, "I pull, I push, I initiate." He expressed concern about the emergence of a "political mafia" centered in Parliament and waged "war at the top" to counter the rise of strong leaders, regardless of whether they were close associates: "That is why I am merciless. My price is losing friends; theirs, losing their posts."

In short, the smashing of the old Solidarity elite, along with the political inexperience of many new party leaders and parliamentary deputies who appeared on the scene in the early 1990s, allowed Wałęsa to bully friends and foes alike. After 1993, however, the pluralist elite emerging in Parliament had honed their skills and were prepared to meet Wałęsa's challenge. His poor relationship with most parties in Parliament cost him the election. His successor, Kwaśniewski, was a consensus-building president who more closely reflected the style of the new elite.

Apart from the president, political leadership also falls to the head of government. Six men and one woman have served as prime minister since General Czesław Kiszczak's failure to forge a last communist cabinet during summer 1989 (Table 3.6 on p. 68). They have included persons of differing socio-occupational backgrounds: a Catholic intellectual and journalist (Mazowiecki), a businessman with a degree in economics (Bielecki), a Solidarity lawyer (Olszewski), a farmer with an engineering degree from Warsaw Polytechnic (Pawlak), a law professor (Suchocka), a Marxist-trained economist (Oleksy), a farmer with a doctorate in law who had been a Fulbright scholar (Cimoszewicz), and a chemistry professor (Buzek).

Relations between presidents and prime ministers have varied. Mazowiecki was originally selected by Wałęsa to serve as prime minister because he promised to rein in the Warsaw intelligentsia, about which Wałęsa had harbored deep suspicions. Soon Mazowiecki proved to be his own man and challenged Wałesa for the presidency in 1990.[29] Mazowiecki was replaced by KLD leader Bielecki, who promised to retain economic reform guru Balcerowicz. Despite this, his government ran up an enormous deficit and, following the October 1991 elections in which the KLD did poorly, had to be replaced. When the candidacy of longtime Wałęsa adviser Geremek was blocked by the new Parliament, the president asked Olszewski to form a new government.

Olszewski was determined to enhance the power of the prime minister and quickly replaced Wałęsa's appointee as defense minister—even though the president had broad constitutional authority over security and defense matters. In February 1992, frustrated by what he saw as an obstructionist Parliament and a meddling president, Olszewski asked the Sejm for emergency powers to govern by decree (this was before the Small Constitution was adopted) but was unable to secure them. Three months later, sealed envelopes were presented to Wałęsa by Olszewski's interior minister. They contained the names of some 60 people who allegedly had been collaborators and agents of the communist regime. Wałęsa's name was on the list, allegedly for signing a loyalty pledge to the secret police after he had been detained during the 1970 unrest in Gdańsk. This was too much for Wałęsa: within days, the president had engineered the defeat of Olszewski's government in Parliament.

Wałęsa's choice to become prime minister was the 33-year-old leader of the PSL. However, Parliament would not let him form a cabinet, and Suchocka was asked to try. Surviving early attacks on her character that asserted that she had been a member of a satellite party of the communists, she was able to establish a relatively stable parliamentary coalition while maintaining a good working relationship with the president. Her

Table 3.6 Political Parties, Programs, and Leaders, December 1997

Party (Acronym)	Policy Orientation	Leaders-PMs
Solidarity Electoral Action (*Akcja Wyborcza Solidarność*, or AWS): part of the electoral alliance, "Agreement of the Right" comprises 30 center-right parties and groups, including: Center Accord (PC), Christian National Union (ZChN), Conservative-Peasant Party (SK-L), Confederation for an Independent Poland (KPN), Nonparty Bloc for Reform (BBWR), Party of Political Realism (SPR), and the Solidarity trade union (*NSZZ Solidarność*)	syndicalist, protectionist, socially conservative	Marian Krzaklewski, Jerzy Buzek
Alliance of the Democratic Left (*Sojusz Lewicy Demokratycznej*, or SLD): electoral alliance based on: Social Democracy of the Polish Republic (*Socjaldemokracja Rzeczypospolitej Polskiej*, or SdRP); 25 smaller parties and groups; and the National Trade Union Accord (*Ogólnopolskie Porozumienie Związków Zawodowych*, or OPZZ)	social market economy, secular	Leszek Miller, Włodzimierz Cimoszewicz, Józef Oleksy and previously Aleksander Kwaśniewski
Polish Peasant Party (*Polskie Stronnictwo Ludowe*, or PSL)	former communist satellite party that supports state intervention, secularism, protectionism	Jarosław Kalinowski, Waldemar Pawlak
Freedom Union (*Unia Wolności*, or UW): 1994 merger of Demo-cratic Union (*Unia Demokratyczna*, or UD) and Liberal Demo-cratic Congress (*Kongres Liberalno-Demokratyczny*, or KLD)	neoliberal: free market orientation centrists: ethical, pragmatic social liberals: statist, intellectual, secular	Leszek Balcerowicz Tadeusz Mazowiecki, Hanna Suchocka Jacek Kuroń
Movement for Poland's Reconstruction (*Ruch Odrodzenia Polski*, or ROP)	nationalist, for decommunization	Jan Olszewski

Source: Prepared by the author.

Table 3.7   Presidents and Prime Ministers of Poland since 1989

Presidents	Took Office	Supported by	Left Office
Wojciech Jaruzelski	August 1989[a]	postcommunists	December 1990
Lech Wałęsa	December 1990	Solidarity	December 1995
Aleksander Kwaśniewski	December 1995	postcommunists	—

Prime Ministers	Appointed	Supported by	Left Office
Tadeusz Mazowiecki	August 1989	Solidarity	December 1990
Jan Krzysztof Bielecki	December 1990	KLD, PC	December 1991
Jan Olszewski	December 1991	PC, ZChN, PL	June 1992
Waldemar Pawlak	June 1992[b]	PSL	July 1992
Hanna Suchocka	July 1992	UD, KLD, ZChN, PSL	May 1993[c]
Waldemar Pawlak	September 1993	PSL, SLD	March 1995
Józef Oleksy	March 1995	SLD, PSL	January 1996
Włodzimierz Cimoszewicz	February 1996	SLD, PSL	October 1997
Jerzy Buzek	November 1997	AWS, UW	—

[a]Jaruzelski was elected indirectly, by the National Assembly.
[b]Pawlak was nominated as prime minister but could not form a government.
[c]Suchocka lost a vote of confidence in May but remained in office until September.
Source: Prepared by the author.

success in stabilizing the government, coupled with a flurry of visits she made to Western European states that enhanced Poland's stature, earned her high popularity ratings in the country.

The 1993 parliamentary elections brought the left to power, and the SLD agreed to let Pawlak of the PSL become prime minister. A "creation" of Wałęsa (according to Wałęsa), Pawlak's prime ministership was destroyed by the president over the issue of who had ultimate power to appoint the defense and foreign ministers. His replacement in March 1995 was not SdRP leader Kwaśniewski, who had his eyes on the bigger prize, but SdRP deputy head Józef Oleksy. Before he bowed out of office, Wałęsa would succeed in removing one more prime minister.

Only a week after Kwaśniewski had been confirmed as the new president and days before Wałęsa was scheduled to leave office, the outgoing president produced a bombshell: he had documents linking Oleksy to the former KGB and its Russian successor, the federal security agency. They purportedly showed the prime minister's collaboration with the KGB from 1983 until March 1995, when he assumed his current position. Oleksy charged that the documents were a forgery. His defenders suggested that they may have been manufactured by the Russian intelligence service to discredit him, because he pursued NATO membership for Poland. The high drama of an incumbent prime minister being investigated for treasonous activity ended when Oleksy was persuaded by Kwaśniewski to step down. Subsequent investigations found no incriminating evidence against Oleksy but noted wrongdoing on the part of agents in the Office of State Security (*Urząd Ochrony Państwa*, or UOP). Since the SLD controlled the investigation process, some doubts remained about Oleksy's role.

Predictably, the conjuncture of an SLD president and an SLD prime minister, Włodzimierz Cimoszewicz (chosen to replace Oleksy), put an end to strained relations between a president and a government. The election of a government based on the AWS brought on a renewed case of political cohabitation. But Kwaśniewski's moderate, low-key, and pragmatic approach to his office suggested that confrontation between executive leaders could be a thing of the past.

When we consider the skills and qualifications of leaders, it seems likely that the very well-educated political elite made up disproportionately of people from the free professions will begin to fade. As educational qualifications slip into second place in a market economy behind entrepreneurial and managerial skills, so elite recruitment is likely to come from successful businesspeople more than from academics and professionals. Poland's leaders in the early 1990s represented what could best be described as a "living museum." They comprised 1950s maverick intellectuals, 1960s student leaders, 1970s trade unionists, and the 1980s dissident underground. By the mid-1990s, these veteran anticommunist protesters were branded as political amateurs by younger, less well-known leaders. Yet they proved their resilience, assuming key ministerial positions after the 1997 elections.

During the 1990s political leaders have emerged sometimes before and sometimes after going into business. The importance of having both political and economic experience is greater than before, but it also breeds suspicion on the part of voters. Ex-communists have been singled out for using connections to launch successful private enterprises, but others in politics have done the same. Successful business entrepreneurs may, in turn, take up political careers, though this still seems to occur less frequently than the reverse process. As a result, Poland may be facing the same questions the United States and other Western democracies have for a long time: Should the economic and political elite overlap? Or should there exist a pluralism of elites that balance one another's power?

Conclusion

As in any democracy, Poland's electorate, political parties, and leaders have shaped the country's institutions, processes, and policies. Working together, these political actors advanced a new constitutional order in 1997 that would put the finishing touch on the transition from communism. Many important questions, especially those related to economics and national security, remain to be resolved. But *how* decisions are to be taken is no longer in dispute. "Democracy is consolidated when it becomes self-enforcing, that is, when all the relevant political forces find it best to continue to submit their interests and values to the uncertain interplay of institutions," wrote Adam Przeworski.[30] Uncertainties will not disappear in Poland, and what to do about them may lead to greater disagreements. But the process leading to political outcomes is neither uncertain nor disagreed upon.

This chapter has highlighted differences in voting behavior, the party system, and the nature of leadership between the early 1990s and the second half of the decade. Changes were the result of an accelerated process of political evolution, where issues related to transition were relatively quickly replaced by issues involving business as usual. There is no reason for electoral behavior, the party system, and the character of leadership to depart so markedly from what it is now in a decade's time. To be sure, leadership is the biggest wildcard and susceptible to the most sudden change. In periods of crisis, voters and parties tend to respond to rather than make strong leaders. But the routinization of politics in Poland signifies that the political initiative rests in the hands of parties and the electorate.

Notes

1. A classic study of the British political system is Jean Blondel's *Voters, Parties, and Leaders* (Harmondsworth, Middlesex, Eng: Penguin Books, 1974), from whom I have borrowed the title.
2. Norman H. Nie and Sidney Verba, "Political Participation," in Fred Greenstein and Nelson W. Polsby, eds., *Handbook of Political Science: Nongovernmental Politics* (Reading, Mass: Addison-Wesley, 1975), 17.
3. For detailed sociological analyses of the 1989 elections, see L. Kolarska-Bobińska, P. Łukasiewicz, and Z. Rykowski, eds., *Wyniki badań, wyniki wyborów* (Warsaw: PTS, 1990); also, R. Kałuża, *Polska: wybory '89* (Warsaw: Wydawnictwo Andrzej Bonarski, 1989).
4. Stanisław Gebethner, "Wybory do Sejmu i Senatu 1989 r.," *Państwo i prawo*, no. 8 (August 1989).

5. Frivolous candidacies included Jerzy Bartoszewski (a lawyer), Edward Mizikowski (a locksmith), W. Trajdos (claiming to be editor of a nonexistent newspaper), and Bolesław Tejkowski (an anti-Semite). Three serious candidates who were unable to obtain 100,000 signatures (0.4 percent of the electorate) to stand included Janusz Korwin-Mikke (Union of Political Realism), Władysław Siła-Nowicki (Party of Labor), and Kornel Morawiecki (Party of Liberty/Fighting Solidarity). Stan Tymiński rose successively from frivolous candidate to one who obtained sufficient signatures to enter the contest as a runoff candidate against Wałęsa.

6. Each party would receive a certain number of seats for a constituency based on (1) the number of seats available multiplied by votes received; (2) the product divided by total votes cast. Remainders were used to distribute the balance of seats.

7. To be eligible for national seats, a party had to have won seats in at least five separate constituencies or have polled 5 percent of the national vote. Alliances between party lists were permitted.

8. *Ordynacja wyborcza do Sejmu i Senatu Rzeczypospolitej Polskiej* (Gdańsk: Temida, 1993).

9. Data are taken from Janina Parandowska, Mariusz Janicki, and Radosław Markowski, "Krajobraz po wyborach: mapa mandatów," *Polityka,* 2 October 1993, 14–15.

10. *MacNeil/Lehrer News Hour,* 20 September 1993. The transcript was carried in the Polish affairs online bulletin *Donosy* in the days following Brzezinski's interview.

11. See John Gibson and Anna Cielecka, "Economic Influences on the Political Support for Market Reform in Post-Communist Transitions: Some Evidence from the 1993 Polish Parliamentary Elections," *Europe-Asia Studies,* 47, no. 5 (July 1995): 765–85.

12. For a more detailed study of the 1995 elections, see my "End of the Wałęsa Era in Poland," *Current History* 95, no. 599 (March 1996): 124–28.

13. Jerzy J. Wiatr, "Wybory prezydenckie 1995," *Myśl socjaldemokratyczna,* nos. 3–4 (Fall-Winter 1995): 18.

14. Zbigniew Nosowski, "Katharsis? Kościół a wybory prezydenckie," *Więź,* no. 447 (January 1996): 67.

15. "Drugie starcie," *Gazeta Wyborcza,* 16 November 1995, 1.

16. Mariusz Janicki, "Nocna zamiana," *Polityka,* 25 November 1995, 15.

17. "Kto głosował na Lecha Wałęsę," *Gazeta Wyborcza,* 20 November 1995, 4.

18. Adam Krzemiński and Ewa Nowakowska, "Suma po wyborach," *Polityka,* 2 December 1995, 4.

19. For a profile of Kwaśniewski's first-round voters, see "Polska Kwaśniewskiego, Polska Wałęsy," *Gazeta Wyborcza,* 7 November 1995, 1.

20. Centrum Badań Opinii Społecznej (CBOS), "Bulletin" (Warsaw: CBOS, April 1994 and January 1996).

21. Radisława Gortat, "Trudny egzamin: partie polityczne w wyborach prezydenckich '95," *Przegląd Społeczny,* nos. 32–33 (January–February 1996): 7. This was a special issue on the 1995 presidential elections.

22. Irena Grudzinska Gross, "Post-Communist Resentment, or the Rewriting of Polish History," *East European Politics and Societies* 6, no. 2 (Spring 1992): 147.

23. On this, see Andrzej Walicki, "Totalitarianism and Detotalitarization: The Case of Poland," *Review of Politics* 58, no. 3 (Summer 1996): 526–27.

24. "Deklaracja Akcji Wyborczej 'Solidarność,'" reported on http://www.news.wow.pl/Czerwca 1996 (10 June 1996).

25. This is the argument of Arend Lijphart, *Democracy in Plural Societies* (New Haven, Conn: Yale University Press, 1977).

26. For the full text of the 1997 constitution, see "Konstytucja Rzeczypospolitej Polskiej," *Rzeczypospolita,* 3 April 1997.

27. On the law, see Frances Millard, "The Polish Parliamentary Elections of October 1991," *Soviet Studies* 44, no. 5 (1992): 838–40.

28. For an analysis of the role of the presidency, see Krzysztof Jasiewicz, "Poland: Wałęsa's Legacy to the Presidency," in Ray Taras, ed., *Postcommunist Presidents* (Cambridge, Eng.: Cambridge University Press, 1997): 130–67.

29. On the origins of the Mazowiecki government, see Zbigniew Domarańczyk, *100 dni Mazowieckiego* (Warsaw: Andrzej Bonarski, 1990); on the role of the intelligentsia, see Voytek Zubek, "The Rise and Fall of Rule by Poland's Best and Brightest," *Soviet Studies* 44, no. 4 (1992): 579–608.

30. Adam Przeworski, Democracy and the Market: Political and Economic Reforms in Eastern Europe and Latin America (Cambridge, Eng: Cambridge University Press, 1991), 26.

FOUR

The Political Activation
of Social Groups

Ewa M. Thompson

An astute observer concluded that in the literature on Solidarity and its aftermath, there is a dearth of quantitative analysis and an abundance of descriptively elaborate but socially inadequate conclusions. Causality is seen as centered in the elite groups of intellectuals and writers whose opinions are treated as evidence that things are thus and so. Literature on the Polish transformation privileges a small group of people whose written *interpretations* of events are seen as *causes* of events by subsequent writers. This static sense of causality has ignored the dynamics of Polish transformation.[1]

Since 1989, much has changed to weaken the above objections. Political parties and civic associations; the struggle of social groups for a share of the shrinking pie; public debates on issues that were taboo under communism; and demonstrations, strikes, and lobbying activities provide evidence that bypasses cultural presumptions of the elite. By comparison with stable democracies, however, literature on the behavior of various social groups in Poland during the 1990s is still excessively dependent on the holistic appraisals of Polish society presented in such periodicals as *Kultura* (Paris) and cultivated by the country's leading intellectuals. In contrast, this chapter has relied on written records about activities rather than assumed attitudes, within the limitations imposed by the aforementioned predilection of Polish writers and journalists, as well as by a corresponding scarcity of systematic sociological research.

As Frances F. Millard has noted, the legacies of Soviet-occupied Poland include not only institutions and structures but also memories and patterns of behavior.[2] Among the latter is the tradition of strange and unusual political alliances. The struggle against totalitarianism temporarily united the intelligentsia and workers, the conservative peasantry and liberal urban dwellers, the Catholic Church hierarchy and militantly secular intellectuals. These alliances fell apart under postcommunist conditions, but not always along the fault lines of economic interest anticipated by the Polish sociologist Edmund Mokrzycki.[3] The disintegration of these alliances during the presidencies of Lech Wałęsa and Aleksander Kwaśniewski led to new ways of self-assertion for all concerned.

The strange alliances just mentioned were operative in Solidarity,[4] although as other writers have demonstrated, the Solidarity movement and its strategies were created in the Gdańsk shipyards, whereas the university-educated advisers came aboard when the movement was already under way. Ever since the creation of the Committee for Defense of Workers (KOR) in 1976, Warsaw and Kraków intellectuals viewed with a watchful and sympathetic eye the developments in Gdańsk, even as they strove to exert their influence on the workers.[5] The Roundtable negotiations with the communists and the semi-free elections to the Sejm (parliament) which followed in June 1989 reflected the antitotalitarian stance of both Solidarity and the intellectuals. It was only to be expected that as soon as the political process became unfrozen in Poland, groups possessed of an agenda and the means to articulate it, as well as groups opposed to other agendas but unable to articulate their own, would assert themselves in a variety of ways. Those groups that failed to get their message across to the media would remain subject to interpretation by the articulate urban elite, and this would cause a secondary wave of social activism such as strikes and demonstrations.

The first sign of disintegration of the Solidarity-led social consensus was given by Tadeusz Mazowiecki, who walked out of Solidarity's Parliamentary Citizens' Club in the first postcommunist Sejm. He and his allies formed their own organization, the Democratic Union (UD) in December 1990, or at the time when another prominent future dissenter from Solidarity, Jarosław Kaczyński, was editor-in-chief of *Tygodnik Solidarność* and worked as an aide to Wałęsa. His Center Alliance (PC), formed with a view to helping Wałęsa win the presidency, evolved into a political party in 1991. In June 1992, the Jan Olszewski faction left the Center Alliance to form the Movement for the Republic (RdR), a party characterized by a vague economic program and a Christian democratic social ideology. The Olszewski group split and renamed itself several times (in 1997, it was called Movement for Poland's Reconstruction, or ROP), while the Democratic Union continued to attract intellectuals and eventually absorbed a good part of the former Solidarity sympathizers, including most of the *Tygodnik Powszechny, Znak,* and *Więź* Catholics (Jan Maria Rokita, Jerzy Turowicz, Tadeusz Mazowiecki, Andrzej Potocki, Andrzej Wielowieyski), and disappointed former communists (Jacek Kuroń, Adam Michnik, Bronisław Geremek, Leszek Balcerowicz). In 1993, the Democratic Union renamed itself Freedom Union (UW) after merging with the Liberal Democratic Congress (KLD) of Jan Krzysztof Bielecki. However, while it gathered intellectual strength, UW kept losing the electorate's support. During 1996 opinion polls, it consistently scored in the single digits, and in the 1995 presidential election, its candidate Jacek Kuroń had received only 9 percent of the vote. In January 1997, Rokita and five other UW members left the party, protesting its leftist orientation. Subsequently, some of them joined the Solidarity Electoral Action (AWS), whose spring and summer 1997 standing in the polls far surpassed that of UW.

The low popularity of the party, whose credentials appear impeccable and whose rank-and-file members' list reads like a *Who's Who in Poland,* has been interpreted by its spokespersons as a sign of immaturity of Polish society. In issue after issue, the Paris *Kultura* advanced this interpretation in articles by Smecz and Krzysztof Wolicki.[6] However, *Gazeta Wyborcza,* which is widely regarded as a mouthpiece for the Freedom Union, continues to be the most widely read tabloid in Poland. In September 1993 elections to the Sejm, a postcommunist majority was elected together with a substantial UW minority (71), giving Solidarity and the parties of the center-right only token representation: 16 out of 460 seats in the Sejm, plus 12 Solidarity senators (out of 100).

After the 1995 presidential election, a realignment of social forces began, reflecting final disintegration of the Solidarity alliance between the conservative working class and liberal intellectuals. This realignment defies the Western pattern of left and right. In terms of economic policies, the former communists (SLD) and the Freedom Union belong to the right side of the political spectrum, whereas Olszewski and Solidarity belong to the left side. From the point of view of philosophical background and social values, however, Poland in 1997 has a two-tier political left and a substantial but disorganized center-right. On the ideological left are the former communists and the leadership, although not always the rank and file, of the Freedom Union. On the ideological right is Olszewski's ROP, various small parties, and the Solidarity labor union.

In social ideology, SLD and UW have taken an increasingly similar position. Both parties favor a secularist state, and their notion of democracy is similar to that represented by the left wing of the Democratic Party in the United States. In terms of economic programs, SLD and UW subscribe to the Leszek Balcerowicz shock therapy supported by the International Monetary Fund (IMF). In contrast, the parties of the center-right, as well as a plurality of the population, are wary of the social costs for such rapid change. They favor slower privatization, hoping that this would keep the workers employed. SLD and UW are staunchly pro-market, whereas parties of the center-right and Solidarity say that so far, privatization has mostly impoverished the workers and benefited the former *nomenklatura*. However, the Solidarity leadership and Olszewski's ROP have failed to articulate details of a "universal distribution of state assets," which they advocate. SLD and UW have defended their position well, and they disproportionately represent Poland abroad and in the media. The Polish Peasant Party (PSL), which entered the ruling coalition in 1993, has increasingly distanced itself from the SLD. The fall 1996 election of Pawlak (representing mostly the poorer farmers) over Jagieliński (representing the wealthier farmers) as head of the PSL signals an attempt on the part of the PSL to position itself vis-à-vis the state as the farmers' labor union.

It is within this framework of conflicting economic and ideological interests that activities of various social groups take place. The largest of these groups are peasant farmers and urban workers.

Farmers

In 1995, about 15 million people lived in the Polish countryside. They were divided among 2,151 districts (*gmina*), consisting of several villages and headed by an elected representative (*wójt*). Over the past twenty years, the rural population decreased by 3.1 percent, whereas the urban population grew by 25.1 percent.[7] In 1996, there were 2,038,000 privately owned farms in Poland, down from 2,168,000 in 1988.[8] Overall, 40 percent of the population lives in villages and small towns. Farmers are traditionally regarded as a monolithic and the least politically active social group: this view was reinforced by dissident intellectuals during the half century of communist rule. In the 1990s, however, farmers' behavior disproved this assessment. Sociological surveys of voting patterns indicate that political behavior in farming communities is similar to that of other social groups in Poland and elsewhere. It is influenced by geography, economic status, and local conditions. A much-publicized split emerged during the 1995 presidential election, when the well-rooted farming communities of the south and southeast voted massively for Wałęsa, whereas the "resettled" farmers of the northwestern voivodships voted for Kwaśniewski.[9] The most prosperous farmers espouse the set of values known as agrarianism, in which self-reliance is a centerpiece. They favor a free market, are conservative in social matters, and do not wish assistance from the state; however, their percentage is still small (7.8).[10] Those least successful expect the state to solve their problems, and they comprise close to one-fifth of the rural population. Unemployment is high: 43 percent of those without work live in the countryside, the highest being among those who worked for state-owned farms (*państwowe gospodarstwa rolne*).[11] This group of rural workers voted mainly for Kwaśniewski, in the hope that government interventionism would alleviate their economic difficulties. At the same time, farmers resent being told that they should leave the land and move to cities so that unemployment in the countryside would go down. PSL deputy chairman Franciszek Stefaniuk has argued that cities have no housing or jobs for these destitute farmers and that relocation is absurd under present circumstances.

In surveys measuring the extent of orientation toward investment as opposed to consumption, farmers and businessmen scored equally high, whereas intelligentsia and workers would rather spend on consumption.[12] This finding contradicts perceived wisdom, which considers peasantry as generally passive and hostile to entrepreneurship. Part-time farmers are divided into hired laborers and small entrepreneurs, and their political behavior varies accordingly. The attitudes of Polish farmers toward the issue of agricultural land sales to foreigners are similar to those of farmers and small businesspeople in countries such as Norway, and they reflect the fear of unfair competition. The dumping practices of Western European companies in Poland have reinforced such fears throughout the capital-starved countryside. From the farmers' standpoint, the policy of marketing in Poland heavily subsidized Western European agricultural products represents not free trade but a blow to the interests of two fifths of the population. Polls have indicated that virtually all parties find adherents in the countryside.[13] In 1996, PSL was poised to join the Solidarity Electoral Action (AWS) in preparation for the 1997 elections, but this did not happen. A substantial number of politicians are of peasant background—a novelty in Poland, where political life was dominated by urban dwellers both under the Second Republic (1918–1939) and under communism.

However, farmers are willing to integrate with Western Europe even when integration is perceived as detrimental to their short-term economic interests. Polls also indicate that Polish farmers behave in a friendly fashion toward those Germans who pay visits to the areas of western Poland where their ancestors lived and from which they were expelled: this despite a hatred of things German with which schools in Soviet-occupied Poland tried to indoctrinate their pupils. According to a 1993 poll, half of all farmers desire some restrictions on imports of food and alcohol, as well as on the right of foreign citizens to purchase land in Poland. However, an even larger percentage supports Poland's integration with NATO and the European Union, even when this integration entails economic disadvantage. According to a sociologist, these contradictory results express the farmers' patriotism, a quality that has been preserved in the countryside much more widely than in the city.[14]

Farmers' ability to organize on a local level and fight what they perceive as unfair decisions of the authorities has increased considerably under conditions of democracy. The farmers are generally opposed to busing and respond to it with sit-in "strikes." In September 1995, at the village of Nowe Polaszki (Gdańsk voivodship), parents hired a private teacher rather than send 28 children by bus to a school miles away. Under leadership of the village mayor, Irena Treder, they picketed county offices for weeks. Parental strikes were also organized in other villages of the voivodship when authorities tried to consolidate schools. Parents presented to journalists tables showing how many babies were born in each village over the past ten years, arguing that the number of births was increasing. They said they planned to inundate the village with babies, thereby forcing the authorities to keep the schools open. When similar attempts to close down schools were undertaken in communist times, however, parents did not dare protest.[15] In October 1996, a PSL member of parliament (MP) visited the middle school in Złoczów (Sieradz voivodship). The town has 2,800 inhabitants, and its population is largely of peasant stock. Students asked questions about the motives for and the functioning of the PSL-SLD coalition, the possibility of the coalition dissolving before the 1997 parliamentary elections, the status of Poland's integration with the European Union and NATO, the justification for energy subsidies for farmers; personal relations between members of parliament representing different sides of the political spectrum; and MP salaries.[16] Such data cast doubt on the famed peasant passivity and an alleged lack of interest in issues transcending village politics.

In contrast, the 1996 local government elections elicited little interest among farmers, drawing between 15 and 44 percent of voters. This indicates that farmers' distrust of state authorities remains high. One reason for such distrust is the unresolved issue of compensation for the so-called nationalization of peasant land during the 1940s and 1950s.[17]

Urban Workers

After 1989, Polish workers found themselves in a no-win situation. Their skills and dedication turned out to be of no use under conditions where they had no influence on the marketing of goods they produced. In addition, outdated technology and the interest of managers collided with workers' interests. Falling wages, disappearing markets, and the growing indebtedness of Polish factories placed workers and Solidarity leaders in a reactive position. The key political activity consisted of strikes and threats of strikes. However, workers and their leaders also have played a role in the battle for the media, in lobbying against abortion, and in other debates on social issues. Demands by factories for cheap credit, a living wage, and the abolition of retroactive taxes on wages have been perceived as regressive by the Polish elite. From workers' standpoint, they are an alternative to hunger. Unlike the professional classes, which have maintained their standard of living, however modest, for workers the issue of privatization has been a matter of getting paid or starving. These perceptions and realities have to be taken into account in assessing the conflict between the Solidarity trade union and the country's political elite during the 1990s. The economic changes inspired by Leszek Balcerowicz and the IMF are perceived by workers as reasons for their miserable condition. Workers' leaders perceive these measures as leading to a near-destruction of Poland's industrial base, and they accuse the ruling coalition of transferring national wealth to the former *nomenklatura*. Insofar as the SLD has continued Balcerowicz-inspired policies, the labor union has transferred this hostility to the Kwaśniewski government. Such are the economic and attitudinal underpinnings of the Solidarity-led electoral coalition that has been gathering strength during the fall of 1996 and into 1997.

The situation is aggravated by the fact that privatization, or transforming factories into "state-owned private companies" with a view to selling them to foreign or domestic investors, has not been accompanied by a radical restructuring of middle and upper management in these companies. Although privatization looks good on paper, the process of management replacement often amounts to the replacement of the old *nomenklatura* (handsomely pensioned off at state expense) by the younger *nomenklatura,* whose conceptions of productivity and efficiency go back to communist times. In the early 1990s, field research in factories disclosed the excellent morale and work habits of workers and foremen, while revealing the disastrous ineptness and passivity of management, whose only occupation seemed to be the collection of salaries.[18] A sociologist has argued that Poland is heading toward the Latin American model of capitalism, where an alignment between the state and the super-rich created monopolies impossible to penetrate by small business competition. Under this kind of capitalism, industrial profits are skimmed off by a relatively small elite, while the management of factories is left in the hands of incompetent but trustworthy underlings.[19] The postcommunist impoverishment of the working classes and the failure of postcommunist governments to quickly restructure factories and enterprises, starting with middle management, are largely responsible for the internal political conflicts under Kwaśniewski's presidency.

The fate of the Ursus tractor factory near Warsaw shows how such conflicts arise. In 1995, Ursus had some 12,000 skilled workers on its payroll. Nationwide, between 120,000 and 140,000 people made a living with Ursus tractors. But the factory was heavily indebted and in danger of bankruptcy, while its workers were not paid a living wage. On 9 May 1995, about half of the workers went on strike. In addition to a 30 percent raise (from $223 to $292 per month), they demanded low-interest credits for the factory to complete outstanding orders and the rescinding of retroactive taxation on wages. In the following days, the strike spread, and so did the demonstrations. On 30 May 1995, Ursus workers were offered a $20 monthly raise but no relief in the matter of credits and debts. Finally, on 11 July 1996, the finance ministry worked out a deal whereby Ursus was transformed into a state-owned private company (a postcommunist oxymoron). Some of the debts to other state-owned factories were canceled, others were converted into ownership shares.

However, these moves turned out to be insufficient to cure the ailing company.[20] Accustomed to a virtual monopoly (70 percent of all tractors owned by Polish farmers were Ursus-made), management neglected to do market research and did not adjust to changing needs. The company became vulnerable to foreign competition that offered smaller tractors—more in demand by Poland's farmers. The result was that in the fall of 1996, Ursus had to trim its work force to stay competitive. As has been the case with the Gdańsk shipyards, the highly skilled Polish workers paid with their jobs for the ineptness of management and its failure to survey the market and keep restructuring during transition years. Increasingly, it is becoming clear that the failing Polish companies are victims of a bureaucracy that acts on the premise that the problems of markets and efficiency should be solved at the ministry level. This is also true of Russia, where "bad" and "horrible" rankings have been given by American researchers to a vast majority of managers.[21] The various ministries have tolerated this passivity because they themselves have been passive. This problem of managerial change has not been addressed to any significant extent either in Poland or in Russia. Therefore, the political activity of workers is often limited to public protests and demonstrations.

Another factor in the apparent excessive readiness of workers to resort to strikes is the shortage of housing in Poland. Under communism, the building of one-family homes was discouraged, and so-called workers' hostels were constructed near factories. They housed single workers under barracks conditions. As time went on and no apartments were built, families with several children vegetated in one-room quarters with no private bath or kitchen.

Television

While workers are preoccupied with survival issues and farmers with local issues, a cross section of Polish society has engaged in several battles over cultural and ideological matters. Foremost among them is the battle for the media, and particularly over who will control television, which plays an increasingly important role in Poland. A 1995 Center for Public Opinion Surveys (OBOP) poll disclosed that 93 percent of teenagers regularly watch TV, whereas only 62 percent read periodicals.[22]

In 1993, Wiesław Walendziak, a respected historian and TV producer, became head of the National Radio and TV Council, a five-person government body supervising national television (TVP). He resigned in February 1996. At this time, his approval rating was 61 percent; just over half of all of respondents considered TVP unbiased and independent, and only one tenth evaluated it negatively.[23] While some commentators felt that Walendziak's departure was a foregone conclusion in view of the 1993 and 1995 election results, others pointed out that the immediate reason for his downfall was that the council's majority of three (two of them representing SLD interests, and one the leftist faction in UW) voted together to sabotage Walendziak's decisions. Such incidents deepened the widening rift between the Freedom Union (UW) and the man in the street. A Solidarity journalist quoted UW's Andrzej Potocki as saying that the party should do anything to "retain its position within the ruling circle."[24] A sociologist has also noted collusion between the former communists and the UW, charging that "[*Gazeta Wyborcza* editor Adam] Michnik has flung himself into the arms of the very generals who had once persecuted him. By his recent behavior he has systematically discredited himself."[25] Such charges indicate that at the very least, the UW displayed careless inattention to the *appearances* of impropriety, and they point to the UW's ambivalent role in the struggle for the media.

Competition from private TV stations caused further difficulties for the ruling coalition. One such station, PolSat, had 30 percent of viewers in the Warsaw voivodship during fall 1996—the largest audience share in that influential area. Walendziak returned to TVP as producer of the popular interview program *Without Anesthesia*. On 10 October 1996, he interviewed Lech Wałęsa, attracting 5 million viewers. The struggle for control over TVP continues.

The Press

The legacy of communism in the Polish press is still considerable. Intellectuals and journalists trained to run state-owned periodicals in People's Poland have largely kept their jobs. When communism fell, its daily organ *Trybuna Ludu*, the name shortened to *Trybuna*, continued publication under the auspices of the SLD, which inherited the physical plant and skilled technical personnel. The communist weekly *Polityka* likewise adjusted to new conditions without any ideological change. According to opposition politicians, in 1997 *Polityka* was supported by money from the finance ministry.[26] Dailies, such as *Rzeczpospolita* and *Życie Warszawy*, were privatized and now are owned by a variety of investors. Some personnel changes have followed. Adam Michnik set up his own daily, *Gazeta Wyborcza*, attracting many left-leaning Solidarity sympathizers, mainly from KOR circles, and distancing himself from the Solidarity labor union. The new weekly *Wprost* imitates *Time* and *Newsweek* in format and ideology. By the time Kwaśniewski became president, SLD and UW sympathizers had gained the lion's share of the periodical market. Apart from *Tygodnik Solidarność*, which remained staunchly unionist, the center-right has been virtually voiceless during the 1990s, being represented in the popular press by the high-pitched *Gazeta Polska*, as well as some small weeklies, biweeklies, and monthlies. On 31 August 1996, during the celebration of Solidarity's establishment, Chairman Marian Krzaklewski said that Solidarity was protesting the left's monopoly in the media.

Why has the center-right done so poorly? One explanation is that it had been frozen out, having had no access to media even under the "reformed" communism of the 1970s and 1980s, when some dissidents were allowed to express themselves publicly. As complete outsiders, whose public relations skills were not honed in the opposition weekly *Tygodnik Powszechny*, the right and center-right, or some one fourth of the population,[27] failed to secure for themselves representation during the initial struggle for the media under the Wałęsa presidency. Thus the grand debates of the 1990s on the economy, the constitution, agriculture, and abortion are channeled into the media, whose orientation reflects the views of the parties currently dominant in the Sejm: the SLD, the PSL, and the UW. The center-right resorts to archaic forms of social mobilization: demonstrations, rallies, open letters, and other ad hoc actions with limited appeal and consequences.

What Divides Them: The Abortion Debate

The abortion issue has played an energizing role in postcommunist Poland. It enabled segments of society that have traditionally been passive to reaffirm themselves, thus broadening political participation. Two consecutive parliaments passed contradictory bills on abortion in 1993 and 1996, and it is widely expected that the Sejm that will emerge after the 1997 parliamentary elections will take on this issue as well.

The anti-abortion bill, passed on 7 January 1993, restricted abortions to cases of incest, rape, major fetus deformity, and direct danger to the mother's health. A striking novelty of this legislation was that it imposed no penalties on the woman undergoing abortion, making only the doctor liable to prosecution, with a maximum penalty of two years in prison. While the number of abortions went down drastically over the next three years, a population increase did not follow, giving credence to the pro-abortion faction's claim that Polish women traveled abroad to get abortions. The anti-abortionists tried to use demographic indicators as well, arguing that the anti-abortion law obviously did not lead to excessive population growth. The decline in abortions in Poland has been gradual, and it began before the anti-abortion law was passed.[28]

After the 1995 parliamentary elections, the stage was set for a reversal of the law. In August 1996, the lower house passed a bill allowing abortions in cases of psychological or financial hardship. In October, the Senate rejected the bill, but the lower house passed it after the second reading. The new bill was signed into law by President Kwaśniewski in November 1996. While the issue was on the legislative agenda, an extraordinary outpouring of anti-abortion sentiment occurred. According to Senator Alicja Grześkowiak, during fall 1996, more than 2 million letters were received by the Sejm, urging the MPs to vote against abortion. Various groups organized sit-ins and prayers before the Parliament building. The press noted that those present included retirees and pensioners—groups that have traditionally been passive regarding issues of no immediate economic interest to them.

Prelates of the Catholic Church entered the debate as well. In October, Poland's bishops sent an open letter to the Sejm urging it to vote against amending the 1993 law. Grassroots lobbying by members of local parishes was particularly visible before the final vote in the lower house. For weeks, delegations visited MPs in their offices, trying to persuade them to vote against changing the law. A Catholic daily published a list of MPs who had voted pro-abortion during the first reading, urging their constituents to press for a reversal. On 23 October 1996, an anti-abortion demonstration of 40,000 took place in Warsaw. The Senate speaker (PSL) said that the SLD had forced the abortion issue on the Sejm in order to cover up its ineptness in economic and social policy.[29] The Polish Medical Association, which rejects abortion on principle, issued a statement saying that the doctors who did not wish to perform abortions should not be forced to do so.

In the week of 15–22 October, when all other party clubs in the Sejm placed the abortion issue prominently on their agenda, only Freedom Union leaders defied the trend. Their club discussed animal rights.[30] This "breaking of the ranks" did not pass unnoticed by Solidarity Electoral Action. Freedom Union is not included in that coalition, which has a good chance of winning a plurality in the next elections. However, in June 1997 in Warsaw, the AWS, the ROP and the UW joined forces in composing a common list of candidates to the Senate in anticipation of the September 1997 elections. In the fall of 1996 and spring of 1997, AWS led in opinion polls.[31] On 4 November 1996, representatives of Solidarity Electoral Action had met with President Kwaśniewski and tried to convince him that he should not sign the bill.

Thus the tactics of the anti-abortion lobby in Poland have been similar to those used in the United States: candlelight vigils, harassment of individual lawmakers, demonstrations, testimonials, and statements by church leaders and doctors. Under communism, no segment of society could afford the luxury of publicly expressing a point of view on social policy matters. The welcome byproduct of the abortion battle in Poland has been the mobilization of citizenry on behalf of a cause that has aroused much controversy in other free societies.

Traditional Expressions of Public Opinion

These are the means of last resort, and they are used when the government is unable to explain its policies to the electorate and when public anger expresses itself without waiting for parliamentary debates. That these forms of social expression retained their usefulness in postcommunist Poland indicates a lack of political equilibrium in the country, not in the sense that the country is about to explode into a civil war but in the sense that proper channels for societal expression have not been found, despite democratic conditions. At the same time, one observes a certain narrowing of goals, as demonstrations and rallies are often used to achieve a specific objective. On 14 October 1996, several dozen handicapped men and women demonstrated in front of the regional office of one of Poland's largest insurance companies in Opole, demanding that Braille-accessible insurance forms be issued and that the building be made accessible for the handicapped. On the same day, inhabitants of Biedrusk near Poznań demonstrated against the use of ashes from a nearby electric power station to fill potholes, claiming that they were detrimental to health. Demonstrators blocked a major road, making it impossible for traffic to proceed. Another grassroots action was undertaken at Białystok. In July 1996, a group of citizens began to boycott vendors who sold pornography. Protests quickly spread to other cities, including Warsaw. In some small towns, sellers of smut have been challenged in the courts.[32] On 31 August 1996, huge rallies marking the fifteenth anniversary of the Solidarity movement took place in Polish cities.

Another traditional form of political participation in Poland is the writing of open letters. In September 1996, *Kultura* (Paris) editor Jerzy Giedroyć wrote a letter to President Kwaśniewski, protesting the incompetence of the culture minister. Before the 1995 presidential elections, the Conference of Polish Bishops issued a letter to the faithful urging them to vote their conscience. Numerous public letters and statements on Chechnya had also been circulated.

At the same time, voter participation in local elections is low. In the 1996 election to agricultural councils, so few people went to the polls that in some voivodships, no councils were elected. Such apathy is a measure of distrust toward the postcommunist authorities. An inability of the electorate to find trustworthy politicians and to rally behind them has resulted in the creation of many ephemeral parties and political groups, formed and dissolved on a nearly month-by-month basis.[33]

What Unites Them: Political and Social Causes

Poles seem united on a number of issues. Foremost is a preference for a democratic system of government and support for other ethnic groups wishing such a system, as well as support for membership in NATO and the European Union (EU). Poles also welcome such innovations as the marketing and advertising of products, but only when they are not carbon copies of Western patterns but take into account local traditions and memories. This unity shows in opinion polls, purchasing preferences, and social work on behalf of causes.

An OBOP poll conducted in the fall of 1996 showed that 78 percent of the population regards democracy as the best form of government.[34] The percentage of people favoring democracy has increased since the polls began to be conducted in the early 1990s. Center for the Study of Public

Opinion (CBOS) polls during 1993–1996 have shown that a solid majority supports integration with NATO and the EU. In a poll conducted during January 1996, about 80 percent of respondents declared that they would vote for Poland's membership in NATO in a referendum on this issue. In a CBOS poll conducted during March 1996, three-fourths of respondents declared they would vote "yes" in a referendum on joining the EU. This compares favorably with Czech responses: in 1996, only 38 percent of Czech citizens favored membership in NATO.[35] At the same time, in regard to the EU, there is a consistent lowering of expectations. Polish respondents who believe that membership in the EU would offer them instant benefits have decreased in number since 1991. However, even those who are skeptical of benefits favor integration, on the premise that it would be beneficial for both Poland and the EU in the long run. As to NATO, a majority of respondents believes that Russian protests should not be a decisive factor in deciding this matter.

A remarkable degree of agreement and financial generosity has been shown in regard to Chechnya and its efforts to gain sovereignty, widely perceived as parallel to the Polish struggle for independence during the nineteenth century. Support has taken the form of conferences and appeals, open letters, and the dispatching of truck convoys with food, clothing, and medical supplies. Ever since *Tygodnik Solidarność* published on 13 January 1995 an open letter to Dzhokar Dudayev (composed by one of Poland's greatest living poets, Zbigniew Herbert, and signed by intellectuals as well as Solidarity rank-and-file members), small donations have been received by Solidarity union offices throughout the country. The editor of *Tygodnik Solidarność* made a trip to Chechnya and reported on it in detail.

During July–August 1996, an international conference was organized by a Polish-Chechen committee. Some Russian democrats attended. During that conference, 62 Polish politicians and intellectuals (including two former foreign ministers and one former prime minister) issued an appeal to world public opinion to help stop the "extermination" of the Chechen people. The appeal alleged that Boris Yeltsin had escalated the rate of extermination after his 3 July 1996 presidential victory. More signatures were collected worldwide during the subsequent 63 days (the length of time of the 1944 Warsaw uprising), and then the appeal was sent to the Council of Europe. On 1 August 1996, Lech Wałęsa wrote to Nobel Peace Prize winners on behalf of the people of Chechnya. He too alleged "genocide," saying that Poland and Chechnya had experienced a similar fate at Russian hands. Both appeals were released on the fifty-second anniversary of the ill-fated Warsaw uprising against the Nazis. The apparent readiness of Poles to rally to the support of Chechens indicates that the pattern of behavior affixed in national memory can be a powerful means of social mobilization.

The Polish response to Western-style advertising usefully gauges the acceptance of the Americanization of public life. Poles have generally welcomed an upsurge in advertising, and private companies spent $505 million for this purpose in Poland during 1995. One famous ad used a scene from Henryk Sienkiewicz's novel, *The Deluge*, to advertise a Polish-made detergent. Two brothers watch a hooligan splash mud on their father's clothes. "Shall we clean his clock?" they ask. "Yes," says the father, "but only with Pollena detergent." The ad received mention in the press as an example of the successful adaptation of modern advertising techniques to local custom, and sales of Pollena soared. In politics and in advertising, Poles seem to respond positively to appeals that activate their historical memory.

The growth of political consciousness and activism in Poland seems to proceed along familiar lines. As various social groups struggle for recognition and discover the political weapons available in a democracy, they begin to lobby for particular legislative action or an administrative decision. Not unlike that in the United States, Polish society is divided along economic, ideological, and geographical lines. The old divisions of country-city, intelligentsia-working class have been replaced by a struggle for presence in the public arena. This struggle brings into the political process new and hitherto unknown players.[36] The intelligentsia continues to evolve into a professional class, and its role as spokesman for society continues to decline.

Notes

1. Lawrence Goodwyn, *Breaking the Barrier: The Rise of Solidarity in Poland* (New York: Oxford University Press, 1991), 443.

2. Frances F. Millard, *The Anatomy of the New Poland* (Brookfield, Vt: Edward Elgar, 1994), 1–28.

3. Edmund Mokrzycki, "Class Interests, Redistribution and Corporatism," in Christopher G. A. Bryant and Edmund Mokrzycki, eds., *Democracy, Civil Society, and Pluralism* (Warsaw: IFiS, 1995), 205–38.

4. Ewa M. Thompson, "The Challenge of Democratic and Nationalist Movements to the Communist Regimes in Hungary, Poland, and Czechoslovakia," in Uri Ra'anan, ed., *The Soviet Empire: The Challenge of National and Democratic Movements* (Lexington, Mass.: D. C. Heath, 1990), 189–210.

5. Important policy differences existed between KOR members and the early Solidarity movement, which are discussed in Roman Laba, *The Roots of Solidarity: A Political Sociology of Poland's Working Class Democratization* (Princeton, N.J.: Princeton University Press, 1991), 109ff.

6. *Kultura* 9, no. 588 (September 1996): 78–91; 10, no. 589 (October 1996): 65–74; and 4, no. 583 (April 1996), 21–28.

7. Barbara Kozińska, "Mniej ludno ale cudno," *Życie Warszawy*, 1 August 1995.

8. Central Statistical Office, as reported by *Gazeta Wyborcza*, 4 November 1996.

9. "Resettled" refers to the fact that after World War II, Poles from Belarus, Ukraine, and Lithuania were forced to migrate to the western voivodships, replacing Germans, who in turn were moved to Germany. Włoclawek voivodship voted 70 percent for Kwaśniewski and Koszalin voivodship, 68 percent. Wałęsa won in the voivodships of Nowy Sącz (76.5 percent), Tarnów (70 percent), and Rzeszów (69 percent). (*Donosy*, 7 November 1996). However, in July 1997, tens of thousands of farmers in western and southwestern Poland were ruined by floods. Angered by government incompetence in managing the emergency situation, these farmers were expected to switch their vote from SLD to AWS in the September 1997 election and did so.

10. Barbara Fedyszak-Radziejowska, "Wieś i jej mieszkańcy," *Arcana* 4, no. 10 (September 1996); 74.

11. Kazimierz Korab, "Hasła i kompromisy," ibid., 89.

12. Fedyszak-Radziejowska, "Wieś i jej mieszkańcy"; Jacek Szpakowski, "Uprawianie wsi," *Tygodnik Solidarność* 42, no. 422 (October 1996).

13. "Wybory-Solidarnościowi chłopi," *Życie Warszawy*, 12 August 1995; "Chłopi w cenie," *Życie Warszawy*, 21 May 1996.

14. Fedyszak-Radziejowska, "Sondaże: zabawa czy manipulacja?" *Arcana* 4, no. 10 (September 1996): 70–82. The percentage of farmers supporting European integration is roughly equal to the percentage of the Polish population supporting such integration.

15. Jerzy Morawski, "Strajk w Nowych Polaszkach—idzie wyż demograficzny," *Życie Warszawy*, 21 September 1995.

16. *Kronika Sejmowa* 140, no. 263, II kadencja, 23–25 October 1996.

17. J. Pawłowski, "Chłopska krzywda," *Życie Warszawy*, 10 September 1996; Roman Strzemiecki, "Chłopski parlament," *Życie Warszawy*, 1 October 1996.

18. James R. Thompson and Jacek Koronacki, *Statistical Process Control for Quality Improvement* (New York: Chapman and Hall, 1993), xii–xiv.

19. Jadwiga Staniszkis, "Wszechwładza oligarchii, czyli co nas czeka," *Tygodnik Solidarność* 31, no. 411 (August 1996): 1, 12–13.

20. See articles about Ursus in *Życie Warszawy* of 10 and 13 May, 12 July, and 18 September 1996.

21. Joseph R. Blasi et al., *Kremlin Capitalism: Privatizing the Russian Economy* (Ithaca, N.Y.: Cornell University Press, 1996), 219.

22. *Życie Warszawy*, 7 August 1995.

23. An OBOP poll, as reported by Beata Pasek in *OMRI Daily Digest*, 6 October 1996.

24. Dariusz Lipiński, "Unia Wolności liczy na furtkę," *Tygodnik Solidarność* 34, no. 414 (1996).

25. Ireneusz Krzemiński, "Defeat of the Silent Revolution," *Periphery* 2, nos. 1–2 (1996): 4–7.
26. Jadwiga Staniszkis, "Wszechwładza oligarchii."
27. Andrzej Nowak, "Nasze zasady, nasz naród," *Arcana* 5, no. 11 (September–October 1996): 7. "Polska Online," on 12 November 1996, reported a Center for the Study of Public Opinion (CBOS) poll according to which 33 percent of Poles declared themselves as right-leaning and 20 percent as left-leaning.
28. According to Lucyna Nowak of the Central Statistical Office, in 1995 about 445,000 births were recorded, or 38 percent fewer than at the high point in 1983. This amounts to a population increase of about 0.1 percent. (Reuters, 1 December 1995). Abortions in 1987 were estimated to number 123,534, although in 1991 there were only 30,878, with a corresponding slide in between. A drastic decline continued after the law was passed, producing 782 abortions in 1994 (UPI press release, 22 October 1996).
29. *Życie Warszawy,* 23 October 1996; *Donosy,* 24 October 1996; *Tygodnik Solidarność* 39, no. 419 (27 September 1996).
30. *Kronika Sejmowa* 139, no. 262, II kadencja, Kluby Poselskie-debaty (Warsaw: Wydawnictwo Sejmowe, October 1996).
31. Interview with Wacław Zawadzki in *Życie Warszawy,* 3 December 1996.
32. Paul Lewis, "Poland's New Parties," in Gordon Wightman, ed., *Party Formation in East Central Europe* (Brookfield, Vt.: Edward Elgar, 1995), 32.
33. An OBOP poll reported by *Życie Warszawy,* 22 November 1996.
34. Jiri Pehe in *OMRI Daily Digest,* 5 December 1996.
35. In a November 1996, OBOP poll probing the preferences of likely voters in the 1997 elections, the newly formed National Association of Retired People scored 5 percent. *Życie Warszawy,* 26 November 1996. The NARP leadership consists mainly of ranking members of the now-defunct Polish United Workers' Party and the party's political opponents' charge that it was formed to increase the influence of the former *nomenklatura* in the Sejm.
36. In a November 1996 OBOP poll probing the preferences of likely voters in the 1997 elections, the newly formed National Association of Retired People scored five percent. *Życie Warszawy,* 26 November 1996. The NARP leadership consists mainly of ranking members of the now-defunct Polish United Workers' Party, and the party's political opponents charge that it was formed to increase the influence of the former *nomenklatura* in the Sejm. However, not a single NARP candidate was elected to Parliament in September 1997.

FIVE

The Presidential-
Parliamentary System

Andrew A. Michta

Democratic institutions established in Poland after 1989 have evolved within the framework of a hybrid presidential-parliamentary system of government, reflecting the formative stages of the country's postcommunist transition. The current system has its origins in the events of 1991 and 1992, when the country's political elite were often deadlocked over the question of constitutional reform; specifically, over the extent and the precise definition of presidential, parliamentary, and governmental authority.

From 1990 until mid-1992, the democratically elected president and Parliament had worked within the confines of the largely irrelevant 1952 communist constitution. Political paralysis in 1991 and 1992 was compounded by the progressive fragmentation of the Solidarity movement and the attendant weakness of the nascent political parties, as well as the growing disenchantment and apathy of the electorate. The absence of constitutional reform, and confusion about the division of powers between executive and legislative branches of government, interfered with the country's ability to govern itself. The "war at the top" between President Lech Wałęsa and the Sejm (lower house of Parliament) over the ultimate shape of Polish democracy was brought into focus during the debate over the wording of the so-called Small Constitution (*Mała Konstytucja*), which in August 1992 replaced the 1952 basic law.

By mid-1992 a form of presidential parliamentarism began to take shape as a compromise solution for Polish democracy. This hybrid system has evolved first under the influence of the Solidarity-era political elite and, after 1993, under the rising influence of the postcommunist parties.

The first phase included the 1990 presidential election, the 1991 parliamentary election, the so-called war at the top between president and parliament, and adoption by the Sejm of the Small Constitution outlining Poland's presidential-parliamentary system of government.

The second phase began with a shift of the Polish political landscape after the 1993 parliamentary election, which removed the Solidarity-era elite from power and ushered in a coalition of the postcommunist Alliance of the Democratic Left (*Sojusz Lewicy Demokratycznej,* or SLD) and the Polish Peasant Party (*Polskie Stronnictwo Ludowe,* or PSL), a new majority in Parliament. After 1993, a struggle over the balance of power between president and Parliament became central to the debate over the future Large Constitution. The office of the president focused the energies of the post-Solidarity center-right and right-wing political parties. The postcommunists, in cooperation with the Polish Peasant Party, pushed to transform Poland's political system into a German-style parliamentary democracy, whereby the presidency would be limited to representative functions.

In late 1995 the issue of how political power in Poland will be divided became temporarily moot by the presidential election in which the former chairman of the Solidarity trade union, Lech Wałęsa, was defeated by the leader of the postcommunist SLD, Aleksander Kwaśniewski. The parliamentary formula for Polish democracy, proposed by the ruling coalition, dominated the constitutional debate. Still, until mid-1997, the question of a systemic framework best suited for Poland remained unsettled. Although both the presidency and the government were in the hands of the postcommunists, the draft of the new Large Constitution awaited a negotiated compromise among the ruling SLD/PSL coalition, the opposition, and the Catholic Church. There was still no agreement on the wording of the preamble, while the approaching parliamentary election called the date of a national referendum on the new constitution into question. Therefore, it was a dramatic breakthrough when, on 2 April 1997, after years of contentious debate, the National Assembly finally passed the amended Large Constitution and set 25 May as the date for a national referendum. Approved by the referendum, the 1997 constitution marks the beginning of the third phase of systemic transformation in postcommunist Poland.

The Roots of the System

In December 1990, the Polish people elected Lech Wałęsa their first democratic president in a run-off against Stanisław Tymiński, an emigré businessman. Wałęsa received close to 75 percent of the vote, which constituted a powerful popular mandate. During the presidential campaign, Wałęsa ran against the "contract parliament" elected under the 1989 Roundtable agreement in which the communists and their fellow travelers had retained a majority. The challenge to Wałęsa by Tymiński, who had attracted more votes than Prime Minister Tadeusz Mazowiecki (the third presidential candidate), served as a warning about the degree of popular discontent in the country. It also demonstrated that the Polish electorate remained quite susceptible to manipulation through populist appeals.

At the time, there was considerable concern among the opposition to Wałęsa, centered on Mazowiecki's Democratic Union (*Unia Demokratyczna,* or UD), that the new president might attempt to exploit his popular mandate to dominate the country's political scene by forming a "presidential party" built around the Center Alliance (*Porozumienie Centrum,* or PC) which had strongly supported Wałęsa's candidacy. The opposition charged that Wałęsa was interested in setting up an "imperial presidency," with the objective of undercutting the Sejm's oversight powers vis-à-vis the executive.[1] These concerns decreased somewhat after Wałęsa's inauguration, when he both reaffirmed his commitment to the market economic program of the Mazowiecki government and distanced himself from leaders of the Center Alliance, although they remained important throughout Wałęsa's five years in office.

Wałęsa asked Jan Olszewski, a lawyer close to Solidarity, to become prime minister. Two weeks later, Olszewski withdrew his candidacy, alleging "significant differences of opinion between the president-elect and himself on the composition of the government."[2] Olszewski had become opposed to the continued presence in the cabinet of Leszek Balcerowicz, a former finance minister and the author of the economic reform program endorsed by the International Monetary Fund (IMF). Wałęsa's next choice was Jan Krzysztof Bielecki, a young businessman strongly committed to continuing the program of currency stabilization and market liberalization. This signaled the president's willingness to continue the Balcerowicz economic reform program, notwithstanding his past criticism of the Mazowiecki government's performance regarding the economy. Still, the protracted negotiation that preceded Bielecki's appointment was a harbinger of an increasingly confrontational relationship between president and Parliament. The question of powers and responsibilities of the Sejm, the prime minister, and the president did come to the fore of Polish domestic politics already in December 1990.

A new parliamentary election to give the Sejm a popular mandate was imperative, but the choice of the election date became another contentious issue between president and Parliament. The election date was set for 9 March. Nevertheless, the Sejm voted 314–18, with 40 abstentions, to continue working through the summer and to hold the election, not in May as Wałęsa had requested, but in October.[3]

Setting the Pattern: "War at the Top"

The parliamentary election of October 1991 was conducted according to a proportional representation formula. This, in combination with the weakness of the nascent political parties, resulted in a fragmented Parliament. No party received more than 13 percent of the vote for Sejm deputies. The fact that almost two thirds of the Polish electorate did not vote raised a disturbing question about the strength of popular support for any government put together by the new Parliament. The two biggest winners were the Democratic Union and the Democratic Left Alliance, which represented clearly different constituencies. The scope of parliamentary fragmentation was best symbolized by the fact that 11 of the 29 political parties represented won only one seat each. Furthermore, the splintering of Parliament reflected a growing ideological division and polarization of the Polish electorate, making the passage of an entirely new constitution (including a bill of rights) a truly formidable task.[4]

The period between October 1991 and July 1992 was characterized by intense confrontation between Wałęsa and the prime minister, supported by the Sejm, over competing claims to executive and legislative authority. Results included constitutional paralysis, a slowing down of the economic reform program, and a growing perception abroad that Poland was becoming politically unstable to a degree that endangered its prospects for continued foreign investment. Described by the media as the "war at the top," constitutional paralysis was evidenced by the collapse of two consecutive governments, led by Olszewski and Waldemar Pawlak. The deadlock appeared to have been finally broken by the majority coalition government under Prime Minister Hanna Suchocka. This was followed on 1 August 1992 by adoption in the Sejm of the Small Constitution, which superseded the 1952 basic law. In the process, an outline of a compromise on the formula for Polish democracy combining elements of presidential and parliamentary systems began to emerge.

The process of selecting the new cabinet after the 1991 parliamentary election became symbolic of the conflict between president and Sejm over their respective prerogatives. The initial decision by Wałęsa to give the Democratic Union the option of naming three candidates for premier (because that party had won the most seats in Parliament), and his selection on 8 November of Bronisław Geremek from the Democratic Union as his candidate to form the new cabinet, were opposed by the center-right parties. The Center Alliance put forward the candidacy of Jan Olszewski. Wałęsa's refusal to accept this proposal set the stage for a stalemate between president and prime minister that would plague Polish politics for months to come.

The impasse over the selection of a new government continued through 25 November 1991, when the resignation of Jan Krzysztof Bielecki (despite Wałęsa's request that he remain) forced the issue. With the Bielecki government now acting as caretaker, and Wałęsa's call for constitutional reform to break the impasse and strengthen the executive unheeded, the center-right coalition mustered sufficient support in Parliament for the appointment of Olszewski. On 5 December, Wałęsa yielded and formally nominated the man as prime minister, in order to "respect the principles of democracy." Even while doing so, he described the new government as inappropriate to the country's needs. Wałęsa's concerns centered on Olszewski's criticism of Poland's economic austerity program, as well as his promise of a "breakthrough" in economic policy—presumably through repudiation of the Balcerowicz plan.

The Olszewski government was confirmed the following day, with 250 votes in favor, 47 against, and 107 abstentions. The cabinet was originally based on a coalition of the five center-right political parties: Confederation for an Independent Poland (KPN), Center Alliance (PC), Liberal Democratic Congress (KLD), Peasant Alliance (SLCh), and Christian National Union (ZChN). However, this coalition proved tenuous from the start, with the Liberal Democratic Congress walking out a week after the government's confirmation on the grounds that the five could not agree on a coherent economic program and on the budget.[5] Also, Confederacy for an Independent Poland—one of the original sponsors of Olszewski—found itself excluded from the government when its composition was presented to the president.

Wałęsa's continued disapproval of the new cabinet led to Olszewski's resignation on 17 December and charges that the president was trying to prevent his government from taking office. Further negotiations, including Olszewski's agreement to retain Krzysztof Skubiszewski as foreign minister (Skubiszewski accepted the offer after consulting with Wałęsa) as well as several expressions of support for Olszewski by the chairman of the Polish Peasant Party (PSL), Waldemar Pawlak, brought about another effort to form a government. On 21 December, almost two months after the parliamentary election, Olszewski finally presented his cabinet and its program to the Sejm. In his speech, Olszewski attacked Bielecki's economic policies as based on a flawed theory of "building a healthy economy on the ruins of state industry." The government was finally approved two days later, by a margin of 235 votes in favor and 60 votes against, with 139 abstentions.

In sharp contrast to Bielecki's tenure as prime minister, from the start Wałęsa and Olszewski failed to develop a working formula for collaboration. Considering that the 1952 constitution did not provide any guidance for the process, nor did it reflect the new political reality in the country, a working relationship between president and prime minister was the sine qua non for effective government. As personal animosity between Olszewski and Wałęsa grew, the lack of a precise constitutional division of power proved debilitating.

Political deadlock at the top was further compounded by the fact that the Olszewski cabinet consisted in large part of relatively unknown nonparty experts; only eight representatives of Olszewski's original center-right coalition remained, as well as four previous members of the Bielecki government. The eclectic composition of the cabinet often led to erratic policies, especially on the question of economic reform. For instance, shortly after taking office, Olszewski reversed himself on his earlier pledge to bring about a "breakthrough" in economic policy, refused to increase government spending, and moved instead toward a dramatic reorganization of the ministerial bureaucracy. The theme that would set Olszewski's administration apart from his predecessors was his call for the "settling of accounts" with the past and for the "beginning of the end of communism in Poland." The government's policy-making process became, to a large extent, dominated by personnel decisions.

Olszewski's move to "decommunize" the country's politics increased the division between former Solidarity activists and politicians tainted by their past association with the communists. Olszewski's strong and unequivocal opposition to the continued participation of ex-communists in the country's administration and in the military forced the Polish population to confront its most recent past to a much greater degree than had been the case during the Mazowiecki and Bielecki governments. Olszewski's criticism of Mazowiecki's decision to defer the issue became especially effective once the Russian and Polish press published accounts detailing the financial assistance channeled after 1989 by Moscow to the communists in Warsaw.[6] Other reports on the past collaboration of various politicians, as well as the release of police files kept by the communists on the opposition (including allegations that Wałęsa himself had been an informer for the secret police), polarized the parties and made it increasingly difficult for Olszewski to retain a base of support in the Sejm.

In February, the prime minister presented his government's 1992 economic program, which called for providing financial help to state enterprises, increasing the money supply, boosting investment, reducing taxes and interest rates, and guaranteeing prices for agricultural products. The program was widely criticized by the opposition in Parliament as inflationary. (Finance Minister Karol Lutkowski resigned his post in protest, warning that the proposed policies would wreck the economy). The plan also seemed to confirm Wałęsa's original fears that Olszewski would abandon the economic austerity program of the Mazowiecki and Bielecki governments. The prime minister's request for special powers to allow him to govern by decree, while he attempted to stabilize the economy (a sentiment echoed by his new finance minister, Andrzej Olechowski), reopened once more the constitutional issue of the division of power between legislative and executive authority, which brought forth the urgent need for constitutional reform.

Olszewski's position was considerably weakened when the Sejm rejected his economic program in a vote on 5 March. It became apparent that the base of support for his coalition had eroded beyond repair and that if his government were to retain even a modicum of effectiveness, the only solution for the prime minister was to seek a new coalition arrangement. Olszewski's efforts to broaden his coalition would continue through the end of April, by which time even he would recognize that the government had failed.

Out of Balance:
The President vs. the Prime Minister

Attempts at cooperation between Wałęsa and Olszewski remained tenuous at best. The relationship was not helped by the president's occasional hints that he stood ready to take over the premiership if necessary. Wałęsa also openly expressed preference for the French constitutional model, whereby the president has substantial executive powers as well as the right to appoint and dismiss the cabinet. In effect, Poland's political scene was increasingly dominated by the assertive president.

Early signs of an impending all-out confrontation between the two men came in January 1992, regarding the question of supervision over the armed forces. The new civilian defense minister, Jan Parys, forced the issue by pensioning off his predecessor (Rear Admiral Piotr Kołodziejczyk). Reportedly, this forced retirement of an officer whom Wałęsa had proposed at a June session of the National Security Council for the position of armed forces' inspector general (the highest position envisioned in the military reform program being considered at the time) was seen by the president as a personal attack against his authority as commander-in-chief. The conflict escalated on 27 February, when Olszewski appointed a 29-year-old journalist, Radosław Sikorski, as deputy defense minister, without seeking Wałęsa's advice. At issue was the question of whether the president or the government had ultimate authority to control the armed forces, including key personnel decisions. The confrontation quickly escalated to symbolize the extent of presidential prerogative vs. the powers of government.

The dispute occurred against the background of Olszewski's concerted effort to purge the senior military establishment of officers who he believed had been compromised by their past close collaboration with the communist regime, in line with his overall objective to "decommunize Polish politics."[7] The purge was announced by Deputy Defense Minister Romuald Szermietiew in a speech at Szczecin to the officers of the Pomeranian Military District. In another move expressive of the government's determination to assert its authority over military matters, Defense Minister Parys rejected the plan presented on 7 February, with Wałęsa's approval, to the National Security Council meeting. It proposed to cut the army by an additional 50,000 soldiers.

The confrontation between president and prime minister reached its denouement when Defense Minister Parys charged in a speech to the General Staff that the army was being used by "some politicians" to bring down democracy in Poland, insinuating that Wałęsa was ready to use extralegal means to dominate Parliament. Two days later, in a newspaper interview, Parys implied that Chief of Staff Mieczysław Wachowski was one of the key conspirators and that Wachowski acted on Wałęsa's orders.[8] Parys alleged that high-ranking army officers had been approached by the president's advisers with a promise of promotions, if they threw their support behind Wałęsa. Wałęsa denied the allegations and countercharged that as commander-in-chief of the armed forces, it was natural for him to have frequent contact with the military. Parys was also attacked in Parliament, where leaders of the opposition parties blamed the government for spreading misinformation about the military being involved in politics. Mazowiecki's Democratic Union was particularly vocal in its criticism of Parys. Amid the gathering political storm, Olszewski was compelled to set up a special commission to investigate the reasons for his minister's comments. The uproar caused by the "Parys affair" in Parliament and the media forced Olszewski to place his defense minister on leave of absence.

At the same time, Olszewski raised the stakes in the confrontation by remarking to the press that the Parys affair reflected "a struggle among president, government, and parliament for leadership of the Polish army." Subsequent newspaper reports, alleging that the National Security Bureau was working in secret on martial law plans, further fueled the crisis. A report in the newspaper *Nowy Świat* on 9 April implied that such plans were being drafted without proper notification of the government or Parliament. These allegations prompted an official denial by Jerzy Milewski, director of the National Security Bureau.

None of the previous confrontations between Wałęsa and Olszewski had cost the latter politically as much as did the Parys affair. Determined to remove Olszewski, Wałęsa addressed Parliament on 8 May, calling for the creation of a strong presidency based on the French system as a necessary step to overcome the paralysis of government. Reportedly, the day after Wałęsa's speech, Olszewski met with Sejm speaker Wiesław Chrzanowski to discuss the government's resignation. Nine days later, Defense Minister Parys officially resigned, after the parliamentary commission appointed to investigate his charges of conspiracy in the army had declared them to be unfounded and recommended his dismissal.

The remnants of Olszewski's power base in the Sejm began to crumble. Increasingly, leaders of various political parties, ranging from the opposition Democratic Union to Wałęsa's own Center Alliance, called for the government to resign. On 26 May, Wałęsa submitted a letter to the speaker of the Sejm in which he formally withdrew his support for Olszewski and asked parliament to replace him. Three days later, 65 deputies from the so-called little coalition of the Democratic Union, the Liberal Democratic Congress, and the Polish Economic Program (*Polski Program Gospodarczy*, or PPG) submitted a motion calling for a vote of no confidence in the government. The last act of the drama was the release of police files that implicated a number of prominent politicians as former communist collaborators, possibly in an attempt to raise questions about Wałęsa's own fitness to remain in office, but to no avail. By bringing down the Olszewski government the president achieved a political victory, while also establishing an important precedent for the future.

Truce: The "Coalition of Seven"

After less than six months in office, the Olszewski government was dismissed on 5 June, when Parliament also accepted Wałęsa's nomination of Waldemar Pawlak from the Polish Peasant Party (PSL) as prime minister. Pawlak pledged to end the strife between premier and president that had bedeviled the previous administration. However, his efforts to build a broad coalition in cooperation with the Democratic Union (UD), the Liberal Democratic Congress (KLD), the Polish Economic Program (PPG), and the Confederation for an Independent Poland (KPN) failed, in part because the last party withdrew from the talks after citing irreconcilable differences over the budget. Wałęsa's attempts to assist the Pawlak coalition by turning to the Christian National Union (*Zjednoczenie*

Chrześcijańsko-Narodowe, or ZChN) also failed because the ZChN refused to participate in a government headed by the PSL chairman. Unable to form a working coalition government, Pawlak resigned on 2 July, after a month of fruitless efforts. Wałęsa's remaining alternative was either to turn to Mazowiecki's Democratic Union or to push for dissolution of the Sejm and a new parliamentary election.

Increasingly confident, in a speech on 3 July, Wałęsa warned that he might resort to extraordinary measures (possibly dissolving Parliament), unless a working coalition government was presented to him within the next few days. The tripartite "little coalition" (UD, KLD, PPG) and five Christian democratic and peasant parties responded two days later by presenting the candidacy of Hanna Suchocka, a lawyer and a Democratic Union deputy to the Sejm from Poznań, as prime minister-designate to form a new government.

The eight parties in this majority coalition represented the entire spectrum of the Solidarity movement. The agreement gave eleven portfolios, including foreign affairs, privatization, finance, and defense to the little coalition, which jointly held 112 Sejm seats. The remaining "group of five" parties, with 115 Sejm seats in total, received 15 portfolios, including two deputy premierships. The Center Alliance, one of the original five, walked out at the last moment in protest, thus reducing Suchocka's majority coalition to seven parties.

The new prime minister proved extraordinarily adept in forging consensus on the question of cabinet appointments and rapidly completed her cabinet list. Within one day, she announced that the ministers-designate had vowed to leave ideological battles to the Sejm. In an interview with the newspaper *Gazeta Wyborcza,* Suchocka pledged to seek a middle ground in her dealings with Wałęsa.

The new cabinet included members of the previous Solidarity governments, such as Jan Krzysztof Bielecki (EC integration), Jacek Kuroń (labor), Janusz Lewandowski (privatization), Jerzy Osiatyński (finance), Janusz Onyszkiewicz (defense), Krzysztof Skubiszewski (foreign affairs), and Gabriel Jankowski (agriculture). The liberal "little coalition" won the key economic and political posts it had demanded, while justice, education, and culture were awarded to the right-wing Christian National Union. In addition to these veteran ministerial appointments, Suchocka brought in deputy ministers with experience from the Mazowiecki and Bielecki governments. Her choice of advisers on the economy reflected a commitment to reaffirm the austerity market economic program, as symbolized by the appointment of Karol Lutkowski, an adviser to Leszek Balcerowicz in the Mazowiecki government and briefly finance minister in Olszewski's cabinet until his resignation in protest over Olszewski's economic program.[9]

Before endorsing Suchocka's cabinet, Wałęsa demanded a written statement from all coalition parties accepting the new prime minister and her nominations. The new government could count on 236 from the total of 460 Sejm votes. With Suchocka's confirmation, Poland acquired a majority government based on a democratically elected parliament. Still, the appointment of the Suchocka government would prove a temporary solution to the systemic problems of Poland's nascent democracy. The perpetual political strife in the fragmented parliament as well as President Wałęsa's continued assertiveness did not bode well for the new government's longevity. When the so-called Small Constitution was finally passed in August 1992, it reflected the experience of the power struggle between Parliament and president that had formed Polish politics of the early postcommunist era. Through his persistence and political skill, in a series of confrontations with parliament, Wałęsa secured for the presidency an important role in Polish politics.

Dilemmas of the Interim Basic Law

Paralysis of government during the last two months of 1991 and half of 1992 brought home the urgent need for a new constitution. Work on the Small Constitution had begun under Mazowiecki's leadership and continued as the war at the top between Wałęsa and Olszewski dragged on. Change of government and the growing realization in Parliament that a democratic constitutional framework remained absolutely essential for Poland's future helped to craft a document acceptable to a majority in the Sejm. The formula that was finally adopted on 1 August 1992, by the required two-thirds majority of votes, reflected the experience of early postcommunist transition, especially Wałęsa's activist presidency.[10]

Since adoption of the Small Constitution in 1992, the political framework in Poland had been delineated by the compromise reached in the early years of postcommunist transition. Reflecting realities of Polish politics at the time, the hybrid presidential-parliamentary system created enough ambiguity concerning the relative powers of president and parliament to allow their precedent-setting decisions to remain within purview of the law. At the core of the power struggle was the presidential prerogative to control the so-called presidential ministries, i.e., defense, foreign affairs, and interior (Articles 33 and 35), and to have a decisive voice on matters of national security and foreign policy. As head of state and commander-in-chief of the armed forces (Articles 29 and 36), upon consultation with the minister of defense, the president appoints the army's chief of the general staff, chiefs of the other services, commanders of military districts, as well as commander of the armed forces. (In previous practice, the minister of defense nominated the chief of the general staff, while the president made the actual appointment). This particular prerogative of the presidency became a bone of contention in 1992 between Wałęsa and Prime Minister Olszewski during the Parys affair; in effect, reaffirmation of presidential control over foreign policy and national security was an explicit victory for Wałęsa.

The Small Constitution institutionalized the emerging presidential-parliamentary system of government. In broad strokes, it reaffirmed the division of power between the legislative and executive branches of government while recognizing the special role of the presidency, apparent after the 1991 parliamentary election.[11] In effect, it was an attempt at a mediated compromise between Lech Wałęsa's desire to build a system centered on the presidency and the Sejm's insistence on primacy of the legislature.

In the course of the constitutional debate, the Sejm also moved to improve its legislative procedures. New parliamentary rules of order limited the number of parliamentary caucuses by setting a minimum requirement of 15 rather than only three deputies required to form one. This change reduced the number of parties in the Sejm that could decide on procedural questions from 18 to ten. In addition, the quorum needed for committee meetings was brought down from 50 to 33 percent. Absent committee members would be fined for unexcused absences, and their names would be publicized. The new rules also forbade last-minute changes to the agenda and imposed tighter limits on speeches, with the goal of accelerating parliamentary debate.[12]

The fight over the division of power in postcommunist Poland was summed up by Lech Falandysz, a lawyer and adviser to Wałęsa, who expressed the president's doubts whether "Sejm-ocracy" was indeed the best option for Poland. In an interview, Falandysz argued that, in practice, the new constitution retained the supremacy of Parliament. As proof of the continued limitation on presidential authority, he pointed to the new requirement for a countersignature by the premier or a minister on some presidential decisions.[13] Wałęsa's continued insistence that the government should be responsible directly to the president (with the Sejm retaining ultimate power through a no-confidence vote) was a clear sign of the kind of systemic change Wałęsa hoped would be introduced by a future "Large Constitution."

At the other end of the spectrum, staunch proponents for supremacy of Parliament over the president and the government argued that the Small Constitution preserved the lion's share of presidential powers. Jarosław Kaczyński, leader of the Center Alliance, which voted against the new basic law, warned that the agreement would eventually lead to a dictatorial presidency or (if government and president found themselves at odds) to a perpetual deadlock within the executive. However, not all political parties represented in the 1991 Parliament shared Kaczyński's view. Some critics of the law, including Leszek Moczulski of the Confederation for an Independent Poland, sided with Wałęsa and opposed the new constitution on the grounds that it allegedly imposed excessive limits on the powers of the president.[14]

On balance, the compromise over the Small Constitution was an expression of the willingness on the part of the Democratic Union, one of the key parties in Parliament and the principal supporter of the Suchocka majority government, to accommodate some of Wałęsa's demands for greater presidential powers. The draft of the basic law had been prepared by the Democratic Union. According to Bronisław Geremek, leader of the Democratic Union parliamentary caucus, the goal of the compromise was to overcome the governmental deadlock and to define clearly the powers and prerogatives of the three branches of government. Geremek expressed the emerging consensus in Parliament that, while being far from perfect, the Small Constitution was "better than the pre-existing situation."[15] However, by blurring the executive prerogatives of the president and the prime minister, the Small Constitution sanctioned divided loyalties within the prime minister's cabinet and encouraged micromanagement of the executive by the president.

Deepening Antagonism:
Wałęsa vs. Resurgent Postcommunists

The Suchocka government outlasted the constitutional compromise by less than a year. Her government collapsed in the spring of 1993, after a no confidence move against her cabinet passed in Parliament by a few votes. After Suchocka's resignation, Wałęsa chose to call a new election rather than appointing another cabinet. Paradoxically, it appeared at the time that all the parties welcomed the prospect of an early election. The parties with their roots in Solidarity, especially the Democratic Union, regarded the dissolution of Parliament as a temporary setback and expected the new election to further strengthen their position in Parliament.[16] They counted on the provisions of a new electoral law passed in June 1993, which set popular vote thresholds for parties and candidates. In order to win seats in Parliament, parties had to clear 5 percent of the popular vote, and coalitions had to win 8 percent.[17] The law set aside 69 seats of the 460 in the Sejm for parties that received at least 7 percent of the popular vote, to be awarded to key party members on the "national lists."

The Democratic Union and other center-right and right-wing parties had hoped to increase their representation in Parliament under the new system, which would allow them to establish a stronger government and give them a sufficient majority in Parliament to pass a new constitution. Postcommunists from the SLD also welcomed the opportunity of a new election because, based on the 1993 preelection polling data, they had hoped to gain additional seats in Parliament. As for the president, in calling a new election, Wałęsa had apparently expected that the new legislature would be more willing to accept his constitutional priorities.

The election showed that initial expectations of the parties with roots in the Solidarity movement had been woefully unrealistic. The 1993 parliamentary vote brought about a dramatic shift in political power away from Solidarity-based parties to the postcommunists. The largest winners in the election were the Alliance of the Democratic Left and the Polish Peasant Party, which jointly received 36 percent of the popular vote. Benefiting from new electoral law provisions, the SLD/PSL jointly obtained 66 percent of the seats in the lower house of Parliament, while together also winning 76 percent of the seats in the Senate. In effect, the postcommunist SLD/PSL coalition had a majority in both houses.

The immediate consequence of the 1993 electoral victory by the postcommunist left was the deepening of antagonism between Parliament and president. The election also marked the end of the post-1989 ascendancy of the Solidarity generation in Polish politics. The SLD/PSL coalition controlled Parliament and government, further confirming Lech Wałęsa's suspicions of the legislature's intentions and pushing him to seek an alternative power base for the remainder of his term. In the post-1993 election period, Wałęsa would confront a Parliament in which the postcommunists had sufficient margins to pass a new constitution. Between 1993 and 1995, the confrontation between Wałęsa and the ruling coalition became the centerpiece of Polish politics and brought to the fore contradictions inherent in the presidential-parliamentary system.

The most serious confrontation concerned civilian control over the military. Wałęsa used his constitutional authority to appoint the General Staff chief and make the senior military his base of political support. The key to this policy was his selection in 1992 of General Tadeusz Wilecki as the new chief of the General Staff. After the dismissal of Parys, Wałęsa approved the reappointment as defense minister of Admiral Piotr Kołodziejczyk, who had served in the same position at the initial stage of Poland's post-communist transition. Constitutional provisions that allow the president the final say on appointments to the so-called power ministries (Articles 29 and 36 of the Small Constitution) made it possible for Wałęsa to turn to the senior military in his struggle against the ruling "red" coalition. The military backed Wałęsa, because it wanted to establish autonomy vis-à-vis civilian structures in the defense ministry. Between the 1992 appointment of Wilecki and the 1994 so-called Drawsko Affair, the military strengthened its position by relying on Wałęsa's direct support. Conversely, the president counted on the army to provide him with a consolidated bloc of votes both in the 1993 parliamentary election through his Nonparty Bloc for Reform (*Bezpartyjny Blok Wspierania Reform,* or BBWR) and during the 1995 presidential election campaign.

The high point of the controversy over presidential prerogative vis-à-vis the armed forces came in the fall of 1994. In September the president attended a dinner at the Drawsko proving grounds with the defense minister and senior military officers, including the chief of the General Staff. Reportedly, in the course of that dinner and in the presence of the president, the officers took a vote of no confidence in Defense Minister Kołodziejczyk.[18] When the story leaked to the media, the Sejm investigated the affair and this time sided with the defense minister, recommending disciplinary action against the officers. Instead, Wałęsa arranged for Kołodziejczyk's dismissal and shielded the officers associated with the Drawsko affair from retribution. Wałęsa also rejected the list of officers recommended by Kołodziejczyk for promotion to the rank of general.

In January 1995, Wałęsa made an all-out attempt to bring the army directly under his control. During an address to the Sejm on 19 January 1995, Wałęsa submitted a draft law that would make the General Staff directly subordinate to the president, i.e., bypassing the defense ministry and parliament altogether.[19] Next, in February, Wałęsa forced the resignation of Prime Minister Waldemar Pawlak, implying that he would not hesitate to dissolve Parliament and call a new election. This confrontation brought Poland to the verge of a constitutional crisis and exposed the weaknesses inherent in the imprecise division of power between president and government. It marked the high point of Wałęsa's bid to shift the balance of power in the direction of the presidency.

Although the governing SLD/PSL coalition backed down from an all-out confrontation during the February crisis, Wałęsa's strong-arm tactics proved costly in the long run. At the height of the crisis, Warsaw was rife with rumors about General Wilecki's impending appointment as Wałęsa's choice for prime minister. The authoritative *Gazeta Wyborcza* even ran a front-page story alleging that the appointment of General Wilecki as prime minister was imminent. A stormy meeting with the parliamentary leadership, which was televised nationally, further weakened Wałęsa's already shaky support base. Wałęsa's assurances that he would not dissolve Parliament, because he was a "Nobel peace laureate," rang hollow. It further alienated from Wałęsa his former colleagues from the anticommunist Solidarity opposition.

The final scandal leading to the presidential election of 1995 came in an August revelation that signatures supporting Wałęsa's candidacy for president had been collected among soldiers of the special Vistula units (*Nadwiślańskie Jednostki Wojskowe*, or NJW) of the Internal Affairs Ministry. An investigation of the matter confirmed that signatures supporting Wałęsa had been gathered in six of the eight units "with the knowledge and approval" and, in some cases, even direct participation of commanding officers. Reportedly, the NJW commander destroyed the petitions after *Gazeta Wyborcza* had run the story. The officer was subsequently dismissed amid allegations that Wałęsa's assistant, Mieczysław Wachowski, had been the principal organizer of the petition drive in the NJW.[20]

Throughout this confrontation, the SLD (and increasingly the opposition as well) insisted that a new constitutional solution limiting the presidency's power and transforming it into a largely ceremonial office was necessary to end the chaos. However, as the chances of Aleksander Kwaśniewski to be elected president increased in late 1995, the postcommunists themselves began to show ambivalence on the subject. In the first election round on 5 November, Kwaśniewski received 35.1 percent of the vote and Wałęsa 33.1 percent, with a voter turnout of 64.8 percent. In the runoff on 19 November, between Wałęsa and Kwaśniewski, the latter won with 51.7 percent of the vote to Wałęsa's 48.3 percent, with a voter turnout of 68.2 percent.[21] The postcommunists were now a dominant force in Polish politics. However, the postcommunist triumph proved incomplete when Premier Józef Oleksy was forced to resign amid allegations that he had spied for Russia.

A New Compromise: The "Large Constitution"

The election of Aleksander Kwaśniewski placed both government and presidency in the hands of postcommunists, thereby making the question of the practical consequences of presidential-parliamentarism temporarily moot. Nevertheless, the institutional framework of the Small Constitution remained, and with it the potential that the process of government could be deadlocked once again. The most significant feature of Polish presidential-parliamentarism (which Wałęsa had used repeatedly in his struggle against Parliament) was the president's control over the ministries of defense, internal affairs, and foreign affairs.

It appears that, on balance, the presidential-parliamentary system of government was a realistic reflection of the distribution of political power in Poland during early phases of the postcommunist transition. The Small

Constitution clearly represented a compromise, but arguably the best one that the existing political conditions in Poland at the time could have produced. However, the evolving political situation in the country, especially the consolidation of Poland's democratic institutions and the maturation of the party system, demanded a revised basic law that would settle the question of presidential vs. parliamentary prerogatives.

On 19 June 1996, the special constitutional commission of Parliament submitted a draft of 221 articles for a new basic law to a subcommittee for final editing before presenting it to the National Assembly. The Large Constitution, work on which had been initiated already in 1992, was still an incomplete document. It lacked the preamble, which had remained a principal bone of contention between the center-left parties and the Catholic Church. Other objections to the new constitution had been raised by the Solidarity labor movement, which demanded that guarantees of employment be written into the basic law. In 1996 the proposed draft came under attack from various, often diametrically opposed political forces. In a vivid testimony to the difficulty of forging a compromise, the Union of Labor (*Unia Pracy,* or UP) even proposed that a partial referendum on the constitution should be held to gauge public opinion on whether the preamble to the constitution should invoke God's name.

The draft of the Large Constitution was defended by the SLD. The opposition parties in parliament, led by the Freedom Union (*Unia Wolności,* or UW),[22] criticized it, while the PSL had been ambivalent in its support of the draft because of the proposed new formula for local administration. The Union of Labor criticized it for not being sufficiently far-reaching in guaranteeing social rights to the citizenry. The Catholic Church criticized it for being anti-Christian. The labor movement, reflecting Solidarity's opposition to the SLD/PSL coalition government, attacked the draft as a product of the "reds." The controversy seemed to suggest that the June version of the Large Constitution would have to be further amended before it could pass in a national referendum.

In a dramatic breakthrough, the Large Constitution was cleared for passage by the National Assembly on 22 March 1997, with a majority of the amendments finally approved on 2 April.[23] The amended version of the new basic law contains 243 articles, which constitute a negotiated compromise on the future of Poland's political institutions. Having been approved by the referendum on 25 May 1997, the Large Constitution will bring about a change in the balance of power between president and parliament. The new basic law retains the Sejm and the Senate as Poland's bicameral parliament. Most important, it takes away from the president the so-called presidential ministries. In a resolution to the long-running political feud concerning civilian control over the military, the defense minister becomes the direct superior of the military (Article 134). The president also loses the power to veto the annual budget. The Large Constitution introduces the universal right to sue for breaches of the constitution, and it gives explicit finality to the rulings of the Constitutional Tribunal (Article 79).

Church-state relations have remained the most divisive issues of Polish politics today. The new constitution places relations between the state and the Roman Catholic Church on the basis of "mutual autonomy and independence" (Article 25). It specifies that "every person has the right to the protection of his/her life" (Article 38), while it also gives parents the right to "raise their children in accordance with their beliefs" (Article 53). The Catholic Church considered these statements insufficient and called for a more explicit inclusion of religion in the new basic law.

Between 1992–1997 the presidential-parliamentary system codified by the Small Constitution served, however imperfectly, to provide the framework for Poland's democratic institutions. The legacy of the 1992 political compromise between Lech Wałęsa and the Parliament proved more enduring than the framers of the Small Constitution had expected at the time. In 1997 the successful passage of the Large Constitution was influenced by the approaching parliamentary elections and the politicians' desire to have the constitutional issue settled before the campaign began in earnest. Nevertheless, it demonstrated that in the end the postcommunists, the peasants, the center and right opposition, and the Catholic Church could reach a compromise acceptable to all. By sending the new constitution to the electorate, the National Assembly took an important step in the country's postcommunist transition. Since the May 1997 national referendum approved the new basic law, adoption of the Large Constitution set the stage for the next phase of democratic consolidation in Poland.

Notes

1. Ewa Rosolak, "Sukces-to prezydent, porażki-to my," *Trybuna,* 16 November 1991.
2. *RFE/RL Daily Report,* 19 December 1990.
3. Ibid., 5 and 11 March 1991.
4. According to Bronisław Geremek, floor leader for the Democratic Union, ideological polarization on issues such as abortion virtually precluded a majority vote on key civil rights guarantees (conversation with the author in Warsaw on 25 May 1992).
5. Małgorzata Subotić and Kazimierz Groblewski, "Liberałowie opuszczają 'piątkę,'" *Rzeczpospolita,* 12 December 1991.

6. Tomasz Rogulski, "Poparcie dla Jana Olszewskiego," *Rzeczpospolita,* 18 November 1991.

7. For an insight into the government's motivation, see the account of his tenure as deputy defense minister by Radek Sikorski, "My Hundred Days," *National Review,* 20 July 1992.

8. Zbigniew Lentowicz, "Czy wojsko będzie apolityczne," *Rzeczpospolita,* 7 April 1992; Zbigniew Lentowicz, "Parys chłodzi nastroje," *Rzeczpospolita,* 9 April 1992.

9. Kazimierz Groblewski, "Wiceministrowie odchodzą i wracają," *Rzeczpospolita,* 20 August 1992.

10. For the text of the Small Constitution, see "Mała Konstytucja: ile komu władzy," *Rzeczpospolita,* 7 August 1992.

11. Senator Andrzej Celiński, in an interview shortly after the election made a case for a strong presidency and a presidential parliamentary system. See Ewa Szemplinska, "W stronę silnej prezydentury," *Życie Warszawy,* 8 November 1991.

12. Louisa Vinton, "Poland's 'Little Constitution,'" *RFE/RL Research Report,* 1, no. 35 (4 September 1992): 25.

13. Eliza Olczyk, "Równowaga czy dominacja?" *Rzeczpospolita,* 4 August, 1992; Danuta Frey, "Prezydent nie może być dekoracją," *Rzeczpospolita,* 10 August 1992.

14. Ibid.

15. Eliza Olczyk, "Coś za coś, czyli sztuka kompromisu," *Rzeczpospolita,* 10 August 1992.

16. Jan Rokita, Suchocka's chief of staff, in a conversation with the author on the eve of the no-confidence vote in Parliament, 1993.

17. "Ustawa z dnia 28 maja 1993: Ordynacja wyborcza do Sejmu Rzeczpospolitej Polskiej," *Dziennik Ustaw Rzeczpospolitej Polskiej,* no. 45 (2 June 1993).

18. The author's interview with Admiral Piotr Kołodziejczyk, 28 March 1995, Gdynia, Poland.

19. "Czyje wojsko?" *Życie Warszawy,* 20 January 1995.

20. "Polish Officers Gathered Signatures Supporting President," *OMRI Daily Digest,* August 31 1995.

21. *OMRI Daily Digest,* November 21 1995.

22. The Freedom Union was created in 1994 after a merger between the Democratic Union and the Liberal Democratic Congress.

23. Janina Paradowska, "Zgromadzenie Narodowe uchwaliło konstytucję: Ekspresem do referendum," *Polityka,* 29 March 1997; and "Polish National Assembly Approves Constitution," *RFE/RL Newsline* 1, no. 3, pt. 2, 3 April 1997.

SIX

Local Government Reform

Joanna Regulska

R obert D. Putnam commenced his study on Italian democracy by posing a question: "Why do some democratic governments succeed and others fail?" Seven years after local self-government reform began to be implemented in Poland, many will argue that despite difficulties and shortcomings, local government reform remains one of the few unquestionable successes of the Polish transition. Although the initial scope of reform has suffered major setbacks and remains incomplete, local government has retained a certain degree of fiscal power, managed to build an impressive record of completed investments, and gained widespread support among citizens.

The successes of local government, however, have only marginally been recognized by policy makers and scholars and only recently have drawn greater attention from political parties. Indeed, what is absent from the majority of analyses on economic and political restructuring is a closer look at the transition process at the local level and at the impact that local institutions have on this process. This lack of acknowledgment that the emergence of local self-government and the formation of new local political spaces play a significant role in the transformation of the Polish state is surprising for at least two reasons. First, fundamental restructuring of the political and economic system cannot take place and ultimately claim success unless the existence of a local state, local institutions, and local power are recognized as legitimate forces that exercise influence over social, economic, and political practices. Second, the performance of the new decentralized local government has been evaluated by citizens very highly in comparison to other Polish public institutions, and this high regard reinforces the notion that any attempt to design the new state needs to include participation and dialogue with local society. Otherwise, these efforts are doomed to fail, because they will result in social alienation and possibly spark unrest.

The year 1989 brought for Poland as well as for the rest of Central and Eastern Europe major attempts to transform political, economic, and social spaces, policies, and practices. To be successful, such a deep transformation required new legislation and institutions but also elicited wide-ranging societal responses. Local government reform became one of the first initiatives undertaken by the newly reconstituted Senate. Already in July 1989, the first parliamentary hearings were conducted on the subject of local government reform, and a debate over the devolution of power opened.

This chapter examines the diverse forces that have carved political and economic as well as social spaces occupied by local governments within the overall governance framework. It argues that although local government has become weaker over the past several years, it nevertheless has gained permanency and solidified its position. Theoretically, national-level instabilities and tensions should have become translated into a local context and affected not only the behavior of local governments but also the perception that citizens hold about them. In reality, despite political instability at the national level and economic fragility, local self-government in Poland not only survived but actually increased in stability and gained steady support from citizens.

Why Decentralization?

The decentralization of power has been promised by all post-1989 Central and East European governments. Since the 1950s, when Stalinist legislation removed what remained from prewar democratic structures, replacing them with a vertical and centralized model of decision making, emerging democratic systems longed for local autonomy and decision-making freedom as well as efficiency and quality of in the delivery of services. A new body of literature from Western democracies argues that decentralization might not be so beneficial as expected and therefore that a certain degree of centralization and central control is essential, especially when service delivery is considered.[1] Nevertheless, East European politicians and governments saw decentralization as essential for dismantling the communist system.

Indeed, a variety of arguments have been presented in support of power devolution to local levels and the provision of autonomy for local decision making. Some officials saw reform of the public sector as essential for achieving efficiency in state management, improving the operational aspects of state administration (information flow, data processing, transparency in decision making), and increasing the effectiveness of public spending.[2] From an economic perspective, decentralization was seen as a means of addressing traditional fiscal issues, such as tax reform and transfer mechanisms, and the realignment of responsibilities among different levels of government. The common aim of these changes was more efficient use of public resources through better mobilization and distribution. Indeed, proponents have pointed out the comparative advantage of local governments' ability to provide and finance a variety of services that directly meet local priorities—priorities that otherwise might not gain this status when considered within the national economic agenda. What also needs to be underscored is that decentralization in the region operates under an expanded mandate as it focuses on issues that emerge as more specific, indeed essential, to countries in transition. Among these issues are privatization reforms, provision of a social safety net, stabilization programs and their subnational fiscal linkages. All have been repeatedly noted as of paramount importance for the success of the reforms.[3]

Within the political sphere, arguments of transparency, political accountability, citizens' participation in the decision-making process, and the consequent development of a political culture (which was absent under communist regimes) have been frequently cited to a much lesser degree. However, other arguments in favor of decentralization, such as political education, leadership, and overall political stability have been utilized in support of restructuring center-local relations. Indeed, along with the broadening of economic reforms and with the increase in political infighting, arguments in support of citizens' participation and a "rebirth of civil society" have slowly faded as priorities.[4] As will be discussed later in the chapter, this development stands in sharp contrast with the increasing support and acceptance that citizens expressed in favor of local government. Decentralization also opens participatory channels for groups and issues that otherwise are underrepresented. This has been the case with women's participation in politics. Not only have women been initially able to gain higher numerical representation in local elected offices (in 1990, 11 percent vs. 9.1 percent; in 1994, 13 percent at all levels), but what is more important, their presence in leadership positions is higher at the local level.[5]

Establishing Local Self-Government

The decentralization process and the establishment of local self-government took place within a cloudy political and economic environment. Politically, reforms in Poland were initiated through semidemocratic parliamentary elections in May 1989 and the subsequent restructuring of national-level institutions and of legislation. Debate over the new Polish constitution was opened in the fall of 1989, with a series of amendments that eliminated the Polish United Workers' Party, established a constitutional foundation for property rights, and passed various measures that removed the remaining pillars of the communist system. From the perspective of local government, new decentralized structures and power assigned to them were reflected in the constitutional amendments that provided for a certain degree of autonomy and, most important, eliminated most of the central tools of control.

Local government autonomy in its first phase was, therefore, the result of legislative modifications rather than of a constitutional drafting process. This development has significant implications for the permanency of change. Constitutions are the most stable legislative documents, most often requiring two-thirds of parliamentary votes, and as a result, they are the most difficult to change. This legislative route may present an advantage for some issues that are sensitive to evolving economies and, therefore, require flexibility. For others, such as the degree of autonomy and overall positioning of local government within the state, it may mean continued vulnerability. Indeed, as will be discussed, such was the case for local government.

Since 1989, Poland has held presidential elections twice, has held three rounds of parliamentary elections (in 1991, 1993, and 1997), and two sets of local elections (in 1990 and 1994). Furthermore, there have been eight prime ministers, some of whom served as long as 16 months (e.g., Pawlak, in office from October 1993 to February 1995, although Prime Minister Cimoszewicz surpassed this record because he successfully governed until the parliamentary elections of September 1997); others served only weeks (e.g., Prime Minister Pawlak in the summer of 1992). The frequent "wars at the top" and a fragmented political party landscape did not create much sense of stability. Election turnout, which represents only one (and definitely not a perfect) measure of citizens' confidence in the country's political system, shows a clear decline. The initial euphoria of the parliamentary elections of 63 percent voter turnout in 1989 declined to 43.2 percent in 1991, although it did increase to 52 percent in 1993. Local elections in 1994 attracted few voters—only 34 percent of the electorate. Similarly, citizens have shown major mistrust in political institutions, such as parties, trade unions, and parliaments, and their ability to represent the public interest. Indeed, at various points over the past seven years, Poland's leading role and its ability to maintain its chosen paths of reform were questioned.

Economic reforms aimed at stabilization, liberalization, and the establishment of market mechanisms. The initial emphasis in 1991–1992 on currency stabilization and the establishment of a legal and regulatory framework subsequently accentuated enterprise restructuring, recapitalization of banks, privatization, and business development, especially of small- and medium-sized firms. While the reforms were successful in some areas, they initially failed to deliver growth, rapidly increased unemployment, and presented the threat of hyperinflation. Depending on their perspective, critics pointed to the failure to move more rapidly, for example, with privatization; to the overemphasis on stabilization and too little progress toward growth; or to the failure to protect citizens from a decline in living standards.[6]

Local self-government was created[7] and began to operate under difficult conditions: The responsibilities, resources, and skills of local government officials were unclear, unpredictable, and weak. Responses were required, not only to the inhospitable external environment but also to local governments' internal difficulties. In this context, at least three impediments should be mentioned. First, the boundaries between the national and the local government were unclear. Although some scholars have argued that the two levels should be examined on a continuum rather than as separate entities, with boundaries that are often blurred,[8] the degree to which many functions were left with conflicting legislative and administrative regulations significantly weakened new local governments. Responsibilities for matters such as urban planning and organization, the local transportation system, water supply and sanitation, health services, and housing, as well as kindergarten and primary education, awaited the outcome of the political struggle between national and local levels. As a result, responsibilities were splintered and lines of accountability were ambiguous.[9] Over time, some of these functions, such as primary education, slowly became assigned to local levels, but the majority remained anchored to central institutions or to the regional level of public administration (*voivodship*). Attempts to complete local self-government reform, by introducing an intermediary level (*powiat*) and therefore reassigning power and responsibility vested in the state administration, failed on several occasions throughout 1992–1997. During 1995–1996, renewed interest in implementing the subnational tier of self-government on the part of the Alliance of the Democratic Left led to immense opposition by its coalition partner, the Polish Peasant Party, to the point of threats by the latter to withdraw from the coalition. In the end, although a large segment of policymakers agreed that decentralization reform would remain incomplete without a second tier, politicians with various fractions managed to effectively dismantle any hopes for establishment of subnational governments.

Second, questions of assigning of responsibility involved not only the issue of political location at the central or local level but, most important, fiscal control. From the beginning, "the Ministry of Finance took a lead role through its budgeting function."[10] Fiscal resources in the initial period were, on the one hand, almost unpredictable and, on the other, tightly controlled by the Ministry of Finance. Almost from the beginning,[11] Poland, like other countries in the region, lacked a powerful office responsible for advocacy and lobbying on the part of local governments. By default, such central institutions as the Ministry of Finance retained a high degree of control.[12] Lack of strong national representation reflected the ambiguity that the first as well as subsequent central governments had toward the establishing a powerful local level of government.

Although the conflict over who pays for particular services has been partly restored over the seven-year period, there remains some ambiguity, as the fiscal powers of local government were never determined clearly. These powers were again increasingly challenged with the attempts to introduce a subregional level of government—the *powiat*.[13] Although initially, issues of planning and budgeting were of primary importance, with mounting fiscal shortages and the increasing likelihood of debt-incurring services to be transferred to the local level (e.g., primary education), local authorities' attention became focused on debt financing, revenue-raising powers, and the management of properties (pricing, contracting, selling).

Third, the experiences and skills of local government officials had been very limited for two reasons: The great majority was comprised of first-time public-office holders, and the institutions for which they worked were newly restructured. Local government officials elected in 1990 did exhibit a strong commitment to the local decision-making process and to addressing local priorities. Although they may not have had a full understanding of the democratic decision-making process, they did have a willingness to adopt new practices. What they lacked the most was practical training regarding both the administrative and operational side of local government management and responsibility for the particular functions that were newly transferred to their jurisdiction.

The professionalization of official local cadres began to be addressed through a mix of practical training, exchange programs, seminars and workshops, and systematic development of professional literature.[14] In 1990 Poland had very few institutions that could fulfill this need, but by 1997 hundreds of training institutes and consulting firms had emerged.[15] They differ in scope and the quality of performed services and are very unevenly distributed across the country, with the greatest concentration in Warsaw, Kraków, Gdańsk, and Łódź. One significant development that has taken place is the slow recognition by major universities that issues pertinent to local governance and public administration are legitimate subjects for an academic curriculum. Although the content of these programs is often divorced from real life and thus students are poorly prepared to be involved in actual decision-making and policy-formation processes, the attempt to link theoretical debates on the state-building process may nevertheless enrich both practice and theory. In this regard, Poland followed in the steps of Western European countries, where the initial training also had a primary practical focus and only subsequently was recognized as academic subject matter.[16] One danger that systematically has been pointed out in Western literature is the possible threat to the democratic decision-making process that professional civil servants will bring with them. General agreement has been, however, that professionalism is needed, even if it opens new questions and produces new tensions, so that local government is on equal footing when dealing with regional or central levels.[17]

A Stable Institution within an Unstable Environment?

Difficulties and constraints that, from the beginning, have challenged the existence of local government and its functioning have no doubt affected its performance. On the one hand, new and still-weak local structures needed to resist political and fiscal pressures from above. Without the subnational level, the potential buffer zone, the *gmina* became exposed to a variety of controlling and supervisory dealings. On the other hand, citizens closely watched and evaluated the performance of their local institutions. In reality, local government began to serve as a buffer zone between citizens and national political events and institutions. Although no systematic studies have been done on the stability and performance of local government, the available data permits the drawing of some general conclusions. In this context, four different dimensions are reviewed.

First, at the national level, through the enactment of pro-local government legislation and the creation of political channels for advocacy and lobbying, political institutions can exercise a supportive role. Indeed, initially this was the case, as both legislative chambers created parliamentary commissions on local government that provided political impetus and support for changes in the laws. What has changed drastically over the years, however, is the degree of commitment to the decentralization process. The most important packet of legislation—fiscal reforms—remained temporary and was subject to renewal on a yearly basis. The initial compulsory transfer of primary education to local government was, at the last minute, extended for an additional two years, under pressure from the teachers' union. A so-called pilot program, under which many responsibilities for social services, education, transportation, infrastructure, and planning were to be transferred (along with their budgets) to 46 urban centers, became the target of various sectoral pressures to a point at which the program became ineffective.[18] These few examples show how an initially supportive political climate at the national level, which could have provided stability, became actively hostile toward local government.

A second group of measures reflects the stability of local offices. They indicate the level of turnover for elected officials in the executive branch and electoral offices as measured through resignations or recalls of presidents and mayors as well as city council chairs and their members.[19] During the first term in office (1990–1994), in both cases—that of the electoral and executive offices—more than 78 percent of the *gminy* did not encounter any changes in leadership positions.[20] Of those that did undergo such changes, urban *gminy* (again, in both cases) were more likely to experience them (33 percent) than rural *gminy* (19 percent). This is not surprising, because city councils are usually much larger (with 80–100 members) and, as a result, are much more politically diverse. Difficulties in reaching consensus were experienced by urban areas. These were further exacerbated by the structural weakness of mayor-council relations and by the lack of negotiating skills among local government officials. Indeed, this is overwhelmingly reflected in the two primary reasons indicated as influencing change: resignation and upon councils' recommendation. Nevertheless, considering that this was their first term in office, these data reflect considerable stability.

A third group includes referenda, currently the only direct mechanism that citizens can utilize to exercise control over local government and force the recall of a *gmina* council. Although citizens have some input into the recall of local officials, ultimately the actual decision is made by the local council. Current law does not provide for any legislative initiative by citizens. This leaves referenda as the only tool. For referenda to be put on the ballot, support must be obtained for a proposal from a minimum 10 percent of eligible voters. The results of a referendum are valid when voter turnout is a minimum of 30 percent.

During the four years, only 76 initiatives have been undertaken.[21] What remains striking is the clear understanding on the part of initiators as to why a particular referendum should take place. They address the essence of self-governance and reflect the arguments that prompted initiation of the decentralization process in the first place. While the notion of self-governance is new, its understanding can be acquired in a relatively short time. Among justifications presented for holding a referendum, the following were most frequently cited: too-great tolerance of a mayor by a council that permitted mismanagement, waste of resources, and poor management of communal wealth; lack of council interest in community matters and disrespect for crucial community needs (unemployment, safety, social services); disregard of citizens' initiatives by a city council; lack of accountability of council members vis-à-vis the electorate; and promotion of private business through public office.

In the end, out of 76 initiatives, five were rejected because of too few signatures. Again, this was predominantly the case in large urban areas: Kraków (twice) and Gdańsk; in 28 other cases, the initiative failed to bring referenda to the voters. Referenda were conducted in 48 communities (in 30 voivodships). Only in three cases (Ostrołęka, Wrocław, Kielce) was the initiative passed. In the remaining cases, the electorate did not go to the polls; in some cases, only a few people voted.

The final, fourth group of indicators reveals citizens' attitudes toward the activities and performance of local government as well as their sense of the extent to which this is a participatory decision-making process. The assumption here is that the higher the stability and better the performance, the greater support for local government is expressed. The strongest backing of this notion comes from public opinion surveys conducted by the Center for Study of Public Opinion (CBOS).[22] CBOS has been conducting regular research on local government since 1988, but it was not until 1992 that local government had been permanently included among political and public institutions whose performance is surveyed through periodic evaluations by citizens. This inclusion, although rather late, no doubt reflects the post-1989 appearance of local government among key public institutions.

Available data unquestionably show that local governments have gained greater citizens' support over time. Moreover, through all these years, those who approved its performance have always outnumbered those who were discontented. This is clearly an achievement, considering the challenges. A closer analysis showed that local government, since its inclusion in the surveys, receives the steadiest ratings among all political institutions (office of the president, national government, and both chambers of Parliament—the Senate and the Sejm). Since 1992, its approval rate has been growing steadily, from 40 percent to 60 percent, with only occasional minor declines of 2–3 percent. Its disapproval rate, while showing greater imbalance, nevertheless remained low and by 1996 was lower than at the beginning of the 1992 (32 percent vs. 28 percent).[23] As a result, the gap between those who appreciated and those who criticized local government performance has been steadily widening. Again, this is the only political institution that has shown not only a consistent increase in ratings but also a significant improvement.

The only other closely comparable ratings are those given to police. Local government represents a political institution and police a public one. These are of a different nature, albeit both are located at the local level. They are the institutions that most frequently interact with citizens and whose actions affect the local population most directly. The approval/disapproval rates of other political institutions show frequent and dramatic changes as they reflect citizens' reactions to various political events, crises, and post election results. The other nonpolitical institutions (although clearly involved in making the political), such as the army, ombudsperson's office, radio, and television, all have higher than local government approval rates (60 percent to 85 percent) and lower disapproval rates (5 percent to 20 percent). As their actions have more limited direct impact on the socioeconomic well-being of large number of citizens (even though radio and television have significant influence over citizens, they do not directly challenge citizens' quality of life), citizens' understanding of these institutions is rather narrow and therefore the ability to evaluate their performance remains restricted.

Endorsement of local government by citizens has been also reflected in the way in which citizens view the degree to which local authorities should have power and influence over the affairs, not only at the local but also at the national level. In the beginning of 1992, CBOS asked whether the influence of local authorities is too small, too large, or adequate. Respondents were very clear that they wished for more influence of local government on national affairs (51 percent vs. 4 percent) and, at the same time, wanted far less of the influence that another local institution exercises—the church (72 percent vs. 3 percent). These results reflect the confidence that citizens have in local government actions, even though one may argue that they also indicate ambiguity in understanding the limits that roles and responsibilities assigned to local government have.

If indeed citizens want to see more influence exercised by local authorities, then it is important to understand whom in particular they have in mind when delegating such power. A survey done by CBOS in mid-1992 asked respondents to indicate whom they believed to have the greatest influence on the affairs of their community.[24] In general, people see a mayor as the most influential person (responses ranged from 39 percent in small villages to 15 percent in large cities), although in large urban areas, where people are more alienated from local authorities, city councils were more frequently perceived as being powerful (23 percent vs. 15 percent). An inquiry into the perception over the influence that citizens have on local affairs indicates the slow development of what one may call the sense of civic responsibility. Those who participate in meetings with local officials, talk to council members, and have been actively engaged in local projects have a greater sense of power. A look at their socioeconomic characteristics confirms that these are newly emerging local elite. They are young, educated, and live predominantly in rural areas; they consider their own material condition as being good, and they positively evaluate the direction of change in the country. Unfortunately, there is no data that would indicate what is happening to these people. Are they engaged in civic activities? Are they becoming leading figures in political or economic life, or have they remained disapproving and discontented with local affairs? The emergence of local elite has become a fact, and their rise is shaping, even if to a limited extent, local discourses. Their emergence signifies the next phase in the consolidation of democracy and the development of political culture that did not exist under communist Poland. It indicates yet another positive impact of the emergence of local self-government.

Research conducted during 1992–1993 showed that citizens feel that they are being noticed and believed that local authorities were truly interested in their problems. Those who valued most highly the effectiveness of self-government authorities also were most ready to cooperate with them. They believe that local authorities do undertake effective actions on behalf of their communities and that local authorities keep their commitments and promises. By 1993, there appeared a very considerable element of trust—nonexistent in 1992—in relations between society and local authorities. This changed again to a certain extent by 1995. The collapse of Prime Minister Suchocka's government and the takeover in the fall of 1993 by the Alliance of the Democratic Left with the Peasant Party brought on a period of increased fiscal and political pressures for local government. This was reflected in a 1995 study by OBOP (Center for Public Opinion Surveys), which indicated that while respondents felt positive that the decision-making process has been brought closer to citizens (52 percent), they were split on the effectiveness with which public funds are managed (39 percent vs. 41 percent) and were considerably angered by the investment decisions that seemed not in line with citizens' expectations (35 percent vs. 48 percent).[25] Furthermore, they felt that citizens do not have adequate influence over the decision-making process (35 percent vs. 55 percent).

Three sets of conclusions may be drawn. First, the results reflect greater understanding and expectations regarding the roles and responsibilities of local government and elected officials. This knowledge is not confined to the economic sphere but rather incorporates the principles of democratic governance: Citizens expect to participate in the decision-making process and to be informed about decisions made by local authorities. Second, the increased dissatisfaction with fiscal management and investment policies indicates, on the one hand, greater knowledge and increased interest on the part of inhabitants in the well-being of their communities and, on the other, the increased top-down pressures that have resulted in more restricted fiscal stability at the local level and have limited local authorities' ability to allocate funds according to local needs. Finally, it should be noted that the dissatisfaction was greater in urban areas, reflecting the fact that in the cities, local authorities are less known and often almost anonymous. This may represent one reason why in small towns, local government has been evaluated much better than in large centers.

What this review confirms is the recognition of local government as a new institution that plays an important role in the formation of political and public discourse. The results reflect both the increased understanding as well as expectations of citizens regarding the roles and responsibilities of local governments and elected officials. At the same time, citizens recognize that in order to claim their newly gained citizenship rights, they have obligations whose fulfillment requires their participation in local affairs. Local governments, then, have not only became embedded in the local political culture but have actually fostered its development. Its existence makes a difference to people. Of course, this is insufficient to argue that the existence of local government has already resulted in building civic traditions. But as R. D. Putnam pointed out, "Citizens in civic communities expect better government. They demand more effective public service, and they are prepared to act collectively to achieve their shared goals."[26] Although in Poland not all of these requirements have been met yet, increased citizens' demands and active participation indicates that in some areas the process of constructing civic engagement is well advanced.[27]

Given that citizens are more engaged, it is not surprising that the survey results show an increased dissatisfaction with the fiscal management and investment policies of local officials. Citizens' greater knowledge and increased interest in the well-being of their communities means closer scrutiny of the actions undertaken by officials. Yet there is another significant explanation of these results: the increased top-down political pressures that have resulted in a more unpredictable fiscal status of local governments that have limited local authorities' discretion to allocate funds according to local needs, in effect undercutting local autonomy.

What Next? Will National Suppress Local?

This chapter has argued that in spite of external and internal difficulties, local governments have made substantial progress. At the same time, while many components are essential for the further stabilization of local autonomy, the increased influence gained by political factors during the past several years calls for greater attention. In fact, they became the major forces in controlling local government reform. The 1993 parliamentary elections were a turning point, and since then, the political sphere has suppressed more strongly changes at the local level. The existence of these new pressures raises several questions: At what scale do political factors inhibiting local autonomy operate? What is the nature of the interactions among these different levels, and what are the consequences for local autonomy? How far can the local political space extend without being restricted by the central level? What strategies are used by the local level to retain the power it possesses?

Most analyses of political decentralization in Poland focus on central-level politics and especially the center's desire to regain and retain power. This approach creates the perception that actions at the central level solely determine the degree of power that the local level possesses. Such analyses theoretically argue for the devolution of power to the local level and, therefore, its empowerment. By omitting the local level it assumes, in practice, a "passive" transfer of power. In other words, while the local level will acquire power through the process of devolution, the presumption is that it will not necessarily use it to sustain itself. This is a critical omission, as it reveals de facto the hesitance of politicians and policy makers to implement decentralization. Considering the fiscal situation of *gminy*, it raises the question of the extent to which Poland may increasingly experience deconcentration of power (the delegation of tasks without the power to fulfill them). The one-dimensional character of this debate calls for analysis of a local government's involvement in retaining and expanding the power that it obtained. It might be that while the central level's actions are significant, the political underdevelopment of the local level presents an important obstacle to strengthening and sustaining local autonomy.

Studies on local autonomy in Western democracies have attempted to identify forces that contribute to political power at the local level. E. C. Page and M. J. Goldsmith[28] have pointed out that the nature of contacts between central and local government actors is just as significant as laws, advice, or grants. They argue that "if local actors themselves have a significant influence on central decisions, they have greater scope of shaping state services than if central decisions were simply the product of an interaction between non-local politicians, bureaucrats and groups."[29] The local elite are then crucial for strengthening of the local political scene and, as has been discussed earlier, are emerging in Poland. The greater the degree of access and influence that the local elite are able to exercise over the higher levels of government, the stronger the probability that such influence will affect local autonomy. This can be achieved through direct forms of influence (contacts of local officials with national-level politicians, civil servants, and policy makers) or indirectly exercised on a collective basis on behalf of local government through a variety of local government associations. These arguments were also echoed in Putnam's analysis of civic traditions at the regional level in Italy.[30]

Other scholars argue, however, that local politics is limited, and therefore in practice local government has little opportunity to influence the national level. P. E. Peterson,[31] in *City Limits,* claims that local political limitations do exist and that they will be displayed, for example, through a narrow scope of local organizing, a lack of strong local lobbying organizations, a lack of ethnic groups, and the absence of strong local parties. In other words, political underdevelopment means that the local level cannot influence redistributive policies: Local politics is limited and its vertical power extends minimally.

How have these arguments been echoed in Poland? Two examples may suffice. One analyzes local government's use of legislative provisions providing the right to organize and to create associations. The second shows the extent to which the local level has been able to resist national-level partisan politics, when forming post-election *gmina* councils in 1994 and electing their mayors. The first case represents a newly gained right, because in the past, freedom of assembly and the freedom to form organizations did not exist. Several general-purpose associations have been created. They include those that unite only rural *gminy* (Union of Rural Gminy) or urban *gminy* (Union of Polish Towns) or bring together *gminy* of a certain site only (e.g., Union of Metropolitan Cities). They include also associations that have a much more regional character and bring together only a few *gminy* that are adjacent to one another (e.g., the Opole Silesia Municipal Union). Probably the most influential and important is the National Assembly of Local Government (NALG), which was created in 1990 and has been lobbying, primarily for fiscal matters, on behalf of local governments.[32] The structure of NALG permits every voivodship to select two representatives to the assembly. These representatives are elected by *gminy* located within each voivodship. Although the general character of the NALG might have prevented it from successfully representing local interests, what brought more power to the association was national fiscal legislation requiring that NALG be consulted in the budget formation process. This anchoring of NALG at the central level makes it permanently visible, albeit also vulnerable, as the assembly became the object and the location of partisan power struggle for political control of its activities.

The special-purpose associations that permit *gminy* to address such issues as roads, environmental problems, waste disposal, or medical service delivery through inter-*gmina* cooperation are other types of groups that were fostered by the new legislation. In 1995, CBOS[33] conducted a survey of local government officials' attitudes toward this type of association. The survey revealed some hesitancy. First, whereas 42 percent of respondents do not see the need to create such organization and more than one third do not belong to any such association, 47 percent do belong to one and 17 percent are ambivalent. At the same time, two thirds of those who do not belong believe that such structures might actually assist in solving local problems, and those that belong to several are overwhelmingly supportive (95 percent) of such cooperation. Second, rural *gminy* are less likely to belong to any organization (42 percent). Often, they did not know about such a possibility (21 percent), and as a result, only 37 percent are members, a substantial number of them belonging only to one organization (27 percent). Rural officials were also more likely to fail to create such an organization (57 percent vs. 30 percent in urban areas). Third, important gender differences are exhibited, as women tend to a lesser degree to believe that there is no need to collaborate (24 percent vs. 42 percent); more often, they see the failure to create such linkages because of an inability to negotiate cooperation agreements with other *gminy* (7 percent vs. 10 percent) and blame their colleagues for such an outcome (8 percent vs. 14 percent). At the same time, women are more skeptical of the benefits once such an association is created (69 percent vs. 62 percent).

These and other results reveal ambiguity among local officials, both male and female, as to the benefits and purposes of working together.[34] Some of this hesitancy comes from the absence of a tradition for working together and the lack of a civic tradition regarding active participation beyond one's borders. To some degree, this is also the result of fear that the scarcity of resources reveals itself in questioning the benefits that such cooperation might bring. Finally, the lack of a lobbying tradition and active participation in the political decision-making process also severely curtails local officials' approaches to development of political strategies.

The outcome of political negotiations after the 1994 local elections raises the question of the local level's ability to develop such political strategies in one particular case: to constrain partisan conflicts that prevail at the national level. The immediate postelection image that was presented by the media stressed the difficulty that the elections of mayors and presidents of large cities present. Moreover, the focus was on partisan politics at the local level and the lack of an established political culture, which undermine local officials' ability to negotiate and build coalitions.

This, in turn, was portrayed as contributing to prolonged political instability at the local level. In reality, however, local government officials evaluated the situation differently. A majority of *gminy* (78 percent) did not have any problems in electing mayors.[35] In rural areas, 89 percent of elections were problem-free. The greater the size of the *gmina*, the more complicated its political landscape and its administrative structure and the greater the need for multiparty coalitions. Indeed, in 46 percent of urban *gminy*, such a formation was necessary.

Contrary to the general belief, however, a majority of council members in such *gminy* felt that they rather than national party headquarters (77 percent vs. 7 percent) have greater influence on the coalition formation process. Respondents stressed that there were indeed conflicts with the national headquarters, as local officials were more often in favor of such a coalition, but ultimately it was their local decision on how to resolve these local conflicts.

What can be concluded from the evidence presented? The absence of organized pressures coming from the local level, through party channels or through independent lobbying, indicates relative passivity at the local level and ambivalence in engaging in democratic consolidation. The question for the future of local government is, then, a two-pronged dilemma: How much the central level can take back will depend on the extent to which the local level is willing to give it up. The still-visible inability to organize and maintain a presence at the national level undermines local government's ability to become an empowered political actor and contributes to the political underdevelopment of the local level. While the process of consolidation is challenged by a deteriorating fiscal situation of *gminy* across Poland, the lack of recognition that the power lies in the ability of *gminy* to mobilize jointly their political resources, to network and cooperate, and to develop joint strategies determines the limited impact that existing associations have achieved so far. Little is known why the local level exhibits limited responses. Besides the factors that have been discussed here, perhaps such a change can only be achieved in response to a crisis situation, and the current status is not yet perceived as such.

Despite some criticism that can be addressed toward local government, the tendency is to increase its stability, although self-government reform is not finished, financial legislation is incomplete, and the position of local government in the new constitution is weaker[36] than was conceived in the post-1989 constitutional amendments. At the same time, citizens' approval rating is high, because local authorities are perceived as representative of local interests. Citizens comprehend self-government as addressing their local needs rather than those of the central administration. Furthermore, local elites are slowly emerging, establishing new political bases and opening new channels of communication with the national level. Still, one dimension of this support calls for attention. Although CBOS surveys showed that citizens believe that local government is close to them, the surveys also indicate that to a much lesser degree, citizens believe they can influence government decisions. The role that citizens can play in the consolidation of power at the local level should not be dismissed. Citizens can become stronger allies of local officials if they have access to local political space. Through voting, NGO activities, the expressed approval and disapproval of people and activities, citizens exercise their political will. As nationwide political events have little impact on the assessment of local government by citizens, it behooves local officials to gain citizens' support and approval. This approval will be complicated by the fact that the consequences of central-level actions may not necessarily be perceived by citizens as a central-local struggle for power but rather as a lack of local government's capabilities to resolve local problems.

This overview of local self-government in Poland indicates that although these new institutions may not have lived up to everyone's expectations, they nevertheless began to alter old patterns of power, both at local and central levels. They initiated local economic development. They fostered the development of political culture and produced what did not exist before—a climate conducive for civic participation. These are not completed tasks, but they are significant achievements and contributions to democratic consolidation, and they should be recognized as such.

Notes

1. I. Elander, "Between Centralism and Localism: On the Development of Local Self-Government in Post-Socialist Europe," *Environment and Planning C: Government and Policy* 15 (1997); T. M. Horvath, "Decentralization without or with Integration," ibid.; R. Prud'homme, "The Dangers of Decentralization," *World Bank Research Observer* 10 (1995): 201–20.
2. M. Kulesza, *Guidelines for Public Administration Reform in Poland* (Warsaw: Office of Public Administration, Council of Ministers, 1993).
3. For an extensive discussion, see R. M. Bird, R. D. Ebel and Ch. I. Wallich, eds., *Decentralization of the Socialist State: Intergovernmental Finance in Transition Economies* (Washington, D.C.: World Bank, 1995).
4. J. Regulska, "Building Democracy at the Local Level: The Case of Poland," *Voluntas: International Journal of Voluntary and Non-Profit Organizations* (forthcoming); J. Kubik, "Culture, Administrative Reform, and Local Politics: Overlooked Dimensions of the Post-Communist Transformation," *Anthropology of East Europe Review* 10, no. 2 (1991): 19.
5. J. Regulska, "Transition to Local Democracy: Do Polish Women Have a Chance?" in M. Rueschmayer, ed., *Women in the Politics of Postcommunist*

Eastern Europe (forthcoming); J. Regulska, "The New State-Gender Relations in Poland," in J. Pickles and A. Smith, eds., *Theorizing Transition: The Political Economy of Change in Central and Eastern Europe* (New York: Routledge, forthcoming).

6. T. Kowalik, "Can Poland Afford the Swedish model?" *Dissent* (Winter 1993): 88–96; J. Lewandowski, "Czy demokracja lubi rynek?" *Przegląd Polityczny* 26 (Winter 1994): 31–34; P. L. Patterson, ed., *Capitalist Goals, Socialist Past: The Rise of the Private Sector in Command Economies* (Boulder, Colo.: Westview Press, 1993); K. Zagórski, "Ekonomia polityczna nadziei," *Przegląd Polityczny* 26 (Winter 1994): 28–30; "Jaki kapitalizm w Polsce?" *Przegląd Polityczny* 11 (Special Issue, 1993).

7. For a detailed history of the design and implementation of local government reform, see J. Regulski, "Polish Local Government in Transition," *Environment and Planning C: Government and Policy* 7 (1989): 423–44; A. Kowalczyk "Basic Information on Local Governments in Poland," in *Local Governments in the CEE and CIS* (Budapest: Institute for Local Government and Public Service, 1994), 145–157; J. Regulska, "Decentralization or (Re)Centralization: Struggle for Political Power in Poland," *Environment and Planning C: Government and Policy* 15 (1997); L. Barbone and J. F. Hicks, "Local and Intergovernmental Finances in Poland: An Evolving Agenda," in Bird, Ebel, and Wallich, eds., *Decentralization of the Socialist State;* A. Coulson, "From Democratic Centralism to Local Democracy," in A. Coulson, ed., *Local Government in Eastern Europe: Establishing Democracy at the Grassroots* (Brookfield, Vt.: Edward Elgar, 1995), 1–17.

8. See I. Elander, "Between Centralism and Localism"; Ch. Pickvance, "Decentralization and Democracy in Eastern Europe: A Skeptical Approach," *Environment and Planning C: Government and Policy* 15 (1997); R. A. W. Rhodes, *Control and Power in Central-Local Government Relations* (Gower, Eng.: Aldershot, Hants, 1981), 33.

9. J. Regulska, "Local Government Reform in Central and Eastern Europe," in R. J. Bennett, ed., *Local Government in the New Europe* (London: Belhaven Press, 1993), 183–97.

10. *Poland: Decentralization and Reform of the State: Country Study.* 10 (Washington, D.C.: World Bank, August 1992).

11. Only during the design and early implementation stage did local government have a central ally in the Office of the Plenipotentiary for Local Government, with the rank of state undersecretary. The only occupant of this position, Jerzy Regulski, although a member of the Council of Ministers during 1989–1990, had nevertheless only restricted power to negotiate during preparation of the 1990 Local Self-Government Act and interministerial agreements. Consequences of unresolved power conflicts at the national level became quickly visible when the Act on Duties and Responsibilities was implemented.

12. J. F. Hicks, Jr., and B. Kamiński, "Local Government Reform," in R. F. Staar, ed., *Transition to Democracy in Poland* (New York: St. Martin's Press, 1993),

85–88; R. M. Bird, R. D. Ebel and Ch. I. Wallich, "Fiscal Decentralization: From Command to Market," in Bird, Ebel, and Wallich, eds., *Decentralization of the Socialist State,* 10–11.

13. D. Głowacka-Mazur and C. Zaremba, "The Pilot Program Six Months After the Beginning of Its Implementation," *Wspólnota* 38, no. 236 (1994): 1, 4–5.

14. The first training institution, the Foundation in Support of Local Democracy, was created in Warsaw during the summer of 1989. Since then, almost 200,000 people have participated in FSLD seminars, workshops, and training courses. FSLD currently coordinates a network of 16 training centers and five colleges of public administration and local government, two of which are accredited by the Ministry of Education and are eligible to award professional certificates. See "Foundation in Support of Local Democracy," *Annual Report* (Warsaw: FSLD, 1992, 1993, 1994, 1995); J. Regulska, "Building Democracy at the Local Level: The Case of Poland," in M. Lazar, ed., *Fortifying the Foundations: U.S. Support for Developing and Strengthening Democracy in East Central Europe* (New York: Institute of International Education, 1996), 32–39.

15. See *Directory of NGO Trainers in Central and Eastern Europe* (Washington, D.C.: Institute for Democracy in Eastern Europe, 1996).

16. For example, in Sweden, public administration was included in the university curriculum only after educational reform had taken place. See T. Magnusson and J. E. Lane, "Sweden," in C. Page and M. J. Goldsmith, eds., *Central and Local Government Relations* (London: Sage, 1987), 14–28.

17. Magnusson and Lane, "Sweden," 26; R. D. Putnam, *Making Democracy Work: Civic Traditions in Modern Italy,* 27–38; R. A. W. Rhodes, *Control and Power in Central-Local Government Relations* (Gower, Eng.: Aldershot, Hants, 1981).

18. J. Regulska, "Decentralization or Deconcentration: Struggle for Political Power in Poland," *International Journal of Public Administration* 20, no. 3 (1997): 643–80.

19. Data presented here cover only the first term of the office, 1990–1994.

20. "Stabilność władz samorządowych w Polsce od czerwca 1990 r. do 15 grudnia 1993" (Warsaw: Biuro Operacyjne, Urząd Rady Ministrów, 1993).

21. *Sprawozdanie z działalności Generalnego Komisarza Wyborczego . . .* (Warsaw: Generalny Komisarz Wyborczy, 1993).

22. "Opinie o instytucjach publicznych kraju," *CBOS Report* (Warsaw: CBOS, 1993), BS/170/138/93; "Stosunek społeczeństwa do głównych instytucji politycznych i społecznych," *CBOS Report* (1992), BS/378/82/92; "Opinie o instytucjach publicznych kraju: Związki zawodowe a rząd," *CBOS Report* (1994), BS/3/3/94; "Instytucje publiczne w opinii społeczeństwa," *CBOS Report* (1995), BS/62/52/95; "Instytucje publiczne—społeczna ocena ich działalności we wrześniu," *CBOS Report* (1996), BS/156/154/96; "Instytucje publiczne—zmiany w ich postrzeganiu," *CBOS Report* (1996), BS/190/188/96.

23. "Instytucje publiczne," *CBOS Report* (1996), BS/190/188/96.

24. "Kto rządzi w Polsce," *CBOS Report* (1992), BS/375/80/92.
25. A. Grobelna and M. Łyszkowska-Cieślik, "Opinia społeczna o samorządzie terytorialnym," *Profile* (Warsaw, 1995).
26. R. D. Putnam, *Making Democracy Work: Civic Traditions in Modern Italy* (1993), 182.
27. An analysis of the unprecedented growth of nongovernmental organizations is beyond the scope of this chapter. It may be sufficient to say that since 1989, thousands of new groups, centers, neighborhood/city/regional organizations, societies, and student/teacher/parent initiatives have developed.
28. E. C. Page and M. J. Goldsmith, eds., *Central and Local Government Relations: A Comparative Analysis of West European Unitary States* (London: Sage 1987), 4–8.
29. Ibid., 7.
30. Putnam, *Making Democracy Work*, 182.
31. P. E. Peterson, *City Limits* (Chicago: University of Chicago Press, 1981).
32. For a detailed history of the NALG, see "Komisje i zespoły problemowe KSST w I Kadencji," *Samorząd Terytorialny I Kadencji* 5 (Poznań: Krajowy Instytut Badań Samorządowych, 1994).
33. "Radni o ankiecie URM, związkach gmin i stosunku sił politycznych do samorządów," *CBOS Report* (1995), BS/22/17/95.
34. For an extensive analysis of the special-purpose associations, see T. Potocki, *Study of Joint Local Initiatives by Special Purpose Associations of Gminas* (Warsaw: DAI, 1996). This survey conducted in 1996 reconfirms the existence of substantial political, social, legal, fiscal, and psychological barriers. Out of 117 associations, 87 percent indicated a variety of difficulties with cooperation.
35. "Radni o wyborze wójta (burmistrza i prezydenta)," *CBOS Report* (1995), BS/33/27/95.
36. The new Polish constitution was approved by Parliament in April and by national referendum in May 1997.

SEVEN

Development of Constitutionalism

A. E. Dick Howard and Mark F. Brzezinski

D uring the late 1980s and early 1990s, the world witnessed a shift from authoritarianism to democratization and a rebirth of experiments in constitutionalism. Within three years, transitions from one-party rule to constitutional democracy began in each of the former Soviet bloc countries, changing the political face of Central and Eastern Europe. One commentator, Judge Wojciech Sokolewicz of Poland's Constitutional Tribunal, reflected on the magnitude of political change ushered in by the postcommunist era: "The changes in Eastern Europe will consist of transition from autocracy to liberal democracy; from the arbitrariness of a Communist Party-controlled State to unconditional subordination of the State to law; and from a loose system of sources of law, their hierarchy obscure in practice, to a coherent and strictly hierarchical one grounded in the national constitution treated as the fundamental source of norms and the supreme law."[1]

Most modern scholars agree that the primary purpose of a constitution is to describe the permissible scope and limits of governmental power and to protect individual liberties. One leading book on the subject offers the following definition: "Constitutions are codes of norms which aspire to regulate the allocation of powers, functions and duties among the various agencies and officials of government, and to define the relationship between these and the public."[2] However, it is important to distinguish between constitutions and constitutionalism.

The former is a written document; the latter is a state of mind, an expectation, a norm under which politics must be conducted in accordance with standing rules or conventions, written or unwritten, that cannot be easily changed; it is a principle whereby all power is limited and whereby forces of power can act and decide only within strict limits defined by the national constitution.

A survey of the constitution-making efforts in Central and Eastern Europe reveals uneven progress toward constitutionalism and the rule of law. Some countries, Bulgaria and Romania, for example, have adopted new constitutions. One must pause, however, especially as regards Romania, before declaring mature constitutional government to be the result. The Czechs and Slovaks agreed, in January 1991, on a bill of rights for their federal republic, but the effort to hammer out a constitutional structure for the federation failed. The Czech and Slovak Parliament ultimately acquiesced in a decision to see the two republics become sovereign entities as of 1 January 1993. In Russia, a new constitution was promulgated in 1993. However, the principal institution for enforcing that document, the Constitutional Court, was suspended by presidential decree in October 1993 for almost 18 months. Afterward, President Yeltsin expanded its membership to pack it with supporters, reminiscent of U.S. President Franklin Roosevelt's infamous idea for doing the same thing to the U.S. Supreme Court.

After 1989, as Poland once again returned to constitutional rule, democratic constitutional arrangements replaced communist political structures put in place in 1952. The first stage of constitutional reform concentrated on amending the 1952 constitution to eliminate the essential features of the communist system and to provide the basis for further evolution of the polity. While the promulgation of an entirely new constitutional order proved politically impossible during 1990–1991, in November 1992 constitutional legislation, colloquially known as the "Small Constitution," came into force. That document provided both a framework within which democratic political processes would operate as well as specific solutions to the institutional dilemmas that had emerged in the first two years of postcommunist government.

In addition to the promulgation of new constitutional provisions, after 1989 new institutions and procedures—foremost among them judicial review—were developed in Poland to make constitutionalism not just an operational reality but a genuinely pervasive institution. Since 1989, the Constitutional Tribunal has actively delimited the lawmaking of the new state and has defined and protected a new understanding of rights and the separation of powers. The tribunal's "activist" jurisprudence has responded to the necessities of Poland's postcommunist transition, defining principled bounds of lawmaking, particularly in those areas untouched by constitutional reform.

This chapter considers the evolution of constitutionalism in postcommunist Poland. Part 1 examines the constitutional reform that accompanied Poland's democratic rebirth in 1989 and describes initial efforts to adopt a new constitution. Part 2 discusses the passage and content of the 1992 Small Constitution and the new institutional framework it created. Part 3 addresses the jurisprudence of the Constitutional Tribunal and discusses the centrality of judicial review in the development of constitutionalism in Poland.

1. Democratic Reconstruction through Constitutional Amendment (1989–1991)

The formal transition from communism to democracy in Poland was precipitated by the Roundtable talks between the communist leadership and the Solidarity-led opposition in the spring of 1989. The talks initially were undertaken to negotiate official recognition of Solidarity, at the time still an illegal organization, in exchange for the opposition's support of the regime's economic policies. However, once the future legal status of Solidarity was settled, opposition negotiators began to push for a bargain that would enable the trade union to participate meaningfully in the country's political life. Throughout the negotiations, the specter of Soviet intervention influenced both the communists and Solidarity leaders, impacting directly on compromises agreed to at the Roundtable.[3]

The Roundtable Agreement and the "April Amendments"

By early April, agreement on most issues had been reached. On 7 April 1989, the Roundtable Agreement was promulgated into law, and the 1952 Constitution was amended (the "April amendments"), providing for important political changes. First, the Sejm officially lifted the ban placed on the Solidarity movement seven years earlier and gave the organization and its sister union, Rural Solidarity, full legal status. The passage of a new electoral law guaranteeing "political pluralism" and independence for all political groups and parties marked the end of the authoritarian phase of Polish political life.[4]

Second, it was agreed that the Sejm would be dissolved and that new elections would be held in June 1989. The preexisting electoral system, fully controlled by the Communist Party, was abandoned. Under the new electoral formula, 65 percent of Sejm seats would be reserved for the PZPR and its allies (the SD and the ZSL). Solidarity would be permitted to compete in genuinely free elections for the remaining 35 percent of Sejm seats. In this way, Solidarity would have representation in the Sejm but only as an opposition party; the communists were ensured of at least 299 of the 460 Sejm seats, giving them the numerical majority needed to thwart any challenges by the new opposition and to control the formation of the government.

The compromise further provided for restoration of the "upper" house of Parliament, the Senate, which the communists had abolished in 1951. With all 100 members freely elected, the Senate was to have considerable legislative powers, including legislative initiative and the right to veto or amend Sejm legislation, which the latter could override with a two thirds majority.[5] With reintroduction of parliamentary bicameralism, laws passed by the Sejm would now be scrutinized and checked within the legislative branch, ending the Sejm's former monopoly.

Third, the April amendments replaced the Council of State with a new, formally quite powerful presidency, elected for a renewable five-year term by the Sejm and the Senate sitting together as a national assembly. As it was assumed that this office would be occupied by General Wojciech Jaruzelski, then-ruling party first secretary, the presidency was seen as an important guarantee of the PZPR's preservation of control over the executive branch and as a safeguard of the interests of the *nomenklatura*. The presidency was given important independent state powers, particularly in foreign and security affairs, at the expense of Parliament, which was no longer regarded as "reliable" by the Party. At the same time, some of the president's constitutional powers (particularly the power of appointment) were ambiguously defined, and there was scope for conflict within the executive branch. The relationship between president and prime minister remained unclear, and some of their functions in defense policy were shared. According to one commentator present at the Roundtable, executive powers were left "deliberately vague on the assumption, current in early 1989, that a communist president would use whatever prerogatives he saw as necessary, since he could rely on the backing of the army, security forces and his Soviet sponsors."[6]

Fourth, the Roundtable Agreement provided guarantees for judicial independence, which it described as "fundamental for a state based on the rule of law and for the protection of citizens' rights and interests."[7] Accordingly, the April amendments resolved that a new national judicial council (*Krajowa Rada Sądownictwa*, or KRS), composed of representatives from all three branches of government (including twelve judges elected by their peers, two senators and four Sejm deputies, the minister of justice, and the president's representative), would be given exclusive power both to select judicial candidates and to propose their candidacy to the president, who could designate as judges only those candidates submitted by the KRS.[8] In order to underline the strictly judicial nature of the Supreme Court, the April amendments provided life tenure for Supreme

Court justices (all other judges had had life tenure since 1957) and abolished the Ministry of Justice's power to promulgate binding directives.

In a political sense, the Roundtable Agreement guaranteed the communists, through the presidency, effective control over the executive branch and the army. At the same time, Solidarity retained a possible veto over communist initiatives through its presence in Parliament. In an institutional sense, the Roundtable Agreement and April amendments together contributed to the restoration of basic elements of the doctrine of separation of powers within a parliamentary system by transforming the unicameral Parliament into a bicameral body, replacing the Council of State with the presidency as part of the executive branch, and providing guarantees of independence to the judicial branch. However, while the democratic opposition's bargain for political power had been successful, it did not anticipate how quickly communist control would collapse.

Implementing the Roundtable Agreement, on 4 June 1989, Poland held its first free national elections since World War II. Solidarity candidates won sweeping victories both in the races for the Senate (99 out of 100 seats) and in the races for the minority of seats open to free election in the Sejm. The ZSL and the SD, once loyal and obedient allies of the PZPR, could not overlook this landslide. Upsetting the communist-led coalition that the Party had hoped to use to control the Sejm, the ZSL and the SD switched their allegiance to Solidarity, giving it an effective majority in Parliament. With this new political equation, the previously rubber-stamp Sejm began to obtain a life of its own. Several influential members of Solidarity demanded leadership of the government as the price of their support for Jaruzelski's presidency.

On 4 July 1989, General Jaruzelski, the only presidential candidate, was elected by the National Assembly to the presidency by a humiliating majority of one vote (after four recounts), a "victory" that the Solidarity leadership had to engineer in order to uphold the Roundtable bargain.[9] Shortly afterward, Jaruzelski designated another communist general, former interior minister Czesław Kiszczak, as prime minister. But without the support of the ZSL and the SD, Kiszczak was unable to form a government. A Solidarity-led parliamentary coalition that included those two parties, eventually formed a government around Tadeusz Mazowiecki, a Catholic journalist and long-time adviser to Lech Wałęsa, who was then the undisputed leader of the coalition. Although Mazowiecki allowed the communists to join the new government and to retain control over the ministries of defense and interior (Solidarity retained the important economic ministries), monolithic communist rule in Poland had come to an end.

The April amendments became outdated by the rapid emergence of the new political order; its patchwork approach to solving fundamental flaws in the 1952 constitution left many important institutional areas cloudy and ill defined. With disintegration of the Soviet bloc and dissolution of the PZPR, the dominant long-term goal became to promulgate an entirely new constitution. But in the meantime, the 1952 constitution, which still explicitly proclaimed "friendship" with the Soviet Union and extolled the "leading role" of the communist party, had to be changed.

The "December Amendments"

On 29 December 1989, the Sejm adopted the so-called December amendments to provide a legal basis for the functioning of democratic institutions and to purge the constitution of symbolic remnants of its Stalinist legacy. The December amendments deleted the constitution's preamble and its first two chapters on the political and socioeconomic system of the Polish People's Republic. They also eliminated the anachronistic clause declaring the Party's "leading role," expunged the reference to Poland's alliance with the Soviet Union, deleted the clause describing Poland's economy as based on "socialized means of production," and introduced the principle of equality for diverse forms of ownership, thus providing a constitutional foundation for private property and the emerging market economy. The original name of the Polish state, Republic of Poland, was restored, and—attacking the heart of Marxist-Leninist phraseology—the term *working people,* for whom the 1952 constitution was allegedly framed, was deleted from Article 2. The new Article 2, modeled on provisions of the 1921 Polish constitution, states that "supreme authority in the Republic of Poland is vested in the Nation."[10] Symbolizing Polish tradition and self-emancipation, the crown was placed back on the head of the Polish national emblem—the White Eagle—where it had been since the fifteenth century.

The most important change introduced by the December amendments is found in the new Article 1, which proclaims that "[t]he Republic of Poland is a democratic state ruled by law, implementing principles of social justice." This provision, and particularly the phrase "state ruled by law," is based on the *Rechtsstaat* principle found in Western European constitutionalism.[11] The *Rechtsstaat* principle hails from nineteenth-century German legal culture and holds that the state has an obligation to be guided by certain principles of justice, fairness, and equity in its relations with individuals. As with the concept of "substantive due process" in America, European constitutional courts have developed a rich jurisprudence through their enforcement and interpretation of the *Rechtsstaat* clause. Poland's new Article 1 was modeled on the *Rechtsstaat* clause of the German constitution, and it became possible for the judicial branch to look to German and other Western European interpretations of the clause. Opportunities to introduce reform measures through this provision were quickly exploited by the Constitutional Tribunal. (See Part 3 for a discussion of the tribunal's *Rechtsstaat* jurisprudence.)

With the April and December amendments, the 1952 constitution was unrecognizable. Poland's constitutional framework was now closer to a liberal-democratic one, with legislative and executive power checked, and with the judicial branch having genuine independence. For most of the 40 years of communist rule, it was not state institutions but Party structures that provided the key to understanding politics. Now the formal institutions of government and constitutional provisions regulating their relations would provide the basic framework within which democratic political processes would operate.

The first stage of constitutional reform was relatively swift and expeditious not only because of the existing political consensus following the Roundtable Agreement but also because PZPR deputies in the Roundtable Sejm had been concerned to demonstrate their "democratic credentials" by producing constitutional changes toward liberal democracy.[12] Unfortunately, dispatch would not continue to characterize the Polish constitution-making process.

The Constitutional Committees

Despite substantial changes, the 1952 constitution as amended was never intended to be the nation's final constitutional structure. The April and December amendments were intended to be temporary, and no effort was made to transform the old document into a permanent basic law of the newly free Poland. As one Solidarity leader (and future prime minister), Hanna Suchocka, stated, "Full cohesion can be reached only in the new constitution, and not on the road of ad hoc changes."[13]

In the fall of 1990, Parliament took the first step toward this end by passing a law providing for a new constitution to be adopted by two-thirds of both houses sitting together as a national assembly and then submitted to a national referendum. To create drafts of the new charter, in December 1989 separate constitutional committees were formed in the Sejm and the Senate.

From the very beginning, however, controversy over legitimacy plagued the Polish constitution-making process. In particular, controversy surrounded the Sejm Constitutional Committee, which was chaired by Bronisław Geremek and composed of 46 Sejm deputies from all parliamentary parties, including the PZPR. Even though Solidarity deputies dominated the Constitutional Committee, a number of Solidarity leaders, including Prime Minister Mazowiecki and Lech Wałęsa, asserted that because the Roundtable Sejm was not the product of fully free elections, it simply did not have the "democratic pedigree" to promulgate a new constitution.[14] The chairman of the Senate Constitutional Committee, the right-of-center Alicja Grześkowiak, claimed that her committee had greater legitimacy to draft the new constitution, as it represented a body that was "more freely" elected.[15] Parliamentary leaders initially hoped to complete the drafting process by 3 May 1991, the bicentennial anniversary of the promulgation of Poland's first constitution. However, fundamental differences over how to achieve legitimacy in the constitution-making process soon made this schedule unrealistic.

Complicating matters further, in 1990 the Sejm Constitutional Committee was additionally assigned the task of drafting a new electoral law. (The existing one had been tailored to the Roundtable Agreement.) This highly divisive project (with smaller parties favoring strict proportionality and larger parties favoring percentage thresholds) considerably slowed the constitution-drafting process and contributed to the dissipation of the spirit of cooperation and consensus that had characterized relations among the diverse groups under the umbrella of Solidarity.

In the fall of 1991, both committees finally produced constitutional drafts. The Sejm draft, modeled in part on the German basic law of 1949, envisaged a parliamentary system with a relatively weak president acting as an arbiter of executive power rather than a chief executive. The Senate draft, inspired in part by the 1958 French model, favored a semipresidential form of government, vesting the president with full government appointment powers. Both drafts specifically provided for the separation of powers and asserted the supremacy of the constitution and of decisions by the Constitutional Tribunal over ordinary legislation. Whereas the Sejm draft contained a broad range of social and economic rights, the Senate draft contained mostly negative rights.[16]

By 1991, however, there had emerged a consensus among the political elite that the Roundtable Sejm, although fully prepared both politically and intellectually to draft a constitution, nevertheless lacked the social legitimacy to promulgate it because the Sejm was the product of a contract with the previous regime and because former communists continued to form a majority in the Sejm. Bronisław Geremek argued in vain that adoption of the new constitution was a vital, immediate practical matter because of lack of clarity in relations among the main organs of the state. He also insisted that circumstances were uniquely propitious, for the communists were still demoralized and Solidarity still unified.[17] Despite this logic, Geremek could not persuade other political elites, and it was eventually decided that the adoption of a new constitution would have to wait until the Roundtable Sejm was replaced with an entirely democratically elected body. When Parliament was formally dissolved in September 1991, both constitutional drafts were put aside.

Although the October 1991 parliamentary elections seemed to negate the initial question of social legitimacy, the results mirrored the breakup of Solidarity into numerous political groupings. Both the Sejm and the Senate emerged highly fragmented, with 29 political parties represented in the Sejm and 13 in the Senate. An electoral system of strict proportionality, without a percentage threshold to keep smaller parties out of Parliament, had been used to enhance the body's "representativeness." The largest party in the Sejm, the Democratic Union (*Unia Demokratyczna*, or UD), controlled a mere 13 percent of the seats. To complicate the equation, the SdRP, the successor party of the former Communist Party, emerged with 12 percent of the vote and was the second-largest party in the Sejm. With this political makeup, it would be difficult to consolidate a stable constitutional majority.[18] By the end of 1991, it was plain that the creation of an entirely new constitution would be a long and drawn-out process.

2. The 1992 Small Constitution

Background: Institutional Dilemmas after 1989

After the dissolution of the PZPR in January 1990, the Solidarity Union and two new political parties, the Center Alliance (*Porozumienie Centrum*, or PC) and the Liberal Democratic Congress (*Kongres Liberalno-Demokratyczny*, or KLD), led a successful movement to replace General Jaruzelski as president. Presidential elections were scheduled for the fall of 1990, and the institution of the presidency was fundamentally strengthened on 27 September 1990, by a constitutional amendment introducing direct popular election for the office (for the first time in Polish history), making the presidency autonomous vis-à-vis Parliament and giving the elected president an independent legitimacy.[19]

While Jaruzelski as president had been unobtrusive (he made no use of his right of legislative initiative and vetoed only one piece of legislation, concerning the sale of state land to foreigners), Lech Wałęsa had assumed he would be a strong activist president (he described himself as a "flying Dutchman" traveling around the country making the necessary repairs). But Wałęsa discovered soon after being elected that while presidential powers were formally rather broad, they did not provide ready tools with which to exert control over the nation's affairs. The sweeping powers implied by the constitution, particularly in the areas of foreign policy, defense, and national security, were not complemented by specific mechanisms necessary to exercise them in practice. The constitution also provided for defense policy making to be shared with the government, because the ministers of defense and foreign affairs had overlapping prerogatives. This cloudy articulation of practical executive powers suited President Wałęsa's opponents, who were anxious to limit what they saw as the president's unpredictability and thirst for power.[20]

An early indication of conflicts within the executive branch and between the executive and legislative branches was the controversy over the president's staff. Soon after he was elected, Wałęsa proposed a new 200-member political council (*Rada Polityczna*) attached to his office to function, as he envisioned it, as a consultative body to ensure continuation of the government's economic reform program. The Sejm leadership expressed fears that the proposed council would become a "super-government" or a "super-Parliament" and encroach upon the constitutional authority of the prime minister. The issue did not become an immediate point of contention because Wałęsa eventually agreed to create a smaller presidential advisory committee. However, it did serve as a harbinger of questions to come concerning the powers of the president, the prime minister, and the Sejm.[21]

The need for a new constitutional framework became even more pressing in the fall of 1991. After the fully free October parliamentary elections had created a Parliament with legitimacy equal to that of the president, the formation of a government coalition over Wałęsa's objections became possible, and the potential for open conflict within the executive branch emerged. Considering that the amended 1952 constitution did not provide any guidance for executive branch cooperation, a working relationship between president and prime minister was the sine qua non for effective government. The selection of a new government after the 1991 parliamentary election became symbolic of the growing conflict between president and prime minister over their respective prerogatives.

President Wałęsa's initial selection on 8 November 1991 of Bronisław Geremek, as his candidate for prime minister, was rejected by center-right parties in Parliament. In November and December 1991, using his constitutional prerogative to nominate the prime minister, Wałęsa delayed for weeks the nomination of Jan Olszewski (PC), despite Olszewski's ability to consolidate the backing of a minority center-right parliamentary coalition. In late December 1991, Wałęsa finally yielded and nominated Olszewski, but he still described the new government as "inappropriate for the country's needs."[22] As personal animosity between

Prime Minister Olszewski and President Wałęsa grew, the lack of a precise constitutional division of power proved destabilizing.

The Olszewski government responded by attempting to end Wałęsa's role as coordinator of security and defense policy. When the president continued to maintain contact with high-ranking officers, Defense Minister Jan Parys accused him of an unconstitutional attempt to subvert control over defense policy making. On 6 April 1992, Parys charged in a speech to the General Staff (broadcast over television) that the army was being used by "certain politicians" to bring down democracy in Poland.[23] Parys alleged that high-ranking army officers had been approached by the president's advisers with a promise of promotions if they joined the conspiracy.

Wałęsa denied the allegations and countercharged that, as the constitutionally designated commander-in-chief of the armed forces, it was natural for him to have frequent contact with the military. The confrontation quickly escalated to symbolize the extent of presidential prerogative versus powers of government, with the authority to control the armed forces, including key personnel decisions, at stake. By the time the Olszewski government was ousted in June 1992, feuding between the government and the president over control of defense policy had brought executive branch operations virtually to a halt.

Drafting and Promulgation of the Small Constitution

While the fragmentation of political alliances during this period complicated work on a new constitution, the need for a clear delineation of power between branches of government, and particularly within the executive branch, became greater. In early 1992, Parliamentary leaders decided to adopt a two-track approach to constitutional reform: (1) the National Assembly (both chambers of Parliament sitting together) would appoint a constitutional commission entrusted with the task of preparing the new, final constitution; (2) the Sejm alone would appoint a separate "extraordinary commission" to prepare an interim Small Constitution (an act having Polish precedents dating back to 1919 and 1947) through a series of amendments to the existing constitutional framework.

In February 1992, an extraordinary commission of the Sejm, under the chairmanship of former prime minister Mazowiecki, began to consider draft legislation for a Small Constitution that had been submitted by the Democratic Union, the largest party in Parliament at the time. The commission's work coincided with and was undoubtedly influenced by the various political crises that had resulted in the fall of the Olszewski government. In particular, the political gridlock that slowed the formation of a new government in late 1991 demonstrated the need to depart from traditional "parliamentary" mechanisms for nominations and dismissals.[24]

On 1 August 1992, less than a month after formation of a government based on a diverse yet solid coalition (ranging from the right-of-center ZChN to the UD) headed by Hanna Suchocka, a constitutional law scholar from the UD, the political parties in the Sejm, still shocked by the events leading to the fall of the Olszewski government, mustered a rare two thirds majority and approved the draft of the Small Constitution that had been submitted by the extraordinary commission in late July.[25] Although President Wałęsa initially claimed that the Small Constitution excessively limited presidential powers, on 17 November he signed the document into law.[26]

The goal of the Small Constitution was both to strengthen the executive branch and to delineate the respective powers of the government and the president in order to prevent a repetition of the conflicts that had erupted between President Wałęsa and former prime minister Olszewski. Although ill will and political ambition also fueled this antagonism, much blame for the conflicts within the executive branch rested with the ambiguities that surrounded the role of the president in the amended 1952 constitution. The framework of government established by the Small Constitution finds its basic model in the German constitution of 1949, although it gives more power to the president than does the German basic law.

From the standpoint of constitutional law, the Small Constitution represents a compromise between presidential and parliamentary systems of government. However, as the drafters wanted to remedy the political paralysis that emerged from the conflicts within Poland's political elite, political practice as well as constitutional theory shaped the terms of the document, with the persona of President Wałęsa being an important point of reference for the document's authors.

"Rationalized Parliamentarism" and the Small Constitution

The Small Constitution is not a complete constitution. It does not address human rights, nor does it establish new instruments to protect them. The 1952 constitution's chapter on rights and the chapter on the Constitutional Tribunal promulgated in 1982 remain in force. The Small Constitution also preserves the basic framework of constitutional structures established by the post-1989 April and December amendments. While the Small Constitution recognizes significant roles for the president, the Parliament, and the government, it attempts to provide a new formula for productive cooperation among the three top state authorities by introducing the concept of "rationalized parliamentarism" into the political structure.

Rationalized parliamentarism has the principle of rewards and punishments as its fundamental underpinning: The Sejm is able to exercise important constitutional powers only if there exists a strong and stable legislative majority. As long as such a majority exists, the Sejm is able to dominate the process of government and the executive branch's ability effectively to challenge parliamentary decisions is restricted. But if no such majority exists, the Sejm's powers are constricted, and other state organs have the opportunity to impose their will on Parliament. The aim of rationalized parliamentarism is to inhibit negative majorities (parliamentary coalitions created only to dismiss a sitting government) as well as the fragmentation of Parliament into many small groups.

Consider, for example, the procedure for forming a new government. The new procedure reinforces the interdependence of the president and Parliament while limiting the possibility that Poland will be without a government for long periods of time. Under the April amendments, the president had the exclusive right to nominate the prime minister, and the Sejm was responsible for voting the nominee into office. Such a division of responsibility led to conflict when the Sejm objected to a nominee preferred by the president (for example, the nomination of Bronisław Geremek in 1991) or when the president objected to a nominee preferred by a Sejm coalition (for example, Wałęsa's reluctance to nominate Jan Olszewski in 1991). The new procedure shifts the burden of choosing a prime minister back and forth between the president and the Sejm.[27] The president is given the first opportunity to name a prime minister, but his nominee's cabinet must receive a vote of confidence by an absolute majority of the Sejm within 14 days. If such a vote is not forthcoming, the responsibility to form a government and choose a prime minister shifts entirely to the Sejm, which may choose its own candidate by absolute majority vote. If the Sejm is successful, the president must accept the prime minister chosen by the Sejm. The president and the Sejm have four alternating chances to nominate. In case of deadlock, the president may either appoint an interim government for a six-month period or dissolve the Parliament and call new elections.

Rationalized parliamentarism is also seen in the new process by which a sitting government can be dismissed. Previously, both the prime minister and ministers could be dismissed by a simple resolution of the Sejm. Now a motion for dismissal must be signed by at least 46 members of the Sejm (10 percent of the chamber), and it must be adopted by an absolute majority of the Sejm. If rejected, the motion may not be resubmitted within three months unless it is signed by at least 115 members of the Sejm (25 percent of the chamber). The Small Constitution also establishes two versions of the no-confidence vote: (1) a "simple" vote of no confidence, which occurs when the Sejm (with an absolute majority of its members present) requires the dismissal of a sitting government; and (2) a "constructive" vote of no confidence, which occurs when the Sejm simultaneously dismisses a sitting government and nominates a new prime minister.[28] Only the latter is binding for the president, who must accept the designated prime minister. In the case of a simple no-confidence vote, the president may choose between dismissing the government and dissolving the Sejm. (In May 1993, President Wałęsa chose the latter alternative.) With these new procedures, the government remains politically responsible to a united Sejm, but it is less vulnerable to volatile parliamentary behavior; the constructive vote of no-confidence, in particular, makes the government less dependent on the purely negative powers of the Sejm.

The Small Constitution also granted the government the right to obtain from Parliament the power to issue decrees having the force of law. The notion of special powers had been advanced as early as 1989, when the first post-communist government was developing its program of "shock therapy" designed to put Poland on the road to a market economy. The Small Constitution authorizes the Sejm to vest the government with the power to issue decrees. In granting such powers, the Sejm must decide which areas of legislation will be the subject of special powers and how long the government's power will be in effect. Important areas may not be the subject of special powers; these include personal freedoms, political rights, the budget, social security and labor benefits (an obvious concession to social democratic traditions), international agreements, and changes in the constitution.[29] The purpose of special powers was to prevent legislative deadlock from hampering the public policymaking process, especially in the area of economic reform.

In most respects, the president's place in Poland's political and governmental arrangements remains much as it was before the adoption of the Small Constitution. But presidential prerogatives are defined more specifically in the new document. The Small Constitution explicitly confers primacy in foreign and defense policy upon the president and guarantees the president's status as commander-in-chief of the armed forces.[30] The president continues to be popularly elected for a five-year term and continues to have the power (shared with others) to propose legislation, the power to veto legislation (subject to the Sejm's power to override by a two-thirds vote), and the right to ask the Constitutional Tribunal's ruling on the constitutionality of legislation.[31] The presidential dissolution power is another important check on Parliament, but the president may dissolve the

Sejm only in certain constitutionally enumerated circumstances, including the failure of the Sejm to adopt the state budget within three months, the failure of the Sejm to form a government, or a vote of no-confidence by the Sejm in a sitting government without simultaneously nominating a new prime minister. Thus, in practical terms, only a weak or fragmented Parliament that fails to fulfill its constitutional duties faces dissolution.

In this new balance of power, the notion of rewards and punishments functions as the theoretical underpinning for almost all of the processes and procedures established in the Small Constitution. As long as the Sejm is able to muster an absolute majority, it has broad powers to replace a sitting government with a new one, and the president must comply with Parliament's decision. As the continued existence of the government in this context depends on continued parliamentary support, it must conduct policy making in a way acceptable to the Sejm majority, even over the president's objections. Further, the government has important controls over the president, as its members may refuse to countersign presidential acts. However, if the Sejm is too fragmented to form an absolute majority, its powers are much more constricted. The president is able to form his own government, the government countersignature does not have political importance, and no-confidence votes allow the president to dissolve Parliament, leaving the country with the president and "his" government.[32]

The Small Constitution is a compromise document firmly rooted in the Polish political realities of the early 1990s. *Gazeta Wyborcza* commentator Dawid Warszawski observed sardonically that "other democratic constitutions in history were generally the result of a compromise between what is and a vision of what, in the opinion of various political forces, should be. Poland's Small Constitution is a compromise between what is and what is."[33] Warszawski went on to argue, however, that the Small Constitution is a positive development if viewed in the proper perspective, "as a giant rule book for solving conflicts."

Importantly, the passage of the Small Constitution confirmed the return to political balance and a spirit of cooperation demonstrated in the formation of Prime Minister Hanna Suchocka's seven-party government in July 1992. From the start, Suchocka emphasized the need for the government to cooperate with President Wałęsa to reinvigorate the public policymaking process; during its existence it achieved an impressive array of policy successes, including the passage of an austerity budget in keeping with the nation's economic reform program and the passage of the mass privatization program in the spring of 1993. The Sejm's activity, despite its political fragmentation, was also impressive. Between August 1992 and May 1993, it passed 62 laws, including vital taxation and banking measures. These and other successes demonstrated the viability of the new institutional arrangements.

After the parliamentary elections of 1993, resulting in a victory for the postcommunist SLD-PSL coalition, the Small Constitution provided the institutional basis for a cooperative relationship between the president and the government and the president and Parliament, an impressive achievement considering that these institutions were occupied by politicians from opposite sides of the political spectrum. Between the beginning of 1993 and the end of 1994, Poland had three governments, two of which were antipodal ideologically with the president. But throughout this period both the new and the (relatively) old holders of power maintained their commitment to the principle of the rule of law and carefully followed constitutional procedures. As Wiktor Osiatyński wrote, "The clever compromise of the Small Constitution constitutes one of the greatest successes of the Polish democracy. This is proof that compromise, despite the representation of interests, can be reached."[34]

Toward a New, "Final" Constitution

Following the promulgation of the Small Constitution, work continued in the Parliament's constitutional commission to prepare a final constitution. However, it soon became obvious that a consensual vision of the political structures in the final arrangement would be difficult to achieve. In particular, agreement required overcoming fundamental substantive and ideological differences regarding three constitutional choices.

First, the political elite was divided over whether the Polish polity should have a presidential or parliamentary system. Those favoring a presidential system, especially Wałęsa while president, argued that it was needed during the present period of national renewal to formulate coherent public policy (particularly in the area of economic reform) and to supervise its execution. But the parliamentary leadership insisted that Parliament, as the most direct representative of the people, should be the supreme organ of government and determine the policy of the nation. A public opinion poll in 1993 revealed that 68 percent of Poles felt that Parliament should have "the most influence over affairs of state."[35]

This debate did not subside with the election of President Kwaśniewski in November 1995. During a 21 May 1996 meeting of the constitutional commission, the president's representative proposed increasing the scope of presidential authority over external and internal state security. The proposal was criticized by members of the opposition, who noted that when Kwaśniewski was chairman of the commission and Lech Wałęsa was president, the former had vehemently opposed shifting the center of state security decision making from the council of ministers to the president. In June 1996, the commission rejected Kwaśniewski's proposal.

Second, while it would seem that the practice of judicial review obviates the question of whether to include positive rights in constitutional text, the drafters faced strong political pressures to include a number of provisions not readily judicially enforceable. With rising unemployment and decreasing social security, a growing segment of society demanded constitutional guarantees of social policies. According to a 1993 public opinion poll, 63 percent of Poles felt that the constitution should provide for positive rights and, in particular, for at least some form of commitment to full employment.[36] Many jurists and scholars, however, believe that a constitution must be very sparing in guaranteeing positive socioeconomic rights, as it would be difficult for a court to ensure that the government observes rights of this kind without taking on the role of a super-legislature (reallocating resources and reshuffling governmental priorities to a degree that healthy democratic systems ordinarily reserve for the legislature and executive). At the same time, it was not certain whether the new constitution would have popular support without specifying social and economic rights; leaving them out could be interpreted as a betrayal by the political elite.

Third, with the collapse of communism, the Catholic Church has re gained a strong voice in political life and has achieved several legislative successes in the areas of abortion and the teaching of religion in public schools. What some see as a legitimate return to the supremacy of "Christian values" after decades of external repression, others perceive as evidence of an impending theocracy and a trampling of minority rights. All of the draft constitutions submitted to the constitutional commission, except that of the SLD, proposed either an "autonomous" (as opposed to *separate*) relationship between church and state, thus presuming at least some symbiosis in public policy making, or for future state relations with the church to be governed by the Concordat, a yet-to-be-ratified treaty between the Polish government and the Vatican that provides for a closer "cooperative relationship" between state and church.[37] Only the SLD draft called for a definitive separation of church and state. But with President Kwaśniewski's election, giving the SLD primacy in both the executive and legislative branches, reconciling the differing positions between political elites on the substance of the new constitution seemed unlikely, and the church and right-wing politicians promised to campaign against the new constitution in the national referendum if a draft were presented that was inconsistent with their positions.

Considering that the passage of a new constitution was the dominant political motivation of Solidarity leaders from the moment of the collapse of communist power, at first glance it may seem surprising that an entirely new comprehensive framework was not quickly enshrined by the new political leadership. But as debate over the nature of the state continued, the "hybrid" constitutional framework created by the April and December amendments and by the Small Constitution provided the groundwork for a modern Polish polity as well as institutional stability during a period of extraordinary politics. Moreover, this hybrid framework has been reinforced by the activist jurisprudence of the Constitutional Tribunal, which has developed constitutional doctrine and principles to complement the existing arrangements.

On 18 June 1996, the constitutional commission finally completed its draft constitution, adopting the final article that defines constitutional amending procedures. The entire project had taken eight years, and the draft proceeded to Parliament for consideration in the fall of 1996. Marek Markiewicz (SLD), who had replaced Aleksander Kwaśniewski as commission chairman in 1995, accelerated deliberations after President Kwaśniewski met with the commission in May 1996 (on the 205th anniversary of the 3 May 1791 constitution) and stressed the need to finish constitutional work because "it is a year free from election campaigns."[38] The draft contained 218 articles.[39]

The draft would establish a strong parliamentary system of government. The constitution states explicitly in Article 79 that "[t]he Sejm exercises control over the activities of the Council of Ministers and the Government." The procedure for appointing a new prime minister is patterned on that provided by the Small Constitution, and according to Article 142, the Sejm may by a majority vote express no confidence in the government based on a motion of at least 46 deputies, with the motion naming a new candidate for prime minister. Legislative initiative belongs to Sejm deputies, the Senate, the president, and the Council of Ministers. According to Article 127, official acts of the president require the signature of the prime minister to be valid, who by signing "becomes answerable to the Sejm."

Parliament's enhanced institutional strength is also evident in the chapter addressing the controversial matter of public finance. The draft would give the Sejm control over levying taxes and determining the laws governing tax exemptions. Moreover, the president would not have the right to veto any budget passed by Parliament. But within two months of receiving the budget from the Sejm, the president may send it to the Constitutional Tribunal to rule on its constitutionality. By giving the Sejm the "power of the purse," its institutional strength vis-à-vis the other branches of government would be strengthened.

The new constitution contains several economic and positive rights. While there is no provision for the right to work, Article 53 provides that "every person has the right to choose his profession and place of work" and that it is the obligation of the state to promote employment. Article 54 guarantees the "right to safe and hygienic working conditions." Every person also has the right to a free education until the age of 18 and to free basic health care provided by the public health service. All Polish citizens have the right to government welfare in the event of work disability or upon reaching retirement age. This catalogue of social rights, however, is not as great as the left-wing parliamentary majority had called for.

The constitutional amendment procedure is relatively easy. Amendments can be proposed by the president, the Senate, or 92 deputies (one fifth) of the Sejm. Article 218 provides that a first reading of an amendment must take place within 30 days following its introduction in Parliament. Adoption of an amendment requires Sejm confirmation by a two-thirds majority of a quorum, followed by an absolute majority of a Senate quorum.

The draft represented a compromise reached among the parties elected to Parliament in 1993, certain strong social organizations, notably the Catholic Church, and nonparliamentary political parties. The preamble invokes God as the "source of truth, justice, goodness and beauty," but it caters to the agnostic sentiment of the postcommunists by recognizing that nonbelievers can draw those universal values from other sources. The church's demand that the charter recognizes natural law as superior to man-made, or "positive," law was rejected. But in a gesture to the church, the constitution does not legalize same-sex marriages and provides guarantees for religious instruction in schools.

Regarding Poland's communist past, the constitution reflects the sentiment of *Unia Wolności* (Freedom Union), the leading opposition party to the governing coalition, by stating that democracy returned to Poland only in 1989, after a long period during which the former communist regime violated "fundamental freedoms and human rights." It also enshrines market economy as the basis of the country's economic system but emphasizes the need for social welfare.

In June 1996, the draft proceeded to the editorial subcommittee of the commission for examination of the legal terminology of the draft. Debate over the more than 200 articles of the draft, as well as the preamble, continued through the end of that year.

Several of the commission's changes strengthened executive power. For example, upon a motion of the undersecretary of state in the presidential chancellery, Krzysztof Janik, the commission adopted a proposal that would allow the Sejm to override a presidential veto with a two-thirds majority. Although Article 18 of the Small Constitution required the same, the draft had initially provided that only a simple majority is required for a veto override.

The commission also adopted Article 19.3, which states that "the relationship between the state, churches, and religious organizations shall be based on the principle of respect for their autonomy and mutual independence of each in their respective field, as well as on the principle of cooperation for human well-being and the common benefit." The amendment left out the phrase stipulating that relations between state and church be based on "mutual autonomy." Poland's Cardinal Józef Glemp said that Catholics would accept this compromise solution and that it was time for Poland to take the historic step of passing a new national charter.

Article 24 was broadened by the commission to state that "the inherent and inalienable dignity of the person is the source of the freedoms and rights of all persons and citizens. Dignity shall be inviolable and the respect and protection thereof shall be the obligation of the public authorities." Article 26.2 states, "No one shall be discriminated against in political, social or economic life for any reason." The commission chose not to list the grounds on the basis of which people may be discriminated against and replaced the relevant article with a provision stating that "rights and liberties originate from the inalienable right of human dignity."

On 22 March 1997, the National Assembly voted in favor of the completed draft. Of the 460 Sejm deputies and 100 senators, 461 voted for the new basic law, 31 against, and five abstained. The following day, President Kwaśniewski was presented with the draft. Kwaśniewski had 60 days to offer to the National Assembly amendments on the draft, but he formally did so within two days.

President Kwaśniewski's amendments focused on limiting the criminal immunity of members of Parliament and called for a presidential prerogative in nominating members of the Supreme Court, the chief of the General Staff, and the commanders of the army, navy, and air force. On 2 April 1997, the National Assembly approved the draft by an overwhelming majority, accepting most of President Kwaśniewski's amendments, including the presidential right to nominate Supreme Court judges and military leaders. However, the assembly rejected limiting the criminal immunity of parliamentary deputies.

Commenting on the draft, former prime minister Tadeusz Mazowiecki said that the proposed charter is "perhaps not ideal, but not bad." He said that the intention of the drafters of the document was "to unite rather than divide Poles."[40]

During the campaign on ratification of the proposed constitution, opposition centered on several issues, including the Catholic Church's concern about the separation of church and state, conservative critics' opposition to Article 90's proviso allowing Poland to cede state authority to transnational organizations, and former president Lech Wałęsa's attack on the reduced power of the president. In May 1997, however, the voters approved the new constitution. With just under 43 percent of the voters turning out, 52.71 percent voted in favor of the proposed constitution, 45.89 percent against.[41]

The Confederation for an Independent Poland (KPN) lodged a protest with the Supreme Court challenging the validity of the referendum. In July, however, the court upheld the results of the referendum. On 16 July 1997, President Kwaśniewski put his signature to the new constitution. "I have signed the Constitution of free and democratic Poland," he said. "The state is thus gaining solid foundations, while the citizens are granted strong guarantees of civil rights and liberties."[42] The new constitution was thus scheduled to take effect on 16 October 1997, with the first meeting of the new Sejm to take place soon thereafter.[43]

3. Enforcing Constitutional Norms and the Rule of Law

In addition to the adoption of new constitutional provisions, central to the development of constitutionalism in Poland and to the success of the transition from communist constitutional practice to a culture of normative constitutionalism, has been the practice of judicial review. The rule of law requires that there be means by which to control the state's use of power, lest use become abuse. Constitutionalism can be a reality only if there are realistic expectations that the norms and principles laid down in the constitution will be respected. It is in this regard that the emergence of a constitutional tribunal takes on such significance.

In 1985, the communist regime created the Constitutional Tribunal because the democratic opposition had increased its pressure for some form of constitutional review of state action. But it was with mixed motives that the regime set up the tribunal: It wanted to create an institution that looked like a real constitutional court but which could be prevented from directly challenging the highest political authorities. Appearance was what counted, as it would be naïve to suppose that the managers of the one-party system, steeped in doctrines of Marxism and Leninism, would seek to bring authentic checks and balances into play. Consequently, the tribunal's practice of judicial review was curbed by limitations designed to ensure that it would not overstep politically acceptable limits. Individual citizens had no right to take a case to the tribunal; access was given only to certain state agencies (including ministries and parliamentary committees). But the most important limitation concerned the effect of a tribunal ruling. While the tribunal's decisions regarding the constitutionality of substatutory acts (such as administrative regulations) have binding effect, if the tribunal finds an act of Parliament to be in conflict with the constitution, that decision does not become final or binding; it simply obliges Parliament to reconsider the statute.

The tribunal was not very active in developing constitutional doctrine during the first three years of operation, but after 1989 its practice of judicial review blossomed. While the limitations on its power of judicial review remained, the tribunal began to instill normative characteristics into Polish constitutionalism by defining and protecting a new understanding of rights and the separation of powers.

The most obvious sign of the tribunal's new role was that it became more aggressive in its review of parliamentary statutes. While previously the tribunal had been reluctant to challenge the Sejm, in 1989 alone it found unconstitutional seven of the eight statutes it reviewed. This trend continued, and from 1990 through the first half of 1994, of 52 statutes the tribunal reviewed, 40 were found unconstitutional, a large percentage if compared to any European constitutional court or even to the U.S. Supreme Court's disposition of statutes. (See Table 7.1 for an overview of the ultimate disposition of tribunal cases between 1986–1994.)

But the most auspicious aspect of the tribunal's practice of judicial review is similar to what the German Constitutional Court has done since the 1970s—developing and protecting substantive rights on the basis of general constitutional clauses. The constitution's *Rechtsstaat* clause is a particularly important tool for the tribunal in this regard. As discussed in Part 1, a *Rechtsstaat* clause was added to the Polish constitution in 1989. The clause's general language ("Poland is a democratic state, ruled by law") was based on the German *Rechtsstaat* clause, and the tribunal has looked for guidance to existing German *Rechtsstaat* jurisprudence as it constitutionalizes norms and principles it sees as essential in a state of law.

This judicial activism became apparent in 1990, when the tribunal held that legislative enactments infringing upon the "principle of nonretroactivity of laws" violated Article 1 of the constitution. The case involved then-president Jaruzelski's challenge to a new pension law that had reduced the pensions of former high-ranking communist officials.[44] While the tribunal found the law to conform with the constitution, it emphasized that the "nonretroactivity of law is one of the basic components of the *Rechtsstaat,* and thus has Constitutional rank."[45]

Since that decision, the tribunal has constitutionalized other due process guarantees on the basis of the *Rechtsstaat.* These include (1) judicial review of service-related dismissals of border guards,[46] (2) judicial review of a

Table 7.1 Review of Laws by the Constitutional Tribunal

Statutes	1986	1987	1988	1989	1990	1991	1992	1993	1994	Total
Unconstitutional	0	0	1	7	3	3	10	20	4	48
Constitutional	1	1	0	1	3	1	3	1	4	15
Review	0	0	0	0	4	1	2	4	1	12
Totals	1	1	1	8	10	5	15	25	9	75
Substat. Acts										
Contrary to	4	2	6	6	2	4	5	5	1	35
Conforming with	0	0	1	0	1	2	0	3	1	8
Review Discon.	1	3	12	11	9	4	6	4	0	50
Totals	5	5	19	17	12	10	11	12	2	93

Note: Between 1986 and July 1994, the tribunal reviewed 168 legal acts, including 75 parliamentary statutes and 93 substatutcry regulations.
Source: Calculated on the basis of *Reports of the Court* (*Orzecznictwo Trybunału Konstytucyjnego*).

government denial of subsidized public transportation for people in need,[47] and (3) judicial review of alien deportations.[48]

Another area where the tribunal has been willing to develop normative principles from the limited language of the constitution is equal protection. The constitution's equal protection clause (Article 68) states that "equal rights [are guaranteed] irrespective of sex, education, nationality, race and religion." This provision is one of the most oft cited in the tribunal's case law, providing a basis for more than 50 decisions.

In developing its equal protection jurisprudence, the tribunal first held that the list of forbidden classifications enumerated in the equal protection clause (sex, race, religion, etc.) is not exhaustive and that equality should be enforced wherever "the rights of individuals belonging to the same category are impacted."[49] Accordingly, the tribunal has found unconstitutional laws differentiating pension privileges according to whether employment occurred before 1945 or after 1945 (or in communist Poland),[50] and classifications imposing regionally disparate tax burdens.[51] In the latter case, the tribunal found a statute imposing an additional sales tax in "tourist regions" unconstitutional. That tax discriminated unfairly between classes equal before the law (citizens of different regions) because it applied not only to tourists but also to all inhabitants of the region, while the inhabitants of other regions were not so taxed.

In its case law, however, the tribunal has not found the principle of equality to be absolute and has permitted differential treatment of otherwise similarly situated individuals, if it found a compelling social interest or human right to do so. In gender discrimination cases, the Tribunal has even *required* differential treatment to ensure "equality in the law."

For example, in a 1989 case, the tribunal found unconstitutional a law permitting male and female miners to retire with full pension only after having worked at least 25 years.[52] Previous statutes had distinguished between men and women, establishing a lower, 20-year minimum for female miners. The tribunal held that for the purposes of equal protection, a mechanically equal application of the laws would not always be sufficient. It wrote that female miners should be allowed to retire at an earlier age because the physical and biological differences between the sexes amount to "objective" and "fair" criteria justifying differential treatment.[53]

But in a subsequent gender discrimination case, the tribunal held that when physical differences between men and women do not justify unequal treatment, both genders should be treated alike. In 1991, the tribunal invalidated a provision of the 1990 Universities Act, which had required retirement at the age of 60 for female instructors and 65 for male instructors.[54] In its decision, the tribunal emphasized that the law could not make an earlier retirement age an obligation where "biological and physical differences" between the genders are irrelevant.[55]

The tribunal's equality jurisprudence has become an effective tool for evaluating the fairness and reasonableness of legislative classifications, and the tribunal has applied the constitution's equal protection clause to strike down an impressive variety of measures, ensuring that the state observes fundamental human rights standards. As in its *Rechtsstaat* jurisprudence, the tribunal has been willing to develop normative principles on the basis of the general language of the constitution. Particularly now in Poland, where the rights provisions of the 1952 Constitution remain in force, the tribunal's activist jurisprudence responds to the necessities of the postcommunist transition, defining the bounds of law-making in an area untouched by constitutional reform.

While the tribunal has played a central role in forging postcommunist constitutionalism, its power of judicial review remains constrained by communist-era legislation.[56] The new president of the tribunal, Andrzej Zoll, commented that "[l]aw must be superior to politics; any other way would be inconsistent with a state ruled by law."[57] Until the tribunal's decisions have the force of finality, the tribunal will not be fully immune to political pressures that accompany controversial cases, and it will not serve as an absolute check on the other branches of government.

Conclusion: From a Constitution to Constitutionalism

Americans sometimes speak of a "constitutional moment"—the era that produced the Federal Constitution and Bill of Rights. Reinforced by such metaphors as Catherine Drinker Bowen's *Miracle at Philadelphia,* this notion of the constitutional moment obscures the fact that the founding period of American constitutionalism was one of trial and error. The state constitutions drafted beginning in 1776 were often quite flawed documents, and the Articles of Confederation (1781) soon proved inadequate to the purposes of the emerging nation.

By the same token, Poland has embarked on a process of trial and error in the development of constitutionalism. First, the 1989–1990 constitutional amendments provided a basis for further evolution of the polity by eliminating the essential features of the communist system and by taking steps to transform the 1952 constitution into a liberal democratic one, with legislative and executive powers checked and with the judicial branch provided genuine independence. While the passage of an entirely new constitution proved politically impossible between 1990–1991, the April and December amendments provided a set of democratic institutions that, for the first time since before World War II, brought political relationships back within the framework of the state.

Second, the adoption of the Small Constitution in November 1992 both clarified and institutionalized a presidential-parliamentary system of government and provided specific solutions to institutional dilemmas that had emerged during the first two years of postcommunist governance. The Small Constitution was clearly a compromise between President Wałęsa's desire for a strong presidency and the Sejm leadership's desire for a classical parliamentary democracy; as such, it defined the division of power between legislative and executive branches of government while recognizing the presidency's special role, which had become apparent after the 1991 parliamentary elections. The document also reflected growing awareness that the government had to be strengthened and made less susceptible to shifting parliamentary majorities if the country was to continue on the path to democracy and a successful market economy. Although the Small Constitution failed to modernize the chapter on individual rights, it went far in addressing popular fears following the "war at the top" in the spring of 1992 that the country could become ungovernable.

Third, in addition to the promulgation of new constitutional provisions, central to the development of constitutionalism in Poland has been the innovative judicial decision and precedent of the Constitutional Tribunal. Since 1989, the Tribunal's activist judicial review has been crucial in forging postcommunist constitutionalism, strengthening Polish constitutional arrangements by surrounding them with binding legal doctrine. Despite significant limitations on its jurisdiction and scope of review, the tribunal has created a normative constitutional jurisprudence characteristic of liberal democracies; it has interpreted the new *Rechtsstaat* clause, a very general, open-ended constitutional provision, to protect additional substantive rights, a practice common in countries with well-established doctrines of judicial review. In addition, decisions interpreting the equal protection clause reflect the tribunal's willingness to develop and uphold general concepts of equality from the basic language of the constitution. Particularly in Poland, where the 1952 constitution's chapter on individual rights remains in force, the activist jurisprudence of the tribunal has responded to the necessities of the postcommunist transition, establishing principled parameters of government action in areas otherwise untouched by constitutional reform.

Completion of a new "final" constitution had been stymied by ideological and substantive differences over constitutional choices; however, the April and December amendments, the Small Constitution, and the tribunal's constitutional jurisprudence provided the fundamental groundwork for a modern Polish polity based on notions of limited government and reflective of European constitutional norms. This framework had proven strong and enduring through an era of extraordinary politics. Since 1989, six governments had stood and fallen according to constitutional rules following free and fair elections. Nothing could have been more volatile than Poland's political cohabitation of the 1993–1995 period, in which the leader of the former opposition movement shared power with a government consisting of former communists and a Parliament dominated by a postcommunist majority. While conflicts over the nature of the postcommunist state are by no means settled, the groundwork for constitutional governance has been laid, experience accumulated, and an impressive measure of institutional stability achieved.

Notes

1. W. Sokolewicz, "Democracy, Rule of Law, and Constitutionality," *Droit Polonais Contemporain* 2 (1990): 5–6.
2. S. Finer, V. Bogdanor, and B. Rudden, eds., *Comparing Constitutions* (Oxford: Clarendon Press, 1995), 1.
3. For example, Bronisław Geremek, one of the opposition negotiators, rejected a proposal for completely free Sejm elections on the grounds that it was too radical for the Soviets. W. Osiatyński, "The Round Table Negotiations in Poland," Working Paper No. 1, Center for the Study of Constitutionalism in Eastern Europe, University of Chicago Law School, 1991, 34.
4. "Ustawa z dnia 11 kwietnia 1989 r.," *Dziennik Ustaw,* no. 37, item 41 (1989).
5. Two senators were to be chosen by the first-past-the-post system in each of the national voivodships. W. Sokolewicz, "Kwietniowa zmiana konstytucji," *Państwo i Prawo* 44 (1989): 3.
6. Z. Sarnecki, "Założenia konstytucji," *Państwo i Prawo* 45 (1990): 5. The president was also empowered to submit legislation to the Constitutional Tribunal for constitutional review.
7. W. Salmonowicz, ed., *Porozumienia Okrągłego Stołu* (Olsztyn: NSZZ Solidarność, 1989), 5.
8. "Amended Constitution of the Republic of Poland," in A. Blaustein and G. Flanz, eds., *Constitutions of the Countries of the World* (New York: Oceana, 1991), Article 60.
9. Several Solidarity senators and deputies had to abstain from voting in order to offset ZSL and SD defections (Z. Pełczyński and S. Kowalski, "Poland," *Electoral Studies* 9 [1990], 351).
10. For the December amendments, see "Ustawa z dnia 29 grudnia 1989 r. o zmianie konstytucji Polskiej Rzeczypospolitej Ludowej," *Dziennik Ustaw,* no. 75, item 444 (1989).
11. W. Sokolewicz, "Rzeczypospolita Polska: Demokratyczne państwo prawne—uwagi na tle ustawy z 29 XII 1989 o zmianie konstytucji," *Państwo i Prawo* 45 (1990): 17.

12. A. Rapaczyński, "Constitutional Politics in Poland: A Report of the Constitutional Committee of the Polish Parliament," 58 *University of Chicago Law Review* 604 (1991).

13. "Sejm Debates Changes," Warsaw PAP, Foreign Broadcast Information Service, Daily *Report: Eastern Europe,* 2 January 1990, 46.

14. J. Majchrowski and P. Winczorek, *La Pologne dans le processus des changements constitutionnels, 1989–1991* (Louvain: Institute de recherches de l'Europe centrale, 1992), 6–7.

15. P. Winczorek, "Pisanie Konstytucji," *Rzeczpospolita,* 16 January 1994, 3.

16. For both constitutional drafts, see M. Kallas, ed., *Projekty Konstytucyjne 1989–1991* (Warsaw: Wydawnictwo Sejmowe, 1992).

17. Majchrowski and Winczorek, *La Pologne dans le processus,* 9.

18. By 1991, some 200 political groups claimed the status of political party. K. Grzybowski, "The Transition of the Polish Party System," in S. Berglund and J. Dellenbrant, eds., *The New Democracies in Eastern Europe* (Aldershot, Eng.: Edward Elgar, 1991), 40.

19. "Ustawa z dnia 27 września 1990 r.," *Dziennik Ustaw,* no. 38, item 73 (1990).

20. W. Osiatyński, "Skazani na oryginalno," *Gazeta Wyborcza,* 29 August 1992, 8.

21. W. Beres and K. Burnetko, *Gliniarz z 'Tygodnika': Rozmowy z byłym ministrem spraw wewnętrznych Krzysztofem Kozłowskim* (Warsaw: BGW, 1991), 110. For a discussion of the conflicts within the executive branch prior to the passage of the Small Constitution, see Frances Millard, *The Anatomy of the New Poland: Post-Communist Politics in its First Phase* (Aldershot, Eng.: Edward Elgar, 1993), chapter 5.

22. J. Rogulski, "Poparcie dla Jana Olszewskiego," *Rzeczpospolita,* 18 December 1991, 1. Wałęsa's concerns centered on Olszewski's criticism of Poland's economic austerity program.

23. W. Fikus, "Incydent wojskowy," *Rzeczpospolita,* 9 April 1992, 1.

24. M. Kruk, *Mała Konstytucja w procesie przemian ustrojowych w Polsce* (Warsaw: Wydawnictwo Sejmowe, 1993), 35–39.

25. "Mała Konstytucja uchwalona," *Gazeta Wyborcza,* 3 August 1992, 1. The Small Constitution was supported by the seven coalition parties plus the communist successor parties, the SLD and the PSL.

26. "Ustawa Konstytucyjna z dnia 17 października 1992 r . . . ," *Dziennik Ustaw,* no. 84, item 426 (1992).

27. Ibid., Articles 57–62.

28. Note that the constructive vote of no confidence hails from German constitutional theory, particularly that of C. J. Friedrich, as applied in the German basic law of 1949.

29. Ibid., Article 23. The decree power has not yet been granted to a government.

30. Ibid., Articles 33–36.

31. Ibid., Articles 28–31.

32. P. Winczorek, "Wartości naczelne Małej Konstytucji," *Państwo i Prawo,* 48 (1993): 3.

33. Warszawski, "Regulamin," *Gazeta Wyborcza,* 4 August 1992, 5.

34. Osiatyński, "Skazani na oryginalność," 8.
35. "Raport z badania 'oceny...,'" Centrum Badania Opinii Społecznej (CBOS), January 1993.
36. "Raport z badania opinii publicznej o projekcie Karty Praw i Wolności," Centrum Badania Opinii Społecznej (CBOS), March 1993.
37. To have force, the concordat must be ratified by the Sejm and signed by the president. In July 1994, Parliament resolved to postpone ratification until after the passage of a new constitution.
38. "Projekt Konstytucji," Rzeczpospolita, 21 June 1996, 1.
39. For the text and provisions of the 1996 draft constitution, see "Projekt Konstytucji z 19 czerwca 1996 r.," Rzeczpospolita, 21 June 1996, 16.
40. "Polish Parliament Passes New Constitution," RFE/RL Newsline, no. 4, pt. 2, 4 April 1997.
41. Washington Post, 27 May 1997, A-11, quoting PAP News Agency.
42. Polish News Bulletin, 17 July 1997.
43. Ibid.
44. "Ustawa z dnia 24 maja 1990 o zmianie niektórych przepisów o zaopatrzeniu emerytalnym," Dziennik Ustaw, no. 36, item 206 (1990).
45. Judgment K 7/90 of 22 August 1990, in Orzecznictwo Trybunału Konstytucyjnego 42 (1990). For a broader discussion of this decision and other Tribunal cases, see M. Brzezinski and L. Garlicki, "Judicial Review in Post-Communist Poland: The Emergence of a Rechtsstaat?" Stanford Journal of International Law 31. No. 13 (1995).
46. Judgment K 8/91 of 7 January 1992, (I) Orzecznictwo Trybunału Konstytucyjnego 76, 1992; henceforth, cited as OTK.
47. Judgment K 17/92 of 7 September 1992, (II), OTK, 133, 1992.
48. Judgment K 1/92 of 3 March 1992, (I), OTK, 29, 1992.
49. Judgment Kw 1/89 of 9 May 1989, OTK 43, 1989, p. 59.
50. Judgment K 1/91 of 28 May 1991, OTK 81, 1991, p. 94.
51. Judgment K 3/89 of 26 September 1989, OTK 84, 1989.
52. Judgment K 6/89 of 24 October 1989, OTK 100, 1989.
53. Ibid., at p. 108.
54. Judgment Kw 5/91 of 24 September 1991, OTK 96, 1991.
55. Ibid., at p. 103.
56. It is remarkable that after more than 100 tribunal decisions declaring parliamentary statutes unconstitutional, the Sejm has overruled the tribunal only five times. Each of these "resurrected" statutes concerned national budget and taxation issues.
57. "O prymacie prawa nad polityką," Rzeczpospolita, 12 April 1994, 5. For a larger study on the development of constitutionalism in Poland, see M. Brzezinski, Law vs. Power: The Struggle for Constitutionalism in Poland (London: Macmillan, 1997).

EIGHT

Macroeconomic Policy during Accession to EU

Nissan Liviatan and Daniel Oks*

The European Union (EU) is likely to focus more on the set of economic reforms that will enhance Poland's prospects for fast and sustained growth than on the strict and premature adoption of Economic and Monetary Union (EMU) convergence criteria (e.g., inflation and interest rate levels), agreed upon at Maastricht. A strong economy will be better prepared to absorb shocks and adhere sustainably to the EMU criteria, while at the same time minimizing the potential budgetary cost of accession to the EU (e.g., social adjustment costs).

Poland has been extremely successful in recovering from the initial posttransformation recession; the economy has entered its sixth consecutive year of economic growth, with inflation declining gradually but persistently to under 20 percent in 1996. However, fast and sustained growth depends on acceleration of reforms, without which investment and continuation of a vigorous supply response could be hampered. Foreign direct investment flows are a core element of the growth strategy; advancing the process of reform is also crucial to attract these flows. However, the key necessary condition of the overall growth and investment strategy is macroeconomic stabilization, which Poland must still consolidate; without it, the uncertainty risk premiums requested by investors will require much higher rates of return and thus much lower rates of investment

---

* Daniel Oks is a regular staff member at the World Bank. However, the ideas expressed in this chapter in no way reflect the views or position of the World Bank on the issues discussed.

than Poland needs to catch up with the EU (at least to reach 75 percent of average EU per capita income—the EU threshold to define a poor region) over the next 20 years.

Fiscal reforms are at the core of any stabilization strategy and, in particular, for meeting the EU requirement (set at the 1993 Copenhagen summit of the European Council) that applicant countries adhere to the aims of the EMU—EMU membership is not a requirement for EU membership. The key distinction between EMU membership and adhering to the aims of the EMU is that in the latter case the country should target the objectives of the EMU (price, interest rate, and exchange rate stability) with a longer horizon to actually fulfill them. Poland should take advantage of this important break to consolidate its reforms and avoid the risk of sacrificing its growth potential by pursuing very tight monetary policies.

The proposed strategy is broadly consistent with the government stabilization plan; the government envisages a gradual reduction of inflation as a result of the process of fiscal and structural reforms that leads, in turn, to sustainable, productivity-driven growth. The biggest risk of the plan is that of entrenchment of inflation at any single inflation step. Consistency of this strategy requires a tighter fiscal policy than currently is planned. It also requires addressing institutional weaknesses (strengthening the independence of the National Bank of Poland [NBP], reducing automatic wage indexation mechanisms in the public sector). Public policy will also be called to play an important "countercyclical" role, e.g., by tightening fiscal and financial policies in the presence of an unsustainable consumption boom which, in turn, could be linked to a surge in capital inflows. The role of fiscal policy as a stabilizing instrument in any case will be heightened after Poland joins the EMU, since the latter implies abandoning domestic monetary policy as a stabilization tool.

Adhering to EMU Goals: Macroeconomic Challenges

Based on its performance, Poland's successful reform and stabilization strategy in the first half of the 1990s puts her in the forefront of candidates for EU accession; its economy has contracted less initially and grown faster than all other Visegrád countries thereafter (see Table 8.1).

Moreover, what adds to Poland's aspirations for EU membership, is that growth has been driven by supply-side reforms, particularly trade and financial liberalization, privatization, deregulation, elimination of most production subsidies, tax reform, and fiscal decentralization. The engine of the economic recovery was the young private sector, whose share of GDP has doubled to 63 percent over the last six years. Poland has

Table 8.1   Comparative Growth Performance in Visegrád Economies (in percentages)

	1990	1991	1992	1993	1994	1995	1996
Czech Republic	−1.2	−14.2	−6.4	−0.9	2.6	4.8	4.1
Hungary	−2.5	−7.1	−3.0	−0.8	2.9	1.9	1.0
Poland	−11.6	−7.0	2.6	3.8	5.2	7.0	6.2
Slovakia	−2.5	−14.5	−6.2	−4.1	4.8	7.4	6.9

Source: World Bank Database (BSD), 1997.

Figure 8.1   Poland, Consumer Prices

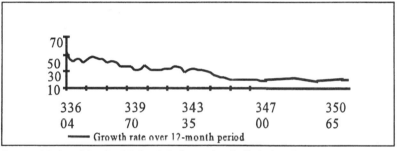

Source: National Bank of Poland, Information Bulletin (1997).

also managed its public finances responsibly: Overall tight fiscal (except in 1991–1992) and monetary policies had also contributed to gradual disinflation (see Table 8.2).

The key macroeconomic requirement for EU accession is adherence to the aims of the EMU (and possibly joining the yet-to-be reformed European Monetary System, or EMS). The current criteria for joining the EMU, often referred to as the Maastricht criteria, are the following: (1) consumer price index (CPI) inflation should not exceed the three best-performing countries in the EU (3–3.5 percent in 1996) by more than 1.5 percentage points; (2) interest rates on long-term government securities should not exceed the average of the foregoing economies by more than 2 percentage points; (3) the general government deficit should not exceed 3 percent of GDP; (4) gross debt of the general government should not exceed 60 percent of GDP, and the exchange rate must be held within the normal fluctuation range of the EMS for two years without a realignment. Although these are the criteria for joining the EMU and are not formally

Table 8.2 Basic Macroeconomic Indicators for Poland, 1990–1996 (in percentages)

	1990	1991	1992	1993	1994	1995	1996
GDP growth	–11.6	–7.0	2.6	3.8	5.2	7.0	6.2
Private sector growth	–3.8	26.7	14.9	9.6	1.6	18.3	15.6
Public sector growth	–14.7	–22.1	–6.3	–1.7	7.9	–15.8	–4.0
Private sector share of GDP	30.9	42.1	47.1	52.0	52.2	59.3	63.5
Inflation end of period	249.3	60.4	44.3	37.6	29.5	21.6	18.5
Fiscal balance share of GDP	3.7	–6.7	–6.7	–2.3	–2.2	–1.8	–2.8
Zloty, money growth	42.1	–8.1	11.2	–6.4	7.1	23.5	13.4
Real exchange rate growth based on CPI	–21.3	56.2	5.4	5.9	1.7	10.5	8.9
Real T-bill interest rates—13 weeks	——	–0.9	–1.0	–1.6	–2.6	–1.7	2.0

Source: National Bank of Poland, *Information Bulletin* (1997).

required for EU accession, being on the right track to meet them will weigh heavily in the decision regarding accession.

The ability to adhere to the EMU in the long run can be interpreted as a requirement to possess a macroeconomic structure that can support sustainable growth and price stability on a permanent basis. Ensuring the robustness of inflation convergence requires that the country must have a broad tax base and good control of public expenditures to ensure fiscal balance on a permanent basis. Since the EMU is likely to take the form of a common currency, it implies also that the budget should possess sufficient built-in flexibility to handle real shocks in a countercyclical fashion, since monetary policy will be unable to do it. A related formulation of the foregoing requirement would be that an applicant should have the capacity of maintaining the Maastricht criteria on a long-term basis and the ability to adhere to them under external shocks. Based on this interpretation, the government's objective should be to create stable conditions for reducing inflation permanently, rather than acting abruptly and possibly risking instability. In turn, this objective can be facilitated if the country has the fundamentals for sustained growth in place.

The main objectives of the government's plan, most recently described in "Strategy for Poland—Euro 2006," are precisely sustainable growth and gradual disinflation to meet the EMU criteria by that year.

Poland has been doing quite well according to the Maastricht criteria, except for inflation and the related interest and exchange rate requirements. The fiscal deficit was just below 3 percent of GDP (although it would exceed the limit if privatization revenues of 0.8 percent of GDP were excluded), and the government debt is below the 60 percent ceiling allowed by Maastricht (see Table 8.2). At the same time, inflation was much above the upper limit, at 18.6 percent in 1996, so that reduction of this rate is one of the major challenges of the medium-term strategy. In view of this relatively high rate of inflation, Poland would not meet either the interest or exchange rate conditions.

Poland has also been doing well on the dynamic side of convergence. However, substantial question marks remain. The fiscal deficit has been fairly stable (below 3 percent of GDP) during 1993–1996, and the public debt ratio has been declining sharply (below the 60 percent limit), mainly as a result of major foreign debt relief, strong real exchange rate appreciation, and fast growth. As will be shown in the next section, however, public finances are still vulnerable (particularly social security expenditures and the large number of enterprises that still belong to the state). Similarly, inflation, after falling rapidly in 1995 (from 37.6 to 21.6 percent), declined rather slowly in 1996.

In short, Poland's largest macroeconomic challenge is to consolidate the strong economic recovery into a path of sustainable growth and price stability to ensure a smooth convergence to the EMU.

Fast or Gradual Disinflation?

Poland has been successful in *gradually* but *persistently* bringing down inflation from close to hyperinflation levels in 1989–1990 to a relatively moderate level of 18.6 percent in 1996 (see Figure 8.1 on p. 165). Government plans are to continue along this path.

The main alternative is a more aggressive disinflation based on a persistent tightening of monetary policy—a tight monetary policy is required under both gradual and rapid disinflation scenarios. One obvious advantage of a rapid disinflation is that it could significantly reduce the macroeconomic country risk and thus have a strong impact on investment and growth. The potential trade-off of the latter strategy, however, is well illustrated by the Spanish experience. In the course of the disinflation process during the preaccession period of 1977–1985, when inflation was reduced from 25 to 9 percent, unemployment jumped from 3.5 in 1975 to a peak of 22 percent in 1985 (double the average of OECD Europe). The sacrifice ratio associated with disinflation was also among the highest in European experience of the 1980s, according to the OECD survey, *Spain 1991–1992*.[1] In the Spanish case, the disinflation strategy was based mainly on tight money, but we find similar recessionary effects in the disinflation process of Ireland during the 1980s, when the exchange rate was used as a nominal anchor.[2] In view of these and similar experiences in Europe, it appears that indeed disinflationary policies based on tight money or hard currency (supported by high real interest rates) have a recessionary potential over the medium run.

However, a gradual disinflation carries risks, too. In particular, a slow pace of disinflation entails a risk of entrenchment of inflation. As mentioned, the pace of disinflation became recently rather slow; a reduction of year-end inflation from 21.6 percent in 1995 to 18.6 percent in 1996 is hardly significant in view of the variance of inflation around an inflation step, as we know it from the experience of other countries. In the cases of Chile and Israel, inflation remained at a rate of about 20 percent for a surprisingly long time—eight years (1984–1991) in the case of Chile, and five years (1986–1991) in the case of Israel. In both cases, the authorities were unwilling to use aggressive stabilization policies after having reduced inflation from high levels.

The entrenchment of inflation could stem from (1) fiscal vulnerability due to (as is the case in Poland) poor tax compliance, pressures for social spending, loss-making state enterprises in the coal sector and some banks; (2) indexation mechanisms, such as those set by the Tripartite Commission (consisting of government, unions, and management), which often combine a forward-looking indexation scheme with ex-post adjustments; (3) the still-high *seigniorage* (around 3 percent of GDP), which could diminish the credibility of disinflation policies; and (4) a shallow financial sector (the M2 and M3 ratios for Poland in 1993 were 22 and 30 percent, respectively, less or about half the corresponding figures for the Czech Republic—66 and 72 percent—and for Hungary—50 and 58 percent), which implies that price shocks can easily fuel inflation (and slow disinflation can in turn slow down financial sector deepening).

The same factors that may hinder disinflation under the gradual disinflation scenario (factors 1–4) will also hinder disinflation under the fast disinflation scenario. In many ways, in fact, dealing with the above factors is more crucial for the success of rapid disinflation than the success of slow disinflation. For example, a persistently tight monetary policy could require as a consistency condition a tighter fiscal policy to minimize the resulting real appreciation of the exchange rate. A faster tightening of fiscal policy is also required to compensate for the loss of *seigniorage* under rapid disinflation. The real issue therefore is assessing how realistic it is to create conditions—over a short period—to tighten fiscal policy rapidly, eliminate indexation mechanisms, and promote the rapid deepening of the financial sector.

The political and social realities of Poland, characterized by expensive social entitlements, relatively high unemployment (13 percent), and unstable political alliances, suggest that pursuing a strategy of fast disinflation can be highly risky. In addition, the completion of Poland's structural reform agenda (in particular, social security, the coal and financial sectors) along with investment requirements associated with EU accession (in particular, approximating EU environmental standards) imply that attaining very low fiscal deficits during the preaccession period would be both unrealistic and undesirable, since many of the costly reforms can bring important long-term fiscal savings. Based on these considerations, a gradual disinflation strategy is more plausible.

There is yet another reason to wait until Poland pursues a policy of rapid disinflation. As EU (EMU) membership gets closer, Poland would be better prepared to benefit from EU (EMU) imported credibility. Based on the lessons from recent experiences of other countries that joined the EU, disinflation policies can be more effective (and less costly) when they are undertaken closer to the EU accession, where the latter requires low inflation as a precondition. In this stage, the disinflation policies may benefit from the EMU-imported credibility (see Box 1).

Box 1. Importing Credibility to Lower Inflation

It is sufficient to look at the experience of the Czech Republic, which succeeded in reducing inflation to single digits by standard macro stabilization (a fixed exchange rate regime backed fiscal tightness) to realize that, with enough credibility, traditional stabilization can be very effective; moreover, the rate of unemployment in the Czech Republic is much lower than in Poland. The more favorable tradeoff between disinflation and unemployment in the Czech Republic is attributable to sounder macroeconomic policies and to greater social cohesion than in Poland, both of which imparted credibility to disinflation policies.

Countries that were not yet in this favorable situation were still able to disinflate by importing credibility from a more stable economy, in the EMS fashion. A similar argument applies to participation in the EMU. That is, the more stringent disinflation steps, such as setting low inflation targets, can be postponed until the time of accession to the EMU, so that the stabilization measures have some measure of credibility.

Something may be learned about the significance of EMU-imported credibility from the experience of the EU in the nineties. Specifically, EU members made efforts to reduce inflation to meet the Maastricht requirements to demonstrate their ability to join the EMU. As in the case of accession of the Central and East European countries (CEECs), these policies were given a priority in view of the great benefits to be gained from further integration with the EU.

In the case of Greece and Portugal, the recognition that inflation will have to be brought down rather soon in the process of EMU accession created the necessary credibility to make the disinflationary exchange rate policies in these countries effective, even though the fiscal deficits and the public debt ratios were still

Box 1 continued on the next page

The Roles of Monetary and Exchange Rate Policy

Poland pursued an exchange-rate-based stabilization approach, the initial step of which was to fix the exchange rate in 1990; the fixed exchange rate regime was modified to a crawling peg in the following year. Flexi-

continued from previous page

high. In Portugal inflation fell gradually as of 1992, when the country joined the European Exchange Rate Mechanism and began to use the exchange rate as a disinflationary instrument (inflation dropped from nine in 1992 to 4 percent in 1995). This process took place with only little support from the fiscal side; while there was a small decline in the fiscal deficit, its level remained in excess of 5 percent of GDP, which is not different from its level ten years earlier, when inflation was 19 percent. The general government's debt ratio was also still high at 71 percent of GDP in 1995.

In the case of Greece, a similar process took place in a much more extreme form. A "hard drachma" policy was implemented in the nineties as a nominal anchor, and inflation dropped from 20 percent in 1991 to 9.3 percent in 1995. The policy received strong support from the fiscal side—the primary deficit and the overall deficit were cut by 10 and 7 percent of GDP, respectively, between 1990 and 1995. However, the level of the deficit was still very high in 1995 (9 percent of GDP), as was the public debt (112 percent of GDP).

The level of the fiscal fundamentals in both countries was clearly not sufficient to lend much support to a reduction in the basic inflationary expectations; presumably, the main reason for the progress in disinflation was the recognition that a quicker pace of disinflation is part of the accession to the EMU in the near future. (Both countries are heavy recipients of structural funds from the EC.) When viewed in this context, the partial steps taken in both countries to reduce fiscal imbalances were apparently taken as being part of a longer term and more fundamental fiscal balancing, which lent credibility to the stabilization effort.

The lesson from these experiences is that disinflation policies are more effective when they are undertaken closer to an EMU accession, where the latter requires low inflation as a precondition. Therefore, the main effort toward attaining low inflation in the CEECs should be postponed until accession is in sight.

---

bilization of the exchange rate regime took an additional step in 1995 with introduction of an exchange rate band of plus and minus 7 percent around the crawling midvalue. At the end of December 1995, the exchange rate band underwent a 6 percent step appreciation. The increased flexibility of the exchange rate was aimed at maintaining the exchange rate as a nominal anchor for price inflation while preventing excessive appreciation that could erode external competitiveness. The rate of crawl decreased over time along with inflation, with causality going probably both ways. The increased flexibility of the exchange rate regime since 1995 came along with heavier reliance on monetary policy as an instrument of disinflation.

Currently, the nominal system is based on the strategy of an inflation target set by the central bank. This strategy targets the supply of base money according to the inflation objective and adjusts the NBP's interest rates in a manner consistent with the target, mainly by open market operations. It also adjusts occasionally the parameters of the crawling band to maintain policy consistency. As in similar regimes in other countries (Israel) that implement multiple nominal anchors, the exchange rate still plays a role in the disinflation process by constraining the movements of the exchange rate in the short run and by signaling the disinflation stance of the central bank through the parameters of the band.

In the government plan, gradual disinflation stems primarily from productivity growth. In this context, nominal exchange rate flexibility can help to translate the long-term real appreciation trend implied by fast productivity growth and capital inflows into lower domestic prices/inflation.[3] Such increase of exchange rate flexibility is consistent with the trend of the exchange rate regime followed in the past by Poland. Although there is an important role for tight money in fighting off destabilizing short-term shocks in this strategy, it should not be used on a continuing basis as a means of "bending" the longer-term inflation trend. The latter function is taken care of by the ongoing process of reform, which generates sustainable growth and disinflation at the same time. Under these circumstances, some variation of the fixed exchange rate, such as a rigid crawling peg, could be inflationary, as it could limit the scope for productivity gains to translate into lower domestic prices.

Strengthening independence of the central bank will lower incentives to use *seigniorage* to finance the deficit. As disinflation policy relies more on setting inflation targets (as set recently in the Euro 2006 plan), there is a growing importance to the *independent status* of the central bank (NBP). This independence can be considered as part of the fundamentals related to macroeconomic stability. However, to be consistent with the government strategy, the central bank should not treat lowering inflation as its sole objective and thus should not pursue aggressive credibility battles with the public over long periods. Its main objective is to resist pressures to provide financing for the fiscal deficit and to exercise its independent status to fight off inflationary shocks even in the face of disagreement with the Treasury. Although the NBP was granted considerable autonomy by the Banking Act of 1989, it has to submit each year its guidelines on monetary policy for approval by Parliament. In addition to this limitation, Parliament still has to approve the law that prohibits financing of the deficit by the NBP. Following EMU membership, there will be no room nor need for an independent monetary policy. However, this does not mean that the NBP should gradually reduce its independence during the transition. After accession, the European central bank would take over the task of maintaining an independent (albeit for the entire EU) monetary policy. Similarly, the transition from a flexible exchange rate to the Euro (the EU common currency) can be accomplished easily once inflation is brought down.

Dealing with Capital Inflows

Within the framework of an inflation target regime, monetary policy is of course one of the main instruments. What should the role for tight monetary policy be in dealing with *short-term* shocks that destabilize the targeted inflation path, in particular, of capital inflows?

Poland, as well as the Czech Republic, experienced in recent years the various features of exchange-rate-based stabilization as described above. In Poland, the incomplete sterilization of the growing capital inflows, through current and capital accounts, increased the total money supply during 1994–1995 much faster than projected; the expansion of net foreign assets became the dominant factor in the expansion of total money supply, accounting for 85 percent of the latter in 1995. At the same time, the contribution of fiscal deficit to money creation dropped drastically, which leaves the capital inflows as a major contributor to inflation from the monetary perspective. (Total foreign reserves, minus gold, increased in 1995 by close to U.S. $9 billion and a further U.S. $3 billion during 1996.)

Part of the capital inflow has been absorbed by a real appreciation of the currency, estimated at about 20 percent in 1995–1996, which is higher than in recent years (around 5 percent in 1993–1994). A reduced rate of intervention by the NBP would have allowed the exchange rate to appreciate more, which would have caused the money supply to grow less and thus contribute to further disinflation. This is essentially a proposal for the medium term, with appropriate qualifications. The policy of keeping the real exchange rate artificially depreciated is especially problematic when the (adjusted) current account was in surplus—3 percent of GDP in 1995. Yet the cautious approach of the NBP is also understandable; the heavy pressure toward appreciation may be temporary, and if this is so, then there is a case for protecting the tradables sector against excessive volatility with spells of "Dutch Disease" difficulties (recession of the tradable sector resulting from a loss of competitiveness as the real exchange rate appreciates). The rapid shift into a small current account deficit in 1996 (just under 1 percent of GDP) and the prognosis of a sizable current account deficit in 1997 indeed validates the cautious approach of the central bank.

In dealing with this dilemma, it is important to distinguish between the short-term and long-term aspects of capital inflows (which is easier done in theory than in practice). Short-term inflows attracted by temporarily high domestic interest rates, as in the case of tight money, or by speculation of further appreciation have a destabilizing potential and provide good reason for temporary sterilization policies. The same is true of a temporary surge of foreign exchange supply originating from the current account—as, for example, was the case in 1995.

Policy considerations with regard to long-term inflows, such as foreign direct investment (FDI), are quite different. When these inflows are expected to continue over the medium term, they alter the sustainable path of the real exchange rate and generate a path of real appreciation as an equilibrium solution. A similar effect on the real exchange rate is generated by a faster rate of productivity growth in Poland than among its trading partners, as was indeed the case in practice. The tendency for real appreciation can be mitigated in the short run in order to ease the transition in industries that are hurt by the process, but in the longer term, the realization of the appreciation is unavoidable. It should be noted, though, that when we speak of the tendency toward an appreciated exchange rate, we refer to the *medium* run. Clearly, in any given year there may be pressures for temporary real depreciation, which may dominate the scene, contrary to the longer-term tendency.

Foreign Savings and Domestic Savings

The proposed strategy puts the FDI and long-term financial foreign investment at the center of the disinflation stage. At present, these flows are relatively small in Poland (as a percentage of GDP), but they can become much larger in the future, as we can learn from the recent experiences of the Czech Republic and Hungary. For example, in 1995, FDI in Poland was about $1 billion, whereas in the Czech Republic and Hungary, which are much smaller economies, the FDIs were U.S. $2.5 and $4.2 billion, respectively. The difference in total capital inflows in 1995 is much more dramatic: while the inflows to Poland were 1 percent of its GDP, the inflows to the Czech Republic and Hungary were 18 and 14 percent, respectively.[4] The flow of these resources is, however, not exogenous to internal developments. We know from other experiences, for example, in Latin America, that these funds are sensitive to domestic reforms and stabilization.

The foregoing connection closes the circle. Growth is needed to support the structural reforms, and the latter facilitate growth and disinflation. However, this virtuous circle requires the participation of domestic saving as well, since otherwise the growth will become unsustainable, because the inflows will be diverted to consumption.

The experience of Spain indicates that the saving propensity of households tends to fall in the early stage of economic integration. This may be due in part to the rise in perceived permanent income without a corresponding rise in current income, and to the relaxation of liquidity constraints associated with financial liberalization. Some development of this nature, which may lead to a consumption boom (in excess of what is warranted by the rise in permanent income), may have taken place recently in Poland. During 1996, in particular, there was a sharp pick-up in private consumption, particularly in durables, that was supported by growth in consumer credit. As a result, the primary domestic counterpart to the increase in foreign financing (5.6 percent of GDP) was a sharp decline in domestic saving (4.1 percent) and only to a lesser degree higher investment (1.5 percent), despite strong investment activity (see Table 8.3).

The pressure toward real appreciation emanating from consumption pressures is clearly undesirable, because it is inflationary and destabilizing; it should, therefore, be offset by a countercyclical increase in public saving.

An additional role for public saving and its associated effect on national saving is to offset excessive real appreciation resulting from speculative short-term inflows, which tend to accompany the basic (equilibrium) trend of real appreciation (linked to differential productivity growth). Some analysts of the Spanish experience hold the view that the excessive appreciation after accession undermined competitiveness

Table 8.3   Savings and Investment (as percentage of GDP)

	1992	1993	1994	1995	1996
Foreign Savings[a]	−1.1	0.6	−2.3	−4.6	1.0
Domestic Savings	16.3	15.0	18.2	22.9	18.8
Public	−3.7	0.2	−0.2	0.0	−1.2
Private	19.9	14.8	18.4	22.9	20.0
Investment	15.2	15.6	15.9	18.3	19.8
Public	3.4	3.3	3.1	3.1	2.8
Private	11.8	12.3	12.8	15.2	17.0

[a]Balance of payments current account, including border trade surplus.
Source: Główny Urząd Statystyczny, *Rocznik Statystyczny* (1997).

and led to excessive deterioration of the current account. This may have contributed to the more severe recession in Spain during the early 1990s. Again, the government may offset these tendencies by a cyclical cut in its expenditures. This can be reinforced with the tightening of supervision applied in particular to financial institutions, with the aim to discourage imprudent lending or unsustainable consumption growth.

What are the implications of a more pessimistic scenario, in which the inflow of foreign investment is small? In this case, domestic saving will have to play the main role in order to generate the required growth in the preaccession stage. In fact, complete reliance on domestic saving was one of the foundations of growth in the East Asian countries, but this is of course a much harder requirement for the Central and East European countries.

It is interesting to note that under this alternative (and less likely) growth scenario, there will be a tendency for the real exchange rate to *depreciate* over the medium term, if the effect of productivity growth in the tradables sector is not dominant. It follows that in order to translate the movement of the real exchange rate into disinflation, it is preferable to have a low crawling peg in the preaccession stage. The real depreciation will then take the form of domestic inflation falling below the crawl of the exchange rate. The creation of fiscal surpluses will be the cornerstone of this policy. These surpluses will also raise national saving. As we know from recent research, there is no complete substitutability between private and public saving.[5] This scenario requires sufficient downward flexibility of domestic inflation to generate the real devaluation in question; the absence of the required flexibility will entail recessionary consequences.

Conclusions

It has been noted that a negative tradeoff between disinflation and growth may be expected, if the former is carried out by tight money policies. In view of the substantial growth potential of Poland in the present stage of integration with the EU, it is desirable not to lose this opportunity by trying to force inflation down by nominal policies. The role of tight money should be confined to *combating the temporary upward deviations of inflation* experienced in the past and to *consolidating the reductions in inflation* that are brought about by other factors, reflecting an approach that consolidates successes.

What are these other factors? It was noted that direct foreign investment and other long-term capital inflows, stimulated by privatization and structural reforms, could be an important source of growth cum disinflation. Productivity growth, again associated with the above factors, is another force that works in the same way.

The risks associated with large capital inflows when consumption falls into an unsustainable path were also pointed out. Countercyclical fiscal policies are the most effective tool under these circumstances. The pressure toward real appreciation in these cases can also be offset by countercyclical fiscal, monetary, and financial policies.

An increase in public savings can stimulate growth by freeing resources to the dynamic private sector. The increased rate of growth from the above sources will in turn contribute to reduction of the inflationary component of the deficit. It should also be noted that higher growth can reduce social tensions if it is shared equitably, which in turn reduces inflationary wage claims and related inflationary pressures. Other sources of sustainable growth, such as reforms in the financial and labor markets, can contribute to disinflation in a similar way. Fiscal reforms that enhance macroeconomic stability also contribute indirectly to growth.

The aggregate effect of the various reforms is likely to precipitate the EU's decision on accession. The increased likelihood of this event will be internalized by the world capital market and be reflected in increased investment and growth in Poland. The implication is that some reforms may be more effective when carried out early, since several reforms may have a strong impact on the advancement of accession, while others, which are credibility-loaded, may be more effective if carried out when accession is near, so that benefits may be realized from the imported EU's credibility, especially in the context of the EMU. During preaccession, Poland will have more scope for policy discretion, vis-à-vis the rules that regulate participation in the EMU; it should use this discretion to implement all those reforms that may help to advance accession. This, in turn, would render inflation targets more credible and would indirectly facilitate disinflation.

To sum up, the main channel for nominal convergence in Poland in the coming years is through the pace of market-oriented reforms and fiscal retrenchment, which stimulate *sustainable* growth cum disinflation. (By contrast, demand-led, nonsustainable growth is a recipe for inflation.) To translate the growth potential into disinflation, the exchange rate regime should remain flexible to allow Poland to absorb productivity increases in a noninflationary manner; at the same time, it will facilitate the absorption of external shocks during the preaccession period, while policy discretion remains at hand. The role of tight monetary policies in this framework is to offset temporary upward shocks to inflation and to help consolidate reductions of inflation caused by the real processes described above. The main role in offsetting destabilizing capital inflows associated with declines in domestic savings is to be played by countercyclical fiscal and financial supervision policies. These are the basic considerations that should underlie Poland's preaccession macro strategy.

Notes

1. Organization for Economic Cooperation and Development, *Economic Survey: Spain, 1991–1992* (Paris: OECD, 1993).
2. Dornbusch, Rudiger, "Credibility, Debt and Unemployment: Ireland's Failed Stabilization," *Economic Policy* 4, no. 8 (April 1989): 173–209.
3. A productivity shock under a fixed rate regime must lead to an increase in inflation since this is the only way of generating a real appreciation; see Matthew B. Canzoneri, Behzad Diba, and Gwen Eudey, "Trends in European Productivity and Real Exchange Rates: Implications for the Maastricht Convergence Criteria and for Inflation Targets after EMU," *Centre for Economic Policy Research Discussion Paper*, no. 1417 (London, June 1996). By contrast, under a flexible exchange rate regime, inflation will decline as a result of the productivity-included growth with a constant money supply. Essentially similar results obtain when we switch from constant levels (of exchange rate and money) to constant rates of change (which in the case of the exchange rate regime takes the form of a fixed rate of crawl).
4. International Monetary Fund, *World Economic Outlook* (Washington, D.C.: IMF, May 1996).
5. Klaus Schmidt-Hebbel, Luis Servén, and Andrés Solimano, "Savings and Investment: Paradigms, Puzzles, Policies," *World Bank Research Observer* 2, no. 1 (February 1996): 87–117.

NINE

Foreign Trade: Policies and Performance

Bartłomiej Kamiński

Poland has made impressive gains in reintegrating into the world economy in general and the EU (European Union) in particular. Its economy has become significantly more open than under central planning. Since 1989, foreign trade has undergone dramatic changes in terms of geography (shift toward the EU) and commodity composition (switch toward manufactures). Foreign direct investment inflows, after a sluggish start during the initial stages of transition, have begun to pick up since 1994, with a positive impact on trade, technology, and know-how.

Yet the task of sustaining an impressive foreign trade performance may become increasingly difficult because of the very slow progress, if not reversal, in institutional reforms, accompanied by creeping state interventionism. The negative impact of these institutional developments is worrying, particularly in view of growing competition in both domestic markets and export markets as a result of liberalization stipulated in the Association Agreement with the EU and the implementation of the Uruguay Round agreements. The Association Agreement provides for duty-free access to Polish markets for industrial products (except for vehicles) originating in the EU by 1999, whereas the Uruguay Round agreements stipulate a significant lowering of barriers to trade in Poland's major export markets. The latter, especially in the EU, where Poland's exports are subject to preferential tariff treatment, will increase competition from other sources.

The slowdown in pace of institutional reforms stems in some part from the capture of several domains, including foreign trade, of economic policymaking by narrow sectoral interest groups. A very strong peasant lobby, represented in the former coalition government by the Polish Peasant Party, had successfully brought agricultural protection to levels almost comparable to those of many highly developed countries and vehemently opposed privatization or opening up of the economy to foreign trade. Free trade does not seem to have many aficionados among politicians in government and in the opposition, as well as among the general public. In the popular perception, exports still tend to be viewed as a virtue and imports as a sin. Moreover, the "socialist" legacy of Marxist thinking—that industrial production is the only source of wealth—is still very much present.

The crux of the matter is that the ability to respond to growing competitive pressures associated with liberalization in market access hinges critically on an improved climate for private sector development and the opening of services to direct foreign investment. Without a reduction in the scope and depth of administrative intervention in the economy and the opening of services to international competition, Polish producers may find it very difficult to cope with increased competitive pressures in domestic and international markets.

However, the specter of bureaucratization, which had been suppressed during the initial stages of the transition, has been on the rise. It has been haunting Poland and its economic policy for the last few years. Despite the Association and Uruguay Round agreements, which limited the discretion of authorities, even the Polish foreign trade regime has not been immune to bureaucratic assaults. It would seem that commitments made under both the European Association Agreement with the EU and World Trade Organization membership would provide a powerful brake on the bureaucratic temptation to micromanage economic processes. This has not always been the case, for Polish authorities have displayed considerable ingenuity in exploiting loopholes and circumventing the corresponding provisions of respective international agreements. Although these developments have not had thus far a devastating impact on Poland's external performance, the accumulation of seemingly innocent bureaucratic interventions may have an adverse impact on Poland's exports in more competitive conditions that may arise in the future.

Section 1of this chapter provides an overview of Poland's reintegration with the international economy, following the collapse of central planning. It shows that Poland has been very successful in coping with the "shock" created by collapse of import demand in the former Soviet Union, thanks to the ability of Polish firms to reorient and develop commercial links with Western partners; that Poland has made great strides in integrating with international markets in general and those of the EU in particular; and that Polish consumers and producers benefited from integration. Section 2 seeks to identify the factors underlying Poland's success in transforming foreign trade patterns. Initially, the liberalization of foreign trade and exchange rate regimes, combined with suppressed domestic and import demand in the (former) Soviet Union, drove developments in Poland's foreign trade. During the later stages of transition, industrial restructuring and improved microeconomic efficiency maintained the competitiveness of Polish exports. Section 3 discusses changes in the evolution of the Polish foreign trade regime, pointing to creeping bureaucratic interventionism. Section 4 asks whether international agreements provide a powerful restraint on the bureaucratic temptation to micromanage foreign trade. Section 5 provides conclusions.

1. External Performance: Reintegrating with World Markets

The key to strong economic performance is integration with the world economy. All success stories of economic development over the past two decades have been based on export-oriented policies combined with low or declining barriers to imports. The foreign sector in countries that have fared well has expanded dramatically. Poland, which recently recorded the fastest growth rates in Europe, is no exception. Its 1990 stabilization cum transformation program set the groundwork for an economic opening. Developments in the external sector have been crucial to an impressive economic growth performance.

With the globalization of production and capital markets, foreign trade is no longer the only linkage between domestic and world economies. Other linkages include inflows and outflows of financial assets, capital in the form of direct investment, and international labor mobility. The stabilization program introduced on 1 January 1990 removed major obstacles that had prevented firms from direct exposure to international markets. The development of capital markets, the removal of various legal barriers to the development of the private sector and the convertibility of the Polish *złoty* have enabled inflows of foreign capital. All these factors have contributed to the fast pace of Poland's reintegration with the world economy.

Foreign Trade: A Shift toward the EU and Manufactures in Line with Comparative Advantage

The dismantling of central planning in foreign trade and the unification of exchange rates combined with initially limited current account convertibility (but subsequently expanded to other foreign transactions) has brought international markets to bear directly on domestic producers and consumers. The response thus far has been impressive, and two-way goods market linkages have had a profound impact on Poland's economy. Foreign trade has provided a boost to recovery, and export earnings financed the expansion in imports. Imports, in turn, have provided higher-quality products, both for consumption and investment. This, combined with competition from imports, has stimulated local producers to improve their performance.

In consequence, the Polish economy has become significantly more open than under central planning, with foreign transactions (the sum of exports and imports divided by two), accounting for around 20 percent of GDP. Although this level is still lower than that in many market economies of a similar size and level of development in terms of GDP, it nonetheless suggests an already high degree of reliance on international markets. In other words, developments in this area strongly affect national economic welfare.

Data on changes in total trade neither fully capture the dramatic transformations that have already occurred nor do they indicate their importance for the Polish economy. While more than doubling the value of total trade turnover over the past seven-year period clearly indicates a double-digit average annual growth rate, this says little about the scope of Poland's transformation in terms of directions of trade as well as its composition (see Tables 9.1 and 9.2). Geographically, it has shifted westward in line with economic considerations. The EU accounts for around two thirds of Poland's total trade—a dramatic increase from its 1989 level of 32 percent. By this measure alone, Poland is more integrated with the EU than are several EU member countries. Germany has replaced the former Soviet Union as Poland's largest trading partner: The share of the former increased from 15 percent in 1989 to 30 percent in 1996, while that of the latter fell from 20 percent to 12 percent over the same period.

Considering the virtual collapse of import demand in Poland's former CMEA (Council for Mutual Economic Assistance) partners in 1991, the scope of adjustment faced by Polish exporters was quite extensive. Countries from the CMEA had accounted for around half of Poland's trade turnover throughout the 1980s. Faced with contracting domestic demand due to macroeconomic stabilization measures, enterprises sought successfully to increase exports to CMEA countries. Exports in this direction surged dramatically during the first six months of 1990. This resulted in significant trade surpluses in nonconvertible currencies. Since these were in fact subsidies to partner countries, the authorities changed the rules governing exports to CMEA partners in order to bring them in line with imports from this area.[1] In consequence, CMEA trade declined, albeit

Table 9.1 Changes in the Direction of Foreign Trade, 1989–1996

	1989	1990	1991	1992	1993	1994	1995	1996 (est)
Total Trade ($mln.)	25,421	27,855	25,993	27,482	29,463	34,736	47,583	54,848
Annual Growth (%)		10	–7	6	7	18	37	15
Growth rate of imports (%)		25	–19	7	–3	25	35	7
Growth rate of exports (%)		–7	11	4	18	12	39	26
Share of EU in total (%)	32	47	53	56	60	60	67	66
Share of the former CMEA in total	41	27	15	12	13	13	17	19

Sources: Derived from the UN COMTRADE database. Estimates for 1996 are based on Polish national data for the first nine months.

Table 9.2   Export Performance in EU Markets, 1990–1995 (in percent)

	1989	1990	1991	1992	1993	1994	1995
Share of Poland in EU imports of manufactures	0.27	0.36	0.43	0.52	0.65	0.70	0.85
Share of Poland in EU total imports	0.38	0.50	0.56	0.63	0.71	0.76	0.85

Source: Derived from the UN COMTRADE database.

much less than in 1991. By 1991, the year of the CMEA's formal dissolution, the share of trade with the CMEA dropped to 15 percent. It seems to have bottomed out at 13 percent during 1993–1994. With the recovery in some former Soviet republics underway and expanding commercial links with CEFTA (Central European Free Trade Agreement) countries, the share has been on the increase.

Exports to the West, mainly Germany and other EU countries, have been an important driving force of Poland's economic recovery. In fact, during the transformational recession of 1990–1992, the only bright spot was exports in that direction; their value surged by 46 percent in 1990 alone and subsequently sustained a double-digit expansion, averaging 11 percent per year over 1990–1996. This expansion has relatively quickly offset the collapse in exports to former CMEA countries: During the first year of the transition, total exports increased by 25 percent; in 1991, they contracted by 19 percent, followed by a 7 percent increase in 1992, a fall of 3 percent in 1993, two years of double-digit growth (25 and 35 percent), followed by a modest increase of 6 percent in 1996.

On the import side, since 1991 the value of imports has been increasing every year. As with exports, the shift was toward the EU. They increased by 6 percent in 1990 and then moved to double-digit levels, recording a record growth rate of 55 percent in 1995. Since Poland's foreign trade balance with the EU has dramatically deteriorated, many observers have complained that the EU received an advantage when it signed the Association Agreement in December 1991. As will be argued later, this is the wrong way to measure the value of the agreement.

To what extent did the switch in the direction of Poland's foreign trade coincide with changes in the commodity composition of her exports? The demise of the CMEA and the shift to hard currency transactions and world prices put an end to the dual external environment for Poland's trade activity, under which one part of trade was subject to market forces and another nurtured by preferential intra-CMEA arrangements. CMEA- and

Western-oriented export baskets were quite distinct, supplying manufactures eastward and primaries westward. Since in the short term, quality could not be significantly improved and Polish exporters had to compete on the same footing in Western markets as other suppliers, one would expect the geographical redirection to induce a commodity shift from the CMEA export basket to the Western basket, with only limited opportunities for redirecting exports of manufactures. After all, Poland's competitive position in non-CMEA markets had significantly declined through the 1970s and 1980s.[2] It was taken for granted that Polish manufactures were mostly CMEA-specific, essentially nonmarketable elsewhere.

These expectations have not been borne out. The change in composition of Polish exports toward manufactures was quite substantial even over the first three years of the transition, that is, during the period when no substantial industrial restructuring could have occurred. Calculations of Poland's revealed comparative advantage indices in Western markets indicate an increased specialization in manufactured products.[3] Among the set of commodities in which Poland had comparative advantage (with revealed comparative advantage index exceeding unity), around 60 percent of the value of exports was accounted for by manufacturers in 1988, and around 70 percent in 1992. Furthermore, export concentration indices, as measured by the share of the top 10 and 30 three-digit Standard International Trade Classification, items in total Western-oriented exports also fell significantly.

The commodity composition of exports has dramatically moved toward manufactures; its share increased from 47 percent in 1989 to 70 percent in 1996. More important, however, Polish exporters outperformed exporters from other countries in markets most important for them—that is, those in the EU. The share of "made in Poland" manufactures in EU imports increased from around 0.3 percent in 1989 to almost 0.9 percent in 1995 (see Table 9.2). One may thus conclude that the export basket of Poland underwent a significant shift away from raw materials and resource-intensive products over this period.

Changes in the commodity composition of imports have been strongly influenced by Polish producers' reintegration into international markets, a trend reflected in the growing dependence on imported industrial raw materials and intermediate products. These account for around 46 percent of total imports. The revival of domestic fixed investment activity has contributed to the increase in imports of capital goods: Their share increased from 13 percent over 1989–1992 to 20 percent over 1993–1995.[4]

Changes in export baskets were accompanied by changes in their relative factor intensities more in line with their respective factor endowments: Analyses of Polish exports suggest a significant shift toward labor-intensive products.[5] This came as no surprise, considering Poland's relatively well-trained labor force and low labor costs.

Benefits from Opening to the World Economy

Benefits from access to foreign goods and services are numerous. These include not only a wider choice of products and services available to consumers and producers alike but also higher levels of competition in domestic markets, bringing about innovation and lower prices. Last but not least, these two-way linkages also improve allocative efficiency, with resources going to the most productive uses. These are standard gains associated with the liberalization of foreign trade.

But the collapse of central planning and of the CMEA has magnified those gains in two additional ways: the former removed internal barriers to foreign trade, whereas the latter eliminated external constraints. The ironic description of the CMEA as the council for mutual exchange of economic inefficiencies is accurate. Dissolution of the CMEA produced efficiency gains associated with liberating foreign trade patterns from the highly destructive Soviet oil grip. Trade within the CMEA, especially with the Soviet Union, may have looked attractive, but only in terms of exchanging manufactures of subpar quality for relatively cheap energy. This trade, however, was in fact highly disruptive. Much of the exchange consisted of Poland exporting energy-intensive and technologically outdated products in exchange for energy—oil. A portion of imported oil was thus shipped back to its supplier. Furthermore, because of the low-quality requirements by importers from supply-constrained economies, the Soviet market was a dumping ground for manufactured goods, thus further removing incentives to efficiency and innovativeness.

This trade pattern, combined with the inward orientation of central planning, contributed to misdevelopment of the Polish economy and its inability to compete in international markets. First, during the 1980s, the high technology content of manufactures fell in comparison with the 1970s.[6] Despite modernization efforts during the Gierek era in the 1970s, the competitive position of Poland, as measured by annual changes in its share of total imports by Western countries, dropped significantly during the 1980s. Moreover, Poland's comparative advantage remained in food and natural resource-intensive products, reflecting the rapidly expanding technological gap.

Second, nothing short of a complete shift away from central planning could have reversed these highly unfavorable trends in Poland's external performance. The process of dismantling the state monopoly over foreign trade had begun well before the collapse of communism in Poland. Yet these various reform measures, falling well short of removing a wall shielding producers from competition, did not reverse the decline in competitiveness of the Polish economy in international markets already evident in the 1970s and exacerbated during the 1980s.

The objective of exports is to secure imports. An economy benefits from these only if imports lower costs to consumers and producers and provide them with products that otherwise would not be available. As can be seen, central planning was strongly biased against foreign trade (possibly excluding that with the Soviet Union). The stabilization cum transformation program launched on 1 January 1990, has weakened, if not completely removed, the institutional foundations of this bias.

The program also has created an environment that mobilized firms to cope effectively with the challenge of adjustment, both domestic and external. The shock of the CMEA collapse negatively impacted Poland's income, as enterprises lost their markets and the money to pay for the oil bill had to be earned in much more demanding international markets. Indeed, Poland's terms of trade (ToT), that is, the ratio of export price to import price, had fallen during the first two years of the stabilization/transformation program (especially in 1990 by 16.3 percent). The income loss—estimated by multiplying the import/GDP ratio by the percentage changes in the ToT for each year—was very sizable, amounting to 3 percent of GDP in 1990 and 1.5 percent in 1992 (see Table 9.3). Poland's ToT recorded a significant improvement in 1992 and 1993 and were flat in 1994–1995. In terms of GDP, a faster rise in prices of exports than in those for imports increased GDP annually by more than 1 percent during 1992 and 1993. Overall, in relation to 1989, the loss in terms of GDP by 1995 still amounted to 1.3 percent.

Nonetheless, it seems that the shock had been fully absorbed by 1995. Consider first that ToT do not account for increases in the volume of exports. These increases may allow a country to generate earnings to pay for even larger imports, even if these become more expensive. The measure that allows to account for it is the purchasing power of exports (ToT multiplied by the index of export volume). As can be seen from Table 9.3, the purchasing power of exports was until 1994 lower than in 1989, but in 1995 it was 37 percent larger than in 1989. Moreover, labor productivity in Poland significantly increased over 1990–1996.[7] One may thus suspect that this was the major source of the growth in export volumes. In other words, export prices may be lower than in the past, but with their lower production costs, the value added generated by these sales is larger. It seems that the ability to import more has not been at the expense of higher domestic costs or as a result of greater effort.

Table 9.3 Terms of Trade and Purchasing Power of Exports, 1990–1995

	1990	1991	1992	1993	1994	1995
Exports, f.o.b. (in millions of US dollars)	15,837	14,953	13,929	13,582	17,121	23,463
Imports, f.o.b. (in millions of US dollars)	12,248	15,104	14,060	17,087	18,930	26,687
Cost (–) or benefits of ToT deterioration/ improvement (annual changes in % of GDP)	–3.23	–1.54	1.52	1.44	0.25	0.36
Purchasing power of exports (1989=100)	95	85	90	96	115	137

Source: Calculations for the impact of terms of trade on GDP on the basis of data in GUS 1996, WDT 1996, and IFS 1997.

The opening to the world economy has had a very positive influence on Poland's economic performance. Good export performance generated earnings to pay for imports, which increased competitive pressures on domestic producers and economic welfare. Thanks to this opening, Poland did not miss the ongoing revolution of the globalization of production and capital. It has already capitalized on it and seems to be well positioned to take advantage of opportunities offered by international markets.

Foreign Trade Imbalances: Dark Clouds on the Horizon?

Many Polish officials and analysts are increasingly concerned with Poland's soaring foreign trade deficit. Indeed, the gap between imports and exports almost doubled in 1995 and more than doubled in 1996. If the past is a guide to the future, then one should not be particularly worried about Poland's external financial position. The country has been running sizable trade deficits since 1990, without resorting to external financing or depleting international reserves (see Table 9.4).[8] This has been mainly because of huge surpluses in trade not recorded by customs. With people freely crossing borders, a large number of international transactions cannot be registered as such. Transborder trade, mainly along the Oder Neisse line (the border with Germany) and the so called suitcase traders from the former Soviet Union, is difficult to trace.

Yet one may estimate the magnitude of these transactions on the basis of amounts of foreign currency exchanged and transactions at "marketplaces" for traders from the former Soviet Union. As for the latter, a particularly well-known site has been a Warsaw Stadium built in 1955 to commemorate the tenth anniversary of the now-defunct Polish People's Republic: Its annual turnover was put at around $1 billion in 1996. As can be seen from data in Table 9.4, unrecorded sales to foreigners (i.e., nonresidents) were quite large. Except in 1993, these more than offset foreign trade deficits.

From the point of view of a country's external financial position, the developments on current account—including foreign trade, services, remittances, investment income, and payments—are more important. Including unrecorded exports, the current account was in surplus during 1990 and 1994–1995. While one may be tempted to challenge the accuracy of the Polish National Bank's estimates, it is important to note that surplus years coincided with large increases in Polish official international reserves. Poland did not run down its foreign exchange reserves to finance external imbalances, except in 1991. Neither did it seek to borrow from banks or foreign governments—repayments exceeded disbursements from foreign creditors in 1990 and 1994. When the reverse was true, i.e.,

Table 9.4 Highlights of Poland's External Position, 1990–1996

	1990	1991	1992	1993	1994	1995	1996
Trade balance	3,589	–711	–131	–3,505	–1,809	–3,224	–7,700
Unrecorded trade			1,183	1,750	3,076	7,754	7,221
Current account	3,067	–2,146	–3,104	–5,788	–2,590	–4,245	–6,700
C/A (unrecorded trade incl.)	3,067	–963	–1,921	–4,038	486	3,509	–2,200
Changes in total reserves	2,178	–859	466	–7	1,750	8,932	2,926
Total reserves	4,492	3,633	4,099	4,092	5,842	14,774	17,700
Foreign direct investment	89	291	678	1,715	1,875	3,659	4,000

Sources: IFS 1997 and estimates from the National Bank of Poland.

disbursements exceeded repayments, the net inflows did not exceed $500 million.[9] As can be seen from Table 9.4, foreign investment alone could not be responsible for this.

Poland, as a developing country, should not be a net exporter of capital. Surpluses on current account can be used to pay sovereign debt, increase foreign reserves, and invest abroad—there is simply no other option. Foreign reserves seem to be now at levels ensuring a buffer against unexpected movements of capital and contraction in foreign exchange earnings. Domestic demand has been growing faster than GDP since 1995, thus reducing incentives to firms to export. Poland's developmental needs are huge, and foreign savings can be effectively used to finance investment. In fact, Poland could have afforded to finance larger purchases of foreign goods and services and, thus, increase its national economic welfare. Consider that Poland's international reserves in terms of imports increased from three months in 1993 to four months in 1994 and seven months in 1995 and 1996. The import equivalent of international reserves might have been too low in 1993 or 1994 but certainly not in 1995 or 1996. It seems, therefore, that under these conditions, Poland should be running current account deficits.[10]

Should the growing gap in current accounts be of concern? The answer is affirmative, only if foreign trade deficit is used by politicians as an excuse to provide inefficient domestic producers with extra protection. There has been a growing tendency among politicians to do this. Parliament obliged the government to submit a program of "all-encompassing and coherent foreign trade policies."[11] While the final shape of the program remains to be seen, there are signs that it may contain measures curbing imports even if "it involves renegotiating international economic treaties."[12]

This is a wrong-headed administrative approach. It fails to recognize that the problems to be addressed, if at all, are in the spheres of public policy rather than foreign trade. Consider first that Poland's macroeconomic stability remains precarious. Public spending is high and geared toward current consumption; subsidies ("state aids," to use EU jargon) eat up around 3–4 percent of GDP; tax and fiscal regimes still await serious reform; and pensions may drive up budget deficits if their funding remains unchanged. Furthermore, the Polish economic regime (including conditions for entry to business activity, regulations and legal framework, foreign trade institutions) is poorly equipped to handle increased inflows of FDI triggered by the prospects of accession to the EU. Hence, unless public finance is strengthened and the climate for business activity improved, the current account deficit may undermine Poland's stability. Last but not least, maintaining and improving the international competitiveness of

Polish firms will be crucial to foreign trade performance; protectionism and state interventionism will not help achieve this goal.

2. Factors Accountable for Improved
External Performance: Is It Sustainable?

The various factors determining the pace of Poland's reintegration with the world economy reflect the progress achieved in establishing market-supporting institutions and policies. The foundation was established by the innovative stabilization cum transformation program launched on 1 January 1990. Other factors included responsible macroeconomic policies pursued by successive postcommunist governments; the growing role of the private sector; rapidly increasing inflows of FDI, and preferential access to EU markets under the European Association Agreement.

The improvement in exports was impressive, but only against the background of the dismal performance in the 1980s. Still, the export boom, driven by manufactures, was an unexpected outcome of the transition and represented a turnaround by Polish export performance in Western markets. The primary force behind the impressive foreign trade performance of Poland was the rapid restructuring of domestic economic systems involving the liberalization of prices, the hardening of budget constraints for state-owned enterprises, and easy entry for private firms. The reforms made the state-owned enterprises more responsive to market signals. By establishing more transparent links between their performance and their financial situation, the reform measures subjected state-owned enterprises to tighter budget constraints. At the same time, the significant liberalization in trade policy exposed all enterprises to foreign competition. Thus, the key to improved export performance during the early stages of the transition was the shift to a demand-constrained economy, accompanied by liberalization of the foreign trade regime.

However, the shift alone would not be sufficient to sustain performance. In fact, during the initial stages, there was good reason the export expansion was only a temporary phenomenon due to diversion from former CMEA markets and the contraction of domestic demand. Expansion of exports would be possible only so long as there would be a further compression in domestic demand, accompanied by devaluations of domestic currency to ensure profitability of exports. Yet although domestic demand did not continue falling and the Polish złoty kept appreciating against major currencies, exports did not contract but kept growing.

The initial export upswing took place in an institutional environment whose full export potential was yet to be tapped. The major institutional constraint related to the dominance of the state-owned sector and weaknesses of institutions supporting private sector development. During the initial stages of the transformation, the export push came from state-owned enterprises with organizational structures inherited from central planning. Privatization of state-owned enterprises, preceded by organizational restructuring to make state-owned assets more attractive to potential investors, increased their capacity to compete in international markets. Indeed, the share of the private sector in exports increased from 20 percent in 1989 to 80 percent in 1995.[13]

Another factor was the impact of rising FDI on Poland's international competitiveness. The total value of FDI exceeded $12 billion by the end of 1996, with inflows over the past two years accounting for two thirds of this total (see Table 9.4). FDI is a powerful vehicle for transfers of technology and the best practices in management and, increasingly, for integrating domestic production capacities into global networks of production and distribution. Although firms with foreign capital generated 12.4 percent of total income in 1995 and accounted for 7 percent of total employment, their share in exports and imports was 34.4 and 42.1 percent, respectively. Among the 100 largest Polish exporters to the EU, accounting for 38 percent of total EU-directed exports, there were 23 firms with foreign capital—13 of these firms were among the top 50 on this list.[14] The ranking is biased in favor of large exporters of heavy chemicals, steel products, and exporters of natural resources (copper, coal, sulfur), which are yet to be privatized and opened to foreign investors. Hence, this share is impressive.

FDI has also contributed to the growth in linkages between Polish firms and their counterparts in the EU by integrating some of them into a global network of production and marketing. This can be observed through increases in intraindustry trade. This trade allows the realization of economies of scale, thanks to greater product specialization in differentiated products. The share of intraindustry trade with the EU, as measured by the Grubbel-Lloyd index (the difference between unity and the quotient of the absolute difference between exports and imports of a given sector and the total of imports and exports for this sector), increased by around one third over 1989–1995 from 0.22 to 0.28.[15] The advantage of intraindustry over interindustry trade remains, because it is less vulnerable to swings in the domestic business cycle, thus assuring a higher degree of stability in export earnings.

Better access to EU markets has also played a role. Initially, the extension of GSP (Generalized System of Preferences) by most Western governments and the elimination of quantitative restrictions maintained by the EU improved Poland's market access. The European Association Agreement, which has placed that country close to the top of the preferential pyramid of access to EU markets, was initially not relevant for the 1990–1991 period, because it went into effect in 1992. Although in terms of tariff preferences, Poland has significant preferential margins over exporters from Most Favored Nation countries (e.g., Japan, the United States, Korea, Malaysia), the edge has been somewhat blunted by the EU's "nondiscriminatory" treatment of Polish exports in terms of nontariff barriers including quantitative restrictions (the Multifiber Agreement or MFA, and agricultural products), voluntary export restraints, antidumping investigations and undertakings, licenses and import surveillance; these probably constrained Polish exports. Finally, the European Association Agreement has given preferential status for Polish industrial exports (excluding initially some sensitive products), but no similar far-reaching concessions were granted in terms of access to EU agricultural markets.

The agreement had a direct impact on FDI inflows because it provided for preferential market access and ensured for investors national treatment and the general right of establishment for most activities. This has sent a strong signal to all potential investors that Poland is open to FDI and is willing to lock this in. FDI has been most common not only in sectors with low production costs due to cheap labor but especially in those sectors considered "sensitive" under the European Association Agreement. In fact, outward processing as a share of Polish exports to the EU has considerably increased in the textiles and apparel industries, where it is estimated that trade related to outward processing amounts to between 70 and 80 percent of total exports. Outward processing seems to have been largely triggered by provisions of the agreement concerning tariffs and restrictive rules of origin. The EU tariffs on reimports of outward-processed textiles were abolished the day that the interim agreement went into force. However, EU customs duties on "ordinary" textile imports were covered by the MFA. Hence, they were subject to both tariffs and quotas. Since none of these barriers applied to outward processing—especially textiles subject to the trade-restrictive MFA—many EU companies transferred production to Poland.

The significance of the agreement does not rest solely on mutual (though asymmetric) concessions in market access. Its provisions compelling the Polish government to harmonize its laws with those in the EU and liberalizing access for products (and services) originating in the EU strike one as much more important. Although the agreement has a number of loopholes and does not come close to the ideal of free trade, the Polish foreign trade regime would have been much less import-friendly without it.

Regarding the question posed in the title of this section, the sustainability of trade performance has become more sensitive to "fine-tuned" economic policies and relies more on new or restructured productive capacities. As for the former, the danger is that these can be easily captured by protectionist domestic lobbying groups unless the right mix of institutions and policies is in place. This section argued that its emergence cannot be taken for granted, as it would reduce the administrative reach of the state. As for the latter, the task ahead is to improve the climate for business activity (among others, through reducing the tax burden thanks to reform in public finance) and attract increased inflows of FDI. As will be argued in Section 3, the irrepressible bureaucratic temptation to micromanage economic processes constitutes a threat to Poland's economic growth performance.

3. Creeping Interventionism

The evolution of Polish foreign trade policy was driven in opposite directions by increasingly better-organized sectoral interests seeking protection from foreign competition, the use of foreign trade concessions to attract FDI, and commitments associated with the European Association Agreement. The result of these conflicting forces are foreign trade institutions and policies distorting the allocation of resources, reducing competition from imports, and creating a social and political atmosphere of corruption and uncertainty.

The foreign trade regime that has emerged in Poland offers ample opportunities for the bureaucracy to intervene through ad hoc management of quotas and tariff exemptions (also known as procedural protection), nontariff measures, including various technical barriers to trade (technical standards), the use of safeguards, and the structure of tariffs. This review commences with the structure of tariffs.

Although dismantling the state monopoly over foreign trade began well before the collapse of central planning, 1990 was a turning point on three important counts. With the introduction of the 1990 stabilization cum transformation program, exchange rates became unified and the złoty became convertible (for current account transactions), access to foreign trade activity fully liberalized on both the import and export sides, and tariffs were applied uniformly to all imports. Tariffs were the major factor shaping access to markets.

The paradox is that Poland had the best trade policy—that of free trade—during the first six months of the 1990 transformation program. Tariff duties were then suspended to curb the monopolistic powers of large, "socialist" enterprises. But even then the new customs law—a component of the transformation program—had not closed all loopholes allowing the imposition of new tariffs, quantitative restrictions, and various surcharges. Despite the suspension of tariffs for six months in June 1990, policy makers were quick to explore opportunities for ad hoc management, as exemplified by extra taxes on imported consumer electronics.[16] Yet the foreign trade regime during these early stages of the transition has been the closest to free trade so far.

Uncertainties associated with the program strongly undervalued the złoty, making imports almost prohibitively expensive and exports very competitive, and initially kept producers at bay. This explains also why, despite the abrupt liberalization, Poland recorded in 1990 a sharp decline in imports accompanied by a surge in exports, mainly to the West. The złoty, however, appreciated strongly, as the exchange rate in terms of the U.S. dollar was kept unchanged (as an anchor to suppress inflation), while domestic prices rapidly increased through 1990. This contributed to an increase in imports, and the foreign trade surplus began to disappear. Responding to pressures from industrial and agricultural lobbies, in early 1991 the government devalued the złoty and linked its exchange rate to a basket of currencies rather than pegging it solely to the U.S. dollar. Although devaluation increased the price of imports and lowered the price of exportables, the pressures to raise the level of protection continued. Poland chose to bind its MFN (most favored nation) tariff rates at a maximum allowable level when it joined the World Trade Organization in 1995, suggesting a further ebbing of commitment to trade liberalization. The share of lines where tariffs were set below their pre-Uruguay Round applied rates (in 1989) is 28.3 percent, with this share particularly low for transport equipment.[17]

By the standards of developing countries, Poland's simple average MFN-applied rate of 27 percent levied on imports from nonpreferential trade partners (i.e., excluding EU and CEFTA member states as well as selected developing countries) is not high. However, its tariff structure is highly diversified. This has two important implications. First, the higher the dispersion in tariff rates, as measured by the standard deviation (absolute dispersion between items), the larger are potential economic distortions—as the variance in tariff rates causes the variation in imported product prices. The overall standard deviation of Polish MFN rates of 28 percent is significantly larger than that in OECD countries—in 1993, the standard deviation of EU MFN tariffs was 6.1 percent; U.S. tariffs were 8.6 percent; and Finland's tariffs amounted to 12.7 percent.[18]

The dispersion is further exacerbated by preferential trade agreements. Imports from preferential partners—the EU, EFTA, and CEFTA countries—accounting for around three fourths of Poland's total imports—are subject to lower tariff rates than those from other sources. Both simple and weighted tariff rates applied against imports from the

EU were in 1996 more than 50 percent lower than those on MFN partners. With the scheduled tariff reductions under CEFTA and the European Association Agreement going deeper than under commitments made when Poland joined the World Trade Organization, the difference will increase rising discrimination against MFN partners.

Second, the diversification in the tariff rate increases the discretion of bureaucracy regarding duties paid on imports. The complex customs clearance procedures increase import costs. Most important, the administrative complexity and the inevitable lack of transparency associated with diversified custom schedules introduce a strong incentive to misclassify products and open the door to corruption. Furthermore, diversified tariffs help to intensify lobbying efforts for protection.

While diversification in tariffs creates the economic incentives for corruption in the customs administration, the practice of tariff exemptions (or, literally, in Polish, duty suspensions) and quotas impedes the state's transformation from an owner and operator to a policy maker and facilitator of private economic activity. Since tariff suspension is only temporary, it creates a patronage relationship between the government and affected firms. Tariff exemptions or quotas, granted by the government usually for a limited period of time, cover a wide range of products (in 1996 around 4,000 categories), including pesticides, electronic components, lightning-protection equipment, building materials, medical equipment, and tractors (for the first six months of 1996).

Official justifications range from addressing alleged deficiencies in the existing tariff structure, the emergency input needs of specific industrial sectors undergoing restructuring (e.g., the telecommunications industry has obtained a permit to import duty-free products and capital goods), and subsidies to government (e.g., quotas on fire engines, medical equipment, and environmental protection equipment imported by local and central government), to dealing with the unintended consequences of such policies, which result in growth in domestic prices for some products (e.g., usually agricultural products but also some chemicals) above world prices or discrepancies between controlled domestic prices and world prices leading to shortages (e.g., oil).

All of these cases represent a misuse of foreign trade policy. Instead of tampering with oil quotas, one should remove price controls. Another instance is the tariff suspension on imports of computer components. With a tariff rate of 10.4 percent on electronic components and a zero tariff rate on computer imports from the EU, Polish firms assembling computers are at a significant cost disadvantage. The problem should be addressed, but there are clearly better remedies for ill-designed tariffs than tariff exemptions. For instance, one might consider either reducing them to zero or bringing them to the EU levels. The main reason for not solving this issue once and for all may be that the existing arrangement seems to offer extra leverage to the central government administration.

The process of managing tariff exemptions and quotas not only lacks transparency and is devoid of clearly defined criteria for granting tariff exemptions but also increases uncertainty and the risk of undue influence on foreign trade policy by rent-seeking private interests. Indeed, there is evidence that exemptions are often granted in response to pressures exerted by domestic lobbies and foreign investors. The exemption of lightning equipment from duties, for instance, coincided with the decision of Philips to invest in Poland. Finally, exemptions offer the administration a proven way to expand its discretionary powers partly lost with the collapse of central planning.

Another area that has witnessed expansion in the state's direct role relates to subsidies offered to firms that meet specified objectives. Fulfilling its obligations under the WTO Agreement on Subsidies and Countervailing Measures, Poland notified the committee in 1996 about five programs falling under its purview: investment-related tax rebates, special economic zones, interest subsidies on bank loans, the credit guarantee scheme, and export insurance government guarantees. These programs are of recent vintage—they were initiated during 1994 and 1995. There does not seem to be a strong demand for these programs, as their scope seems to be rather limited: The credit guarantees in 1995 (by end-November) amounted to around $250 million, well below the $1.9 billion budgeted for 1997. In the same period there was not a single case of disbursement under the interest subsidy program, despite a budget commitment of $8 million. Nonetheless, these examples illustrate the bureaucratic temptation to micromanage economic activity.

In fact, the focus of foreign trade policy recently has been on finding ways of maintaining, if not increasing, protection in face of declining border protection (mainly tariffs), as required by international treaties, rather than on finding ways to increase the scope of free trade. For example, in Poland the product groups that are subject to a very extensive web of special nontariff restrictions include beverages and tobacco, live animals for meat, and motor vehicles. Nontariff measures on agricultural products testify to the political power of the agricultural lobby as represented by the former co-ruling Polish Peasant Party, whereas measures relating to automobiles illustrate the misuse of trade policies as a way to attract FDI. In 1995 these two sectors accounted for 83 percent of all imports affected by nontariff barriers to trade.

In addition, Poland is about to introduce new antidumping legislation, even though its customs law already has antidumping provisions and the authorities can easily resort to other safeguard instruments. Although all highly developed countries have extensive protection against dumping, this is one of these rare areas where economists agree that the case for antidumping is political, not economic.[19] This initiative seems redundant and amounts to a waste of bureaucratic resources, especially because with EU accession the locus of foreign-trade policy making will move to Brussels. Furthermore, there are strong pressures from Parliament, which do not seem to encounter opposition in the executive branch, to introduce measures restraining imports.

Third, instead of adopting EU product standards, safety regulations, and certification procedures, Poland has imposed its own rules covering more than 1,400 product categories. Products listed in the certification law account for a large percentage of all products consumed and produced in Poland. Legislation covers steel products, nonferrous products, capital equipment, precision products, transport equipment, electronic products, engineering products, chemicals, construction materials, glass and ceramic products, wood and paper products, textiles and clothing, and leather products. The refusal to accept foreign firms' self-certification of conformity with domestic standards forces producers to undertake lengthy testing procedures in designated units. If it is not extended to all trading partners, an (incomplete) agreement with the EU only, in which Polish authorities would have agreed to accept the EU safety certification (the CE mark) for some products, would exacerbate already existing reverse discrimination because of preferential or discriminatory trading agreements. The official rationale—protecting the consumer—does not seem very convincing: Rather, its objective is to give ailing ministerial institutes empowered to conduct testing some extra revenue and to protect domestic producers.

Finally, the existing institutional arrangement protects domestic producers at the expense of consumers and producers using imported inputs. Two examples illustrate this point: a recent reorganization of the central government establishing one super-economy ministry; and the rule allowing foreign trade officials to take seats on boards of industrial companies. The latter is due to Poland's mixed-up corporate control, with the state owning all or part of more than 3,000 companies. Among board members appointed to represent state interests are high-level government officials; these appointments are attractive because they are well remunerated and constitute an important addition to a ministerial salary. The conflict of interest is evident: Officials will represent industrial companies rather than national economic interests.

The reform of central government, implemented on 1 January 1997, merged the Ministry of Economic Cooperation with the Ministry of the

Abroad (which in many countries pays greater attention to impacts of nontariff barriers and tariffs on national economic welfare) into a new, (super) Ministry of the Economy. Decisions regarding access to Polish agricultural markets are assigned to the Ministry of Agriculture, which amounts to asking a fox to guard a henhouse. While the Antitrust Office in Warsaw compares favorably to competition authorities in OECD countries in terms of its influence in foreign trade matters as they affect domestic competition, its status and resources are too limited to have a decisive impact. Since there are no independent institutions that would balance the interests of import-competing sectors against those of exporters and consumers, the danger of protectionist interests capturing the foreign-trade policy-making process has, if anything, greatly increased. With no internal constraints on protectionist impulses, the question is whether international agreements provide a buffer against resurgent bureaucratic pressures to micromanage foreign trade and erect barriers against imports.

4. How Effective Are International Agreements in Curbing Bureaucracy?

International economic agreements are not specifically designed to ensure that policies and institutions maximize the national welfare of their signatories. They may contribute to it. But their purpose is to ensure that the national interests of signatories are taken into account. In other words, their focus is on preventing negative externalities rather than on compelling the Polish government to adopt policies that would increase national welfare. Thus, the WTO or the trade component of the EU Association Agreement aim mainly at areas affecting market access. Provisions in the Association Agreement, going further than those of the WTO, are too limited to tame the special interests of politicians and import-competing sectors (a litmus test for the quality of foreign trade institutions and policies), especially if these do not directly affect trade between Poland and the EU. Furthermore, treaties usually have safeguard provisions allowing for a temporary suspension of disciplines. Hence, they cannot be fully relied upon to address this problem.

But interventions by Poland's foreign trading partners that have special treaties with Poland and the commitments made under these treaties, as well as the discipline embodied in the WTO provisions, have provided some measure of restraint on protectionist impulses of the economic bureaucracy and politicians. For instance, due to pressures from major trading partners (including CEFTA members), implementation of the law on technical standards was temporarily suspended. As products identified in the law account for a very large share of Poland's manufactures imports, this would have erected a formidable barrier to imports.

Another area in which international agreements have contributed to sustaining liberal reforms in foreign trade are tariffs. Poland's relatively low tariffs owe much to preferential trade agreements under CEFTA and the European Association Agreement. Both agreements envisage duty-free trade areas, at least for manufactures with negotiated schedules to attain this goal by 1999 (with some exceptions). These commitments have certainly contributed to lower tariffs which, however, are increasingly replaced with other measures to reduce competition from imports (see Section 3).

The drawback of regional liberalization is that in contrast to the widening gap between tariffs on imports from CEFTA, EFTA, and the EU, those on MFN contribute to increased discrimination of exporters from MFN countries and trade diversion in favor of regional suppliers. The EU is both an economic superpower and Poland's natural trading partner. But it does not necessarily produce all products and at the lowest cost worldwide. Those that are not and yet are sold in Poland only thanks to high MFN tariffs obtain rents at the expense of their Polish users. In other words, Polish consumers of these products pay higher prices with the extra profit pocketed by preferential suppliers. Considering that Polish producers are already exposed to competitive pressures from EU imports and the level of protection would not change significantly, it is rather surprising that free trade has not spread yet to Poland under MFN trade policy. One may only explain this by a deeply entrenched aversion to free trade among Polish policy makers.

Although the Association Agreement stipulates elimination of tariffs and quantitative restrictions on industrial imports, it also provides provisions allowing withdrawal from obligations under the Europe Agreement to safeguard (protect) specified interests. The Europe Agreement does not ban the use of nontariff measures under specified circumstances. Derogations from free trade are allowed especially for sensitive products. Poland and the EU alike can resort to any of eight safeguard clauses contained in the Europe Agreement. Two of these can be employed under explicit conditions, and six are specific to particular groups of products or circumstances regarded by Association Agreement signatories as unique to an economy in transition from central planning. Since the safeguard clauses are nontransparent, weakly disciplined, and loosely defined, they are virtually open to unconstrained administrative discretion.

In fact, the Association Agreement provides weaker discipline on the use of safeguard measures than do those of the GATT. The CEFTA agreement, albeit encompassing countries at a rather similar level of development, retains also all the safeguard clauses included in the Europe Agreement. A restructuring clause was used to justify increases in tariffs—not to exceed the respective MFN applied rate and up to a three-year period—on imports from free-trade partners of telecommunications equipment (since 1994); of petroleum products (in 1996 raised from 12 to 15 percent); oil (raised to 25 percent in 1996); and trucks, trailers, special vehicles and chassis bodies (tariff rates raised from 30 to 35 percent). In the cases discussed above, no injury to domestic producers from adopted measures had to be demonstrated. Such derogation from trade liberalization envisaged in the agreements did not constitute part of a comprehensive program for restructuring, because there was none. Rather, it resulted from pressures either to protect domestic producers or to attract foreign investors.

5. Conclusion

Considering that Poland has been so successful in integrating with world markets, especially those in the EU, and has had very high economic growth rates, should one be concerned with a bureaucracy successfully reclaiming some areas of control lost as a result of the collapse of central planning? This research seems to suggest a positive answer to this question for the following reasons.

First, the negative impacts on economic efficiency of foreign trade-related administrative measures tend to accumulate over time. They contribute to the erosion of exporters' competitiveness. In the emerging post-Uruguay Round global environment, Poland will be in danger as competition in world markets intensifies. Consider that with the EU lowering its external barriers to trade in line with Uruguay Round commitments, Polish exporters will enjoy declining preferential tariff margins as EU markets become more open and competitive. The Round has produced deep tariff cuts and the outlawing of nontariff barriers, such as the MFA and voluntary export restraints. The average MFN import-weighted applied tariff rate on industrial products in the EU will decrease by the year 2000 by 2.9 percent.[20] Tariff reductions are particularly high for some Polish exports. For instance, the post-Uruguay Round applied rate on wood and furniture imports will be reduced by 5.5 percent and on metals by 3.3 percent. As a result, those Polish producers of industrial products who were able to compete in EU markets mainly thanks to preferential tariff margins (i.e., the difference between an MFN rate and a tariff rate offered in the European Association Agreement) will face difficulties in maintaining their market shares, unless they increase their efficiency.

Second, although the momentum in FDI inflows now works in favor of Poland, these may contract once the threshold of a tolerable administrative penetration spreading around from foreign trade is exceeded. Since FDI has provided a boost to Poland's reintegration with the world economy, its contraction would negatively affect Poland's competitiveness in world markets. A liberal foreign trade regime is an important component of an overall business climate. The international experience suggests that attracting FDI by a liberal and investment-friendly environment is the only efficient tool for developing new industries and restructuring existing sectors. Improving the environment for private business activity, both foreign and domestic, is a necessary precondition for achieving this goal.

Third, economic performance so far has been impressive. If the annual GDP growth rate of 6–7 percent is sustained over the next two years, it would place Poland close to the performance of such East Asian tigers as Taiwan (6.3 percent over 1990–1996) or Indonesia (7.2 percent over 1990–1996). Yet it would not be enough to match the growth performance of Singapore (8.3 percent), South Korea (7.7 percent), Malaysia (8.8 percent), Thailand (8.6 percent), not to mention China (10.1 percent). It is impossible to provide evidence regarding how many percentage points in terms of GDP growth would be added more by open, liberal, foreign-trade policies. It seems, however, that creeping interventionism has already generated welfare loss, whereas the growing bureaucratization of economic regimes (including that of foreign trade) may make the task of sustaining the earlier economic growth performance very difficult to achieve.

Notes

1. B. Kamiński, "The Framework of Soviet-East Central European Economic Relations in the 1990s," in Richard F. Staar, ed., *The USSR and East Central Europe* (New York: St. Martin's Press, 1991).
2. K. Poznanski, "The Competitiveness of Polish Industry and Indebtedness," in P. Marer and W. Siwinski, eds., *Creditworthiness and Reform in Poland* (Bloomington: Indiana University Press, 1988).
3. B. Kamiński, Z. K. Wang, and L. A. Winters, *Foreign Trade in the Transition: The International Environment and Domestic Policy* 20, Studies of Economies in Transition Series (Washington, D.C.: World Bank, 1996).
4. Główny Urząd Statystyczny, *Mały Rocznik Statystyczny* (Warsaw, 1996).
5. B. Kamiński, "How the Market Transition Affected Export Performance in the Central European Economies," *Policy Research Working Papers,* no.1179 (Washington, D.C.: International Economics Department, World Bank, September 1993); M. A. Landesmann, "The Pattern of East-West European

Integration: Catching Up or Falling Behind," Research Report no. 212 (Vienna: Institute for Comparative Economic Studies, Vienna 1995); P.C. Padoan and M. Pericoli, "The Single Market and Eastern Europe: Specialization Patterns and Prospects for Integration," *Economic Systems* 4, no. 17 (1993): 279–99.

6. Poznanski, "The Competitiveness of Polish Industry."
7. P. Havlik, "Exchange Rates, Competitiveness and Labour Costs in Central and Eastern Europe," *Research Reports*, no. 231 (Vienna: Institute for Comparative Economic Studies, 1996).
8. International Monetary Fund, *International Financial Statistics* (Washington, D.C.: IMF, 1996 and 1997).
9. *World Debt Tables: External Finance for Developing Countries*, vol. 2, *Country Tables* (Washington, D.C.: World Bank, 1996).
10. B. Kamiński, "Are Current Accounts a Threat to Poland's Macroeconomic Stability?" University of Maryland, College Park, 1997, mimeographed.
11. Polish Press Agency, 22 April 1997.
12. Ibid.
13. Główny Urząd Statystyczny, *Mały Rocznik Statystyczny*.
14. "Eksporterzy do Unii Europejskiej," *Gazeta Bankowa* (October 1996).
15. B. Hoekman, "Intra-Industry Trade, Foreign Direct Investment, and the Reorientation of East European Exports," *Center for Economic Policy Research Discussion Paper*, no. 1377 (London, 1996).
16. D. Rosati, "Institutional and Policy Framework for Foreign Economic Relations in Poland," in M. Kaser and A. M. Vacic, eds., *Reforms in Foreign Economic Relations of Eastern Europe and Soviet Union* (New York: UN Economic Commission for Europe, 1991).
17. J. M. Finger, M. D. Ingco, and U. Reincke, *The Uruguay Round: Statistics on Tariff Concessions Given and Received* (Washington, D.C.: World Bank, 1996).
18. Organization for Economic Cooperation and Development, *Indicators of Tariff and Non-tariff Trade Barriers* (Paris: OECD 1996).
19. J.M. Finger, *Controlling Antidumping* (Washington, D.C.: World Bank, 1995).
20. Finger et al., *The Uruguay Round*.

TEN

The Prospects
of Regional Cooperation

Sarah Meiklejohn Terry

Historically, in East-Central Europe, political stability and national autonomy have proven fragile and short-lived in the absence of a broader framework within which both to mediate contentious issues left by fallen empires and to focus energies on common needs and interests. Already twice this century—first in the immediate aftermath of World War I, and again during World War II—cooperation in this part of Europe has fallen victim to some combination of negative forces: domestic instability and political fragmentation; regional conflicts based on territorial, economic, and ethnic disputes, and diverging perceptions of national interest; the longstanding imperial ambitions of Russia or Germany or both; and the benign (or malign?) neglect on the part of Western powers, to which the new and fragile states in the region looked for support and protection.

Now, almost a decade after the collapse of Central Europe's communist regimes in the fall of 1989, the question remains to what extent all parties to the region's past turmoil—East, West, as well as the Central Europeans themselves—are now committed to the creation of new and more viable forms of cooperation both within and beyond the region. A second and equally important question concerns the synergy (or lack thereof) between cooperation at the regional or subregional level, on the one hand, and at the broader interregional or pan-European levels, on the other. The argument that multiple levels of cooperation are not only compatible but mutually reinforcing has been most eloquently expressed by a senior Polish diplomat, Józef Wiejacz: "The rise of a new united Europe and a new security system . . . will be a long and difficult process, constructed like a mosaic. A new and important phenomenon . . . is the formation or activation of various groups and associations, more or less formal, bringing together different states on the basis of regional interests and . . . shared fundamental values. There is no contradiction [between the "new regionalism" and] the tendency toward integration and unification of the continent."[1] While this view has enjoyed substantial rhetorical support, it has also, as we shall see, encountered skepticism and outright rejection from those who either saw an intensification of relations with their immediate neighbors as an unnecessary (even undesirable) detour from their "road to Europe," or feared that genuine success at the regional level would simply let the West off the hook on the question of integration at the European level, once again excluding them from the European mainstream.

In addressing these issues, this chapter focuses primarily on the four core Central European states—Poland, Hungary, and the now-separate Czech and Slovak Republics—and examines their attempts both to develop new forms of cooperation among themselves and to forge strong links with broader European structures, most important, the European Union (EU) and NATO. The analysis covers three main periods: the formative years of 1990–1992, characterized by early optimism over the speed of the transition despite a highly fluid domestic and international environment; the watershed year of 1993, which saw developments that altered the dynamics of both intraregional and interregional relations, significantly diminishing prospects for the former; and the years since 1994, which have witnessed the collapse or attenuation of once-promising regional initiatives as a result not only of their inherent internal weaknesses but also of Central Europe's quest for integration into Western institutions and for security in the face of a reassertive Russia.

1990–1992: False Optimism, Tentative Beginnings

In the first three years after the collapse of Central Europe's communist regimes, the evolving status of relations among the successor states can be likened to changing images in a kaleidoscope, in which appealing patterns emerge, shine brightly for a moment, and then dissolve into new combinations and configurations. This period saw the evolution of the Central European Initiative (CEI), efforts to enhance the institutional structures of the Conference on Security and Cooperation in Europe (CSCE), and the formation of the Visegrád Triangle. In this fast-changing environment, the dynamics of regional relations can best be grasped chronologically, with the years between late 1989 and the end of 1992 broken down into overlapping but distinct phases corresponding roughly, if imperfectly, to the calendar years 1990 to 1992.

1990

Despite strong personal ties among a number of the new political leaders that were forged in earlier dissident days, 1990 was not an auspicious year for regional cooperation. The dyspeptic state of relations among the then three core Central European states at the beginning of the year was evident on all sides. Poland in particular found itself somewhat isolated and vulnerable, while its two neighbors to the south saw themselves on a fast track toward inclusion in the European Community (or EC, as the EU was then known). In part this was due to the deceptively benign international environment in which the Soviet Union, still intact and under the leadership of President Mikhail Gorbachev and Foreign Minister Eduard Shevardnadze, was for most of the year cooperating in the controlled deconstruction of its "external empire." In Czechoslovakia and Hungary, this climate encouraged a false euphoria over the ease and speed of their "return to Europe." The Hungarians especially were convinced that their long history of reform efforts and substantial lead in attracting foreign investment gave them preferential status. Indeed, despite official denials, there was a palpable sense of competition among the three—a race to join Europe that was perceived as a zero-sum game in which if one wins, the others must lose, "as if all were courting the same woman."[2]

But the reluctance of the Central European states to forge closer links also had deeper and more structural roots. Four decades of forced cohabitation in the Soviet bloc only compounded a long history of mutual grievances and mistrust. Cultural and ethnic differences had been allowed to fester under a blanket of denials and ritualized protestations of fraternal friendship, or were exacerbated by policies of overt or covert assimilation. Moreover, the shared pathology of Marxist-Leninist rule, misdirected development, and flawed "integration" within the confines of a Moscow-dominated CMEA left all with a familiar litany of economic woes, ranging from technological obsolescence and redundant capacities to inefficient trading mechanisms. Thus, it should have come as no surprise that they saw each other as inappropriate and undesirable partners or that trade among them plummeted following the fall of their communist regimes. As a Polish journalist commented, "When a blind man takes the hand of a lame man, they create a pair which together can move forward more easily. Those afflicted with the same handicap do not have that chance."[3]

Other divisive factors concerned demographic, economic, and geopolitical asymmetries between Poland, on the one hand, and Hungary and Czechoslovakia, on the other. From a demographic perspective, Poland, with a population of 38 million (nearly 50 percent more than the other two countries combined), was seen as a potential heavyweight in the region, "both too large and too risky a partner for other Central European nation-states." Furthermore, "Poles are generally disliked in other Central European countries for their cockiness . . . [and] pretentious sense of self-importance."[4] From an economic perspective as well, Poland was out of step with the others, not only due to the country's crushing external debt and decades-long history of political and economic instability, but also because the Poles were the first to bite the bullet of free-market austerity. Given the near-term impact of the radical reform program introduced early in 1990—deep recession accompanied by surging unemployment and inflation—Poland temporarily (and unfairly) became "exhibit A" of how not to undertake the transition.

Through much of 1990 the Poles were perceived both by themselves and by their neighbors as uncomfortably exposed on both their western and eastern flanks. In the West, uncertainty over a reunited Germany's continued recognition of the Oder-Neisse boundary (defining Poland's post–World War II western frontier) caused Warsaw, reluctantly and temporarily, to view the continued presence of Soviet troops as a guarantee of the territorial integrity of the country at a time when Budapest and Prague were negotiating rapid withdrawals of their Soviet garrisons and pushing for early termination of all Warsaw Pact activities. In the East, Moscow's acquiescence in the demise of allied regimes in Central and Eastern Europe did not mean that it had yet accepted a loss of influence in the region, as evidenced by concerted efforts well into 1991 to negotiate new bilateral treaties with all the countries in question, including a special security clause prohibiting them from joining alternative alliance systems that the Soviet side deemed hostile. By virtue of size and strategic location, Poland again became the target of unwanted attention. According to one source, "The Soviets [were] resigned to allow two separate regional confederations, one in the North, with the Baltics and Scandinavia, and one in the South, over former Hapsburg lands, but neither embracing Poland."[5]

A final asymmetry, this one political, stemmed ironically from the April 1989 Roundtable Agreement that led to the installation of the first noncommunist government in Central and Eastern Europe in more than 40 years. Having been the front-runner in 1989, Poland found itself saddled with an anachronistic compromise struck at a time when both the communists and the Solidarity opposition assumed a continuation of Soviet hegemony over the region. In the spring of 1990—as Czechs, Slovaks, and Hungarians were voting their former communist rulers out of office in fully free elections—the Poles were stuck with an unfinished housecleaning: in particular, the "contractual Sejm," in which 65 percent of the seats in the more powerful house of Parliament were reserved for parties in the old communist-led coalition; a newly established executive presidency expressly designed for General Wojciech Jaruzelski, the man who had imposed martial law in 1981; and four former communists in key security-related cabinet posts. In postcommunist Central Europe, Poland seemed oddly out of synch.

Thus, throughout 1990, cooperation was focused primarily at the interregional and pan-European levels, specifically on enhancing two existing organizations: the Adria-Alpine Group (as the CEI was originally known) and the CSCE. The Adria-Alpine Group was a unique organization in a divided Cold War Europe. Formed in 1978, it provided a limited forum for discussion and coordination of largely nonpolitical issues among neighboring provinces of four countries: neutral Austria, communist but nonaligned Yugoslavia, NATO/EC member Italy, and (by the early 1980s) Warsaw Pact member Hungary. Joint concerns included regional planning, environmental and health issues, economic and agricultural problems, as well as cultural cooperation. Despite its apolitical character, and especially as the Cold War waned in the late 1980s, participation assumed added significance for Hungary as a vehicle for pursuing its strategy of "stealth neutrality." It was no accident, therefore, that at a meeting in Budapest in November 1989, as Eastern Europe's communist regimes were unraveling—a meeting attended for the first time by the foreign ministers of the four member states—the group was reconstituted from a subnational organization to one operating at the state-to-state level. It was only a matter of time before the questions of expanded membership and a broader agenda would arise.[6]

Adria-Alpine's appeal to other states in the region was obvious. As a group spanning the two alliance systems as well as the nonaligned world, membership would not imply an explicit break with Moscow (still a politically impossible, if not unthinkable, move); but it would mean formal affiliation with states outside the Warsaw Pact and a tentative first step toward the shared goal of EC membership. For Poland, in particular, it could also have meant the first step toward realization of a long-nurtured dream of building a network of cooperative links along a North-South axis to offset the pressures from East and West. Both Prague and Warsaw expressed interest in joining, but only the Czechoslovak application was accepted. The reasons for excluding Poland at this point went unstated. Possibly, the others were wary of being drawn into the uncertainties over the Polish-German boundary or the still-unresolved status of Soviet troops in the country; it is also possible that they were sensitive to Moscow's objections to Poland's participation in any independent regional grouping. But an element of Polish-Czechoslovak rivalry cannot be excluded. In his speech to a summit of Polish, Hungarian, and Czechoslovak leaders in Bratislava on 9 April, President Václav Havel referred to his own country's pending admission to the "Adriatic Community"; then, turning to Poland's status, he noted that "our brothers the Poles know that they do not belong to the historic Danube area" and suggested that they look to "some kind of North or Baltic equivalent of the Adriatic Alliance with Czechoslovakia as the geographically logical connecting link" between the two.[7]

At its Venice summit, held 31 July–1 August, the group, now officially renamed the Pentagonale, set itself an ambitious agenda through 1992. Five formal working groups were either confirmed or newly established (road transport, telecommunications, environment, small enterprise development, and culture and tourism), and plans for two more (on energy and migrations) were announced. On a more political level, the policy statement adopted at the summit described the Pentagonale as a "geographically circumscribed" initiative within the broader spectrum of European organizations, "represent[ing] a level of cooperation which will be helpful in bringing those member countries not yet participating in—or candidates to—the EC closer to the European Community." It also foresaw "a regular exchange of views . . . on matters of a political nature," interparliamentary cooperation, and support for contacts among nongovernmental organizations of member states. While not excluding involvement of nonmembers in specific Pentagonale projects, "particularly those dealing with the environment," the statement appeared to preclude further expansion, echoing Havel's Bratislava speech by suggesting that "encouragement must be given to the creation of other regional associations to the North and Southeast, with which profitable cooperation" could be established.[8]

The second major initiative of 1990, also spearheaded by Havel and his foreign minister, Jiři Dienstbier, involved a proposal to transform the CSCE into a pan-European security system that would gradually replace the Warsaw Pact and NATO alliances. In a memorandum distributed three days before the April summit in Bratislava, Czechoslovak leaders outlined a three-stage plan for "institutionalizing our joint efforts within CSCE and creating effective mechanisms of a new type." The centerpiece of the first stage was to be a European Security Commission, with headquarters in Prague, to "provide a permanent all-European platform for the consideration of questions relating to security on the continent, and for seeking their solution." The commission would meet regularly at the level of permanent representatives and at least once a year at the level of foreign ministers, and it would also have a military subcommittee. Stages two and three foresaw the emergence, first, of a treaty-based Organization of European States (including the United States and Canada) and, finally, of a "confederated Europe of free and independent states."[9]

There can be little doubt that all former Soviet bloc states attached enormous importance to the CSCE process, of which they were charter members by virtue of being signatories to the 1975 Helsinki Agreement. Not only had it played a facilitating role in their liberation from Soviet domination, it was also their only formalized link to the full North Atlantic community—in particular, to a continued American military and political presence in Europe, which most saw as a provisional guarantee of their future security in a very uncertain climate. Most did not share Prague's idealism (even naïveté) about the obsolescence of the traditional alliance systems, and especially of NATO. Indeed, the gaping hole in the Havel/Dienstbier proposal centered on the promise of "effective mechanisms of a new type." In fact, no specific amendments were offered to replace the unanimity rule in CSCE decision making; the Prague memorandum stated only that the proposed commission would "operate on the basis of consensus." As a more somber Havel admitted a year later, "Everything appeared to us to be clear and simple."[10] In the end, the CSCE's November 1990 summit in Paris—the most important result of which was the signing of the long-awaited conventional forces in Europe (CFE) arms reduction agreement—did approve the establishment of a secretariat in Prague and a crisis prevention center in Vienna but made no changes in the unanimity principle that hindered effective enforcement.

1991

The second year of postcommunist transformation was marked by brightening prospects for cooperation at both the regional and pan-European levels. For Poland, the most important development was the end of its quasi-isolation, first with the formation in February of the Visegrád Triangle (comprised of Czechoslovakia, Hungary, and Poland) and, later, with Warsaw's belated inclusion in the Pentagonale (thereafter Hexagonale). It was also a year in which the three states made important strides toward inclusion in the broader European community. By year's end, they had reached provisional association agreements with the EC and had been included in the newly formed North Atlantic Cooperation Council (NACC)—although both achievements fell short of their hopes. On the negative side, however, 1991 was a year of nasty surprises that demonstrated in manifold ways both the tenuous nature of past achievements and the enormous difficulty of constructing a new architecture for European cooperation and security.

The reasons for the sudden rapprochement in Central Europe were related both to changing internal situations in each of the three countries and to a substantially altered international climate. At the domestic level, the political and economic asymmetries that had weighed so heavily on relations were considerably reduced in at least two senses. First, Poland had weathered its first year of "shock therapy" far better than many had feared; at the same time, Czechoslovakia and Hungary were beginning to feel the pinch of declining production accompanied by rising inflation and unemployment. Moreover, all three economies were staggering under the impact of slumping trade with the Soviet Union. Second, the anomaly of former communists still occupying high political office in Poland was largely resolved with the December 1990 presidential elections, in which Solidarity leader Lech Wałęsa replaced General Jaruzelski, and with the appointment of an entirely noncommunist government.

Changes in the external environment were even more significant in ways that both pushed and pulled the three states together. On the "pull" side, the November 1990 signing of a treaty in which a united Germany formally recognized its postwar boundaries with Poland narrowed the gap between Warsaw on the one hand, and Prague and Budapest on the other—and not only over policy toward Germany. It also allowed the Poles to open negotiations with Moscow over the withdrawal of Soviet troops and to take a stance parallel to that of its neighbors on dissolution of the Warsaw Pact. On the "push" side, by the beginning of 1991, all three had a more realistic appreciation of the long time frame, as well as stringent conditions in terms of domestic legal and economic adjustments that the EC would impose for admission. They also seemed to recognize that none stood to be admitted on a preferential basis and that further pursuit of competitive tactics would only be counterproductive.[11]

But the most important push toward closer regional cooperation almost certainly came from a renewed sense of threat from the East. The conservative backlash in Moscow that first appeared in the waning months of 1990 and culminated in the abortive coup against Gorbachev in August 1991 shattered the perception of a relatively benign international climate that had prevailed a year earlier. Like a wounded bear, the Soviet military began showing its frustration over loss of empire by exerting mounting pressure on Gorbachev's reform leadership to reverse course. Most alarming for the Central Europeans were the dramatic resignation of Foreign Minister Shevardnadze, the man most responsible for the peaceful implosion of the USSR's external empire, as well as the blatant attempt to evade CFE arms limits and the January 1991 military crackdown against breakaway Lithuania.

In addition, all three Central European governments were finding Soviet negotiators increasingly truculent over a whole range of issues related to troop withdrawals, the termination of Warsaw Pact activities, and preparation of new bilateral treaties. Warsaw, which had reached an agreement to open withdrawal talks only at the end of 1990, was told that a large contingent of Soviet troops would have to remain in Poland until the completion of the much larger-scale withdrawal from the former German Democratic Republic in the mid-1990s. Budapest and Prague, both of which supposedly reached final withdrawal agreements already in 1990, suddenly found themselves in testy arguments over demands for reparations for alleged "improvements" on former Soviet bases and rejections of counterclaims for environmental damages. Finally, all three had become alarmed over the repeated postponement in the second half of 1990 of the promised Warsaw Pact meeting to discuss the time frame for dissolution of the alliance and even more so over Moscow's repeated insistence on the inclusion of the special security clause (mentioned earlier) in the new bilateral treaties. Indeed, this last point was formalized as a core tenet of Soviet policy in a January 1991 resolution of the CPSU Central Committee that reiterated Moscow's opposition to the inclusion of any Central or Eastern European country in Western European security structures and advocated the use of economic leverage (e.g., oil supplies) to maintain a Soviet sphere of influence in the region.[12]

This heightened threat perception, even more than the shared aspiration for early EC membership, provided the main driving force behind the limited cohesion the Visegrád states were able to develop. Finding themselves in a "security vacuum," they saw the virtue of occupying that uncomfortable space collectively—on a single sofa, so to speak, instead of separate armchairs. This new, more somber attitude was reflected in their quick response to the Lithuanian crisis in January. Within days, the three foreign ministers met in Budapest and issued a joint appeal for the immediate dismantling of the Warsaw Pact's military structures, as well as a stepped-up timetable for ending its political activities and disbanding the CMEA.[13] On the same day, 21 January, Hungary and Czechoslovakia signed a bilateral military cooperation agreement; similar Czechoslovak-Polish and Polish-Hungarian agreements were signed on 27 February and 20 March, respectively, marking the beginning of a pattern of intensified coordination on defense and security issues.[14] At a follow-up meeting on 2 August, the three defense ministers signed an additional "defense coordination" agreement, providing for a "system of regular consultations at all levels of their military establishments." While scrupulously maintaining that they had no intention of creating a new military alliance and that their cooperation was "not aimed at any other country," the reaction of the three to the attempted coup in Moscow just two and a half weeks later "indicated that there might have been greater depth to their military cooperation than they were willing to make public."[15] Another round of post-coup consultations led to a joint appeal, at a summit on 6 October, for the "direct inclusion of Poland, Czechoslovakia, and Hungary in the activities of the [NATO] alliance"—a status short of full membership but one that presumably would have implied the extension of a security umbrella over the Triangle.[16]

It was also the perceived security vacuum that prompted Poland's admission to the Pentagonale. Already in late 1990, Warsaw had been invited to participate in two working groups and to appoint a permanent representative to the organization. Now in January—again, only days after the violence in Vilnius—the Italian foreign minister told a meeting of parliamentarians from the Pentagonale countries that in light of "the present international situation" (a reference to the deteriorating situation in the USSR), "it is impermissible for us to leave Poland between two great powers when the formation of a new pan-European security system is still quite a long way off." Poland's membership was subsequently approved in May and became official with the next (now Hexagonale) summit in August. By this time, two new working groups had been added, and others had had their mandates expanded.[17]

At the broader European level, 1991 saw some forward movement in NATO-Visegrád relations. By the time of his visit to Brussels on 21 March, Havel's attitude had come full circle from the year before in Bratislava. Rather than seeing NATO gradually dissolving into a pan-European security organization built around the CSCE, he now recognized that, "as the only working and time-tested defensive alliance" in Europe, it was NATO that must be the "nucleus" or "cornerstone" of a pan-European system.[18] This brought Prague into closer alignment with views adopted earlier by both Budapest and Warsaw and set the stage for a more coordinated approach to the Western alliance (as seen in the October appeal). For its part, NATO already in mid-1990 had invited all Warsaw Pact members to establish diplomatic relations with the alliance; in 1991, amid growing instability to the east, NATO showed a greater willingness to expand mutual visits and consultations specifically with the Central European military establishments—a move that undoubtedly contributed to security cooperation within the Triangle.[19] Nonetheless, the alliance remained reluctant—as it had been before the dissolution of the Warsaw Pact—to establish any formal ties with Central Europe. The stated reason was that to give preference to some former WTO members over others would be an affront to Moscow that might complicate ongoing arms control talks or upset the delicate balance of power in Moscow. But a second reason was obviously that NATO members, already at odds over the alliance's role in "out of area" conflicts, were unwilling to accept any real responsibility for the region's defense. In November, the North Atlantic Council rejected Visegrád's October appeal in favor of establishing the broader but more amorphous North Atlantic Cooperation Council (NACC) as a forum for consultations among all NATO and former WTO states.[20]

Ironically, trilateral cooperation in the political and economic spheres in 1991 yielded more mixed results than in the security area. Ironically, because the 15 February summit, held in the provincial Hungarian town of Visegrád, from which the Triangle took its name, was hailed at the time as a major breakthrough in Central European cooperation. Indeed, it was a breakthrough in the sense that by comparison with the 1990 Bratislava summit, which lacked a clear focus and which produced no agreed program of action, Visegrád ended with an ambitious agenda focused four goals: restoration in full of each state's independence, democracy, and freedom; the dismantling of the economic and spiritual structures of the totalitarian system; the building of parliamentary democracy and a modern constitutional state, and respect for human rights and fundamental freedoms; and total integration into the European political, economic, security, and legislative order. These goals were to be achieved through multilayered collaboration at the European, regional, and subregional levels in at least eight priority areas. In addition to the "harmonization" of relations with European institutions, these included initiatives to foster intraregional cooperation and understanding at the social, cultural, and local governmental levels; free movement of capital and labor, interenterprise cooperation; joint strategies for attracting foreign investment; improvements in transportation infrastructure, telecommunications and energy networks; environmental cooperation; and the creation of "optimum conditions" for ensuring minority rights.[21]

The reality proved quite different. Instead of becoming an organization for promoting intraregional cooperation as well as integration at the European level, the Visegrád process became fixated exclusively at the latter—in effect, a vehicle for coordinating Central Europe's "road to Europe," while development of closer ties within the region languished on the back burner. At the European level, the Triangle's effort were rewarded in December with the signing of association agreements with the EC, but only after very difficult negotiations (and an initial veto by France). Moreover, although they offered the prospect of full membership within ten years, with a gradual lowering of trade barriers and partial protection for Central European markets in the interim, the agreements were seen by the Visegrád states as consolation prizes. Particularly distressing was the EC's refusal to open its markets to exports in the "sensitive" areas of steel, textiles, and agricultural products.[22]

The reasons for the lack of progress within the Triangle were several. Most important at this point was the shared fear that successful collaboration at the regional level would be used as an excuse to delay or even derail integration into the EC. A second set of issues concerned the emergence (or reemergence) of ethnic and interstate conflicts: between Czechs and Slovaks over the latter's demands for greater autonomy and a slowdown in the pace of economic reforms; between Hungarians and Slovaks both over the status of the Magyar minority in Slovakia and the controversial Gabčikova-Nagymaros dam on the Danube; at a lower level of contention, between Poles and Czechs over cross-border trade and the small Polish minority in Czechoslovakia; and on all sides, the perpetuation of mutually negative stereotypes of each other. Still a third disincentive to closer trilateral relations was apparently "friendly" advice from Moscow, at least to the time of the failed August coup, not to "spoil" relations with the East.[23]

At the official level, the response to these concerns was a joint effort to deny any intention of "institutionalizing" Visegrád; instead, it was most often described as a "political club." In fact, however, there were serious discrepancies on this point. The Poles in particular were eager for closer cooperation. As Wałęsa told an interviewer in September, "Should we [not] strive to make the most rational use possible of the comparable potential of comparable economies for better cooperation among the CSFR, Poland, and Hungary, and then on this basis attempt a more effective approach toward an integrated Western Europe?" In effect, it meant "training hard in the second league and then breaking through to meet the very best competition." As sensible as this point of view might have seemed—Wałęsa would raise it again in an expanded form a year later—it was not one shared in Prague or Budapest, where insistence on maintaining the informal nature of trilateral cooperation remained firm.[24]

1992

It quickly became clear that 1992 would be a year in which the hard-won gains of 1991 were jeopardized by developments within and beyond Visegrád. First, domestic preoccupations—a complicating factor in trilateral relations from the start—became a major stumbling block as all three countries found themselves in the throes of internal crises of quite different sorts. In Poland, fully free elections in October 1991 had yielded a badly fragmented Parliament, resulting in more than a year of political gridlock that came close to derailing economic reforms and undermining international confidence won over the previous two years. In Czechoslovakia, the issue of full independence for Slovakia versus maintenance of a looser federation was effectively decided by the June 1992 elections, which saw the victory in each republic of the party most determined to split the federation—Václav Klaus's rigorously free-market Civil Democratic Party in Prague and Vladimír Mečiar's populist-nationalist Movement for a Democratic Slovakia in Bratislava. In the meantime, Hungary remained mired in economic recession, its national psyche increasingly fixated on the status of Magyar minorities in neighboring states and on the volatile issue of "Hungarianness," with all of its anti-Semitic and xenophobic overtones, at home. By year end, Hungarian-Slovak relations were further exacerbated by the breakup of the CSFR, which the Hungarian minority in Slovakia saw as leaving it exposed to greater discrimination, and by the Danube dam, which the Slovaks rushed to finish in November and which Budapest regarded not only as a violation of its territorial integrity but also as a looming environmental disaster.

Disarray at a number of levels beyond Central Europe also affected relations among the Visegrád states. The Hexagonale, renamed the Central European Initiative at the beginning of 1992 to accommodate the growing number of post-Yugoslav states, disappeared from view for most of the year, resurfacing only in late November. Already in 1991, there had been no evidence of high-level activity after the August summit at which Poland was formally admitted—something that could be explained by the fact that the designated chair for that year was Yugoslavia, then in the process of disintegration. The reasons for the organization's dormancy through most of 1992, when the chair passed to Austria, were less obvious; nor was it clear if the technical working groups had continued to function.[25] As for the CSCE, to which Havel had attached so much importance two years earlier, the combination of an expanding membership (from 34 to 52 states with the breakup of the USSR), its nascent and toothless crisis-prevention mechanisms, and the absence of a back-up commitment from NATO, left the organization paralyzed in the face of the escalating Yugoslav crisis.

The breakup of the USSR also had a differential impact on the Visegrád states. While all shared a sense of relief over the collapse of the Soviet center, only Poland found itself bordering four post-Soviet states: Russia (in the form of the highly militarized Kaliningrad *oblast'*), Lithuania (with which relations were strained over the status of the Polish minority), plus Belarus and Ukraine (both of which also have sizable Polish minorities). By contrast, Hungary and Czechoslovakia bordered only on one, Ukraine, and the Czech Republic alone on none. This discrepancy not only left the

Poles more exposed in the event of widespread disorder in the east but also gave Warsaw a greater incentive to build a network of political, economic, and security ties with its new neighbors as a means of fostering their independence and stability. In both official and unofficial commentaries, there was a growing awareness that Poland had a choice between providing a bridge between East and West with strong links in both directions or risk seeing that bridge built over them and, most likely, again at their expense.[26]

A final external factor affecting trilateral relations at this point was the unexpected disarray in the EC. The December 1991 Maastricht Treaty, which was supposed to inaugurate the final stage in the creation of a single market by the end of 1992, instead ushered in a year of wrangling over everything from monetary policy to agricultural trade and larger subsidies for the EC's poorer southern tier. In brief, "Europe 1992" was not going to happen on schedule and, as defined by Maastricht, might not happen at all; in the interim, complications in the process of "deepening" EC integration could only postpone a "widening" of the community. Prospects that Brussels would step up the pace of trade liberalization (especially in the three sensitive areas of steel, textiles, and agriculture) were slim. In addition, two other factors clouded EC-Visegrád relations. First, the queue of aspiring members, mostly the small and prosperous EFTA (European Free Trade Association) countries, was already long; moreover, while they would add significantly to Community coffers, less-developed EC states had already indicated they would oppose expansion to the east—to countries that would impose a heavy long-term burden on the EC budget—until their own development needs had been more fully met.[27]

The combined effect of these developments on the Visegrád states was to sharpen the differences among them on the question of deepening their own cooperation even as they continued to coordinate relations with the EC, NATO, and the CSCE. Again, the critical dividing line was over institutionalizing relations within the Triangle. As before, Warsaw was the lone proponent both of deepening and widening cooperation as the best means of promoting greater stability and faster economic recovery in the region until full integration at the European level could be achieved. At the other extreme, and especially after leadership passed from Havel to Klaus, Prague remained steadfastly opposed and, as the year closed, increasingly intent on "jumping the queue" to the EC at whatever cost. Thus, 1992 was a year of decidedly mixed results in trilateral relations, with achievements in some areas offset by setbacks in others.

Not surprisingly, the most progress was made in the security area, where the pattern of regular consultations established in 1991 continued undisturbed even by the pending breakup of Czechoslovakia. Indeed, new areas for cooperation were agreed on, including air defenses and confidence-building measures within the framework of the CFE and "open skies" agreements. Nonetheless, a serious discrepancy in approaches to regional security arose shortly before the September defense ministers' meeting, when Warsaw floated the idea of a "NATO-bis" or "NATO-2," comprising not only of the Visegrád group but also several post–Soviet states (potentially the Baltics, Belarus, and Ukraine), as well as Romania and Bulgaria. The concept reflected both Poland's greater exposure to potential instability in the East and a growing conviction that the CSCE and the NACC were too passive and symbolic to be of practical significance. As presented by Wałęsa's top security adviser, Jerzy Milewski, the rationale was not to create a new alliance system as an alternative to NATO; indeed, he specifically stated that a guarantee of eventual NATO membership would be a precondition of any new regional alliance. Rather, Milewski foresaw NATO-2 as a transitional organization to defuse conflicts in the region and prepare the way for more rapid entry into NATO-1. On the latter point, he noted that "we will be welcome in NATO to the extent that NATO reaps an advantage from our membership, and . . . [that] we show that our relations with the East are good. Our trump card will be well-established cooperation with the countries of our region, as is the case within the 'Visegrád Triangle'." Thus, members of this transitional alliance would be required to renounce all territorial claims and contribute to the formation of a joint peacekeeping force.[28] In any event, Prague and Budapest summarily rejected the idea of a military pact either within the triangle or on a broader regional basis—although Warsaw's initiative would be revived in slightly different form and under different sponsorship barely six months later.

On the economic front, trilateral cooperation remained focused, as it had been in 1991, on the joint effort to speed up access to Western markets and set a timetable for full integration with the EC. That effort yielded limited success with the March 1992 decision to put the gradual trade liberalization features of the association agreements into effect, pending ratification by all 12 EC members. Beyond that, however, repeated appeals for a clear commitment to early EC membership met with repeated rebuffs, first at a London meeting of EC and Visegrád leaders in late October and later at the EC's Edinburgh summit in December.[29] In light of its internal economic difficulties, the EC's reluctance to take on the burden of a rapid absorption of Central Europe was understandable. On the other side, however, hard-pressed governments feared that the ten-year time frame for integration foreseen in the association agreements was undermining their fragile stability and sapping popular support for closer ties with the West. As Polish Prime Minister Hanna Suchocka told a German interviewer in November, "Most people here want to realize their chances in the EC in the next one or two years."[30]

Frustration over the slow pace of trade liberalization, both with the EC and within Visegrád, led the Poles to float a second trial balloon. A year after Wałęsa had first spoken of the potential advantages of "training hard in the second league" before taking on the main competition, a group of his closest advisers proposed a Central European trade initiative—in effect, a kind of EC-2 as the economic counterpart of NATO-2. Like the latter, EC-2 (which also would have embraced countries beyond Visegrád) was not intended as an alternative to full EC membership but as a transitional arrangement "to fill the vacuum left by the collapse of CMEA . . . that will exist until Poland (and similar countries) are integrated with the [EC]."[31] The potential benefits for Poland were obvious. Not only were Polish exports the most adversely affected by the remaining nontariff barriers within Visegrád; a restoration of trade ties with neighboring post-Soviet states was also seen as vital to the country's continued economic recovery. However, the idea fell on deaf ears, especially in Prague, where, with the approaching separation of the Czech and Slovak republics, Klaus was making it increasingly clear that cooperation even within Visegrád would henceforth be "no more important" to the Czechs than bilateral relations with other countries. By this time he had also rejected the decision taken at the May 1992 Prague summit—a meeting that proved to be the high point of Visegrád cooperation—to coordinate their applications to the EC; the official Czech position now was that each country should enter when it was "ready."[32]

Despite their failure to see eye to eye on broader economic cooperation, the Visegrád states did manage to conclude a Central European Free Trade Agreement (CEFTA) among themselves, but not without difficulty. The agreement in principle, arrived at in November 1991, to begin talks on a free-trade zone, was motivated more by loss of markets in the east and constraints on access in the west than by a genuine commitment to regional integration; negotiations dragged on for more than a year, complicated by the split between Czechs and Slovaks and by Klaus's dyspeptic attitude toward the whole enterprise. With the help of EC pressure to keep the Czechs from pulling out of the talks, CEFTA was finally signed in late December and scheduled to come into effect in March 1993.[33] Officially hailed as a major breakthrough that would promote intraregional trade and attract more foreign investment, unofficially it was widely recognized that a phased reduction of tariffs would have little impact in the presence of nontariff barriers left untouched by the agreement and provisions for the continued protection of agricultural markets.[34]

One positive development as 1992 came to a close was the surprise reappearance of the Central European Initiative (CEI), with a meeting at the foreign minister level on 20–21 November in the Austrian city of Graz. Its working groups had continued to function during the yearlong hiatus in high-level meetings and had elaborated more than 100 projects. A major constraint on CEI activities had been a lack of financial resources, but by the time of the Graz meeting the group had reached an understanding with the European Bank for Reconstruction and Development (EBRD) for assistance with at least seven infrastructure projects. Just what prompted member countries to call attention to the CEI at this point is not clear, but there appear to have been at least three agendas at work—one overt and two hidden or less obvious. One purpose clearly shared by all was to coordinate their responses to the Bosnian crisis; exactly a month after the Graz meeting, four of the foreign ministers traveled to New York to appeal directly for UN intervention.

A second, less explicit Polish agenda may have been to gain acceptance in a different forum for their vision of broader and more institutionalized regional cooperation embodied in the earlier EC-2/NATO-2 proposals. Therefore, Foreign Minister Krzysztof Skubiszewski's emphasis on the need for the CEI to be "open for cooperation with all interested states"; hence also the significance of the presence for the first time of observers from Bulgaria and Romania as well as Ukraine and Belarus. Still a third agenda, this one specifically Hungarian (and in all probability not articulated at Graz), appears to have been Budapest's intent to use a reenergized CEI, of which it would be the chair in 1993, as a forum for bringing pressure on Slovakia on both the Danube and minority issues. In an interview shortly after the Graz meeting, the Hungarian official designated as coordinator of CEI activities for 1993 singled out "cooperation along the Danube" as Budapest's priority; other intriguing points in the interview were a less-than-subtle hint that Hungary might try to use the breakup of Czechoslovakia as leverage to force the successor states to reapply for membership in CEI, his emphasis on the increasing salience of political issues, and his reference to the "special problem" of national minorities.[35]

A final noteworthy development in 1992 was the establishment of a new regional grouping, the Council of Baltic Sea States (CBSS), which evolved out of a 1990 Polish-Swedish initiative to convene a meeting of prime ministers of all Baltic Sea states. The following year, an Association of Baltic Cities was formed, and in March 1992, at a foreign ministers' conference in Copenhagen, the CBSS was created. Of the ten members, five belonged to some combination of NATO, the EC, and the EFTA

(Denmark, Germany, Norway, Sweden, and Finland); of the other five, Poland was the only Central European state, the remaining four being the former Soviet republics of Estonia, Latvia, Lithuania, and Russia. In addition to an annual meeting at the foreign minister level, the council's institutional structure included an executive body (the Committee of Permanent Representatives), and a parliamentary forum. The agenda adopted in Copenhagen was similar to that adopted by the CEI in its emphasis on practical tasks, such as infrastructure modernization, as well as cooperation in energy, health, and environmental policy. Another important aspect of the CBSS's declared agenda was the salience given to "support for new democratic institutions." Like the CEI also, the CBSS stressed the synergistic nature of regional cooperation—that in "the creation of a Baltic identity" it would be contributing to a pan-European architecture rather than seeking to build an alternative to it.[36]

1993: A Watershed Year

From the outset, 1993 brought developments that fundamentally altered not only the internal dynamics of the region but also its relations with both East and West. Within Visegrád, the breakup of Czechoslovakia had consequences that went far beyond the mere squaring of the Triangle, effectively undermining what remained of its political cohesion even as CEFTA began to take hold. Similarly, broader regional initiatives, such as the CEI, flagged in the face of the Bosnian conflict and other ethnic tensions. To the east, the reappearance on the international stage of an assertive Russia, intent on reclaiming its dominant position not only in the near abroad but potentially also over its former Warsaw Pact allies, coincided with the debut of Ukraine—equally intent on eluding Moscow's clutches—as an aspiring regional actor. To the west, both the EC and NATO took tentative steps toward eastward expansion, although without specifying timetables or entry requirements. By year-end, the net effect of these developments was to accentuate the disincentives for intraregional cooperation and to rivet the attention of the Visegrád states on integration with Euro-Atlantic institutions.

It was hardly a surprise when Klaus seized on the moment of the formal separation of the Czech and Slovak republics to reject once and for all the notion of synergy between cooperation within Visegrád and EC integration. In early January, he told *Le Figaro* that the Triangle had been an artificial construct from the start, imposed on Central Europe by the West; in a second interview at the World Economic Forum in Davos later that month, he argued that to focus on cooperation with non-EC members (by which he clearly meant Visegrád) would deflect the Czech Republic from its primary goal of joining the Community—positions that were vehemently disputed by the Poles.[37]

While the increasingly vocal disinterest of the Czechs was the primary impetus for the unraveling of Visegrád, other question marks hung over the group in 1993, of which the most nettlesome was the "Mečiar factor." No longer constrained by Prague, the mecurial Slovak prime minister was free to pursue his populist-nationalist brand of politics which, apart from his reluctance to implement meaningful economic reforms, included policies aimed at limiting the cultural and political rights of Slovakia's Magyar minority (more than 10 percent of the population) and an ambiguous foreign policy that mixed pro-Western rhetoric with a distinct tilt toward Moscow, on which an unreformed Slovak economy was still heavily dependent. The ethnic tensions, complicated by the unresolved issue of the Danube dam, not only exacerbated relations with Budapest but also caused Prague and Warsaw to view Bratislava with reserve. By the end of the year, another development sapped Visegrád's cohesion—this time, the return to power of the postcommunists in Poland in September, with the likelihood of a similar electoral result in Hungary in spring 1994. Klaus was again quick to seize on these shifts to tout Prague's "front-runner" status.

Despite their differences, Prague did join the others in yet another appeal to the EC, on the eve of its Copenhagen summit in June, to "set the date and define conditions" for membership. This yielded partial success when the summit extended a formal, if guarded, invitation to those "associated countries in Central and Eastern Europe which so desire" to become members, but with no timetable and only generally worded conditions for eligibility—and with the further stipulation that admission would be subject to "the Union's capacity to absorb new members while maintaining the momentum of European integration."[38] In essence, Brussels' position remained unchanged—deepening must come before widening. For the Visegrád four, this meant that the group's one achievement of the year was a major disappointment. Otherwise, it was a year of declining activity. In what proved to be a bad omen for the future, 1993 was the first year since the group's founding in which it failed to hold a summit. It was also a year in which what little high-level activity there was took place in other forums—such as the March foreign ministers' meeting with EC and NATO officials in Brussels and the May defense ministers' meeting in Rome (not attended by the Czech minister) during a session of the West European Union.[39]

For the CEI, the year began auspiciously with the establishment of a secretariat, sponsored jointly by Italy and the EBRD, to provide technical assistance and funding for some projects. But it did not take long for the divisive minority rights issue to surface. In March, the foreign ministers endorsed a Hungarian initiative to organize a conference on nationality questions, setting the stage for a prolonged stalemate at top levels of the CEI and diverting attention from its practical agenda. Dissension erupted at the Budapest summit in mid-July over whether the organization should adopt legally binding norms for the treatment of minorities within member states. In particular, an Italian draft, strongly supported by Hungary, endorsed the right of minorities to set up autonomous territorial units and would have prohibited any redrawing of administrative boundaries to the detriment of minorities—positions that were clearly unacceptable to Slovakia. The issue was made even more acrimonious by an ill-fated attempt on Budapest's part to enlist Prague's support against Bratislava. Already miffed by a Hungarian attempt to delay Slovakia's admission to the Council of Europe, Klaus demonstrably sided with Mečiar, arguing that minority issues were not in the CEI's purview and should be left to all-European organizations, such as the Council of Europe or the CSCE.[40]

In the end, no document was adopted; nor was the proposed conference on minority rights ever held. If there was any positive outcome of the situation, it was to engage the Council of Europe in monitoring the status of minorities in both Slovakia and Romania as a condition of their membership—although this did not prevent the issue from continuing to dominate CEI meetings. Meanwhile, a statement issued by the parliamentary committee at its November session called attention to serious systemic defects in CEI coordination. Expressing "profound dismay that communication problems between the [governmental and parliamentary] forums have not been resolved, the statement called for "joint working sessions between CEI ministers and parliamentarians" as a "fundamental element" of the CEI framework. It also noted the need for "greater awareness" of EBRD priorities "so that projects suitable for EBRD support [could] be elaborated," proposed that "committees of national parliaments . . . be included in the activities of working groups," and expressed regret that no agreement on the financing of the working groups had yet been reached.[41]

On balance, the CEI's record to this point was more positive than negative in that it had brought together ten countries, most newly independent and some just new, in search of mutually beneficial solutions to shared problems. It had, in contrast to Visegrád, established institutional structures that at least in principle represented the diverse interests of member states. At the same time, cracks were appearing in the CEI's structure that would jeopardize its future success: half of its now ten members (Macedonia was admitted in July) were either directly involved in or potentially threatened by the escalating Bosnian tragedy; other political and ethnic tensions within the region were threatening to politicize the agenda and deflect energies from the CEI's original pragmatic goals; finally, the two most prosperous members, Italy and Austria, were by themselves incapable of meeting its daunting funding needs.

By the second half of 1993, however, these disparate developments in regional relations were increasingly overshadowed by larger security concerns as the Visegrád states pressed for accelerated membership in NATO to offset what they perceived as a renewed threat from the east. The issue burst into public view in late August with Russian president Yeltsin's unexpected declaration in Warsaw (repeated also in Prague and Bratislava) that the entry of Poland and other Central European states into NATO would not be seen as contrary to Moscow's interests—followed only a few weeks later by his equally stunning retraction.[42] In retrospect, it is clear that the emergence of the issue of NATO's eastward expansion and Russia's seemingly confused response were rooted in developments dating back to the closing weeks of 1992, in particular, the shift to the right in Russian politics with the defeat of reformist prime minister Yegor Gaidar (and indirectly Yeltsin) and Moscow's increasingly assertive stance in both domestic and foreign policy.

Two aspects of Russian policy, neither well recognized in the West, were especially important here. The first was Moscow's creeping redefinition of the "near abroad" to include not only the former Soviet republics but its old Warsaw Pact allies as well. The second was (and remains) the central place of Ukraine in the fine-tuning of Russia's policy toward the Visegrád states. Indeed, Yeltsin's flip-flop on NATO membership for the latter cannot be understood without reference to Moscow's resolute determination to head off efforts by the former to reorient itself westward as a counterweight to pressures for closer integration within the CIS.

The first point was most clearly articulated by then Russian foreign minister Andrei Kozyrev in an interview with the Warsaw weekly *Polityka*. Reminding Kozyrev of his own conceptualization of Russia's "three circles of good neighborliness"—the former Soviet republics (or near abroad), the developed countries of the northern hemisphere, and the southern arc from the Near East to China—the interviewer asked where Central and Eastern Europe fit into this picture, whether this region "which played a critical role in the foreign policy of the USSR" was being pushed into the background. Kozyrev's answer was both revealing and blunt: "Eastern Europe has not been pushed to the background by us. The countries of this region have never fallen out of Russia's field of interest. Considering their geographical proximity and traditional centuries-long ties, *we include them rather in the first circle*. The goal of our policy toward Poland, the Czech Republic and Slovakia has been to

maintain the existing infrastructure of mutual relations while simultaneously changing the basis on which these relations operated [emphasis
added]." Kozyrev went on to warn the three countries that joining NATO
would strengthen reactionary forces in Russia and transform the region
into a "buffer zone that could be crushed in any situation"; instead,
Poland and its neighbors should form a neutral "bridge" linking Russia
with Western Europe.[43]

Another reference point is the "Foreign Policy Concept of the Russian
Federation," adopted in January 1993, which directly linked relations with
the near abroad with policy toward Eastern Europe: "East Europe does
not just retain its significance for Russia as an historically formulated
sphere of interest. The importance of maintaining good relations with the
countries of this region has become immeasurably greater with the formation of the belt of sovereign states—Ukraine, Belarus, Moldova,
Lithuania, Latvia, and Estonia—the interrelation with which cannot help
but be influenced by the effect of the nature of our ties with East Europe."
The document went on to state that the "strategic task at the current stage
is to prevent East Europe from turning into a sort of buffer zone, isolat-
ing us from the West." It further noted that "This is a task which is well
within our powers," considering that these states are economically and
culturally "still oriented as before toward Russia and the other CIS countries." A later section dealing with general European security spelled out
Moscow's opposition to "subregional organizations," especially those that
might include other CIS states without Russia's participation.[44]

That Ukraine and Poland, as the relative heavyweights on each side of
the CIS-Central European divide, were prime targets of this new assertiveness should have come as no surprise. Although Warsaw's September 1992 proposal for an extended security cooperation in Central
and Eastern Europe had fallen on deaf ears among its Visegrád partners,
Kiev clearly took note. Not only did Ukraine express interest in closer cooperation with Visegrád and the CEI, then-president Leonid Kravchuk
also launched his own plan for a Baltic-to-Black Sea security zone. First
broached on a state visit to Hungary at the end of February 1993,
Kravchuk's initiative was presented to all four Visegrád states and the
CSCE over the next four months and was based on assumptions and
anxieties similar to those that had motivated President Wałęsa: that the
security vacuum in Central and Eastern Europe had created a situation
of "latent military and political instability, that Western security structures were "not yet ready to enlarge their 'zone of responsibility,'" and
that an "all-European security space" could only be created when regional stability had been reestablished. While Kravchuk's proposal did
not preclude Russian participation, several of the conditions he wanted

participants to accept were clearly at odds with Moscow's goal of re-asserting its dominant position in the former Soviet republics. These included the "inadmissibility of strengthening one's own security at the expense of others' security"; "strict respect for political sovereignty and territorial integrity . . . in Central and Eastern Europe"; and the "inadmissibility of deploying foreign troops in territories of other states without their clearly expressed consent."[45]

Moscow did not wait for Kravchuk's diplomatic offensive before moving to preempt Ukraine's westward reorientation. On a visit to Warsaw in January (as the foreign ministry was finalizing its concept paper), Yeltsin adviser Sergei Stankevich warned his hosts that Moscow was opposed to close military ties between Poland and Ukraine.[46] In addition, in a meeting at the Polish Senate, a question concerning Ukraine's possible membership in the Visegrád group elicited the following elliptical response: "In no case would we wish that post-communist Europe create any structures aimed . . . at constraining Russia [or] her alleged aggressive designs. *We have no aggressive intentions and operate on the principle that Russia has never had any such intentions* [emphasis added]." Stankevich then warned against the formation of any groups for which "Russia might be the object of joint actions" and put Warsaw on notice (more than six months in advance of Kozyrev's *Polityka* interview) that Moscow would oppose Poland's quest for membership in NATO.[47]

This consistency in Moscow's statements over the preceding six months, not only in opposition to NATO's eastward expansion but also on recouping its position in the near abroad, raises an intriguing question concerning Yeltsin's motives in signing the August declaration. In addition to dropping Russia's objections to Poland's membership in NATO, he also gave his blessing to the "development of subregional cooperation" within the framework of Visegrád and the CEI—in both cases contradicting his foreign minister.[48] Clearly, Yeltsin must have needed something very badly—a quid pro quo to justify a high-visibility reversal (albeit temporary) of well-established policies. What that something was remains a matter for speculation, but in this observer's view, Moscow's first priority had to be to derail the Kravchuk initiative—to drive a wedge between Ukraine on the one hand and the Visegrád states (and especially Poland) on the other. How better than by offering the latter the prospect of a green light (or blinking yellow) to pursue the NATO option in exchange for adopting a hands-off approach toward Ukraine?[49]

In all probability, the concession was a calculated move on Yeltsin's part in the expectation that he could retract it at a later date or perhaps, in light of the nascent state of debate over enlargement within the alliance at that point, that NATO would not be responsive. What he almost certainly did not anticipate was that it would spark a full-fledged debate in NATO capitals or that, barely two weeks after Yeltsin's Warsaw visit, NATO Secretary General Manfred Woerner would test his sincerity by stating that "the time has come to open a more concrete perspective to those countries of Central and Eastern Europe which want to join NATO and which we may consider eligible for future membership. I am happy that President Yeltsin also sees it in this way. We intend to build bridges and not barriers. Nobody will be isolated."[50] The speed with which enlargement captured the public's (especially the media's) attention sent Moscow into rapid retreat. On 1 October, in the midst of a final showdown with his conservative parliament, Yeltsin sent simultaneous letters to the four major NATO capitals "reinterpreting" his understanding of the Warsaw declaration. The earlier acceptance of NATO's eastward expansion was now framed in the "wider context of the central role Russia must plan in the future security of Europe." An expanded alliance without simultaneous membership for Russia was unacceptable. Alternatively, NATO and Russia could provide "joint security guarantees" for Central and Eastern Europe—a variant that these countries clearly viewed as unacceptable.[51]

But the die had been cast. The fallout from Yeltsin's flip-flop was three-fold. First, it led directly to the creation of the Partnership for Peace (PfP), with the Russian president as unwitting midwife. Caught between raised expectations in the Visegrád capitals and members' reluctance to confront Moscow, NATO had little choice but to come up with a face-saving compromise. PfP, adopted at the alliance's January 1994 summit, offered to extend political consultations begun two years earlier under the NACC into areas of military cooperation. The initial reaction of the Central Europeans was one of deep disappointment, not only over being lumped together again with Russia and other CIS states but also because the new program failed to offer a security guarantee or to set clear criteria and a timetable for membership. However, PfP also posed a dilemma for Moscow. Precisely because it was open to all WTO and Soviet successor states, Russia could either join on equal terms or stand aside as other former republics—Ukraine among the first—got in line. In effect, Yeltsin's August "concession" had opened a Pandora's box that he (or any other Russian leader) would find difficult to close.[52]

At the same time, it is not too much to say that the shift in Russian policy in 1993 delivered the final coup de grâce to the Visegrád process. For the Poles and other Central Europeans, Russia's new assertiveness dramatically narrowed their options and raised the stakes in their race to join the West. Ironically, while fears of a resurgent Soviet Union had been one of the main catalysts for the formation of the Triangle in 1991, the emergence three years later of an assertive Russia contributed to the group's demise, prompting the less exposed Czechs to abandon even the pretense of a coordinated strategy. Not only was the notion of an expanded Central and East European cooperation zone (whether in the form of Wałęsa's NATO-2/EC-2 ideas or Kravchuk's Baltic-to-Black Sea initiative) now a dead letter; the region also faced the possibility that at least some post-Soviet states along its eastern borders could effectively lose their independence, leaving the Central Europeans in all too familiar and uncomfortable proximity to Russia—a situation these countries were incapable of dealing with on a strictly regional basis. In brief, Central Europe alone was too lacking in resources, too weak militarily, and too burdened by the multiple legacies of the past to shape itself into a viable regional entity without the economic and security umbrella that only the West could provide.

Third, the structure of the partnership plan also contributed, perhaps inadvertently, to the demise of multilateral cooperation within Visegrád. The proposal, to be based on bilateral agreements between NATO and each nonmember "partner," played neatly into Klaus's game plan. Thus, when Warsaw, Budapest, and Bratislava called for a meeting of defense ministers to coordinate their stance in advance of NATO's January 1994 summit, the Czechs were represented only by a deputy minister. A follow-up summit in Prague on 11–12 January, at which the four heads of state met with U.S. President Bill Clinton, was also arranged (much to the displeasure of the others) to underscore the bilateral as distinct from the regional dimension.[53] Two days later, the Czech defense minister pronounced Visegrád "obsolete," adding that "associating entry into NATO with military cooperation among the Visegrád countries is nonsense."[54]

1994 and Beyond:
Toward Fragmentation and Integration?

The decline in genuine multilateral cooperation in Central Europe that was readily apparent in 1993 became more pronounced in subsequent years. Of the two most visible regional initiatives, Visegrád as a forum for political coordination faded into its still nascent (though growing) economic offspring, CEFTA, while the CEI was increasingly paralyzed by the war in Bosnia. In their place, interactions among the Central European states are now conducted for the most part bilaterally, with each individually engaging prospective partners to the west and east. This final section addresses the following questions: Should more have been expected from these early regional cooperative ventures? If so, what went wrong? And what are the implications, not only for regional cooperation but also for broader European integration in the future?

Despite attempts by Warsaw, Budapest, and Bratislava to use the Clinton meeting to reenergize Visegrád as a vehicle for coordinating relations with EU and NATO, January's "antisummit" effectively marked the end of this once promising initiative.[55] The name virtually disappeared from official Czech discourse. Among the other three, there was a good deal more nostalgia over its demise; but the hope, initially expressed by Wałęsa, that they could sustain the group without the Czechs, and possibly even expand it to new members, proved a non-starter. That Slovakia—the weakest and least progressive of the three—was now the only connecting link among them was in itself an impediment to continued cooperation; equally important, however, was the fact that relations between Budapest and Bratislava continued to be confounded by prolonged negotiations over the basic treaty. Even the signing of the treaty in March 1995 (after extensive Western mediation) and its quick ratification by Hungary did nothing to improve relations as the two sides continued to dispute the interpretation of its minority rights provisions and as Mečiar delayed submitting it to the Slovak Parliament until he could pass a language law undermining those portions of the treaty.

The fallout from Visegrád's demise has not been entirely negative. First, CEFTA remained as a partial surrogate, with a more limited mandate to be sure, but with a potentially broader membership. Second, despite (or perhaps in part because of) ongoing strains in Hungarian-Slovak relations and the increasing isolation of Bratislava, the last several years have seen an unexpected warming of Polish-Czech relations. And, third, in the face of the escalating verbal offensive out of Moscow and in the absence of effective multilateral alternatives, Warsaw has begun moving to engage its immediate neighbors to the east, most important, Ukraine.

By early 1994, the leading CEFTA skeptic, Czech prime minister Klaus, had at least two reasons to rethink his position. First, the breakup of the CSFR had disrupted economic relations between the two successor republics, leaving Prague with a rising trade deficit and extending the postcommunist recession. Second, it had now become clear even to Klaus that the Czech Republic had no chance of being included in the EFTA round of EU expansion, that negotiations for Central Europe's accession would begin only after completion of the EU's Intergovernmental Conference (IGC) scheduled for 1996–1997, and that in the meantime the prevailing view in Brussels was that these countries should "not disturb the EU market with excessive exports of the so-called sensitive goods . . . but should intensify cooperation among themselves.[56] Starting in March 1994, CEFTA adopted a series of amendments to the original 1992 agreement that accelerated and broadened trade liberalization and tentatively opened its doors to new members, provided they belonged to GATT and had concluded association agreements with the EU. On paper, the measures were impressive: for all but a small fraction of industrial goods, the date for creating a fully free trade zone was moved up from the beginning of 2002 to the beginning of 1997; in the contentious area of food and agricultural products (passed over in the original agreement), 50 percent of such products became duty free as of 1 January 1996, with step-by-step reductions up to 50 percent on the remainder; in addition, at its September 1995 meeting, CEFTA agreed to open talks on liberalizing trade in services and capital flows. That same meeting saw the admission of Slovenia as the fifth member of the group, while Romania, Bulgaria, and Lithuania were represented for the first time as observers.[57]

Despite these successes, the level of trade among CEFTA members, while rising from severely depressed levels, has remained disappointingly low. With the exception of Slovakia, which still conducts some 30 percent of its trade with the Czech Republic, trade within CEFTA is in the range of 5–8 percent of total turnover for each country (for Poland in 1995, a mere 5.5 percent). In addition, discordant notes over the future direction of CEFTA development remain. Poland would like to see faster liberalization of trade in services (especially construction) and consideration of freer labor flows, both of which would help to close its current trade deficit within CEFTA but which others fear would inundate them with large numbers of unemployed Poles. Members also differ over the pace and direction of expansion; Warsaw is especially interested in bringing Lithuania into the fold, while others favor a go-slow approach or an orientation toward the southeast. Another difference has been over the extent to which CEFTA should become a substitute for integration into the EU. Finally, although most members view CEFTA (as they did Visegrád) as a "self-obsolescing" form of cooperation that will end with full integration in the EU,[58] Mečiar, no doubt motivated by Slovakia's growing isolation and declining prospects of being among the first tier of Central European states to be invited to join either the EU or NATO, tried to use his position as CEFTA chairman for 1996 to push for greater institutionalization of CEFTA, with the creation of a secretariat in Bratislava and expansion to some of the weaker Balkan states that are also unlikely to qualify for early EU membership, such as Bulgaria. Nonetheless, CEFTA's overall record of progress has already sparked speculation that it could eventually provide the impetus for a revival of the more broadly based, multilayered cooperation that Visegrád was originally intended to foster.

A second byproduct of Visegrád's demise was the surprise rapprochement between Prague and Warsaw that began in late 1994 and has continued unabated to the present, and which has forced Klaus to put aside not only traditional Czech suspicions of Poland but also his initial disdain for its postcommunist leadership. Klaus's motives were several: most important was his recognition not only that integration with the West would be delayed but also that the special importance accorded Poland by Bonn and Washington made good relations with Warsaw a priority; that Klaus was locked in a prolonged if subdued struggle with Germany over mutual wartime grievances (settled only in January 1997) provided another reason for seeking support from the Poles.[59] Still a third factor was Prague's growing estrangement from Bratislava, where Klaus's initial efforts to prevent Slovakia's isolation, even in the face of profound policy differences, soon gave way to a need to distance himself from Mečiar's aberrant behavior and the rising flood of negative attention from Brussels. A final factor was apparently the more modest style adopted by Polish diplomacy whereby in place of Wałęsa's sometimes overbearing attempts to speak for the region as a whole, two successive foreign ministers in 1994 and 1995 took a more consultative and conciliatory approach.[60] Whatever the mix of motives and personalities, the change in the tenor and substance of Polish-Czech relations could not have been more striking. Consultations at the presidential, head of government, and ministerial levels have become more frequent, especially in the area of military cooperation. Personality factors have also played a role; the November 1995 presidential elections in Poland, which saw the defeat of Wałęsa (long disliked by Klaus) by the social democratic leader Aleksander Kwaśniewski, brought together two likeminded technocrats in what can best be seen as a calculated partnership to advance their common interest in integration with the West.[61]

More fascinating and potentially even more important than the shift in Polish-Czech relations has been a similar turn in Polish-Ukrainian ties. After the rejection of Kravchuk's Baltic-Black Sea initiative in 1993, Kravchuk himself was defeated in Ukraine's 1994 presidential elections. Motivated by the interdependence of the two economies, the new president, Leonid Kuchma, had campaigned on a platform of rapprochement with Russia and found most of his support in the heavily russified parts of the country. It looked as if Ukraine's brief flirtation with a westward orientation was over. In addition, the postcommunist social democratic-peasant party coalition that came to power in Warsaw in September 1993 was initially more inclined to cultivate Moscow than to risk ruffling Russia's feathers by engaging the former republics too closely.[62]

Little more than a year after his election, however, Kuchma was again looking west to escape Moscow's relentless political and economic pressures for integration within the CIS—which his foreign minister described in an October 1995 letter as "in practice washing out CIS states' sovereignty, making their activities subordinate to Russia's interests and restoration of a centralized superpower." At the same time, Ukraine announced that it had applied for full membership in the CEI.[63] Since then, the level of cooperation between Ukraine and its immediate neighbors to the west has increased across the board; in addition, it has shown interest in becoming an observer in CEFTA. But it is the Warsaw-Kiev link that promises to become, in Kuchma's words, a "strategic partnership." From Kiev's perspective, "the most important task . . . is for us the confirmation of Ukraine as a Central European state with full rights," and clearly Kuchma sees (just as Moscow fears) an engaged Poland as Ukraine's most reliable route to Central Europe and out of its current Eastern European limbo. Warsaw's interests are equally clear. It views a democratic and independent Ukraine as a sine qua non of regional stability and a bulwark against a possible renewal of Russian imperialism; Warsaw also believes that close cooperation—including military cooperation—with Ukraine will be the best answer to Moscow's contention that NATO expansion could lead to a new Iron Curtain along the Bug River. Polish-Ukrainian relations are not, of course, problem-free. In particular, Kiev, while no longer opposed to NATO enlargement, is concerned that it take place in a way that will not further compromise Ukraine's security.[64] But on balance, the rapprochement between the two countries since mid-1995 represents a kind of historical reconciliation similar to that which has taken place between Poland and Germany since 1990.

Finally, a few observations concerning recent developments in the CEI: On the positive side of the ledger, it has continued to hold regular meetings at the prime minister and foreign minister levels, with a rotating chair. It has grown from ten member states in late 1993 to 16 at the end of 1996—the new members in addition to Ukraine being Albania, Bulgaria, Romania, Belarus, and Moldova. On the negative side, however, expansion has brought a political and geographical diffuseness that cannot help but erode its organizational and programmatic cohesion. In particular, the increase in Balkan membership has shifted its center of gravity to the southeast and—in light of the protracted Bosnian war—has forced the CEI to focus much of its energy and limited resources on conflict resolution and postwar reconstruction. It is thus of declining relevance to Poland and other Central European states, although it may regain its momentum as a broader regional enterprise in the future, provided adequate funding is found for its ambitious list of prospective projects.

In this respect, it is useful to compare the CEI's experience with that of its Baltic counterpart, the CBSS. Despite its diverse membership embracing a combination of prosperous Nordic states and postcommunist states in varying stages of transition, the CBSS's more defined geographic and thematic focus—namely, the shared interests in restoring the health of the Baltic Sea as well as fostering the stability and development of all states that border on it—offers much better prospects for achieving its goals. The CBSS's second major advantage over the CEI is that it has largely been able to avoid politicization of its agenda; indeed, it has played an active role in easing tensions between Russia and the Baltic states over testy questions of troop withdrawals and minority rights.[65] Third, unlike the CEI, the CBSS can fund the projects it proposes, either through its own budget or through "special Baltic funds" set up within the EBRD by the Nordic states.[66]

Thus, not quite eight years after the collapse of communism in Central and Eastern Europe, the state of relations among the successor states presents a mixed picture. Some former adversaries have reached genuine reconciliations, while others are painfully moving in that direction and others still remain mired in ancient animosities. Once-promising regional initiatives have faded or are struggling to sustain themselves, while most eyes are fixed on Western institutions as the panacea that will cure their ills and insecurity. Could the Central European countries have done more to promote regional stability and cooperation? Or would stability and cooperation have been better achieved by integrating these countries into Western institutions sooner rather than later? And what are the implications of the looming proximity of a once imperial Russia that has not yet fully relinquished its expansionist tendencies? In addressing these questions, it is useful to recall the statement by Ambassador Wiejacz cited at the beginning of this chapter, in which he described a new Europe and a new security system that would have compatible and mutually reinforcing levels of cooperation.

Both Visegrád and the Central European Initiative could no doubt have accomplished more had they adhered more closely to their original mandates. With respect to Visegrád, Prime Ministers Klaus and Mečiar were the odd couple most responsible for bringing the group down—Klaus with his arrogant belief that the Czechs were better than their neighbors, Mečiar with his blatant exploitation of domestic tensions for personal political advantage at the expense of Slovakia's internal stability and external interests. The CEI, too, fell victim in part to the actions of individual members who saw advantage in pursuing their own parochial agenda over the shared goals of the whole. Yet even without these impediments, was either Visegrád or the CEI capable alone (or even together) of anchoring Central Europe's transition? The answer is clearly no, any more than CEFTA—despite laudable steps to liberalize trade among its members—can compensate for barriers to markets outside the region.

Responsibility for the problems besetting regional cooperation lies also with external actors. Strategies pursued both by the EU and NATO since 1993 have proven to be disincentives to policy coordination, especially among the Visegrád states, although for quite different reasons—the EU due to the long time frame for integration and the fear that continued cooperation at the regional level would force the front runner to wait for the laggards for admission, NATO due to the bilateral nature of its PfP initiative. Further south, the inaction of the West, in the face of the deteriorating situation in the former Yugoslavia, prolonged that conflict and helped derail progress within the CEI. To the east, Russia's influence has also been detrimental. Ironically, while fears of a resurgent Soviet Union had been one of the main catalysts for the formation of the Visegrád group in 1991, the reemergence of an assertive Russia three years later contributed to the group's demise, prompting the less exposed Czechs to abandon even the pretense of coordinated strategy and convincing others that regional initiatives were insufficient to counter Moscow's ambition.

Viewed in a longer perspective, however, the present disarray in the region may only be temporary—part of what Wiejacz called the "long and difficult process [of] construct[ing] a mosaic"—a mosaic in which elements of regional cooperation blend with integration at the pan-European level. Despite initial expectation, however, it now seems more likely that the latter will reinvigorate the former. Already, NATO's PfP has encouraged an expanding pattern of cooperation on military and security issues among partner countries. Nor is the pending decision to invite at least three Central European states—Poland, Hungary, and the Czech Republic—to become full members of the alliance likely to slow down this process. Progress in enlarging the EU will be slower as it struggles with its own internal organizational and monetary reforms; but even here, any moves that bring the Central Europeans closer to admission are much more likely to foster rather than discourage intraregional cooperation. In brief, the closer the Central Europeans come to becoming full-fledged members of Western institutions, the more favorably they will view cooperative relations with one another.

The most important remaining question is Russia's reaction to these developments and especially to the prospect that Ukraine and other former Soviet republics may become parties to them. Despite its diplomatic offensive over the past several years against NATO enlargement—coupled with persistent attempts to cajole or dragoon its former republics and Warsaw Pact allies back into political and economic dependence—there are signs of movement here as well. The conclusion of a NATO-Russia charter in May 1997 is the most positive indication yet that Moscow has begun to understand that its own security and prosperity would be better guaranteed by mutually acceptable cooperative relations with its neighbors than by territorial control and political domination. It is to be hoped that the glass is more than half full rather than half empty.

Notes

1. Józef Wiejacz, "Ugrupowania regionalne w nowej Europie," *Polska w Europie*, no. 11 (April 1993): 110. At the time of writing, Ambassador Wiejacz was an adviser to the Polish foreign ministry on regional relations.
2. Joanna Solska, "Grupa Wyszehradska," *Polityka*, 1 January 1993, 3.
3. Ibid.
4. Grzegorz Górnicki, "Is Poland Really in Central Europe?" *East European Reporter* 4, no. 2 (Spring–Summer 1990): 57–58.
5. Ibid.
6. For background on the Adria-Alpine Group, see Johnathan Sunley, "Alpe-Adria," *East European Reporter* 4, no. 2 (Spring–Summer 1990): 65–66.
7. For the text of Havel's speech, see ibid., 59–61.
8. Concerning expansion of the Pentagonale, see *East European Reporter* 4, no. 3 (Autumn–Winter 1990): 54–56. For a candid expression of the feeling of rejection in Warsaw, see the interview with Polish journalist Grzegorz Musiał, "An End to Solidarity?," ibid., 59–60. Concerning possible reasons behind Poland's exclusion and the unlikely prospects at this point for a Baltic equivalent to the Pentagonale, see Robert Sołtyk, "Penta, hexa czy wcale?" *Gazeta Wyborcza*, 11 July 1991.
9. The text of the memorandum is translated in the same issue of *East European Reporter* as Havel's speech (see note 6 above), 62–63.
10. Havel's speech at NATO Headquarters, 21 March 1991, in *East European Reporter* 4, no. 4 (Spring–Summer 1991): 65; concerning his continuing commitment to the "futurological" promise of the CSCE, see the abridged text of his address to the Conference on European Confederation, held in Prague on 12–16 June 1991, in *East European Reporter* 5, no. 1 (January–February 1992): 42–46.
11. See, e.g., Grzegorz Górnicki, "Visegrád: The Three-Cornered Umbrella," *East European Reporter* 4, no. 4 (Spring–Summer 1991): 68–69.
12. See especially Rudolf L. Tokes, "From Visegrád to Kraków," *Problems of Communism* 40, no. 6 (November–December 1991): 104–07. The resolution of the CPSU CC, "On the Development of Conditions in Eastern Europe and Our Policy in This Region," dated 22 January 1991, was published in *Izvestiia TsK KPSS*, no. 3 (1991): 12–17.
13. Both Foreign Minister Skubiszewski (in a January 1991 speech at the Royal Institute of International Affairs) and Havel (at NATO in March) used the term security vacuum; see their respective texts in *East European Reporter* 4, no. 4 (Spring–Summer 1991): 61–68. Concerning the 21 January foreign ministers' meeting, see Jan B. de Weydenthal, "The Visegrád Summit," *Report on Eastern Europe* 2, no. 9 (1 March 1991): 29.

14. The agreements provided for consultations on a wide range of issues, from the development of new military doctrines and the inculcation of democratic values to such practical problems as maintaining aging Soviet weapons systems and the possible coproduction of military equipment; see Douglas L. Clarke, "Central Europe: Military Cooperation in the Triangle," *RFE/RL Research Report* 1, no. 2 (10 January 1992): 42–45.

15. At a hastily called meeting on 20 August, the day after Moscow announced the coup, senior Visegrád officials agreed on "concrete measures regarding cooperation in the areas of immigration, border protection, and the exchange of political information." It was later disclosed that at least Warsaw had issued standby mobilization orders and that "constant liaison" had been maintained among the three capitals throughout the crisis (ibid).

16. Jan B. de Weydenthal, "The Cracow Summit," *Report on Eastern Europe* 2, no. 33 (25 October 1991): 27–29; also "The Triangle," *East European Reporter* 5, no. 1 (January–February 1992): 44.

17. See Józef Wiejacz, "Grupa Pentagonale i miejsce Polski," *Polska w Europie*, no. 5 (June 1991): 79–88; also Sołtyk, "Penta, hexa, czy wcale?"

18. See note 9 above.

19. Tokes, "From Visegrád to Kraków," 108–9. The most important demonstration of Western concern over Central European security was NATO Secretary General Manfred Woerner's appearance at a Prague conference about the future of European Security on 25 April, at which he expressed the need for "a new modern and comprehensive concept of security."

20. Concerning dissolution of the Warsaw Pact and formation of the NACC, see Christopher Jones, "The Security Policies of the Former Warsaw Pact States," in Andrew Michta and Ilya Prizel, eds., *Postcommunist Eastern Europe: Crisis and Reform* (New York: St. Martin's Press, 1992), 112 and 125–26; also *NATO: Communiqués 1991* (Brussels: NATO Office of Information and Press, 1992), 26–39.

21. For the text of the Visegrád Declaration and commentaries on the summit, see de Weydenthal, "The Visegrád Summit"; also *East European Reporter* 4, no. 4 (Spring–Summer 1991): 68–70.

22. For details of the Association Agreement signed between Poland and the EC, see Mieczysław Nogaj, "New Principles of Trade with EC Countries and Changes in Customs Regulations in Poland," *Polish Foreign Trade*, nos. 3–4 (March–April 1992); similar agreements with the CSFR and Hungary were signed the same day.

23. Concerning the various structural, economic, and psychological obstacles to closer cooperation within Visegrád, see Rafael Wiśniewski, "Po Wyszehradzie—Środkowoeuropejskie perspektywy," *Polska w Europie*, no. 5 (June 1991): 66–78; and Stanisław Pużyna, "Trójkąt środkowoeuropejski—wyzwanie i szansa," *Polska w Europie*, no. 6 (September 1991): 82–88. See also comments by Jerzy Marek Nowakowski et al., especially concerning Moscow's "advice," in the report of a conference held at the Center for International Studies of the Polish Senate in October 1991, in

Polska w Europie, no. 7 (November 1992): 53–58. An overview of the first year of Visegrád cooperation from perspectives of all three member states appears in a special section on the Central European triangle, *RFE/RL Research Report* 1, no. 23 (5 June 1992): 15–32.

24. Tokes, "From Visegrád to Kraków," 110–11.

25. See, e.g., Katarzyna Kołodziejczyk, "Inicjatywa środkowoeuropejska'" *Rzeczpospolita,* 21–22 November 1992. In his wide-ranging review of Poland's foreign policy priorities to the Sejm in June 1992, Foreign Minister Skubiszewski made no mention of the CEI; see his "Droga do Europy 1992," *Polska w Europie,* no. 9 (July–September 1992): 5–12.

26. See, e.g., excerpts from former prime minister Jan Krzysztof Bielecki's talk delivered at the Institute of Economic Affairs in Brussels (9 March 1992) and Jerzy Marek Nowakowski, "Polska i Europa środkowa," both in *Polska w Europie,* no. 8 (April 1992): 5–8 and 20–26; also Edward Wende, "W europejskiej tradycji," *Polska w Europie,* no. 9 (July–September 1992): 13–15.

27. Concerning the burden that the East-Central European states would impose on the EC, see *Is Bigger Better? The Economics of EC Enlargement* (London: Centre for Economic Policy Research, 1992); according to CEPR estimates, early integration of the Visegrád states would cost the EC states 8 billion ECUs (approximately $10 billion) annually, while Bulgaria and Romania would add another 5 billion ECUs.

28. See interviews with Milewski in *Rzeczpospolita,* 8 September 1992, in FBIS-EEU-92-177 (11 September 1992), 14–16; and 28 October 1992, in *RFE/RL Research Report* 1, no. 44 (6 November 1992): 61. Despite Milewski's references to the NACC and CSCE as "passive" and "symbolic," Warsaw remained committed to taking advantage of the opportunities offered by the former and to strengthening the crisis-prevention potential of the latter. See, e.g., Skubiszewski, "Droga do Europy"; the foreign minister's statement at the December 1992 CSCE meeting in Stockholm, in FBIS-EEU-92-246 (22 December 1992), 1; and an interview with the deputy defense minister on Poland's defense goals and relations with the NACC, in FBIS-EEU-92-192 (2 October 1992), 22.

29. The most important initiative was the submission of a joint memorandum to the EC, in anticipation of the London and Edinburgh meetings, in which the Visegrád countries appealed for further trade concessions (especially in the "sensitive" sectors), an agreed timetable for beginning negotiations on full EC membership, expanded political dialogue at all levels, and more financial aid, especially for small- and medium-size enterprises; *Rzeczpospolita,* 12–13 September 1992, in FBIS-EEU-92-183 (21 September 1992), 23–24. See also the follow-up report from the Polish Press Agency, in FBIS-EEU-92-206 (23 October 1992), 3. Concerning the Edinburgh summit's failure to act on the Visegrád appeal, see Marek Ostrowski, "Po szczycie w Edynburgu," *Polityka,* 19 December 1992, 2.

30. Markus Ziener, "Warsaw Calls for More Western Commitment," *Handelsblatt* (Düsseldorf), 5 November 1992; in FBIS-EEU-92-220 (13 November 1992), 12.

31. Arkadiusz Milewski, "Nostalgia na CEMA?" *Nowy Świat*, 15 September 1992; in FBIS-EEU-92-183 (21 September 1992), 24–25.

32. See Klaus's statement in Vienna on 15 December, in FBIS-EEU-92-244 (18 December 1992), 9. This was the first time he had stated this position so bluntly but hardly the first time he had presented the Czech Republic as more qualified for rapid integration into the EC than the other Visegrád states. On the issue of nontariff barriers, the most serious tensions were between Poland and the CSFR over the latter's tight border controls to prevent Poles from buying up subsidized Czech goods following the adoption of free-market reforms by Warsaw. As former foreign minister Jiři Dienstbier lamented: "It was terrible. The borders went down with the West and up in the East;" quoted in William Echikson, "Falling from Grace in Eastern Europe," *Boston Sunday Globe*, 31 January 1993.

33. Details of the agreement were summarized in *Gazeta Wyborcza*, 23 December 1992, in FBIS-EEU-92-250 (29 December 1992), 32; see also Karoly Okolicsany, "The Visegrád Triangle's Free-Trade Zone," *RFE/RL Research Report* 2, no. 3 (15 January 1993): 19–22.

34. For press commentaries that took a less favorable view of the agreement than official statements, see Joanna Solska, "Grupa Wyszehradzka," *Polityka*, 1 January 1993, 3; Leszek Mazan, "Trójkąt biedy," *Polityka*, 21 November 1992, 19; and Zsuzsa Regos, "Forced Integration—What is in the Visegrád Covenant?" *Nepszabadsag*, 9 December 1992, in FBIS-EEU-92-240 (14 December 1992), 27–28.

35. For general coverage of the Graz meeting and Skubiszewski's remarks, see Kołodziejczyk, "Inicjatywa środkowoeuropejska"; for the interview with the Hungarian official, Andras Szabo, see FBIS-EEU-92-239 (11 December 1992), 16–17. Szabo's approach to broadening CEI cooperation was also more cautious than Skubiszewski's; referring specifically to the four observer states, he noted that "this does not mean the expansion" of the CEI, only that they could participate in some working groups.

36. Concerning the founding and activities of the CBSS, see Józef Wiejacz, "Ugrupowania regionalne w nowej Europie," *Polska w Europie*, no. 11 (April 1993): 112–18.

37. For Klaus's view, see *RFE/RL New Briefs* 2, no. 4 (11–15 January 1993): 12, and no. 7 (1–5 February 1993): 10. Skubiszewski was quick to contradict Klaus on the origins of Visegrád, restating that it remained for Warsaw "a valuable tool" for improving Central Europe's leverage with Western institutions; see Milada Anna Vachudova, "The Visegrád Four: No Alternative to Cooperation?" *RFE/RL Research Report* 2, no. 34 (27 August 1993): 41–46; see also Wiejacz, "Ugrupowania regionalne" (cited in note 1 above).

38. Desmond Dinan, *Ever Closer Union?* (Boulder, Col.: Lynne Rienner Publishers, 1994), 479–80.

39. See *RFE/RL News Briefs* 2, no. 12 (8–12 March 1993): 12, and no. 23 (24–28 May 1993): 11. By now, sending lower-ranking officials to foreign policy and defense consultations had become a frequent practice for the Czechs, no doubt a way of reinforcing Prague's disinterest in Visegrád.

40. For coverage of CEI activities through the summit, see Alfred A. Reisch, "The Central European Initiative: To Be or Not to Be?" *RFE/RL Research Report* 2, no. 34 (27 August 1993): 30–37; also *RFE/RL News Briefs* 2, no. 30 (12–16 July 1993): 17 and 19, and no. 31 (19–23 July 1993): 9–10 and 17. By this time, Klaus had become as dismissive of the CEI as he was of Visegrád, stating that the group would be of "little use" if it did nothing but "build highways and railroads through neighboring states."

41. See FBIS-EEU-93-225 (24 November 1993), 1; also the report of the November foreign ministers' meeting, in *RFE/RL News Briefs* 2, no. 48 (22–26 November 1993): 10–11, where it was announced that Ukraine had applied for membership and that Belarus, Bulgaria, and Romania wanted to participate in some working groups.

42. For reports of Yeltsin's visits to Warsaw, Prague, and Bratislava, see *RFE/RL News Briefs* 2, no. 35 (23–27 August 1993): 16, 18; also FBIS-EEU-93-163, 164 and 165 (25–27 August 1993), 23–25, 12–14, and 7–8, 17–19 and 23–24, respectively. See also Suzanne Crow, "Russian Views on an Eastward Expansion of NATO," *RFE/RL Research Report* 2, no. 41 (15 October 1993): 21–24; and Alfred A. Reisch, "Central Europe's Disappointments and Hopes," *RFE/RL Research Report* 3, no. 12 (25 March 1994): 21. The full text of the declaration was carried by ITAR-TASS on 25 August; see FBIS-SOV-93-164 (26 August 1993), 13–15.

43. The interview was given on the eve of Yeltsin's visit, but extensive excerpts were published only after Yeltsin's apparent concession. See "Nie chcemy poprawiać geografii," *Polityka*, 9 September 1993.

44. *FBIS Report: Central Eurasia* [FBIS-USR-93-037] (25 March 1993), 10–12. Concerning Moscow's distrust even of the Visegrád group, see Reisch, "Central Europe's Disappointments and Hopes," 20.

45. Ukraine never issued an official document outlining Kravchuk's proposal; however, the Ukrainian Embassy in Warsaw did issue a press release on 22 April 1993, entitled "To Strengthen Regional Security in Central and Eastern Europe: Initiative of Ukraine." For another account of the initiative, see Roman Solchanyk, "Ukraine's Search for Security," *RFE/RL Research Report* 2, no. 21 (21 May 1993): 1–6.

46. Solchanyk, "Ukraine's Search for Security," 3.

47. "Stosunki polsko-rosyjskie—wyjście z cienia Katynia . . ." *Polska w Europie*, no. 11 (April 1993): 71–92.

48. By some accounts, these concessions were extracted from Yeltsin only after hard bargaining at the last minute and over the strenuous objections of his entourage, including Kozyrev. Concerning the latter's somewhat embar-

rassed retraction of positions taken in his interview less than a week earlier, see Ryszard Malik, "Czas rozpocząć odliczanie na nowo," *Rzeczpospolita,* 26 August 1993. Rumors at the time that Yeltsin made the concession on NATO only because he was inebriated do not stand up in view of similar statements made on later stops in Prague and Bratislava.

49. It is worth noting that after his visits to Warsaw, Prague, and Bratislava, Yeltsin returned home via Kiev. We can only imagine that his message to Kravchuk was the Russian equivalent of "Gotcha!"

50. For excerpts of Woerner's 10 September speech to a high-profile conference of the International Institute for Strategic Studies, see his op-ed piece, "What We Now Know," *Wall Street Journal* (European edition), 13 September 1993.

51. Roger Cohen, "Yeltsin Opposes Expansion of NATO in Eastern Europe," *New York Times,* 2 October 1993; and Vladimir Lapskiy, "Russian President Urges West Not to Expand NATO by Incorporating East Europe," *Izvestiia,* 2 October 1993, in FBIS-SOV-93-190 (4 October 1993), 12. In the intervening weeks, Kozyrev's August reference to Central Europe being "crushed" was repeated in an even more menacing way by a middle-level Foreign Ministry official, who stated that despite the breakup of the USSR, Russia would continue to play the leading role in Eastern Europe, adding that "whether they like it or not, the small nations of Eastern Europe will be forced with time to resign [their] separatism and conclude an alliance with Russia because otherwise they will be crushed politically and economically by Germany." From *Segodnia,* 14 September 1993, quoted in "Albo sojusz z Rosją, albo stłamszenie przez Niemców," *Gazeta Wyborcza,* 15 September 1993.

52. See "NATO Partnership for Peace: Invitation" and "Framework Document" (Brussels: NATO Press Service), 10 January 1994; the document was noticeably reticent about future enlargement, saying that it would come only "as part of an evolutionary process, taking into account political and security developments in the whole of Europe." See also Michael Mihalka, "Squaring the Circle: NATO's Offer to the East," *RFE/RL Research Report* 3, no. 12 (25 March 1994): 1–9.

53. Concerning the defense ministers' meeting on 7 January, see *RFE/RL News Briefs* 3, no. 3 (27 December 1993–7 January 1994): 22–23; also the interview with Hungarian foreign minister Géza Jeszenszky, "Nastroje w poczekalni," *Polityka,* 15 January 1994. The latter notes that at the closing dinner (after departure of the Americans), the Czech hosts sat each of the four Visegrád delegations at its own table.

54. From *Lidove Noviny,* 14 January 1994, in FBIS-EEU-94-012 (19 January 1994), 12.

55. The apt phrase "antisummit" was coined by Milada Anna Vachudova in her unpublished Ph.D. dissertation, "Systemic and Domestic Determinants of the Foreign Policies of East Central European States, 1989–1994" (St. Antony's College, Oxford University, 1997), 267. For the divergent perspectives of the

242   •   Sarah Meiklejohn Terry

Visegrád states on the utility of the group, see FBIS, *East Europe Daily Report,* issues for January 1994, especially the 5th through the 14th.

56. As quoted in Marian Szczepaniak, "Współpraca gospodarcza państw Grupy Wyszehradzkiej: Trzy lata funkcjonowania CEFTA," *Przegląd Zachodni* 52, no. 3 (July–September 1996): 57.

57. For an overview of CEFTA's development, see ibid., 56–76. FBIS, *East Europe Daily Report,* carried extensive coverage of CEFTA activities between 1994 and 1996.

58. See Vachudova, "Systemic and Domestic Determinants," 266.

59. See Elizabeth Pond, "A Historic Reconciliation with Poland" and Steve Kettle, "Czechs and Germans Still at Odds," in *Transition* 2, no. 3 (9 February 1996): 9–11, 22–25, and 64; also Craig R. Whitney, "Germans and Czechs Try to Heal Hatreds of the Nazi Era," *New York Times,* 22 January 1997.

60. See, e.g., "Współpraca gospodarcza Europy środkowej—wstęp do integracji?" (Skrócony zapis dyskusji na konwersatorium Fundacji "Polska w Europie," 8 listopada 1995 roku), *Polska w Europie,* no. 20 (May 1996): 76–86; also Jósef Vesely, "The Czech Republic and Poland: An Attempt at Having Another Go," *Tyden,* 21 August 1995, in FBIS-EEU-95-189 (29 September 1995), 14.

61. See e.g., FBIS-EEU-96-008 (11 January 1996), 12–13; and FBIS-EEU-96-112 (10 June 1996), 19–20.

62. For background, see P. K., "Poland-Ukraine: Heightened Activity After Stagnation," *Rzeczpospolita,* 6 July 1995.

63. For two summaries of the letter, which was in direct response to Yeltsin's 14 September 1995 decree outlining Russia's strategic concept of relations within the CIS, see FBIS-SOV-95-195 (10 October 1995), 71–72.

64. See, e.g., Kuchma's 26 June 1996 speech to the Polish Parliament and Polish commentaries, in FBIS-EEU-96-125 (27 June 1996), 31–35; also "Military Cooperation with Ukraine Discussed," in FBIS-EEU-95-196 (11 October 1995), 54–55; and "Geremek Interviewed on Eastern Policy," in FBIS-EEU-96-156 (12 August 1996), 45–48.

65. See note 36 above; also *RFE/RL News Briefs* 3, no. 22 (22–27 May 1994): 17.

66. European Bank for Reconstruction and Development, *Annual Report 1996* (London: 1997), especially 74–80. These funds—one for investment and a second for technical assistance—are designed primarily for private sector development, with an emphasis on small and medium enterprises, in Estonia, Latvia, and Lithuania. With respect to funding for CEI projects, the EBRD report is silent. Its cumulative disbursements through 1996 show that less than 10 percent of the total went to (unspecified) "regional" projects, but the CEI is not mentioned as a cooperating or co-funding organization.

ELEVEN

Western Assistance: Changing Mindsets and Relations

Janine R. Wedel

When the Soviet bloc collapsed in the fall of 1989, a mood of triumph swept West and East alike. After eight years of underground struggle in Poland, the communists had relegalized the Solidarity movement, and in June, Solidarity won by a landslide in the country's first semifree vote in half a century. Through the autumn of 1989, one communist regime after another had fallen, until the whole East bloc toppled: The long-suffering peoples of Eastern Europe had risen up en masse. The region Ronald Reagan had christened the "Evil Empire," the West's nemesis of the postwar era, had collapsed, remarkably and unexpectedly.

The West had won not only a political but also a moral and ideological victory. It now had an unparalleled, historic opportunity to spread the fruits of freedom and free markets, to unite Europe, and to break down isolation between the two worlds. Certainly, it seemed, there was a meeting of the minds at last: The West had supported the spirit of resistance embodied in the movement led by Polish Solidarity leader Lech Wałęsa, and in the aftermath of its success, the people of Poland embraced the democratic ideals and financial support offered by the West.

In both East and West, the idea that Poland should look to the West not only for financial help and political models, but for economic strategies and cultural identity as well, stood nearly unchallenged. "Democracy," "freedom," "markets," "civil society," and "return to Europe" were the bywords of 1989 and the early 1990s. Western capitalism and democracy were seen as the only possible choices after abandonment of communism. As Poland adopted Western models, so its people expected the West to open its doors and accept new responsibilities: to come in with accolades and affirmation and aid promises.

The Marshall Plan was the reference point for the kind of aid that the West would provide to the "other Europe." Leaders and commentators in both East and West compared post-1989 aid to Eastern Europe with the post–World War II effort to rebuild Europe. Offered as an economic life raft by the United States to the ravaged states of Western Europe after World War II, the Marshall Plan had helped to reconstruct the region. Now, a post–Cold War "Marshall Plan" would accomplish similar objectives. Both Marshall Plans celebrated and even symbolically consummated America's winning of a war: first in a literal sense and, 50 years later, in a symbolic sense. Both Marshall Plans were to assist "First World" Europeans: first to remake Western Europe and, 50 years later, to bless East Europeans in their "return to Europe." The words "Marshall Plan" became almost a metaphor for America's role as a white knight.

The most generous outlines for the new Marshall Plan featured the same kind of capital investment that had been provided to rebuild postwar Western Europe. Across the West, donor nations, agencies, and individuals expressed their commitment to helping Poland and the other Eastern European nations. The Group of Seven (G-7) countries (Canada, France, Japan, United Kingdom, Germany, Italy, and the United States) convened meetings to organize multilateral activities. The European Union (EU) established PHARE, the largest aid program to the region. PHARE stands for Poland-Hungary Aid for Restructuring the Economy and reflects the EU's initial focus on those two countries. (After the first year of operation, the PHARE program broadened its target to include other countries in the region, but the old acronym was retained.)

In the United States, legislation was enacted on the very heels of communism's collapse. In the last days of November 1989, the U.S. Congress rushed through the so-called SEED (Support for East European Democracy) Act. SEED allocated $2 billion to promote the private sector, democratic pluralism, and economic and political stability in Poland and Hungary. In addition, then-president George Bush established a Citizens' Democracy Corps and other initiatives that would make American know-how available to these nations. There was strong bipartisan support for aid to America's former Cold War rivals.

Western development agencies were similarly galvanized into action, reorienting resources and diverting personnel from the Third World nations of Africa, Asia, and Latin America to the Second World of Eastern Europe. Assignments in the Second World were "where the action is," or at least where it was at the moment. By 1993, the G-7 countries had committed nearly $35 billion in aid to help Central and Eastern European nations.[1] The United States had obligated $1.3 billion in aid, of which nearly half was targeted for Poland.[2]

The West offered aid, and Poland accepted it. Politicians on both sides showed their support, and their populations supported them in turn. How did it happen, then, that in just a few short years, this promising era of cooperation soured, fostering much disillusionment and frustration? Lack of funding, lack of communication about the character of the aid effort and the type of aid that would be sent—and perhaps most important, the West's lack of understanding about the legacy of communism in the East—all played their part. The original Marshall Plan had been widely seen as a success, but in the 1990s, the new one would fall far short of its promise.

One of the factors that few appeared to consider at the time was how ill prepared the West was to send development aid to any region that was not in the Third World. Following 40 years of Cold War foreign aid, during which capitalist and communist leaders sent aid to the Third World in an attempt to buy loyalties, what was available were development models, programs, and implementation strategies tried in the Third World. The usual packages combined multinational aid (mostly loans from international financial institutions, notably the International Monetary Fund [IMF] and the World Bank), some bilateral assistance, and assistance supplied by an array of "private" providers, often nongovernmental organizations (NGOs) largely funded by donor governments. So despite attempts to resurrect a First World model through a type of Marshall Plan, a Third World model was largely implemented.

Unfortunately, both of these models ignored Poland's political, social, and historical context. They did not, crucially, address the effects of more than 40 years of communism. Yet the legacy of Eastern European communism was a key ingredient in how aid relations would unfold in the 1990s. The huge gulf that had developed between East and West during nearly a half century of isolation, as well as a lack of strategy, commitment, and funding in the West also contributed to less-than-optimal outcomes. Ironically, perhaps, both the successes and failures of aid relations have their roots in the aftereffects of communism and the Cold War.

The West as Saint and Demon

Two generations of isolation under communism had made the West a potent symbol in Poland, of both good and evil. The idea of the West as demon, for instance, was woven into the fabric of communist ideology. Years of rhetoric about Western imperialism and interference had been hammered into the Polish mindset. As anthropologist David A. Kideckel explains,[3] "Generations of communist state leaders used images of the West as *bête noire,* manifestly for consolidation and maintenance of their own power in society. For example, the chronic economic difficulties and shortages in the socialist states were regularly blamed on the machinations of the imperialist powers, Wall Street bankers, and financial lackeys like the International Monetary Fund."

This image of the West was promulgated through the state-controlled media. However, these media were seldom taken at face value: Many Poles found the official form of the news aired on television and printed in most newspapers suspect and in conflict with the facts of daily life. Nonetheless, the media had a powerful effect; often, people reactively believed the opposite of whatever the media presented. In the early 1980s, one Polish physicist who was a visiting scholar in the United States was surprised to learn that racial discord was a genuine problem in South Africa. She had assumed that the Polish media had invented apartheid.[4]

Partially as a result of this undercurrent of disbelief, the image of the West as a saint appeared in Poland. America was a land of milk and honey, a symbol of prosperity, due in part to waves of immigration to the New World and considerable contact between Poland and the United States. Particularly for people who had not traveled to the West, it was a place where one lived the good life—or at least where one lived a less trying life.

Through years of relative isolation and selective and sporadic contact with Western peoples and products, images of the prosperous West were refined to commercial icons: Imported Swiss chocolates, French perfume, German wine, Viennese coffee, Bic razor blades, and Marlboro cigarettes could be purchased only in Pewex stores for hard currency. Associations with the West, including Western products or relatives living there, were status symbols.

The fact that the West was a source of gifts (goods and money) also contributed to its image as saint. For generations, many Poles had traveled to the West and brought back goods. After World War II and during the martial law imposed throughout Poland in the early 1980s, millions of households received relief parcels both from private relatives abroad and from religious and charitable organizations. For Poles, an important experience with Western gift giving was the West's funding for the Polish opposition and the Solidarity movement during the late 1970s and throughout the 1980s. Western involvement and financial support had largely sustained the opposition. According to one prominent Polish oppositionist,[5] "The Opposition's main source of financial support was the West. Donations came from inspired individuals, from subscriptions, trade unions, social and political organizations, as well as from corporations, Polish emigré organizations, and government bodies such as substantial grants [about $1 million] from the U.S. Congress."

Poles admired and envied the West not only for its ability to deliver precious gifts but also for its freedom and democracy. Many Poles gained status in the eyes of their peers, because they had worked or studied or simply traveled to the West and made friendships with Westerners. Indeed, Poles identified with and aspired to be part of the West. As Polish psychologist Zbigniew Necki noted during the early 1980s, "We compare ourselves to Western countries, the most developed ones such as the United States, Japan, France, Sweden, and the Federal Republic of Germany."[6]

The considerable intellectual independence and freedom to travel that Poles and Hungarians had enjoyed since 1956 gave them closer contact with the West than, say, Romania and Bulgaria, where travel and intellectual freedom were much more restricted. Cultural and religious identification were also factors: Poland, with its Roman Catholic tradition, looked West. In Poland, as in the other Eastern European nations, however, the isolation, relative unavailability of consumer goods, and generally lower standards of living contributed to idealized views of the West.

So did American actions of apparent compassion during the Cold War. The West's tradition of warm welcome for defectors from Poland and other Eastern European countries, the sympathy expressed by Western diplomats for the "casualties" of communism, and the benevolent image of America presented on Radio Free Europe and Voice of America broadcasts led many in Poland to believe that the West was anxiously waiting to come to their assistance. As the Berlin Wall fell, these idealized views crystallized to form an even more potent image. The concept of Western aid became inextricably entwined with ideas about Western thought, culture, and people. In the months after the revolutions of 1989, the West became much more than a saint. It became a savior.

There was little in the environment to dampen the high regard for the West and its role in Poland's transition to free markets and democracy. In discussions with international lending institutions and Western governments, Polish officials naturally tended to have views different from those held by peasants. Yet even among the highly educated and well-traveled elite, few had much knowledge of Western assistance goals, institutions, and results. The new officials could not draw on the experiences of several generations of aid recipients, who had learned to tailor aid to their own purposes.

Idealized views of the West and the Poles' predisposition to the idea that the West cared and would fulfill its promises contributed to the willingness to accept, at least initially, Western promises of assistance. With historical and cultural ties to the West, and the idea that the nation had been torn from Europe by the politics of the Cold War, Poles fully embraced the West's sentiment and rhetoric. The concepts of a civil society and a return to Europe were made more alluring by history and the end of communism, which made such a return finally possible.

And so Cold War isolation, followed by the heady events of 1989 and the steady stream of visitors from the West conveying their willingness to help, nurtured high expectations. The reputation of the West as saint inspired a whirlwind of goodwill and anticipation.

Cousins in the East

Just as the East had high expectations of the West, so the West had high expectations of the East and what its aid efforts could achieve. These goals were higher and different from the West's expectations of the Third World. The idea of Eastern Europe as an aid recipient upset the worldview of development planners. They could not readily classify the region as either underdeveloped or developed—the traditional development scheme.

At first glance, the reasons for helping both the Second and Third Worlds appeared to be much the same: to ensure economic and political stability, create markets, and promote friendship with the West. But all nations are not equally tied to one another. Analyzing the psychological underpinnings of aid, Pascal Bruckner has concluded that "our estimation of a nation is tied in with our capacity to identify with it, to project ourselves in it."[7] There was a familial feel to Western interest in helping Poland. Aid to Poland presented an historic opportunity for partnership with the West's "cousins."

To begin with, Poles were European. In the Western view, then, the region's transition involved simply the recovery of an ill patient with whom "we" had close cultural and historical bonds and from whom "we" had been separated only by an accident of history. There was to be integration and partnership between East and West, concepts much more easily understood with regard to Eastern Europe than, say, Africa. The more developed Visegrád countries of Poland, Hungary, and what was then Czechoslovakia were thus categorized almost as Western European countries that simply needed to catch up a little. These countries bolstered the view that they were nearly part of Western Europe through a number of actions, including their "Visegrád declaration" of February 1991, which called for three nations to move toward a common goal of joining the European Community. Polish president Lech Wałęsa, Czechoslovak president Václav Havel, and Hungarian prime minister József Antall met in an ancient castle on the banks of the Danube River to sign the declaration, taking care not to annoy their giant eastern neighbor—at that time, still the Soviet Union.

Not all of the newly independent countries of the Second World of Europe, especially those of the former Soviet Union, were considered candidates for joining Europe. As nations and regions came to the attention of the aid community, decisions about their status had to be made. To resolve this ambiguity, aid officials eventually placed these countries into conventional First World or Third World development schemes.

As part of Europe, the Visegrád countries were to receive special aid so that they could be economically "reintegrated" with the West. The more equitable term *partners* often replaced the terms *donor* and *recipient*, which had a ring of Third World aid. And one of the West's key criteria for its partners was the extent to which a particular country figured in the West's security and political considerations. These reasons, too, had a different nuance than security and political considerations in Third World aid. Given the fall of communism, the idea was no longer just to keep these nations out of the clutches of the East. They would be invited to reintegrate with the West to the extent that they might eventually be welcomed into the EU and NATO. Thus, it was understandable, natural, and practical to help "our cousins." This sentiment was enhanced by the fact that the communist bloc collapsed at a time during which the idea of European unity had gained momentum and was a major focus in the West.

In addition to the assumptions the West made about the peoples and the dramatic revolutions of Eastern Europe, the desire to excise the legacy of communism, and finally the winning of the Cold War and the new security and political situation this had created all converged to form higher and different expectations and to cause Poland (along with select other Visegrád nations) to be regarded as a unique breed of aid recipient.

Just what did the West hope to achieve in the region? The overarching aid goal appeared to be to eradicate the legacy of communism—a quest that implicitly required more dramatic and wide-ranging change than had been expected of the Third World or was later to be expected of most underdeveloped republics of the former Soviet Union. Aid to India, as an example, tended to be couched in terms of economic growth, not institutional change. But erasing the legacy of communism in Poland required changing the very nature of recipient institutions. Poland was to shift course entirely.

The Western missionaries of change came armed with slogans to conceptualize, justify, and promote radical and rapid change. The oft-repeated allegorical slogans of the transition emphasized both the difficulty and the necessity of wholesale change: Suppose the British were to decide to switch from driving on the left side of the road to the right side? Would you recommend that they do so gradually, starting with trucks one year and cars a year later?[8]

Change was not only supposed to be comprehensive but was also to be accomplished quickly, according to economic analysts and pundits: "You can't cross a chasm in two jumps [you have to cross it in one]."[9] Both economic and political reasons underlay the demand for rapid change. Many economists held that every change in the system would affect every other part of the system and lead to still more adjustments, so that all of the changes should be made at once. Many attuned to politics argued that opposition to reform would be more likely to arise if reforms were made in a leisurely fashion: The window of opportunity to effect change would be narrow. Thus it was imperative to demonstrate support for economic reform through aid that would deliver quick and tangible results.

And so Poland and the West were, at least in the early days of Polish independence, agreed: The West would help Poland, and Poland would show its gratitude through quick reform and unswerving loyalty. In all the discussion, virtually no alternatives to Western capitalist models of reform, such as those espoused by the International Monetary Fund (IMF), were seriously entertained on either side. Jan Krzysztof Bielecki, prime minister of Poland during 1991 (and also a minister in the subsequent government), emphasized that no one in the relevant policy circles, from foreign advisers sent by international institutions such as the IMF to local officials, considered alternatives. At that time, "nobody [in the donor community] raised the issue of a social safety net," said Bielecki, which he found startling in retrospect. "We forgot, donors forgot. [No Eastern European aid recipient asked] the donors to insist on a social [safety] net." The fact that nobody "took it into consideration as a necessary political factor" ultimately "strengthened ex-communist forces in these countries." Bielecki was only one of the politicians in Poland and the region to be voted out within a short period of taking office.[10]

Part of the reason for this single-mindedness was that Poles were looking for simple answers. With little warning of impending difficulties from within or from the West, they hoped that their transition to democracy and free markets would be easy. Having finally attained their long-awaited Holy Grail of independence, they expected that their new leaders could transform their devastated economies over night with a little monetary help from their friends in the West. Again, however, the legacy of communism intervened.

Where's the Gift?

If communism had led Poles to embrace the West as a saint, it is not surprising that a key problem with Western aid was the perception in Poland that it was hopelessly inadequate. The aid actually delivered was regarded as deficient in scale and structure. Despite the lofty talk of a Marshall Plan for Eastern Europe, few Western policy makers had talked about a serious aid commitment on the order of tens of billions of dollars in strategic capital investments. (The Marshall Plan appropriated $13.3 billion over four years in 16 countries equal to 87.5 billion 1997 dollars.[11]) A Marshall Plan-style bailout for Eastern Europe (implying long-term and strategic planning, commitment of high-level officials, and above all, massive capital assistance in the form of grants) was simply not in the political and economic cards of the day. This reality was acknowledged in the aid and development community, using the idiom of the Marshall Plan. "We didn't do a Marshall Plan" was a way of saying, "We couldn't come up with the money," or "We didn't create a comprehensive aid package."

News reports in 1990–1991 that the West was sending billions of dollars in aid to Poland neglected to explain that the aid included export credits and loans that would have to be repaid. As Poland's chief coordinator of foreign assistance, Jacek Saryusz-Wolski, explained in 1991, at the height of the country's frustration with aid efforts: "When people in Poland hear that billions of dollars come to Eastern Europe, they expect that Poland gets one-half or one-third of that money. Very often people ask us what happened to it."[12] In 1992, Polish president Lech Wałęsa articulated the growing resentment when he spoke at the European Parliamentary Forum in Strasbourg, charging that "it is you, the West, who have made good business on the Polish revolution. The West was supposed to help us in arranging the economy on new principles, but in fact it largely confined its efforts to draining our domestic markets."[13]

Where indeed? There was a considerable gap between donors' allocations and actual disbursements in the region. In 1992, only an estimated 11 percent of the committed monies had actually been disbursed.[14] Not only was there a wide gap between what the rhetoric of the Marshall Plan suggested and what the donors actually promised, but there was also another huge chasm between what the donors promised and what they delivered.

Furthermore, Eastern Europeans did not view the type of aid that was sent as help. In Poland, the word "help" had come to mean either tangible goods like relief packages or in the context of an active, organized underground resistance, huge dollar sums to fund opposition activities. Poland has long had a sophisticated system of informal reciprocity and an elaborate etiquette of exchange. Bearers of gifts from outside were lavished with hospitality and presents. The realization that Western help now meant people, not cash, hit hard. The fact that the Polish word for help (*pomoc*) also was commandeered to mean foreign aid may have further frustrated the issue.

Initially, when the West announced its intentions to provide aid, its Polish partners expressed their gratitude with the graciousness of people schooled in Old World culture and civilization. For its part, the West assumed that the East would take whatever was offered up: After all, the aid was a gift. But the two sides had differing expectations for what the gift would consist of and just what constituted help.

The issue was a critical one. Marianne Gronemeyer argues that the success of many aid efforts depends on whether and to what degree aid is interpreted as help by the recipients:[15] "However obviously fraudulent use of the word 'help' to describe development aid may be, the word continues to be taken as the gospel truth, not least by those upon whom the fraud is committed."

Poles began to doubt the idea of foreign aid as help both because donors supplied primarily technical assistance, not capital assistance, and because of the dubious nature of much of the technical assistance. Bilateral donors and the EU supplied primarily technical assistance through advisers who provided expertise and training for aid recipients. Although some aid officials argued that there was a division of labor between the technical assistance provided by bilateral donors and the capital assistance provided by international financial institutions, the latter came in the form of loans that had to be repaid (often not regarded as aid in Eastern Europe), and there was little coordination between loans and technical assistance.

The technical assistance itself was often flawed. The Marriott Brigade was a term the Polish press[16] coined for the short-term "fly-in, fly-out" consultants who delivered technical assistance; they stayed at Warsaw's pricey new Marriott and hurtled among other five-star hotels across Eastern Europe. In contrast to long-term consultants, who often stayed for six months to two years, members of the Marriott Brigade appeared in Eastern Europe for several weeks or less. They were nattily dressed, quick with words and promises—and in time they left many official contacts in Eastern Europe filled with disillusionment and frustration.

At first, Eastern European officials, most of whom were new at their jobs, had welcomed the Marriott Brigade. Their doors were always open in those early days. Yet after hundreds of "first meetings" with an endless array of short-term consultants from the World Bank, the IMF, USAID, and other aid organizations, many officials concluded that a certain degree of skepticism should be in order. As early as 1991, the honeymoon was largely over in Warsaw, as well as in Budapest and Prague.

What went wrong? The consultants generally came with little knowledge of the countries in which they were to intervene or the context of the problems they were to address. Unlike long-term consultants, who often were committed and acquired enough knowledge of the local landscape to be genuinely useful, the short-term consultants tended to be ignorant of and even uninterested in local conditions. And they often were ill prepared. The U.S. General Accounting Office (GAO), which is charged by the U.S. Congress with monitoring how appropriated monies are spent, investigated a project in which volunteers spent four to six weeks in Poland working on specific tasks. One volunteer charged with helping Polish legal associations to establish a commercial law library was "an American divorce lawyer with no Polish language skills," as the GAO put it. The lawyer "had difficulty getting the legal associations to work together effectively. [In time] USAID officials acknowledged that the person in charge was 'not the best person' for the job."[17]

Some consultants came with ready solutions that did not take into account the starting point for reform: the planned economies and state socialism of Eastern Europe. And, crucially, despite the pretense of Eastern Europe as a Second World candidate for First World status, many short-term Western consultants applied assumptions and experience they had gleaned from work in the Third World. These assumptions not only constituted a deep insult to a people who considered themselves exemplars of European culture and civilization; they also reinforced the widely held view that Western consultants generally were unfamiliar with the institutions peculiar to postcommunist economies. In 1990, the vice minister of Poland's Ministry of Finance, Stefan Kawalec, criticized the approach of Harvard economist Jeffrey Sachs to the Polish economy: "There were and still are many question marks [about] how the economy will respond. In this, Sachs had no knowledge at all because he was not familiar with communist economies. He tried to treat this economy the same as Latin American ones."[18]

In short, the contributions of consultants were often suspect. The GAO reported that "[Polish] officials told us that in the early stages of reform, many consultants came to Warsaw for 1-to-2-week stays, interviewed some officials, and then produced reports that merely repeated everything they had been told."[19]

By January 1992, a chorus of Polish and Hungarian officials (whose countries at that point had received the most U.S. aid) had concluded that their countries were "technically over-assisted," as Marek Kozak, a Polish official who monitored foreign aid, put it, and that the assistance was doing more harm than good. Overburdened top-level officials, often working without benefit of trained support staff, complained that they could not do their jobs because they had to spent so much time meeting with fact-finders and consultants. Kozak went so far as to suggest that the main benefit derived from the Marriott Brigades was not the expertise they provided but the hard currency they contributed to the local economy.[20]

Furthermore, local perceptions of the consultants called into question the motives of Western aid in general. Not surprisingly, many Polish enterprise managers and workers viewed the "neutral" technical advice they received from Western experts as anything but neutral. Charges of industrial espionage were common. High-ranking officials in the region sometimes suspected advisers sent from Western bodies, ranging from the IMF and the EU to multinational corporations, of spying to assess the Eastern European nations' potential competitiveness with regard to certain products. Such officials even intimated that the advice they received could be intended to sabotage their nation's future competitiveness. One Polish manager who worked with foreign consultants was convinced that Eastern Europe had become a "paradise for [Western] spies." The deputy director of NIK (the Supreme Control Board, which is the Polish government's chief auditing agency and equivalent to the U.S. General Accounting Office) confirmed in 1994 that "[a] few years ago the [consulting] firms had an industrial espionage quality to them. They came and got all [the] valuable information about the enterprises—the state of the firm, the amount and cost of production, and so on—and after this they disappeared. This is also the fault of Polish officials. Today there are fewer naïve officials who allow this to happen."[21]

Thus, the aid Eastern Europeans received bore little resemblance to the Marshall Plan in form as well as in scale. Few Polish citizens, including officials, had anticipated that the assistance would take this form. Minister Witold Trzeciakowski, Poland's first aid coordinator, who in 1989 had called for a Marshall Plan to Poland, said that he had had in mind not only the amount of money but also that the aid would resemble the original Marshall Plan in that it would consist largely of grants, not loans and technical assistance. It was not until 1993, he said, that it finally became clear that a new Marshall Plan would not be forthcoming.[22]

As people became more suspicious of and ambivalent toward the aid effort, latent images of the West as demon began to resurface. A workers' slogan that decorated the main entrance to a factory expressed popular sentiment: "A Foreign Elite Steals From Us While The Polish People Are At The Bottom."

Polish Pride

The Polish perception of consultants as arrogant and patronizing appears to have encouraged a defensive national pride. Minister Jacek Saryusz-Wolski, responsible for aid coordination in several governments, said in 1992 that the West's approach to assistance was "paternalistic, like a parent giv[ing] to a child."[23] It was easy to see why such an approach offended a people whose culture and civilization were centuries old and whose educational systems were exemplary, especially in comparison with those of the Americans, the "teachers," who were viewed as cultural neophytes with dubious claims to intellectual or cultural superiority.

Poland's experiences with the Marriott Brigade and others of its ilk led to problems in bilateral relations. Specifically, they contributed to difficulties in negotiating the terms of U.S. bilateral aid relations. When the United States presented boilerplate aid agreements typically made for the Third World to Central and Eastern European recipients and expected them to sign on the dotted line, all of the Visegrád countries evinced reluctance to do so. The reluctance appeared to be due in large measure to the recipients' perceptions of being treated like Third World peoples—perceptions that had wounded their pride and left them wary of Western overtures of help.

The draft agreements also included requests for aid workers to be exempted from income taxes and duties on alcohol and tobacco—a request that also was viewed as an attempt to take advantage of recipients and thus was received poorly. The Visegrád countries responded by delaying by at least several years the completion of bilateral negotiations. These countries refused U.S. requests for American diplomatic immunity. Their officials indicated that no other donor countries had made such requests and that although such arrangements might be justified in Third World settings, they were not in Central and Eastern Europe. As one official remarked, "We have flatly refused [the request for diplomatic immunity]. It is the product in our eyes of some bureaucrats who have difficulty distinguishing the Czech Republic from Shangri-La [an imaginary place inspired by Nepal]."[24] Although an August 1992 cable from the U.S. Department of State addressed to the ambassadors of all Central and Eastern European posts urged them to conclude bilateral agreements as quickly as possible,[25] two years later (in July 1994) protracted negotiations were still under way in the four Visegrád countries. In Poland the agreement was never signed, although the Polish government eventually agreed to grant consultants privileges through other means.[26]

The obvious question to the observer was the following: if the consultants and aid agencies are such a problem, why not send them home? But that was not an option that recipient officials generally entertained. They did not wish to antagonize the donor countries. And some officials conceded that "occasionally, [the consultants'] advice is useful" or "their contacts are useful" or "we need the equipment that the consultants bring." (Equipment and technical assistance often come as a package.) In other words, accepting aid became chiefly a matter of maintaining good relations and contacts, and of receiving useful hardware from time to time. For the most part, though, as one official put it, "The donors pretend to help us, and we pretend to be helped."

The tendency of donors through all this was to assume that whatever was offered would be welcomed by the recipients. After all, it was a gift. Why were they complaining? What the donors failed to see was that to many Poles, a gift was something designed to benefit and serve the needs of the recipients. Because they felt that the post-1989 version of aid did not constitute "help," they felt they were being asked to accept a gift that was a ruse: to pretend to have received and benefited from something they had neither received nor benefited from.

If on the Polish side the issue was "where's the gift," on the Western side, the issue could be summed up as "where's the gratitude?" Both were seen as less than fully forthcoming and fulfilling.

Moving On

Despite myriad mistakes and complaints, changing views in Poland about Western aid and intervention were already in evidence during 1994. Much of the antagonism present in the first years of the aid effort had dissipated. Recipients adapted as their experience with donors grew: After early frustration and resentment about the inadequacies of foreign consultants and the aid they offered, Polish officials became better at identifying their needs and more selective about foreign (and local) advisers. As Salvatore Pappalardo, an American consultant in Poland, observed in 1994, there were "a lot of carpetbaggers early on. At this stage of the process Poles are more aware of the things they know and, most importantly, of the things they don't know. They've learned to clarify their needs."[27]

One result of this evolution was that Poles requested more capital and less technical assistance.[28] The capital assistance generally was not forthcoming from bilateral donors. However, the EU did begin to supply more capital assistance to finance trans-European network projects in the form of railway lines, roads, and border infrastructure. As one EU official explained, "Investment finance is more visible to the public. That's one of the reasons we're going into it. [Investment] can be seen and touched."[29]

Over seven years of aid to Poland, both donors and recipients began to turn the "learning curve." Regardless of whether much of the technical assistance rendered was effective, a natural progression occurred. As Poles developed technical capacities, the need for foreign aid-sponsored technical assistance diminished. They developed new skills for dealing with the donor community and became more realistic about what aid could and could not do for them. In some cases, they concluded that the costs of working with an aid program, in terms of timing and meeting donor requirements, outweighed the benefits, and they chose not to get involved.

A related positive development was the blurring of distinctions between donor and recipient personnel. Initially, it had been possible to detect who was who by nationality, language, and style. By 1994, however, many Western consulting groups, including accounting firms, were hiring more local citizens and expatriates who spoke Polish. Donors also recruited some formerly high-level Polish officials who had served in the first postcommunist governments. As an example, the Polish-American Enterprise Fund hired a former deputy minister of privatization and a former undersecretary in the ministry of industry and trade to be vice presidents. Marek Kozak, who, two years earlier, had criticized Western aid efforts from his vantage point as a recipient official, headed a private-sector development initiative for the EU.

Emerging from the isolation of the Cold War, both West and East were perhaps destined to have great expectations that could not be fulfilled: Polish frustration and resentment over assistance were real, if largely temporary. To the extent the nation has prospered, it appears to be largely despite foreign assistance rather than because of it.

Yet despite its mixed legacy, aid has been part of a broader process of establishing "normal" relationships between Poland and the West, and aid programs have contributed to the interchange of people and ideas. Even if both sides initially came away disappointed, person-to-person contact helped to reduce the isolation stemming from the Cold War. Both sides reaped some benefits from the general increase of contact.

Today, as Poles match and even outdo their Western counterparts in extravagance, it is sometimes hard to remember the time when the excesses of the Marriott Brigade were universally perceived as offensive. This is not to say that all potential for antagonism toward the West has dissipated, especially not in the regions that are doing relatively poorly. Whether as saint or demon, the West will continue to play an important role in Poland's development.

Still, the lines of polarization within Poland appear different now, because they are primarily between those who have become wealthy during, or at least survived, the transition from communism and those who have not. These lines appear different now, because Poles are increasingly claiming a place in European and international organizations and activities. Polish consultants serve as representatives of the West on EU delegations in Romania and Ukraine. More often than not, they are treated as partners, if not with deference. One EU official in Poland explained his reluctance to criticize a particular Polish official this way: "One day he might be my boss [at the EU]."

Notes

1. This figure, which is based on the April 1993 G-24 Scoreboard, covers the period from January 1990 through December 1992. U.S. Department of State, *SEED Act Implementation Report: Fiscal Year 1993* (Washington, D.C.: U.S. Department of State, January 1994), 278.
2. Ibid., appendix, 1.
3. David A. Kideckel, "Us and Them: Concepts of East and West in the East European Transition," *Cultural Dilemmas of Post-Communist Societies*," Aldona Jawlowska and Marian Kempny, eds. (Warsaw: IFiS Publishers, 1994), 135.
4. Cited in Janine Wedel, *The Private Poland: An Anthropologist's Look at Everyday Life* (New York: Facts on File, 1986), 129.
5. The oppositionist is "Tadeusz Wróblewski," a pseudonym to protect identities. His article is "The Opposition and Money," in Janine Wedel, ed., *The Unplanned Society: Poland during and after Communism* (New York: Columbia University Press, 1992), 239.
6. Zbigniew Necki quoted in Wedel, *The Private Poland,* 163.
7. Pascal Bruckner, *The Tears of the White Man: Compassion as Contempt* (New York: Free Press, 1983), 80.
8. Jeffrey Sachs, "The Economic Transformation of Eastern Europe: The Case of Poland," *American Economist* 36 (Fall 1992): 5.
9. Jeffrey Sachs, quoted in George M. Taber, "Rx for Russia: Shock Therapy," *Time,* 27 January 1992, 37; cited in Walter Adams and James W. Brock, *Adam Smith Goes to Moscow* (Princeton, N.J.: Princeton University Press, 1993), 40.
10. Interview with Jan Krzysztof Bielecki, 14 December 1995.
11. U.S. Department of State, "The Marshall Plan: Origins and Implementation" (Washington, D.C.: Office of the Historian, June 1982), 30; "The Marshall Plan," *Boston Globe,* 3 June 1997, A-8.
12. Cited in Janine R. Wedel, "Beware Western Governments Sending Gifts," *Wall Street Journal* (European edition), 14 January 1992.
13. Reported in Blaine Harden, "Poles Sour on Capitalism," *Washington Post,* 5 February 1992, A-1.
14. This figure represents average disbursement rates by nine G-24 countries and the EU for total committed assistance to Central and Eastern Europe (Raymond Barre, William H. Luers, Anthony Solomon, and Krzysztof J.

Ners, *Moving Beyond Assistance* [New York: Institute for East-West Studies, June 1992]).

15. Marianne Gronemeyer, "Helping," in Wolfgang Sachs, ed., *The Development Dictionary: A Guide to Knowledge as Power* (London: Zed Books, 1992), 55.

16. See, for example, Jacek Kalabiński, "The Marriott Brigade in Action," *Gazeta Wyborcza,* 21 June 1991; and "The Misfortune of the Marriott Brigade," ibid., 18 October 1991.

17. U.S. General Accounting Office, *Poland: Economic Restructuring and Donor Assistance* (Washington, D.C.: GAO, August 1995), 43–44.

18. Stefan Kawalec, quoted in Janine R. Wedel, "The Economist Heard around the World," *World Monitor* (October 1990): 40.

19. U.S. General Accounting Office, *Poland,* 66.

20. Marek Kozak, cited in Janine R. Wedel, "The Unintended Consequences of Western Aid to Post-Communist Europe," *Telos,* no. 92 (Summer 1992): 133.

21. Interview with Piotr Kownacki, deputy director of NIK, 29 April 1994.

22. Interview with Witold Trzeciakowski, 10 May 1997.

23. Jacek Saryusz-Wolski, quoted in Janine R. Wedel, "Beware Western Governments Sending Gifts," *Wall Street Journal,* op. cit.

24. Interviews with and documents provided by Zbigniew Lewicki and Zdzisław Ludwiczak of the Polish Ministry of Foreign Affairs; Jitka Cenková of the Centre for Foreign Assistance at the Ministry of the Economy of the Czech Republic; Jarmila IIrbáčková, Andrea Matisová, and Lubo Lubina of the Slovak Ministry of Foreign Affairs; and Kornél Kováts and Ágnes Nádházi of the Assistance Coordination Secretariat at the Hungarian Ministry of International Economic Relations.

25. The cable stated that "at this time only Albania has signed the draft bilateral transmitted . . . and we have no hard information (other than possibly re the CSFR) that we are close to signing anywhere else. The time has come for all posts to make a serious overture to the appropriate host government officials involved at the highest appropriate level and to agree on an imminent timetable for execution of these agreements, so that the program can continue without interruption" (cable from Lawrence Eagleburger, Acting Secretary of State, 10 August 1992).

26. Interviews with Zdzisław Ludwiczak, deputy director, Department of the Americas, Ministry of Foreign Affairs, 31 August 1995 and 12 May 1997.

27. Interview with Salvatore Pappalardo, 13 April 1994.

28. Interviews with Paweł Samecki, director of the Bureau for Foreign Assistance, Polish Council of Ministers, 29 April 1994; also with Ágnes Nádházi and Kornél Kováts, Hungarian Ministry of International Economic Relations, 27 April 1994.

29. Interviews with Klaus Schmidt and Andrew Rasbash, EU delegation in Poland, 7 April 1994 and 22 April 1994; interviews with John Kjaer and Pierre Mirel, PHARE, Brussels, 4 May 1994.

TWELVE

NATO: Hopes and Frustrations

Arthur R. Rachwald

The end of Soviet domination in Central and Eastern Europe
opened up new opportunities and presented new dilemmas for all
former members of the communist bloc. Poland's status as a component part of the multinational political and military structures of the
Warsaw Pact had come to an end. For the first time in fifty years, the
country could pursue its independent foreign policy priorities, defined in
terms of national interest rather than a foreign ideology forcefully imposed by Soviet troops deployed in Poland and neighboring states.

The country regained independence in an orderly manner during
April 1989 as the Roundtable negotiations between Solidarity and the
regime terminated the constitutionally guaranteed communist monopoly
of power. It finally became free to shape its own domestic political and
economic systems as well as its foreign policy goals. As expected, Poland
immediately adapted to the international realities of the 1990s while incorporating the political vision and aspiration expressed half a century
before by the last legitimate Polish government-in-exile at London during
World War II. Poland had fought the war as a partner of the Big Three,
contributing in the hope of winning real independence and, by extension,
the opportunity to reconstruct the country as a democratic republic, a
good neighbor, and a dependable member of the European community of
nations. However, the sovietization of Poland and reduction of the country to satellite status over four decades resulted in a fundamental reposi-
tioning of domestic and foreign policies that became antithetical to the
original ideals championed by the people.

The foreign policy objectives that the first Polish postcommunist government put forward reflect a remarkable continuity in perception of national interest. They remain unaltered today, despite several changes in

the ruling coalition. At the top of Poland's priorities is the comprehensive incorporation into Western European political, economic, and military structures, especially NATO. Second, Poland has attached special importance to the peaceful settlement of all outstanding issues with its neighbors in order to ensure stability throughout the region. Particularly critical was the final conclusion of the Polish-German dispute over the Odra-Nysa (Oder-Neisse, in German) border, recognition of the Ukraine, Belarus, and Lithuania as independent states, and implementation of the Soviet military withdrawal from Poland. In less than two years, Poland addressed the complex legacies of the past with its neighbors, all of them new political entities, and successfully avoided political entanglements that otherwise might have impeded its first stages in the transition to democracy and a free market economy.

These main priorities were, in fact, related. The close attention to local issues during the first few years of independence also played another role as a preparatory phase in a larger strategic objective of complete integration into Western political, economic, and military institutions. Most important, Poland proceeded to qualify itself for membership in the European Union and NATO. With this agenda, Poland managed to link its domestic and foreign policies together into a comprehensive Western foreign policy in order to take full advantage of the exceptionally beneficial international circumstances at the end of the Cold War.

On the domestic front, fifty years of combined Nazi and Soviet occupations did not affect the Western cultural and social profile of the Polish nation. Indeed, shaped by the spiritual guidance of the Roman Catholic Church and intensive resentment of the Soviet-Russian occupation, Poland's commitment to Western values intensified during the decades of communist rule. As in 1919, Poland was once again free of outside domination and, together with other states of the region, proceeded to make every possible effort to permanently make itself independent from the shadow of Russian political domination, authoritarianism, and economic and social backwardness, as well as the pervasive threat of unpredictability inherent in the political processes taking place in Moscow. At the same time, in order to establish itself permanently in Europe, Poland had to bury once and for all its involvement in the east, namely the Ukraine, Belarus, and Lithuania.

The breakdown of the Soviet empire and the subsequent independence of Central and Eastern European nations, combined with the emergence of newly independent states out of former Soviet republics, produced a fundamental transfiguration in the global and European balance of power for the first time since 1919. The times of Yalta-like unchecked dominance of major powers in Europe came to an end, as the geopolitical balance turned instead to favor independence of small- and medium-sized nations.

In order to integrate itself successfully with Western institutions, Poland had to address several specific issues of strategic partnership and new relations with its two historic enemies, Russia and Germany. First, Poland has anchored its security into a multilateral alliance of nations rather than relying on a bilateral arrangement with a superior and expansionist neighbor (Germany in the 1930s and Soviet Russia during the Cold War) or reluctant partners (France and Britain in 1939). As Poland discovered through tragic experience, bilateral security agreements that were directed against a single or group of states often forced it to take sides first, then pay the consequences for another country's political objectives. Poland's experience with France between World War I and World War II, as well as the lessons it learned from the Cold War, were instructive enough to avoid any excessive entanglement with any other state after communism's collapse.

To be sure, Polish authorities initially contemplated reconstruction of historic French-Polish ties. However, the "French orientation" was soon discovered to be unproductive, as France had its own individual and frequently anti-American agenda in Europe; consequently, instead of becoming a champion of pan-European and transatlantic unity, Poland might have appeared to side with a maverick frequently committed to el evating its own narrow interests. As a candidate for membership in European institutions, Poland preferred to avoid entanglement with internal political arguments among member states. Furthermore, another unwanted implication of a special Versailles-like relationship between France and Poland would have been a suspected plot against Germany that promoted a "deepening" rather than "widening" of Europe. At this stage of political and economic integration on the continent, Polish interests are actually much better served by a widening of the regional system to include Central European nations rather than remaining within the narrow scope of a Western-dominated region. Last, Warsaw considers the American presence in Europe as absolutely essential for regional stability and security, since neither French nor British conventional and nuclear deterrence can substitute for the political and military presence of the only remaining superpower. Thus, French aims at displacing the United States in Europe are fundamentally antithetical to Poland's expectations for the future of the continent.

Poland also had to reformulate its relationship with Germany, which received special attention in Poland's *Westpolitik* since the conclusion of the 1991 border agreement. In turn, this treaty set the stage for comprehensive political, economic, and cultural relations, ultimately closing a painful history in mutual relations that began with the protracted Polish-Prussian hostility culminating during World War II, in the death of more than six million Polish citizens, the expulsion of some nine million Germans from territories acquired by Poland, and the integration of four million Poles from the Soviet-seized provinces. The significance of German-Polish normalization, however, goes far beyond immediate bilateral relations. As French-German reconciliation in 1963 became a cornerstone of Western European security and integration, the end of animosity between the two largest Central European states provides the necessary political infrastructure for eventual integration of Central and Western Europe. After the disintegration of Soviet imperial hegemony in the region and the liquidation of the East German state (and its Prussian authoritarian-military legacy), Poland and Germany could face each other as neighbors bound by a whole spectrum of mutual concerns and interests.

From the Polish point of view, Germany has become a friendly and valuable neighbor, by and large free of its nationalistic past. The second unification of Germany was accomplished peacefully, as the totalitarian German Democratic Republic became integrated with democratic West Germany and its Western political and military institutions. The last institutional bastion of Prussian authoritarianism ceased to exist when communist East Germany was dissolved into a unified Federal Republic of Germany. Since the end of World War II, the Federal Republic has played a fundamentally constructive role in European politics. Its membership in NATO and the EU has guaranteed that Germany would no longer attempt a destabilizing independent foreign policy course, through acquiring nuclear weapons, adopting a "new Rapallo" treaty with Russia, or promoting a revival of nationalistic sentiments.

Although today's Germany is a direct successor of the West German state, unification has brought several profound domestic and international implications. First, it produced a notable geostrategic shift toward the east, making united Germany a Central European state, rather than exclusively West European, with important security and economic interests east of the Odra-Nysa line. At the same time, Germany has become more powerful, more sovereign, and more willing to express its national interest along traditional lines of West German peaceful engagement in the east, known as *Ostpolitik*. The geopolitical elevation of Germany has also produced several destabilizing political and social repercussions. Unification brought with it the inclusion of a significant number of citizens unfamiliar with democratic ideas and procedures and resentful of economic dislocation during the transition to a free market economy. As a result, the process of East German political assimilation may not be completed for another generation or even longer.

In addition to this source of internal instability, a united Germany is confronted with an uncertain international situation beyond the Odra-Nysa line. Except for its borders with Poland and the Czech Republic, Germany is enveloped in a chain of friendly and democratic states. This loose end in Germany's international security system is potentially destabilizing, since it makes it easy to import instability into Germany by provoking nationalistic and authoritarian political trends. One of the most frightening prospects for Europe, not surprisingly, is a possible revival of chauvinism in Germany. This threat to German and European well-being provides the strongest common security link between Germany and Poland, a bond based on mutual determination to eliminate the gray area of international security from the map of Europe.

Central and Eastern Europe had become a gray area of international security with the demise of the Soviet state and its European empire. In the West, this region of the continent borders directly with NATO and the European Union and indirectly with nuclear powers like the United States, France, and Great Britain. On its eastern side, Central and Eastern Europe is confronted with the Russian Federation, an entity that is a diminished version of the Soviet empire plagued by its habitual conflicts with minorities, mafias, and political and economic instability. Moreover, traditional imperialism continues to find very strong appeal among a sizable portion of the Russian public, which is still unable to accept the breakdown of the Soviet Union. This school of Russian nationalism now looks toward the Commonwealth of Independent States (CIS) as a vehicle for reintegration of the former republics and the idea of "far abroad" as an excuse for strategic hegemony over Central-Eastern European states. Restoration of the imperial domain to its pre-1989 borders receives much higher priority among the Russian elite than the material well-being of the population. In the spring of 1993, just two years after the breakdown of the USSR and less than four years after the demise of the Soviet empire, Moscow declared Central and Eastern Europe as its special "sphere" of security interest and claimed special rights to carry out "peacekeeping" operations, after first fomenting ethnic animosities. At the same time, the "new" military doctrine of the Russian Federation announced that Moscow's security aspirations remained global, despite the profound domestic crisis and the recent failure of the Soviet experiment.

In practice, the new Russian "Monroe doctrine" has provided Moscow with an excuse to either incite local conflicts or to meddle in already existing civil strife in order to force lost near-abroad states to rejoin the

CIS. The West has unofficially recognized Russia's rights to engage in the near abroad as a self-appointed peacekeeper by not expressing any diplomatic protest against Russian actions. Indeed, some U.S. politicians have even offered the absurd comparison of Russian aggression with the American Civil War, showing not only a complete ignorance of both Russian and American histories but also a disdain for human rights and national self-determination.

In truth, a renewed round of Russian "land gathering" has already begun, and some politicians in the West have already volunteered to provide patronage for Russian neocolonialism. What these individuals have neglected to realize, however, is that a no-man's land in Europe and the threat of renewed Russian hegemony up to the Odra-Nysa line would entail a military confrontation, possibly engulfing the entire continent. Furthermore, domestic political debate has not focused on improvement of the Russian standard of living but on the maintenance of extensive international involvement as a great power prerogative. In fact, the collapse of Marxist-Leninist ideology left an enormous intellectual vacuum in Russia, which had always been an empire and never a nation-state. Consequently, the only common ideological denominator left for Russians is the idea of their greatness. Russians have not yet emerged from a nation-building stage and are experiencing a deep national identity crisis, which in turn propels them to give priority to foreign rather than domestic political issues. Russian anxiety over international isolation, wrought by its "surrender" as a great power, has overshadowed any social or economic agenda. As a result many Russians, including intellectuals, cannot conceive of themselves as great people without domination over other nations based on a self-given right to invade and occupy independent states.[1]

Historically, this is not the first Russian attempt to establish a gray security area in Central and Eastern Europe. Some Western states, especially Great Britain, have realized that such an arrangement could produce strategic advantages for them. British policy at Vienna in 1815 and Versailles in 1919, as well as American policy at Yalta in 1945, favored the establishment of weak, dependent states in the region where Western and Russian influences could overlap. This chain of weaker states ("pygmy" states, as Russians often say) between Germany and Russia would force them to be pro-Western without the need for a reciprocal commitment, while their relative weakness would restrain them from an effective pursuit of their own international ambitions. Above all, they would provide the West with an early warning against the rise of either Russian or German imperialism. For centuries, Russians and Germans encountered each other on Polish territory, either as enemies or as friends, but always at

Poland's expense, generally resulting in the liquidation of the Polish state. Vladimir Zhirinovsky, leader of the nationalistic Liberal Democratic Party, has made similar pronouncements recently, as have the Russian communists under the leadership of Gennadii Zyuganov.

The countries of Central and Eastern Europe, including Poland, have displayed an extraordinary degree of determination, initiative, and forcefulness to never again become a guinea pig for Europe. Among the principal fears of these countries is an entrapment between NATO and the CIS that could lead to an entanglement in a strategic competition over influence. Central and Eastern European nations are unable to assume an assertive and independent position in global or continental politics. Rather, they tend toward a traditional cultural preference of belonging to regional security and economic organizations for fear that they might otherwise become a "football" in the international power game. Moreover, an undefined international status leads to profoundly destabilizing domestic repercussions and promotes unfavorable attitudes toward democratic processes, as internal issues become scrutinized from their foreign policy implications (e.g., as either pro-Western or pro-Russian) rather than from an objective evaluation of national interest.

Russian interests in a Central-Eastern European "gray zone" also were at the heart of Gorbachev's conception of a common European house, namely with cross-guarantees of regional security that both threaten de facto resatellization and prescribe permanent economic inferiority vis-à-vis the West. In principle, the Russian objective is to arrest the process of pro-Western integration of the region that could eventually leave two strategically linked alliance systems in Europe, NATO and the CIS. This division could come to resemble another Warsaw Pact, as the relative increase of Russian power will enhance Moscow's presence in Central Europe and vis-à-vis Western Europe. In this respect, the Russian position is not much different from the Soviet attitude expressed in 1945 at Yalta, the main source of the protracted Cold War conflict on the continent. At the same time, more than six years after the breakdown of the Soviet empire in Europe, not a single one of the Central European nations was offered an unequivocal security or economic commitment from the West, giving rise to the possibility that an anti-Western backlash could arise and seek political and military accommodations with Russia as the only realistic alternative available.

Furthermore, another abandonment by the Western democracies could foment xenophobic nationalism, rather than democracy and socioeconomic development, which could in turn fuel ethnic conflict and other symptoms of instability. Combined with a skepticism about the Central and East European nations' ability to govern themselves,

Russia could find a convenient excuse to reassert its regional hegemony through peacekeeping in the near abroad peripheries of the Russian state. Some indications of this attitude are already evident, as Moscow has consistently been refusing involvement in any bilateral dialogue on security issues with the Central European nations, instead negotiating these matters directly with NATO and appealing directly to Western public opinion. In the West, Russia is basically trying to develop a two-tier policy, a Moscow-Washington axis and a Moscow-Berlin axis, both designed to reduce international relevance and outmaneuver the Central and Eastern regions of Europe by securing a broker's position in international affairs. The short-term Russian objective (until Moscow is again economically able to sustain a global presence), therefore, is to maintain security zones in Central Europe, the Balkans, and the Far East that will facilitate future expansion.

In April 1996, when Poland's president, Aleksander Kwaśniewski, visited Moscow, the exchange of views on security-related issues was limited to a recognition of fundamental differences on the Polish desire to join NATO. Moscow, however, has become increasingly concerned with the complete and irreversible geographic shift in Poland's foreign trade. Specifically, it fears that the Polish move toward full membership in the European Union and the reduction of tariffs within the Central European Free Trade Association (CEFTA) would permanently impair bilateral trade relations. In order to reverse this trend, Moscow favors the creation of a free trade zone between both countries, as well as closer cooperation in the construction of gas and oil pipelines, highways and railroads. The Polish side, on the other hand, believes that a free trade zone between Poland and Russia could hinder Polish aspiration to join the EU. Still, the total volume of Polish-Russian trade in 1996 jumped to $4 billion from only $1 billion in the preceding year. During his November 1996 visit to Moscow, Polish prime minister Włodzimierz Cimoszewicz concluded agreements to settle mutual debts and joint air-sea search and rescue operations, with negotiation of a comprehensive economic cooperation treaty on the long-term agenda.

In short, after three years of scornfully ignoring Poland and other Central European states, Russia has proceeded to take a more positive attitude and engage some former Soviet bloc nations in bilateral economic relations. This is to some extent a "can't beat them, join them" attitude in Moscow, which is becoming more aware of its inability to stop Poland's accession to NATO and the EU. From an economic point of view, however, Russian relevance to the development of the Polish economy is not very significant. Its exports to Poland are almost exclusively limited to raw materials and energy, as Warsaw remains careful to restrict its dependence on Russian resources to avoid the possibility of political blackmail in the future. Regarding efforts to join NATO, Prime Minister Cimoszewicz stated, "I would like the main message of this visit reaching ordinary Russians to be that Poland wants good relations with Russia. We want to cooperate, but that we don't forget we also have rights."[2]

Despite its defeat in the Cold War, and unlike Great Britain, France, or Germany, postcolonial Russia appears unwilling to define its identity alone within the framework of a nation-state role because it continues to pursue its imperial aspirations. To fulfill this objective, Russia needs tacit American cooperation in the form of renewed global consensus over mutual spheres of influence. Specifically, this requires identifying the entire geographical area of the former Soviet empire as primarily a Russian area of special foreign policy prerogatives. Both Moscow and some politicians in Washington remain unable to grasp the new contemporary reality of self-determination and the international role of small- and medium-sized states, preferring instead some form of global condominium in which the United States would accept Moscow's claim to both near abroad and far abroad. As of now, Russia claims the right to military intervention vis-à-vis at least 14 countries, all of them members of the United Nations.[3]

Moscow already has begun treating the independent nations of Central Europe as objects of security consideration in Europe, without any attention given to their own needs and objectives. It does not hesitate to conclude bilateral economic agreements in the expectation that economic ties would increase the region's overall dependency on Russian resources, energy in particular, providing Russians with an effective lever to exercise political influence. Furthermore, its economic policies in Ukraine provide clear clues to understanding Moscow's long-term plans in the region. Russia, regardless of whether she is red or white, totalitarian or protodemocratic, cannot stop looking at all nations west of its borders as a near abroad periphery of limited sovereignty. This persistent refusal to recognize the post–Cold War reality of independent Central Europe places Russia on another collision course with both the countries of the region and the Western states. The end of the Cold War and the Soviet Union are still not enough for Moscow to discontinue playing spheres-of-influence power games with the West in Europe.

Part of Russia's calculation is that the United States will again follow World War II Rooseveltian policies toward Central Europe. In essence, it is a "Russia first" perspective, willing to recognize Moscow's special political and military preponderance in Central Europe, while only paying lip service to America's support for democracy to appease domestic electoral constituencies. It was the deceitful Yalta formula of "free and unfettered elections" lacking international supervision that plunged the region into more than four decades of a communist nightmare and the world into the Cold War, except that in Central and Eastern Europe, the term Cold War is a misnomer. For the West, it was a cold war, but for the Central and East European nations it was a true hot war with heavy casualties, especially during the initial period of sovietization, invasions, martial law, socioeconomic backwardness, and national humiliation. In addition, the nations of Central and Eastern Europe provided the front line for the offensive Soviet posture against Western Europe, and they were expected to pay the highest price for any military miscalculation of Moscow.

Today, the region looks toward restoration of a Wilsonian outlook in Washington, with a genuine emphasis on independence, democracy, and unity rather than another division of the continent. This approach requires, first and foremost, recognition of the new political reality in Europe instead of persistent stereotyped thinking in terms of Cold War patterns and arbitrary solutions that disregard the relative strength and importance of medium-sized states. Emancipation of Central and Eastern Europe from Russian control is a fact, as is its democratic transformation and its rapid development of free-market economic systems. These nations will no longer be satisfied with a status of reduced security, trapped between a hermetically closed but stable and affluent West and an unstable, backward, and expansionist Russia. In short, the NATO countries face a choice of either exporting stability across the Odra-Nysa line or importing instability from the East.

A renewal of Wilsonian attitudes in the White House started at the end of 1994, following the CSCE summit in Budapest (which created the OSCE), as the Clinton administration finally began to understand that Russian interests in regard to special relations with the United States were driven by several ominous long-term goals: gaining endorsement for expansionist actions on the territories of the former Soviet Union; liquidating NATO (that is, American presence in Europe) by imposing a Russian veto on enlargement, or at least subordinating NATO to OSCE; and in fact returning to the 1815 Congress of Vienna international security pattern, in which five powers (this time, the United States, Russia, Britain, Germany, and France) would assume an oversight position to police smaller states. More recently, President Clinton took another step toward a more proactive foreign policy by appointing Madeleine Albright as the secretary of state, despite concerns over her Central European origin voiced in Moscow. Unlike her predecessor, Albright has a strategic vision, familiarity with European affairs, and a strong commitment to bringing the Central European nations into NATO. Her declared priority is building a democratic and united Europe, linked with Russia through strategic partnership, rather than dividing Europe again into Western and Russian spheres of influence. In her eyes, only a Europe that is unified, integrated, and permanently allied with the United States can assure stability on the continent by leaving Russia no alternative to peaceful cooperation. As recent events have shown, the mere prospect of NATO enlargement prompted countries of Central and Eastern Europe to stabilize their democratic institutions, promote political and economic reforms, and establish close and friendly relations with one another.

The anti-enlargement zealots in Washington appear to believe that the future of security in Europe can be devised by a partial undoing of the reality created by the 1989 revolutions in the region, that is, a limited reintroduction of Russian strategic and economic hegemony on some 140 million unwilling people of Central and Eastern Europe. A small but vocal "Russian party" of several retired American diplomats and some academics is in fact more pro-Russian than the Russians, repeatedly advancing arguments based on ethnic bias and the distant geographic proximity of the region. It is coded in the "would you die for Bratislava?" question (an echo of the 1939 appeasement cry, "would you die for Danzig?"), which disregards consequences of this policy, namely the 52 million people that had been killed by 1945. Additionally, these individuals assert that democratic stability in the proximity of the Russian Federation would threaten or somehow endanger prodemocratic evolution within Russia!

In this strategic context, the main focus of a new Polish foreign policy is, first, to establish a network of bilateral political and economic contacts with all neighboring states, designed to normalize mutual relations, enhance stability along Poland's borders, and initiate mutually beneficial political and economic cooperation. Second, Poland has attached special importance to a comprehensive involvement in a European and global network of treaties and agreements designed to strengthen the United Nations' system of collective security and global arms control and disarmament agreements. Finally, Poland has placed its aspiration for membership in NATO, the West European Union (WEU), and the EU at the forefront of its international objectives, including a special partnership with Germany and France.[4] At the same time, it has repeatedly voiced readiness to initiate direct talks with Russia on all matters of European security.

Poland's determination to join NATO is a product of careful calculation. Historical experience has taught the Poles all possible perils of either acting alone or relying on bilateral defense guarantees or membership in an undemocratic multinational alliance like the Warsaw Pact. Instead of defending its members, the main function of the Warsaw Pact was to coerce them by intimidation or direct invasion. As World War II made clear, the optimal security option for Poland is membership in a democratically structured collective security system in Europe that would also recognize the Western orientation of Polish culture. Also implied in these objectives is an overall strengthening of the country's internal and external position. On the domestic front, the rapid transformation of the Polish economy into a dynamic free-market system has helped to integrate it with the most industrialized nations of the world. Internationally, Poland has proceeded to become an active, visible contributor to security and stability on the continent, stressing the importance of international organizations, the rule of law, and unswerving commitment to Western cultural values.

Under peaceful conditions in Europe, Poland has several important assets as an international actor. Its geographical location on the main route between Western and Eastern Europe, along with its size, has guaranteed the country's relevance to the continental system of international security. Perception of Poland's importance as the "key to European security" might be somewhat overstated, but there is substantial historic evidence to assert that a strong and direct link exists between the security of Poland and the security of the entire continent. Both World War II and the Cold War started over the Polish issue, and the rise of Solidarity during the 1980s proved a decisive factor behind the breakdown of the Soviet bloc and the Soviet state. Its significance also means that a politically stable and economically prosperous Poland can make an immense contribution to further peaceful European integration, security, and economic growth.

The success of shock therapy during Poland's postcommunist transition has made its economic policy an integral part of the country's foreign policy. This radical form of transformation from socialism to a free market has reaped generous dividends as the rapid pace of structural change, including privatization, has produced an impressive rate of economic growth (which in 1995 exceeded 6 percent), the highest in Europe. Poland was the first Central European state to emerge from recession, quickly earning the reputation of a Central European "tiger" and attracting more than $10 billion of private foreign investment. Furthermore, it is expected to receive an additional $20 to $30 billion in foreign investments during the next five years. Despite some spells of political turbulence, frequent changes of government, and the ascension to power of former communists, a political consensus in Poland has formed that believes a strong economic performance will be the chief national asset in support of membership in the European Union and NATO. Indeed, the vibrant economic performance of Central Europe's largest and most populous state has generated interest and enthusiasm in the West to support a nation that had been gripped by economic paralysis only a few years earlier.

The new wave of foreign investment has a qualitatively different character than in previous years, when the country had attracted a large number of relatively small foreign economic ventures. Poland is bringing large investors in who are willing to finance billion-dollar projects, such as the Daewoo Group, which pledged $1.5 billion by 2001; General Motors, which plans to introduce its new European car production in Poland; and Hormel Foods, which has entered into a joint venture with a leading Polish manufacturer of meat products. After some initial hesitation, the Japanese have also decided to invest in Polish electronic, motor, shipbuilding, and steel industries. These are tangible indications of foreign confidence in the Polish economy and its ability to produce Western-quality goods for both Western markets and the rapidly growing demand from some 40 million domestic consumers.

Most important, foreign investments in Poland are viewed as a yardstick of Western confidence in the country's economy *and* political stability, especially its future as an independent, pro-Western nation. The current share of foreign investment in Poland's equity market has reached approximately 25 percent, which is considered to be relatively low due to unfinished privatization. Small- and medium-size economic enterprises in Poland were successfully privatized within the first three years of full independence, but the restructuring and privatization of large, monopolistic state firms that employ hundreds of thousands remains a highly sensitive political issue. As a result, many of these socialist giants have been left untouched by reform. However, the last stage of privatization is planned to begin during 1997, with the objective to partially or fully privatize 115 companies, including the national airlines, the monopoly telecommunications giant, several oil refineries, and coal mines in order to expand the scope of the stock market and attract more foreign investors. Progress to meet commitments under the Uruguay Round and Europe Agreement is one of the central objectives of Polish foreign policy, and it is expected that by 1999, most imports of industrial goods from the EU could enter Poland duty free; by January 1997, well over 70 percent (that is, more than 85 percent of total export) of Poland's industrial export, including steel products and textiles, had become free of EU tariffs.[5]

It should not be concluded that Poland has managed to overcome all of its economic problems and begun an uninterrupted course of continuous success. On the contrary, Poland has reached a critical juncture on the road to a Western-style economic system, and unless radical methods are applied once again, heavy subsidies demanded by unions, farmers, heavy industries and social services could produce a "reform-killing gridlock."[6] Without another round of bold and socially painful economic restructuring and the breakup of large, state-owned monopolies, the annual inflation rate driven up by government subsidies to inefficient enterprises and vast investments into the antiquated infrastructure, which is running above 20 percent annually, the Polish economy could again start falling behind the West without any hope of closing the gap in the near future. The strategic objective of Poland is to become a member of the European Union as early as the year 2000. At this point, fortunately, the country has already joined the OECD and met two out of three Maastricht criteria, with an annual budget deficit below 3 percent and total public debt below 60 percent of its GDP. The agricultural sector, however, continues to be a major drag on Poland's economy; some one fourth of the labor force is employed in this sector but contributes only 8–9 percent to the nation's GNP. If it can overcome these obstacles, however, membership in the European Union would fulfill the national aspiration of permanent association with the most successful international economic and political organization in the world. With such an attachment, Poland would receive the best possible guarantee for domestic stability, democratic viability, and international security. Between 2000 and 2005, Poland has a realistic chance of joining the most successful political and economic organization in Europe. EU membership is therefore a top foreign policy priority for Poland and an integral part of the national strategy to bring the country up to the industrial level of the West.

As part of its EU agenda, the Polish government is currently preparing a National Integration Program, a detailed outline of steps designed to prepare the country for entry into the European Union. This ten-year plan, known as Euro 2006, is expected to be presented to the Polish Parliament at the beginning of 1997. The plan contains strong anti-inflation measures to enable the country to meet the EU's five Maastricht criteria on public debt, budget deficit, inflation, interest, and foreign exchange rates by 2004. In addition, Poland is expected to qualify for membership in the EU no later than 2005. In fact, domestic political processes in Poland are organized around the paramount national objective, namely, integration within NATO and the EU. As President Aleksander Kwaśniewski has noted, "We believe both [EU and NATO] are structures that may help us to exist in a stable and democratic Europe. Nothing should be done to slow economic growth. Nothing should happen which would make our joining NATO more difficult."[7]

Nevertheless, however welcome and beneficial for the country, Poland has never regarded economic prosperity gained from expected EU membership as a substitute for the political-military security guarantee of national independence that the North Atlantic alliance would ideally provide. The current security imbalance between Central and Western Europe is seen as a deeply destabilizing development on the continent, especially given the absence of any effective structural mechanism for preserving peace and stability. Poland, along with many other European countries, does not share the Russian view that the Organization for Security and Cooperation in Europe should assume an exclusive responsibility for all security-related issues in Europe. The OSCE has no institutional structure and resembles a periodic foreign affairs workshop of some fifty nations. Moreover, it could be easily dominated by Russia, which is the most powerful nuclear state on the continent, while the American presence in Europe would quickly come to an end with a potential disintegration of NATO. Although the OSCE provides a convenient pan-European forum for discussion of various security-related developments, it should not, under any circumstances, be regarded as a substitute for NATO. Russian preference for OSCE is in essence another expression of opposition to NATO, namely, the presence of American troops in Europe, and caters to Russian ambitions of acting as a policeman in all issues affecting Europe. In other words, the international objectives of Russia toward Europe have remained the same, despite the Soviet collapse. As a result, this ominous continuity has provided additional incentives for Poland and all other Central and East European nations to seek the enlargement and strengthening of NATO.

In short, Poland believes that the Euro-Atlantic structure of Western democracies, rather than a "Europe from the Urals to the Atlantic," serves as the only multinational organization that can effectively protect the country from an outside threat, maintain stability in Central Europe, and ensure that democratic and free market trends remain irreversible. NATO is not only a political and military reality but also an institution with a powerful legacy of historical success. Almost half a century of democracy, stability, and prosperity in Western Europe, with most of those years passed under stressful Cold War conditions, has been possible because of NATO's defensive umbrella. This protection has also symbolized moral values in international affairs, especially in the context of self-invasions practiced by the Warsaw Pact and recent Russian military interference along its borders.

The key to understanding the Polish position on the expansion of NATO is that the main national objective is to establish a framework for permanent stability in Europe under existing peaceful and secure conditions of the immediate postcommunist period. However, there are Russian and Western critics of expansion who present this policy as an attempt to contain and isolate Russia, when in reality the primary purpose of expansion is to eradicate a geopolitical vacuum on the continent while engaging Russia in all European security-related matters by concluding a strategic partnership between NATO and the CIS. It is not, as expansion critics would have it, an attempt to create new lines of division in Europe but just the opposite: to eliminate all divisions between free societies through extension of the Western security umbrella over Central Europe. Stability of Central and Eastern Europe is in the best interests of security and democracy in Russia, which in the past justified its expansionist practices by allegations of threat from the West. A democratic Russia is not an adversary, and NATO is not an offensive military organization. However, new Russian threats to stability have appeared: a resurgence of anti-Western and neo-expansionist forces; sale of conventional, chemical, bacteriological, and nuclear arms to countries like Libya, Syria, Iran, and Iraq; the global expansion of Russian mafia activities; and the general inability of the Russian state to proceed with either political or economic reforms.

Although President Clinton's Partnership for Peace proposal in October 1993 proved to be disappointing, Poland initially hoped that the PfP would provide an opportunity to qualify for full membership in NATO. Consequently, Poland was one of the first to apply for PfP and one of the first to agree on individual partnership with NATO. This provided numerous opportunities for Polish armed forces to either host or to participate abroad in military exercises sponsored by the Atlantic alliance. Moreover, Poland's proactive attitude toward the PfP has more easily facilitated the purchase of Western military hardware to expedite the standardization and modernization of weapons, as well as to advance compatibilities in military equipment, communications, command, and control. The PfP has become a learning experience for Poland on NATO approaches to international security, planning, budgeting, and civilian control over the military. In other words, the organization enabled Polish armed forces to master daily routines of the alliance in order to facilitate the eventual transition to the status of an ally protected by a collective security guarantee, as specified in Article 5 of the Washington Treaty. Working together with NATO, Poland has already developed close and successful relations with the alliance, while its allies have had plenty of opportunity to become more familiar with the armed forces and politics in Poland. This constructive experience was instrumental in moving the internal debate from *whether* to invite some new European democracies to join NATO to *when and how* the expansion should take place.

Inspired by PfP program, Poland also made important changes in its civilian-military relations. The 1996 reorganization reduced the powers of the general staff by subordinating it to the defense ministry. In this way, Poland departed successfully from the Soviet model, which was designed to give Moscow military control beyond that of Polish civilian authorities: it adopted NATO-style organizational structures in which the military command is a department of the defense ministry.

Another advantage of PfP was the reassurance to Russia that NATO had neither a hidden agenda directed against Moscow's legitimate security interests nor a nontransparent, undemocratic enlargement procedure. PfP is based on the declaration that the alliance has no offensive anti-Russian objective; rather, it welcomes Russian participation in the promotion of peace, security, democracy, and a free-market economic system in all of Europe. Albeit with reluctance, Russia joined the PfP with the reassurance that it would have a voice but not a veto power in the enlargement process, and that the eastern extension of the alliance would include a parallel strategic partnership between Russia and NATO. As Robert E. Hunter, permanent representative of the United States on the North Atlantic Council explained, this approach "can create the necessary political basis for extending Western security commitments eastward, without weakening the Alliance. It can help draw nations into the West, embed them organically in broader institutions, and help shape the attitudes and practices needed to underpin a vocation of peace."[8]

Constructive experiences with the PfP, further enhanced by Central European contributions to the IFOR peacekeeping in Bosnia, helped convince many American politicians during mid-1996 to support the appropriation of $60 million in military assistance to Poland, Hungary, and the Czech Republic for modernization of their armed forces. In Congress, this bill received an overwhelming majority of votes (353–65 in the House and 81–16 in the Senate). For the first time, these three Central European nations won recognition for their individual contributions to promoting NATO's objectives in Europe. At the same time, congressional debate over the bill signaled how the polemics over NATO expansion had developed. As in 1949, when the Truman administration sought Senate ratification of the North Atlantic Treaty, the vote on NATO enlargement faced similar opposition from three factions: isolationists, defense hawks, and liberal internationalists. Today, ultraconservative Republican isolationists could join forces with Republicans concerned over the budgetary consequences of enlargement and liberal internationalists opposed to any military commitments of the United States. The last group, which includes some members who favor the dissolution of NATO, has a propensity to idealize the domestic situation in Russia and will likely resist an eastward extension of the alliance. The most effective political strategy to secure the two-thirds majority necessary for amending the Washington Treaty, therefore, would be to present enlargement as a "broader referendum on whether the United States should continue to lead NATO or even remain a member."[9]

President Clinton's position on the issue of NATO enlargement began with an initial reluctance to address the problem, while his administration, and particularly Deputy Secretary of State Strobe Talbott, tested the notion of a strategic partnership with Russia. More recently, however, the president has come to endorse a careful step-by-step effort toward inclusion of new members. For its part, the Republican Party has officially endorsed the idea of enlargement in a number of political statements, including its Contract with America and the party platform in San Diego, and accused the Democrats of stalling and caving in to the Russian lobby in Washington by placing imperial Russian interests above those of the United States and its European allies. Indeed, the administration first embraced a rather ambiguous position in the weeks preceding the 1996 presidential campaign in Moscow. However, the U.S. presidential race soon compelled President Clinton to take a clear-cut position on the future of NATO—not only for American voters but also for our allies in Europe.

The official presidential endorsement for the extension of the Atlantic alliance came at the very end of the 1996 presidential campaign, in a major foreign policy statement delivered in Detroit. President Clinton declared that "by 1999—NATO's 50th anniversary and 10 years after the fall of the Berlin Wall—the first group of countries we invite to join should be full-fledged members of NATO." Without naming the countries that would be invited first, the president continued that "NATO should remain open to all of Europe's emerging democracies who are ready to shoulder the responsibilities of membership." The United States, for its part, is prepared to provide "the most solemn security guarantee to our new allies," that is, to extend its nuclear umbrella eastward in Europe. At the same time, the president pointed out that "NATO enlargement is not directed against anyone," and he invited Russia to take advantage of "the best chance in history to help to build that peaceful and undivided Europe, and to be an equal and respected and successful partner."[10]

Despite such statements, complications remain. It may appear that the United States decided to proceed with enlargement regardless of what the Russians say, but a new fear has emerged: a charter of cooperation between NATO and Russia might lead the United States to accommodate Moscow by giving Russia political membership in NATO. In this way, Russia would take part in all NATO activities except those specified under Article 5 of the Washington treaty. This American approach is not popular in Europe because it could create a "Big Five" club within the alliance that would make decisions at the expense of smaller states. Thus, the extent and future scope of Russian influence in NATO has become a cause of transatlantic friction within the alliance.

Furthermore, there are indications that Moscow has in fact accepted extension of NATO to Poland, the Czech Republic, Hungary, and perhaps Slovenia, while its unending campaign of threats to deploy more nuclear weapons or to violate arms-control treaties with the West are designed to avert any additional eastern enlargement of the alliance. Some Central and Eastern European nations, and especially the Baltic states, are not included in the first enlargement. These so-called have-nots are expected to mount an aggressive diplomatic campaign for continuing growth of the alliance into the domain of the former Soviet Union. Moscow seems determined to secure guarantees that the first enlargement would also be the last and that enlargement of NATO would take the form of negotiations with Russia that would extract from the West the best possible price. So far, in the proposed NATO-Russia security charter, the United States has offered such arrangements as the exchange of military liaison officers, the creation of joint crisis-management mechanisms, and regular ministerial meetings—or "just about everything, short of giving Russia a veto over NATO's activities."[11]

By the summer of 1997, NATO is expected to officially invite the first three Central European countries to join the alliance and to begin formal negotiations on membership immediately thereafter. Despite the fair certainty that Poland would be included within the first group of countries considered for eventual membership, the Poles have asked for an early endorsement from several major European states, including Britain and Germany, to strengthen their case. In doing so, German defense minister Volker Ruehe stated that "Poland is a country where there are no doubts at all that they are very much at the forefront when it comes to becoming a member of NATO and also a member of European Union."[12] At the same time, however, it is possible that Germany may try to delay Poland's admission into the European Union up to 2005, due to the fear that the low cost of labor in Central Europe would worsen unemployment in the West. Furthermore, it is clearly understood that the Central European nations trying to join the European Union "could not expect special favors on entry terms and that the bloc's most ambitious expansion yet could take place in several stages."[13]

In conclusion, seven years of independence have been used productively to overcome the tradition of regional animosities and to recast Poland's international image from that of a political troublemaker and an economic failure within the Soviet empire to that of a stable democracy with a rapidly developing free-market economy. In this relatively short period of time, Poland became a Western state, successfully disentangling itself from patterns and institutions of the Soviet period. Even the successor of the former Polish United Workers' (communist) Party has fully adopted democratic ideas and style, leading the country toward Western institutions and programs. Political and economic changes in Poland are irreversible, and for all practical purposes, there is no procommunist or pro-Russian political constituency left in the country.

However, Poland's enthusiasm, energy, and commitment to Western-ization have received only limited appreciation in the West. Procedural issues and the time required for admission to the European Union is a cause of frustration and disappointment, and the slow manner in which the NATO enlargement issue is moving ahead in Washington, together with strongly anti-Polish—bordering on ethnic bigotry—polemics that saturate the American press and some academic debates, is a painful reminder that Poland is still living in the shadow of Russian imperialism and is in danger of becoming a playground for Russia's organized crime groups, which appear to be firmly in control of the authorities in Moscow.[14]

Nevertheless, the country consistently proceeds with its program of complete incorporation into the Western economic, political, and military institutions that will once and for all remove Poland from any future contest between European and Russian cultural domains. Thus, the country is rapidly acquiring the characteristics of a Western European state, becoming present, visible, and influential in the network of political and economic relations on the continent. For this reason, Poland is confident that despite a very powerful Russian effort to again transform Central Europe into its special sphere of strategic influence, the extension of NATO and the EU to include countries like Poland, the Czech Republic, and Hungary will succeed eventually. This expectation is the driving force behind Poland's domestic and foreign policies. Eventual membership in NATO and the EU would be a crowning fulfillment of political and cultural ambitions that can be traced back to Poland's participation in the Napoleonic Wars two hundred years ago.

The historical decision to invite Poland, together with the Czech Republic and Hungary, to join NATO was officially pronounced at the 8 July 1997 NATO summit in Madrid. Following some discussion of whether two additional countries, Romania and Slovenia, should also be included among the first invitees, the unanimous Summit Declaration recognized Polish, Czech, and Hungarian contributions to democracy and a free-market economy, and limited invitation to these three states. At the same time, the final communiqué from Madrid pointed out that both Romania and Slovenia had also made progress toward greater stability and would be considered for NATO membership during the second wave of enlargement, expected to begin as early as the end of 1999.

The invitation to start accession talks with NATO was received in Poland as the most important news of the century or even as the most important development since the adoption of Western Christianity more than ten centuries ago. The very essence of the Polish aspiration to join NATO was most clearly expressed by President Clinton during his 10 July visit to Warsaw, when he told an enthusiastic crowd, "Never again will your fate be decided by others—Poland is coming home."[15] That is, Poland, together with other countries of Central Europe, was recognized as a fully independent security partner of the West, including the United States.

At the same time, the invitation to negotiate membership in NATO was received with a high degree of realism and common sense. Polish authorities and the public are fully aware that accession talks will be long and difficult, and that the country must designate $150 to $200 million annually for modernization of its armed forces to achieve compatibility with NATO standards in such areas as telecommunications and the command structure.

Finally, Poland is aware that the final test is yet to come in the form of the U.S. Senate vote on enlargement at the end of 1998. The main battle for the destiny of Europe and the American leadership in the world is yet to come.

Notes

1. For example, Irina Kobrinskaia, "*Vnutripoliticheskaia situatsia i prioritety vneshnei politiki Rossii,*" a study prepared for the U.S. and Canada Institute, Moscow (1992), 13 ff.

2. "Polish PM Visits Moscow, Signs Trade, and Economy Pacts," *New Europe,* 17–23 November 1996, 8.

3. Henry Kissinger, "Beware: A Threat Abroad," *Newsweek,* 17 June 1996, 21.

4. Prime Minister Włodzimierz Cimoszewicz, "Building Poland's Security: Membership of NATO a Key Objective," *NATO Review,* no. 3 (May 1996): 3–4.

5. Organization for Economic Cooperation and Development, *OECD Economic Surveys, 1996–1997: Poland* (Paris, 1996), 123; "Treasury Minister Wants to Fine-Tune Privatization," *New Europe and the World,* 10–16 November 1996, 9.

6. Daniel Michaels, "Miracle Interrupted," *Wall Street Journal Europe's Central European Economic Review* 4, no. 9 (September 1997): 8–9.

7. "NATO, EU Entry Key Government Objective," *New Europe,* 1–7 December 1996, 9.

8. Robert E. Hunter, quoted in "Enlargement: Part of a Strategy for Projecting Stability into Central Europe," *NATO Review,* no. 3 (May 1995): 6.

9. Jeremy D. Rosner, "NATO Enlargement's American Hurdle," *Foreign Affairs* 75, no. 4 (July–August 1996): 15.

10. President Bill Clinton, quoted in Brian Knowlton, "Clinton Targets '99 For NATO Growth," *International Herald Tribune,* 23 October 1996, 1.

11. "Can Russia Ever Be Secure?," *Economist,* 7 December 1996, 30.

12. Volker Ruehe, quoted in *International Herald Tribune,* 30 October 1996, 1.

13. "Eastern Hopefuls Warned There Are No EU Favours For Entry," *New Europe,* 1–7 December 1996, 6.

14. Richard Staar, "How the Mob Moves In on Moscow," *Washington Times*, 27 November 1996, A-15.

15. *News from Poland* 3 (July–August 1997): 1; Embassy of the Republic of Poland, Washington, D.C.

Name Index

Subject Index